Treasury Of The Rule Of Law

Edited by RICHARD W. NICE

*Author of "Dictionary of Criminology"
and "Crime and Insanity"*

1965

LITTLEFIELD, ADAMS & CO.

Totowa, New Jersey

1965 Edition

By LITTLEFIELD, ADAMS & CO.

Originally published as *Treasury of Law* and copyrighted in 1964 by the Philosophical Library, Inc.

Library of Congress Catalog Card No. 64-20425

Printed in the United States of America

Looking back at antiquity, the Dark Ages, the Feudal Era, or even observing modern times, one shudders not at what people did unlawfully, but rather at what crimes were committed in the name of the law.

—DAGOBERT D. RUNES

CONTENTS

INTRODUCTORY NOTE

Since the beginning of time men have sought to establish rules and regulations in order to control their conduct within their particular societies. Some of the earliest attempts to regulate human behavior sprang from powerful, primitive religious influences that governed matters of ethics and morals. Examples of these types of ancient legal systems may be found in the Code of Hammurabi (Babylonia) and the Mosaic Code (Palestine).

The first "pure" law can be traced back through classical history to Solon and to Lycurgus, as well as to the Law of the Twelve Tables, which was the forerunner of Roman law. Under the Emperor Justinian, Roman law became an elaborate, highly developed system of government that had an immeasurable effect upon the evolution of modern Western law.

The advances and influences of Roman law subsequently contributed heavily to the development of the complicated Canon Law of the Catholic Church (although Mosaic law remained at the heart of Catholic dogma) and even more heavily to later feudal law, which placed most of its emphasis on the individual's rights and privileges rather than on a concern for the state.

As European civilization progressed into the Renaissance and international commerce became an important facet of governmental life, legal reform was concentrated on advancements in maritime law and resulted in such documents as the *Consulado del Mar*, The Law of Oleron, and the English Black Book of the Admiralty.

Following the Norman conquest, feudal law was eventually replaced by the authority of royal courts, i.e. the King's Bench.

From this developed common law, which adhered primarily to the concepts of precedent and equity.

* * *

In this volume I have endeavored to assemble as many as possible of the meaningful and significant documents that contributed to man's determination to govern his conduct in inter-personal and international affairs. Most, it will be observed, reflect early attempts to establish some form of regulatory practice in dealing with specific problems of the times.

Particularly noticeable are the number of legal documents that grew out of religious convictions and moral principles; they reflect the influence of religion on early attempts at government. The reader will also note, interestingly enough, that many of the documents reproduced here were the direct result of some form of internal revolution or international war.

I might conclude by stating that because of space limitations I was, on more than one occasion, compelled to omit what some readers might consider material that should be included in any compendium on law. I do feel, however, that my attempt to include as many representative documents as practicable, so as to offer a broad sampling of man's legal tradition, was successful.

R. N.

ACKNOWLEDGMENT

The Editor wishes to acknowledge with thanks the many individuals who helped make this work possible. Without the help and forbearance of the librarians of the New York City Library, the Columbia Law Library, the Rutgers Law Library and the Library of Congress, this work would have been impossible.

Specific material sources, other than public documents on file with the Library of Congress, are as follows:

Ancient Codes & Laws of the Near East, ed. Driver & Miles, Vol. II, Oxford Press, 1955. From pages 7-37.

The Code Napoleon, being The French Civil Code translated by Robert Samuel Richards, London, Widdy & Sons.

Consulate of the Sea, translation of the Chapter CCLXII of the Consulado del Mar, relating to prize law, London, W. Wilson for J. White and J. Butterworth, 1800, translated by Sir Christopher Robinson.

Naval War College, *International Law Topics,* Declaration of London—pp. 169-193, 1909.

Year Book on Human Rights for 1946, U.N. Publications, 1948, XIV, 1, pp. 1-6, 107.

A Digest of International Law, John Bassett Moore, Vol. VII, Washington, Government Printing Office, 1906, pp. 561-562.

English Historical Documents, ed. by David C. Douglas, New York, Oxford University Press, 1953, pp. 847-850, 854-866.

Documents of American History, Commager, 6th ed. 1-2, pp. 15-16; 224-227.

Lipit—Istar's Law in *Ancient Codes & Laws of the Near East,* Driver & Miles, Vol. II, Oxford Press, 1955, pp. 306-307, 309, 311, 313.

Magna Charta, the Bill of Rights with the Petition of Right, London, published by J. Bailey.

Treasury Of The
Of Law Rule

I.

LAW IN THE HEARTLAND

THE REPORTS OF GALEOTTO PERERA*

An early example of the Chinese legal system as being extremely law-abiding and peaceful is chronicled by Perera, a Portuguese merchant, in Macao about A.D. 1560. A group of merchants including Perera had been mistaken for pirates and were arrested, during which time they offered resistance which resulted in the death of several Chinese. The strangers were first charged with piracy and secondly with resisting officers. Perera and his followers were found not guilty by trial, the officers who unjustly arrested them as pirates were disgraced and the individuals who had done the killings were found guilty of homicide. The following is Perera's comment on the type of Chinese justice he and his companions received.

A FOREIGNER'S EXPERIENCE AS ACCUSED IN A CHINESE COURT

I shall have occasion to speake of a certaine order of gentlemen that are called Louteas. I wil first therefore expound what this word signifieth. Loutea is as much to say in our language "Sir" . . . Such Louteas as doe serve their prince in weightie matters for justice, are created after trial made of their learning . . . Now will I speake of the maner which the Chineans doe observe in doing of justice, that it may be knowen how farre these Gentiles do herein exceed many Christians, that be more bounden then they to deale justly and in trueth . . . In the principall Cities of the shires be foure chiefe Louteas, before whom are brought all matters

*From the Reports of Galeotto Perera. Reprinted in Hakluyt, *Principal Navigations,* VI, 1904. Through the courtesy of the West Publishing Company and the heirs of the late Professor John Henry Wigmore, editor of *Panorama of the World's Legal Systems.*

of the inferiour Townes, throughout the whole Realme. Divers other Louteas have the managing of justice . . . These Louteas do use great diligence in the apprehending of theeves, so that it is a wonder to see a theefe escape away in any City, Towne or village. . . .

The Louteas observe moreover this: when any man is brought before them to be examined, they aske him openly in the hearing of as many as be present, be the offense never so great; thus did they also behave themselves with us. For this cause amongst them can there be no false witnesse, as dayly amongst us it falleth out. This good commeth thereof, that many being alwayes about the Judge to heare the evidence, and beare witnesse, the processe cannot be falsified, as it happeneth sometimes with us . . . Againe, these Louteas, as great as they be, notwithstanding the multitude of Notaries they have, not trusting any others, do write all great processes and matters of importance themselves. Moreover one vertue they have worthy of great praise, and that is, being men so wel regarded and accompted as though they were princes, yet they be patient above measure in giving audience. We poore strangers brought before them might say what we would, as all to be lyes and fallaces that they did write, ne did we stand before them with the usuall ceremonies of that Countrey; yet did they beare with us so patiently, that they caused us to wonder, knowing specially how litle any advocate or Judge is wont in our Countrey to beare with us. For wheresoever in any Towne of Christendome should be accused unknowen men as we were, I know not what end the very innocents' cause would have. But we, in a heathen Countrey, having our great enemies two of the chiefest men in the whole Towne, wanting an interpreter, ignorant of that Countrey language, did in the end see our great adversaries cast into prison for our sake, and deprived of their Offices and honour for not doing justice,—yea not to escape death: for, as the rumour goeth, they shal be beheaded.

CONFUCIUS*

Confucius was born 551 years before the Christian era. His parentage, though respectable, was not distinguishable for honor, wealth or position. His father was a soldier in the service of the government. The son, when not teaching, was occupied much of the time in the employ of the Empire, first as storekeeper, but subsequently in positions of far greater responsibility and trust. Under the government his abilities and faithfulness were appreciated, and later in life his counsel and advice were eagerly sought by his superiors in authority. He was plain Confucius—plain K'ung-Fu-tsze, or Chung-ne; a man represented to be of excessive modesty, making no profession of perfection, but constantly lamenting his shortcomings and want of ability. He was an earnest scholar "constantly striving after the good and to know the truth." The wisdom and insight of which he was possessed were the same, he claimed, as all could possess by allowing their natures, through virtue, to unfold and by keeping close to the laws of their being; differing, possibly, in degree, but not in the nature or manner of acquiring.

He is represented to have been a great lover of antiquity and claimed to have been largely in its debt. With all his great learning, he seems to have lived much in the past. He is represented as having been a strict observer of the ceremonies of his time and of the rules of propriety as instituted in the country in which he lived, to such an extent that he may be said to have been almost a "stickler" even to the point of punctiliousness.

Confucius is said to have had "no foregone conclusions, no arbitrary predeterminations, no obstinacy, no egoism." While he is not accredited with having been the founder of any in-

*From *Confucius, the Secret of His Mighty Influence,* edited by Thomas Whitney, Chicago, 1901.

stitution of learning, like Aristotle or Plato, he is accredited with having upon the roll of his school as high as 3,000 students at a time. Appreciated by both scholars and disciples while living, he was practically unknown to the mass of his countrymen. This he is said to have felt keenly. Just before his death, he is said to have repined: "Of all of the princes of the Empire, there is not one who will adopt my principles or obey my lessons," but before two centuries had passed he had become the idol of all China, and today his name is revered by more than one-third of the population of the globe.

Confucius taught that the perfection of being, the perfection of manhood, is the true purpose of life. The seeking after happiness, which is a prompting of our natures, he considered a result proceeding from true being, and not an end. He taught that the making of the perfect man, the Superior man, as he termed it, is the chief end of life, and that this can only be reached through the practice of perfect virtue. Virtue, therefore, with him, was the all in all, a necessity to the spiritual development of man. It is the atmosphere, he claimed, in which man's spiritual nature grows and unfolds, and the only surrounding atmosphere in which it can grow and unfold; it is to the spiritual what food is to the physical nature—that in which it finds nourishment. Without it, he thought, man could not unfold spiritually, and with it there was no limit to his unfolding.

Confucius believed that while pleasure was to be derived from the gratification of the senses, happiness was only to be found in man's bringing himself into harmony with the laws of his being —into harmony with the "Will of Heaven"—and that this can only be attained through the practice of perfect virtue. This attainment he considered the highest enjoyment of life, the *summum bonum* of human existence, the thing to be prized above all else. To him there was nothing miraculous or supernatural about this. The law of the unfolding of man's spiritual nature was to him as natural as the law of the unfolding of the oak from the acorn, a provision of our nature, innate, the same as is the full fruit in the germ of the seed. For this reason, therefore, he would seek virtue, because through it man can become godlike, and without it, it is as impossible as for the plant or tree to unfold upon an entirely barren rock.

Sincerity, faithfulness and truthfulness were the groundwork of all of Confucius's teachings. With him these constituted not alone the cornerstone, but the foundation stones in the building up of character. He could listen to nothing which bore the air of insincerity.

When asked if there were not one word which would serve as a rule of practice for one's life, he said, "Is not reciprocity such a word? What you do not like when done to yourself do not do to others." When asked concerning the principle that injury should be recompensed with kindness, he replied: "With what, then, will you recompense kindness? Recompense injury with justice and recompense kindness with kindness." "To love those whom men hate and hate those whom men love, this is an outrage of the natural feelings; calamities cannot fail to come down on him who does so. He who recompenses injury with kindness is not careful of his person."

Confucius knew nothing of what is termed original sin. While he considered striving after perfection to be the true purpose of life, he did not consider that it could ever be reached by the finite. Perfection he ascribed to the Infinite alone. *He believed development to be the order or law of Nature—that man was created to develop physically, mentally and spiritually—each essential to the other, but the spiritual the crowning manifestation of all.* He did not consider this life probationary, that its purpose or object was preparation, upon this plane of existence, for life upon another of which he could know nothing, but that its purpose is development upon this state of being in accordance with Nature's laws. He held that it is the duty of every individual to cultivate to the utmost his or her nature along this line, and to strive constantly after the perfect. Sin was to him the cultivation of one's nature upon the plane of the small, the mean, the selfish, the animal man. This, he considered, might be due largely, if not mainly, to heredity—to the accident of birth, or environment, or education, or ignorance, over which the individual might have had no control and for which he or she might not be accountable. He believed that every act in life carried with it its own compensation, no less inevitably in the spiritual than in the physical world; that the individual received the penalty for violating a spiritual law, at the time of its infraction, as unerringly as for violating a physical law. In his view, therefore, everyone received reward or punishment, at the time of commission, for all deeds done, whether good or bad, those living in accordance with the laws of their being receiving noble character with contentment and happiness, and those living upon the plane of the low and the animal, ignoble character with anxiety and unhappiness. This latter he considered a misfortune, for the reason that by so living, either through will or ignorance, the individual debars himself or herself from the enjoyment of that patrimony for which he or she was created, and in this way suffers, in his view, the severest penalty for misdoing which it is possible for a human being to experience.

The following are a few only among the many of Confucius's sayings and aphorisms:

"In the Book of Poetry are three hundred pieces, but the design of them all may be embraced in that one sentence— Have no depraved thoughts."

"Fine words and insinuating appearance are seldom associated with true virtue."

"To be able to practice five things everywhere under the heavens constitutes perfect virtue—gravity, generosity of soul, sincerity, kindness and earnestness."

"Hold faithfulness, truthfulness and sincerity as first principles."

"Is he not a man of complete virtue who feels no discomposure tho men may take no note of him? Only the sage is equal to this."

"Perfect virtue is, in retirement, to be sedately grave; in the management of business reverently attentive; in intercourse with others, to be strictly sincere."

"Virtue is not left to stand alone; he who practices it will have neighbors."

"To be true to the principles of our nature and the benevolent exercise of them to others—this and nothing more."

"When a man holds fast to virtue without seeking to enlarge it and believes in right principles, but without firm sincerity, what account can be made of his existence or nonexistence?"

"The superior man is satisfied and composed; the mean man is always full of distress."

"What the superior man seeks is in himself; what the mean man seeks is in others."

"The superior man has neither anxiety nor fear. When internal examination discovers nothing wrong, what is there to be anxious about—what is there to fear?"

"The superior man is disturbed by want of ability; he is not distressed by men's not knowing him."

"Riches adorn a house and virtue adorns the person—the mind is expanded and the body is at ease."

"The way of the superior man is threefold, but I am not equal to it. Virtuous, he is free from anxieties; wise, he is free from perplexities; bold, he is free from fear."

"The sage and the man of perfect virtue, how dare I rank myself with them? It may simply be said of me that I strive to become such without satiety and teach others without weariness."

"In letters I am, perhaps, equal to other men, but the character of the superior man—carrying out in his conduct what he professes—is what I have not yet attained to."

"I am not one who was born in the possession of knowledge; I am one who is fond of antiquity, and earnest in seeking it there."

"When one cultivates, to the utmost, the principles of his nature and exercises them upon the principle of reciprocity, he is not far from the path."

"Have no friends not equal to yourself."

"Between friends, frequent reproof makes the friendship distant."

"If the scholar be not grave, he will not call forth any veneration, and his learning will not be solid."

"The scholar who cherishes the love of comfort is not to be deemed a scholar."

"When you know a thing, to hold that you know it, and when you do not know a thing, to allow that you do not know it—this is knowledge."

"When you have faults, do not fear to abandon them."

"See what a man does, mark his motive, examine in what he rests; how can a man conceal his character?"

"What truly is within will be manifest without."

"By nature men are nearly alike; by practice they get wide apart."

"A man can enlarge the principles which he follows; those principles do not enlarge the man."

"If a man take no thought about what is distant he will find sorrow in store."

"Learning without thought is labor lost; thought without learning is perilous."

"Wealth gotten by improper ways will take its departure in the same way."

"What is the good of being ready with the tongue? They who meet men with smartness of speech for the most part procure for themselves hatred."

"To see what is right and not to do it, is want of courage."

"Benevolence is to love all men—knowledge to know all men."

"Ornament is as substance and substance is as ornament. The hide of a tiger or leopard stripped of its hair is like the hide of a dog or goat stripped of its hair."

"Do not be desirous of having things done quickly. Desire to have things done quickly prevents their being done thoroughly. Do not look at small advantages."

"Men of principle are sure to be bold, but those who are bold may not always be men of principle."

"The superior man has dignified ease without pride; the mean man has pride without dignified ease."

"He who speaks without modesty will find it difficult to make his words good."

"The ways of heaven and earth may be completely declared in one sentence: They are without any doubleness and so they produce things in a manner that is unfathomable."

"I will not be afflicted at men's not knowing me (personally). I will be afflicted that I do not know men."

"I am not concerned that I am not known; I seek to be worthy to be known."

"At 15 I had my mind bent on learning. At 30 I stood firm. At 40 I had no doubt. At 50 I knew the decree of Heaven. At 60 my ear was an obedient organ for the reception of truth. At 70 I could follow what my heart desired without transgressing what was right."

DHAMMAPADA*

Dhammapada (which, according to the Chinese gloss, may be rendered "Scriptural Texts" or "Verses") is a work of importance in the study of Buddhism. It contains, as its title signifies, authentic texts gathered from ancient canonical books—and these texts are generally connected with some incident or other in the history of Buddha, helping to illustrate everyday life in India at the time when they were written, as well as the method of teaching adopted by the founder of this religion. Not only does the general tone pervading these verses illustrate the spirit of Buddha's doctrine, but by a critical examination of particular passages, we are enabled to solve some of the difficulties which always attend the interpretation of words and phrases used in a religious sense.

Chinese Version of *Dhammapada*

There are four principal copies of *Dhammapada* in Chinese. The first, approaching most nearly to the Pali, was made by a Shaman "Wei-chi-lan" (and others), who lived during the Wu dynasty, about the beginning of the third century of the Christian era.

The title by which it is known is *Fakheu-King* that is, "The Sutra of Law Verses." The symbol *kheu* does not necessarily mean "a verse," but is applied to any sentence or phrase: the rendering "law texts" or "scripture texts" would, therefore, be more correct were it not that in the preface to this work the symbol is explained by "Gatha," which is stated by Childres (*sub voce*) to mean "a verse or stanza" or generally "a cloka or anushtubh stanza."

*From *Texts from the Buddhist Canon, Commonly Known as Dhammapada,* translated by Samuel Beal, London, Trubner & Co., 1878.

The Buddhist works in China are of great value for an exact knowledge of that religion, because they are faithful versions of works everywhere known in India, not only during the early period of its history, but also throughout its development—or, to put it into plain figures, the books found in China afford us a consecutive catena of writings dating from at least 100 B.C. to A.D. 600, that is, during a period of 700 years. More than this can scarcely be desired for a perfect study of any religious system.

The *Fakheu-King* contains thirty-nine chapters against the twenty-six of the Southern edition, and 760 stanzas against 423. We are told, however, in the preface that the original work consisted of twenty-six chapters and 500 stanzas; and as in Buddhist calculations the next highest round number is frequently used to denote the exact number intended, we have in this statement sufficient evidence to show that the original from which our translation was made consisted of the same chapters, and probably the same number of verses, as that known in the South.

CHINESE		PALI	
Title of Chapter	No. of Verses	Title of Chapter	No. of Verses
1. Impermanence	21	1. Twin Verses	20
2. Inciting to Wisdom	29	2. Reflection	12
3. The Sravaka	19	3. Thought	11
4. Simple Faith	18	4. Flowers	16
5. Observance of Duty	16	5. The Fool	16
6. Reflection	12	6. The Wise Man	14
7. Loving Kindness	19	7. The Venerable	10
8. Conversation	12	8. The Thousands	16
9. Twin Verses	22	9. Evil	13
10. Carelessness	20	10. Punishment	17
11. Thought	12	11. Old Age	11
12. Flowers	17	12. Self	10
13. The Fool	21	13. The World	12
14. The Wise Man	17	14. The Awakened	18
15. The Rahat	10	15. Happiness	12

From the ninth chapter to the thirty-fifth (with the exception of the thirty-third) the two works contain the same succession of subjects, whilst there are seventy-nine more stanzas in the Chinese than in the Pali throughout the chapters common to each.

360

Restraint in the eye is good, good is restraint in the ear in the nose restraint is good, good is restraint in the tongue.

361

In the body restraint is good, good is restraint in speech, in thought restraint is good, good is restraint in all things. A Bhikshu, restrained in all things, is freed from all pain.

362

He who controls his hand, he who controls his feet, he who controls his speech, he who is well controlled, he who delights inwardly, who is collected, who is solitary and content, him they call Bhikshu.

363

The Bhikshu who controls his mouth, who speaks wisely and calmly, who teaches the meaning and the Law, his word is sweet.

364

He who dwells in the Law, delights in the Law, meditates on the Law, follows the Law, that Bhikshu will never fall away from the true Law.

365

Let him not despise what he has received, nor ever envy others: a mendicant who envies others does not obtain peace of mind.

366

A Bhikshu who, though he receives little, does not despise what he has received, even the gods will praise him, if his life is pure, and if he is not slothful.

367

He who never identifies himself with his body and soul, and does not grieve over what is no more, he indeed is called a Bhikshu.

368

The Bhikshu who acts with kindness, who is calm in the doctrine of Buddha, will reach the quiet place (Nirvana), cessation of natural desires and happiness.

369

O Bhikshu, empty this boat! if emptied, it will go quickly, having cut off passion and hatred, thou wilt go to Nirvana.

370

Cut off the five (senses), leave the five, rise above the five? A Bhikshu, who has escaped from the five fetters, he is called Oghatinna, "Saved from the flood."

371

Meditate, O Bhikshu, and be not heedless! Do not direct thy thought to what gives pleasure! that thou mayest not for thy heedlessness have to swallow the iron ball (in hell) and that thou mayest not cry out when burning "This is pain."

372

Without knowledge there is no meditation, without meditation there is no knowledge; he who has knowledge and meditation is near unto Nirvana.

373

A Bhikshu who has entered his empty house, and whose mind is tranquil, feels a more than human delight when he sees the law clearly.

374

As soon as he has considered the origin and destruction of the elements (khandha) of the body, he finds happiness and joy which belong to those who know the immortal (Nirvana).

375

And this is the beginning here for a wise Bhikshu: watchfulness over the senses, contentedness, restraint under the Law; keep noble friends whose life is pure, and who are not slothful.

376

Let him live in charity, let him be perfect in his duties; then in the fulness of delight he will make an end of suffering.

377

As the Vassika-plant sheds its withered flowers, men should shed passion and hatred, O ye Bhikshus!

378

The Bhikshu whose body and tongue and mind are quieted, who is collected, and has rejected the baits of the world, he is called Quiet.

379

Rouse thyself by thyself, examine thyself by thyself, thus self-protected and attentive wilt thou live happily, O Bhikshu!

380

For self is the lord of self, self is the refuge of self; therefore, curb thyself as the merchant curbs a good horse.

381

The Bhikshu, full of delight, who is calm in the doctrine of Buddha, will reach the quiet place (Nirvana) cessation of natural desires and happiness.

382

He who, even as a young Bhikshu, applies himself to the doctrine of Buddha, brightens up this world, like the moon when free from clouds.

II.

FROM THE ORIENT

THE CODE OF HAMMURABI, 2100 B.C.*

The only thoroughly complete pre-Hebrew code of law was that
compiled by the king of Babylonia, Hammurabi, somewhere
around the year 2100 B.C. Although the code is somewhat strong
and harsh in its retribution features, which follows the "eye for
an eye" concept, it remains one of the greatest of ancient laws.
The code itself was discovered at Susa carved on a diorite column
in 3,600 lines of cuneiform. It is one of the most ancient known
legal documents.

When the exalted Anum king of the Annunaki (and) Illil
lord of heaven and earth, who allots the destinies of the land,
allotted the divine lordship of the multitude of the people
unto Marduk the first-born son of Ea, magnified him amongst
the Igigi, called Babylon by its exalted name (and) so made
it pre-eminent in the (four) quarters of the world, and
stablished for him an everlasting kingdom whose foundations
are firmly laid like heaven and earth, at that time Anum and
Illil for the prosperity of the people called me by name
Hammu-rabi, the reverent God-fearing prince, to make
justice to appear in the land, to destroy the evil and the
wicked that the strong might not oppress the weak, to rise
indeed like Shamash over the dark-haired folk to give light
to the land.

I, Hammu-rabi the shepherd, called of Illil, who gathers
together abundance and plenty, who accomplishes everything
for Nippur 'bond of heaven', the reverent (prince) who

*From *The Laws of Moses and the Code of Hammurabi,* by
Stanley A. Cook, London, Adam and Charles Black, 1903.

cares for Ekur, the able king, restorer of Eridu, cleanser of the shrine of Eabzu, who has stormed the four quarters (of the world), who magnifies the fame of Babylon, who gladdens the heart of Marduk his lord, (who) has borne the charge of Esagil all his days; the seed royal which Sin has created, giver of abundant riches to Ur, the humble (prince) deep in prayer, the bringer of overflowing wealth to Ekishshirgal; the king endued with authority, obedient to Shamash (and) powerful (?), the stablisher of the foundation of Sippar, who clothes the dark abode of Aya in green foliage, designer of the house of Ebabbar which is as the habitation of heaven; the hero who showed grace to Larsa, renewer of Ebabbar for Shamash his helper: the lord the reviver of Uruk, provider of abundant waters for his people, raiser up of the top of Eanna, gathering together rich provision for Anum and Ishtar; the (protecting) shade of the land, gatherer together of the scattered people of Isin, giver of plentiful abundance to the house of Egalmah; the dragon amongst kings, the faithful servant of Ilbaba, sure founder of the habitation of Kish, who surrounds Emeteursag with splendors and perfects the grand accoutrements of Ishtar, overseer of the house (of) Harsagkalam; the net ensharing the enemy, whose desire Nergal his companion has satisfied, giver of pre-eminence to Cuthah, who grants all increase for Mishlam; the sturdy wild ox who gores the foe, the beloved of Tutu bringing jubilation to Borsippa, the reverent (prince) ceaseless in care for Ezida; a god amongst kings, endued with knowledge and wisdom, who enlarges the tilth of Dilbat, who heaps the garners (full of corn) for the mighty Urash; the lord whose proper ornaments are the sceptre and crown wherewith Mama the wise (goddess) has invested him, who has laid down the groundplan of Kish, bountiful provider of holy feasts for Nintu(d); the gracious arbiter (?) who has allotted pasture-land and watering-place to Lagash and Girsu, who maintains great offerings for Eninnu; who takes strong hold of the adversaries, the favorite of the most high (goddess), who fulfills the oracles of Hallab, who rejoices the heart of Ishtar; the prince pure (in heart) whose hands uplifted (in prayer) Adad regards, appeaser of the heart of the heroic Adad in Bit-Karkara, who sets in order the ornaments of Eudgalgal; the king the giver of life to Adab, the watcher over the house of Emakh; the manly (king) amongst kings, the warrior whom none can resist, he who has granted life to Mashkan-shabrû, the giver of (the waters of) abundance to Mishlam to drink; the profoundly wise (ruler) who bears the charge of government, who has attained the source of wisdom, protector of the people of Malgûm from annihilation, who has firmly laid (the foundations of) their habitations (and supplies them) with abundance (of good things) for (the pleasure of) Ea and Damgalnunna; the magnifier of his kingdom, [who] has allotted pure sacrifices for ever; the foremost amongst kings, the subduer of (the dwellers in) the towns beside the Euphrates by the oracular command of Dagan his creator, who showed grace to the people of Mari and Hit; the reverent prince who lightens the countenance of Tishpak (and) provides holy feasts for Ninazu; who brings together his people in distress (and) by his friendly act stablishes their foundation in the midst of Babylon; the shepherd of the people whose deeds are pleasing to Ishtar, who stablishes Ishtar in Eulmash in the midst of the mart of Agade; who makes the truth to appear, guiding the folk aright, restoring its favorable guardian spirit to Asshur, subduer of rebels; the king who has made the titles of Ishtar to appear in Emishmish in Nineveh; the reverent (prince) deep in prayer to the great gods; the scion of Suma-la-el, the powerful heir of Sin-uballit, the everlasting seed royal, the powerful king, the sun-god of Babylon who makes the light to rise on the land of Shumer and Accad, the king who also brings the four quarters of the world to obedience, the favorite of Ishtar am I.

When Marduk commanded me to give justice to the people of the land and to let (them) have (good) governance, I set forth truth and justice throughout the land (and) prospered the people.

At that time:

§ 1

If a man has accused a man and has charged him with manslaughter and then has not proved (it against) him, his accuser shall be put to death.

§ 2

If a man has charged a man with sorcery and then has not proved (it against) him, he who is charged with the sorcery shall go to the holy river; he shall leap into the holy river and, if the holy river overwhelms him, his accuser shall take and keep his house; if the holy river proves that man clear (of the offense) and he comes back safe, he who has charged him with sorcery shall be put to death; he who leapt into the holy river shall take and keep the house of the accuser.

§§ 3-4

If a man has come forward in a case to bear witness to a felony and then has not proved the statement that he has made, if that case (is) a capital one, that man shall be put to death.

If he has come forward to bear witness to (a claim for) corn or money, he shall remain liable for the penalty for that suit.

§ 5

If a judge has tried a suit, given a decision, caused a sealed tablet to be executed, (and) thereafter varies his judgment, they shall convict that judge of varying (his) judgment and he shall pay twelve-fold the claim in that suit; then they shall remove him from his place on the bench of judges in the assembly, and he shall not (again) sit in judgment with the judges.

§ 6

If a man has stolen property belonging to a god or a palace, that man shall be put to death, and he who has received the stolen property from his hand shall be put to death.

§ 7

If a man buys silver or gold or slave or slave-girl or ox or sheep or ass or anything else whatsoever from a (free) man's son or a (free) man's slave or has received (them) for safe custody without witnesses or contract, that man is a thief; he shall be put to death.

§ 8

If a man has stolen an ox or a sheep or an ass or swine or a boat, if (it is the property) of a god (or) if (it is the property) of a palace, he shall pay 30-fold; if (it is the property) of a villein, he shall replace (it) 10-fold. If the thief has not the means of payment, he shall be put to death.

§§ 9-13

If a man, some of whose property is lost, seizes his lost property in a man's possession, (if) the man in whose hand the thing belonging to him is seized states 'A seller sold (it) to me; I bought (it) before witnesses', and the owner of the lost property states: 'I will produce witnesses who know my lost property', (if) the buyer produces the seller who sold (it) to him and the witnesses before whom he bought (it) and the owner of the lost property produces the witnesses who know the lost property, the judges shall examine their statements and the witnesses before whom the sale was made and the witnesses who know the lost property shall declare what they know before a god, and the seller (is) a thief; he shall be put to death. The owner of the lost property shall take his lost property; the buyer shall take the money (which) he has paid from the house of the seller.

If the buyer does not produce the seller who sold (it) to him and the witnesses before whom he bought (it) the owner of the lost property produces the witnesses who know his lost property, the buyer (is) a thief; he shall be put to death. The owner of the lost property shall take his lost property.

If the owner of the lost property does not produce witnesses who know his lost property, he is a felon since he has uttered a slander: he shall be put to death.

If the seller (meanwhile) goes to (his) fate, the buyer shall take 5-fold (the amount of) the claim in that suit from the house of the seller.

If that man's witnesses are not at hand, the judges shall grant him a period (of adjournment) up to 6 months, and, if he has not haled his witnesses within 6 months, that man is a felon; he shall remain liable for the penalty for that suit.

§ 14

If a man kidnaps the infant (son) of a (free) man, he shall be put to death.

§ 15

If a man has let a slave of a palace or a slave-girl of a palace or the slave of a villein or the slave-girl of a villein escape by the great gate, he shall be put to death.

§ 16

If a man has harbored a lost slave or slave-girl of a palace or of a villein in his house and then has not brought (them) out at the proclamation of the herald, that owner of the house shall be put to death.

§§ 17-20

If a man has caught either a slave or a slave-girl fugitive in the open country and hales him to his owner, the owner of the slave shall give him 2 shekels of silver.

If that slave does not then declare (the name of) his owner, he shall hale him to the palace; the facts of his case shall be found, and they shall restore him to his master.

If he detains that slave in his house (and) afterwards the

slave is caught in his possession, that man shall be put to death.

If the slave escapes from the hand of him who has caught him, that man shall take an oath by the life of a god for (the satisfaction of) the owner of the slave and he then goes free.

§ 21

If a man has broken into a house, they shall put him to death and hang him before the breach which he has made.

§ 22-4

If a man has committed robbery and is caught, that man shall be put to death.

If the robber is not caught, the man who has been robbed shall formally declare whatever he has lost before a god, and the city and the mayor in whose territory or district the robbery has been committed shall replace whatever he has lost for him.

If (it is) the life (of the owner that is lost), the city or the mayor shall pay one maneh of silver to his kinfolk.

§ 25

If a fire has broken out in a man's house and a man who has gone to extinguish (it) has coveted an article of the owner of the house and takes the article of the owner of the house, that man shall be cast into that fire.

§ 26

If a runner or a fisher who is commanded to go on a mission of the king has not gone or has hired a hireling and sends (him as) his substitute, that runner or fisher shall be put to death; his hired (substitute) shall take and keep his house.

§ 27

If the field or the plantation of either a runner or a fisher, who is taken captive in the armed forces of the king, has afterwards been granted to another who performs his service, if he returns and regains his city, they shall render his field and his plantation to him and he shall himself perform his service.

§ 28-9

If either a runner or a fisher, who is taken prisoner in the armed forces of the king, has a son able to render his service, the field and plantation shall be given to him and he shall perform his father's service.

If his son is an infant and is not able to perform his father's service, a third part of the field and plantation shall be given to his mother for him, and his mother shall bring him up.

§ 30-1

If either a runner or a fisher has abandoned his field his plantation and his house because of his service and decamps (and) another afterwards has occupied his field his plantation and his house and performs his service (for) 3 years, if he returns and will demand his field his plantation and his house, it shall not be given to him; he who occupies (it) and performs his service shall himself perform (it).

If he decamps only for one year and returns, his field his plantation and his house shall be given to him and he himself shall render his service.

§ 32

If either a runner or a fisher, who is taken captive on a mission of the king (and) a merchant has ransomed him and so has enabled him to regain his city, has the means for ransoming (himself) in his house, he shall himself ransom himself; if there are not the means of ransoming him in his house, he shall be ransomed out of (the resources of) the temple of his city; if there are not the means of ransoming him in the temple of his city, the palace shall ransom him. His field his plantation and his house shall not be given for his ransom.

§ 33

If a recruiting officer or adjutant levies men exempt from service or has accepted and dispatches a hired man as a substitute for a mission of the king, that recruiting officer or adjutant shall be put to death.

§ 34

If a recruiting officer or an adjutant takes (any) article of a runner, oppresses a runner, hires out (the services of) a runner, delivers a runner into (the power of) a great man in a law-suit, (or) takes the gift which the king has given to the runner, that recruiting officer or adjutant shall be put to death.

§§ 35-6

If a man buys cattle or sheep, which the king has given to a runner, from the runner, he forfeits his money.

The field the plantation and the house of a runner a fisher and a rent-payer shall not be sold.

§§ 37-40

If a man buys the field the plantation or the house of a runner a fisher or a rent-payer, his tablet shall be broken and he forfeits his money; field plantation or house shall revert to its owner.

A runner a fisher or a rent-payer shall not assign any (portion) of the field the plantation or the house of his fief in writing to his wife or his daughter, and he shall not give (them) for his bond.

He may assign any (portion) of a field a plantation or a house, which he may buy and acquire, in writing to his wife or his daughter and may give (it) for his bond.

A priestess a merchant or a foreign fief-holder may sell his field his plantation or his house; the buyer shall perform the service of the field the plantation or the house which he buys.

§ 41

If a man has acquired the field the plantation or the house of a runner a fisher or a rent-payer by exchange (for other land) and has given an additional payment (to equalize the exchange), the runner fisher or rent-payer shall return to his field his plantation or his house and shall take and keep the additional payment which has been given to him.

§§ 42-3

If a man has taekn up a field for cultivation and then has not raised corn on the field, they shall convict him of not having done the (necessary) work on the field and he shall give corn corresponding to (the crops raised by) his neighbors to the owner of the field.

If he has not cultivated the field but leaves (it) waste, he shall give corn corresponding to (the crops raised by) his neighbors to the owner of the field and shall plough the field, which he has left waste (and) harrow (it), and he shall render (it) to the owner of the field.

§ 44

If a man has taken up a waste field for three years for opening up and has been slack and does not open up the field, in the fourth year he shall plough the field, hoe (and) harrow (it), and he shall restore (it) to the owner of the field, he shall pay 10 gur of corn for every bur (of land) .

§§ 45-7

If a man has given his field for rent to a cultivator and further receives the rent for his field, and Adad afterwards inundates it or a flood has then carried away (the soil) , the loss (shall be that) of the cultivator.

If he does not receive the rent for his field, whether he has given the field (in return) for a half or a third share (of the crop), the cultivator and the owner of the field shall divide the corn which shall be raised on the field in the agreed proportion.

If the cultivator, because he has not recovered his costs in the foregoing year, states that he will (again) cultivate the field, the owner of the field shall not refuse(?) ; his cultivator shall cultivate his field and at the harvest shall take corn according to his contract.

§ 48

If a man incurs a debt and Adad inundates his field or a flood has carried away (the soil) or else (if) corn is not raised on the field through lack of water, in that year he shall not render (any) corn to [his] creditor; he shall not pay interest for that year.

§§ 49-52

If a man has taken money from a merchant and has given a field prepared for corn or sesame to the merchant and has stated to him; 'Cultivate the field, and heap up take and keep the corn or sesame which may be raised,' if a cultivator raises corn or sesame on that field, at the harvest it is the owner of the field who shall take the corn or the sesame which may be raised on the field and shall give corn for his money, which he has received from the merchant, and the interest on it and the costs of the cultivation to the merchant.

If he has let a cultivated field [of corn] or a field of sesame, it is the owner of the field who shall take the corn or the sesame which may be raised on the field and shall repay the money and the interest thereon to the merchant.

If he has not money to repay, he shall give [corn or] sesame to the merchant up to the value of his money which he has received from the merchant and the interest thereon at a rate in accordance with the ordinances of the king.

If the cultivator does not raise corn or sesame on the field, he shall not vary his contract.

§§ 53-4

If a man has been slack in maintaining [the bank of] his [field] and has not maintained [his] bank and then a breach has occurred in his [bank], and so he has let the waters carry away (the soil on) the water-land, the man in whose bank the breach has occurred shall replace the corn which he has (caused to be) lost.

If he is not able to replace the corn, he and his goods shall be sold and the tenants of the water-land, whose sesame the waters have carried away, shall divide (the sum so obtained).

§§ 55-6

If a man has opened his trench for irrigation (and) has been slack and so has let the waters carry away (the soil on) his neighbor's field, he shall pay corn corresponding to (the amount of the crop which) his neighbor (has raised).

If a man has released the waters and so has let the waters carry away the works on his neighbor's field, he shall pay 10 gur of corn for every bur (of land).

§§ 57-8

If a herdsman does not make an agreement with the owner of a field to let his sheep graze the green shoots and lets the sheep graze the field without (the consent of) the owner of the field, the owner of the field shall reap his field; the herdsman, who has let his sheep graze the field without (the consent of) the owner of the field, over and above shall give 20 gur of corn for every bur (of land) to the owner of the field.

If, when the sheep come up from the water-land (and) the cord (?) closing the pen (?) is drawn through the great gate, the herdsman has put the sheep on a field and so has let the sheep graze the field, the herdsman shall (be set to) guard the field on which he has let (them) feed and at the harvest he shall pay 60 gur of corn for every bur (of land) to the owner of the field.

§ 59

If a man has cut a tree in a man's plantation without (the

knowledge of) the owner of the plantation, he shall pay ½ a maneh of silver.

§§ 60-3

If a man has let a field to a gardener to lay out a plantation (and) the gardener has laid out the plantation, he shall raise trees on the plantation for 4 years; in the fifth year the owner of the plantation and the gardener shall divide (the proceeds) in proportion; the owner of the plantation shall choose and take his share.

If the gardener has not fully laid out the field and has left (part) waste, they shall reckon the waste (part) to him in his share.

If he has not laid out the field which has been let to him (as) a plantation; if (it is) arable land(?), the gardener shall pay rent for the field for the years which it has been left waste according to (the amount of the crop raised by) his neighbors, and he shall do the (necessary) work on the field and render (it) to the owner of the field.

If the field is waste land, he shall do the (necessary) work on the field and shall render (it) to the owner of the field and shall pay 10 gur of corn for every bur (of land) for one year.

§§ 64-5

If a man has let a plantation to a gardener to pollinate, the gardener, so long as he is occupying the plantation, shall give two-thirds of the produce of the plantation to the owner of the plantation; he himself shall take one-third.

If the gardener has not pollinated the plantation and so has diminished the produce, the gardener [shall pay] rent for the plantation [to the owner of the plantation up to (the amount of the crops raised by) his neighbors and shall restore the plantation to the owner of the plantation].

LAWSUIT OF BUNANITU vs. AKABU-ILU*

About 550 B.C. a record of a lawsuit which raises points of law readily appreciable under our present modern legal system was found. In the case of Bunanitu vs. Akabu-ilu a widow sues her brother-in-law. The widow and her husband, having no children, adopted a young boy. They bought land, paying for it with, in part, the wife's dowry. On the death of the husband the brother-in-law claimed the estate on the ground that there had been no male heir. The widow maintained that the land belonged to the adopted child and herself. The six-judge court decided in her favor.

Bunanitu, daughter of Hariza, comes to the judges of Nabonidus, king of Babylon, and says:

[*Plaintiff's Pleading.*] "Bin-Addu-natan, son of Nikbata, had me to wife, receiving 3 silver mana as dowry, and I bore to him one daughter. I and Bin-Addu-natan, my husband, traded with the money of my dowry, and then with 9⅓ silver mana, including 2½ silver mana borrowed from Iddin-Marduk, we bought 8 rods of land, and a ruined house, in a large estate in Borsippa. We made this purchase jointly, in the fourth year of Nabonidus, king of Babylon. Now my dowry had been in the hands of Bin-Addu-natan, my husband. But I asked for it, and Bin-Addu-natan, in the kindness of his heart, deeded and entrusted to me for future maintenance the 8 rods of land and that house in Borsippa. Then in the fifth year of Nabonidus, king of Babylon, I and Bin-Addu-

*From the translation by H. F. Talbot, *Records of the Past,* XI, 101 (London, Samuel Bagster).

natan, my husband, adopted Bin-Addu-amara as our son, and executed a declaration of adoption and provided that the dowry of my daughter Nubta, when she would marry the adopted son, was to be 2 mana 10 shekels of silver and the furniture of a house. Fate then took my husband. On account of this, [his brother], Akabu-ilu, son of my father-in-law, now claims to inherit the house and everything which my husband had deeded and entrusted to me, and also claims the slave Nabu-nur-ili who we had bought by the agent, Nabu-ahi-iddin, for money. I have brought the case to you for judgment."

[*Judgment.*] The Judges heard the parties' statements, and examined the tablets and documents which Bunanitu produced in court. They held that Akabu-ilu [the brother] had no title to the house in Borsippa, which had been entrusted to [the wife] Bunanitu in place of her dowry; nor to the slave Nabu-nur-ili, whom she and her husband had bought for silver; nor to any property of [his brother] Bin-Addu-natan. [The widow] Bunanitu and the son Bin-Addu-amara, pursuant to the terms of their tablets, are to possess them. Iddin-Marduk is to be repaid the 2½ silver mana which he had loaned as part of the purchase price of that house, and to discharge his claim. Then [the widow] Bunanitu is to be repaid the 3½ mana, her dowry. [The daughter] Nubta, besides her own property, is to have the slave Nabu-nur-ili, according to the agreement of her father.

Judgment entered accordingly.

LIPIT-ISTAR'S LAW, 2207 B.C.*

Lipit-istar, King of Isin, recently was discovered to be the author
of a collection of Sumerian laws and is thought to be the author
of a section of laws written in the old Babylonian dialect and
not thoroughly unrelated to the laws of Hammurabi. In fact,
the reader will note that the text agrees almost word for word
with section seven of the laws of Hammurabi.

A

§ 1

If a son says to his father 'Thou art not my father,' he may
shave him, he may put the slave-mark on him [and] sell him.

§ 2

If a (!) son says to his mother 'Thou art not my mother,'
they shall shave half his head and lead him round the city and
put him out of the house.

§ 3

If a father says to his son 'Thou art not my son,' he forfeits
house and wall.

§ 4

If a mother says to her (!) son 'Thou art not my son,' she
forfeits house and furniture.

§ 5

If a wife has hated her (!) husband and says 'Thou art not

*From *The Babylonian Laws,* edited by G. R. Driver and John
C. Mills, Oxford, Clarendon Press, 1955.

my husband,' they shall throw her (!) into the river.

§ 6

If a husband says to his wife 'Thou art not my wife,' he shall pay ½ maneh of silver by weight.

§ 7

If a man has hired a slave and he has then died (or) escaped (or) fled (or) struck work or fallen sick, he shall pay 1 *ban* of corn by measure as his daily hire.

B
§ 1

If he does not pay silver, he shall pay him grain by measure at the current rate.

§ 2

If he will not pay grain, he shall add 10 *še* on every 1 *gur* as interest thereon and shall pay . . . grain [by measure].

§ 3

If he does not pay silver and (the price of) corn falls, at the expiry of the year he shall pay the corn and the interest on it by measure.

§ 4

If he is able (to pay) silver, he shall add 1 maneh 12 shekels in silver as interest.

§ 5

If he does not pay silver, he shall pay 1 *gur* of corn by measure for every 1 shekel of silver.

THE EDICTS OF ASOKA *

Asoka was an Indian emperor and conqueror of the third century who was afflicted by repentance after the short and sanguinary Kaliṅga war. He revealed himself a philosopher in the consequences he draws from his repentance—a political philosopher who expressed himself in proclamations and laws, bounding his country with Rock Edicts to publish his ideals and aims to his neighbors and to his subjects along the frontiers, erecting Pillar Edicts in the important places of his empire to express his moral and social objectives, and dedicating in the Cave Edicts places for religious observance. He became a moral philosopher who found a substitute for conquests by arms in conquest by Dharma, by righteousness and morality.

PUBLIC ADMINISTRATION: THE PROMULGATION OF MORALITY AND THE ADMINISTRATION OF JUSTICE

Rock Edict III

King Priyadarśī says:

Twelve years after my coronation I ordered the following:

Everywhere in my dominions local, provincial and state officials shall make a tour of their districts every five years to proclaim the following precepts of Dharma as well as to transact other business:

Obedience to mother and father; liberality to friends, acquaintances, relatives, priests, and ascetics; abstention from killing living creatures; and moderation in spending money

* The present selection is from *The Edicts of Asoka*, edited and translated by N. A. Nikam and Richard McKeon, and reproduced by permission of the University of Chicago Press.

and acquiring possessions are all meritorious.

The Council shall direct local officials concerning the execution of these orders in accordance with my instructions and my intention.

Rock Edict V [continued from IV, 2]

In the past there were no officers charged with spreading Dharma. I created these posts in the thirteenth year of my reign.

These officers are commissioned to work with all sects in establishing and promoting Dharma, in seeing to the welfare and happiness of all those devoted to Dharma, among the Yōnas, Kambōjas, Gandhāras, Rāṣṭrikas, Pitinikas, and other peoples living on the western borders of my kingdom. They are commissioned to work among the soldiers and their chiefs, the ascetics and householders, the poor and the aged, to secure the welfare and happiness and release from imprisonment of those devoted to Dharma. They are also commissioned to work among prisoners to distribute money to those who have many children, to secure the release of those who were instigated to crime by others, and to pardon those who are very aged.

They have been assigned everywhere—here [at Pāṭaliputra], in all the provincial towns, and in the harems of my brothers and sisters and other relatives. These officers in charge of spreading Dharma are at work everywhere in my dominions among people devoted to Dharma, whether they are only inclined to Dharma or established in Dharma or duly devoted to charity.

I have commanded this edict on Dharma to be inscribed so that it may last forever and so that my descendants may conform to it.

Pillar Edict IV

King Priyadarśī says:

I ordered this edict on Dharma inscribed twenty-six years

after my coronation.

I have appointed provincial governors [Rājūkas] to serve as administrators over hundreds of thousands of people.

In order that they may be fearless and impartial in administering the welfare and happiness of the people of the provinces and in bestowing favors among them, I have left to the discretion of these governors the award of honors and the infliction of punishments.

They shall learn the sources of the people's happiness and misery, and they shall admonish the people of the provinces, with the help of those who are devoted to Dharma, to lead lives that will gain them happiness in this world and the next.

The provincial governors are, of course, ready to obey me. They shall also obey the officers of higher rank [Puruṣas], who are acquainted with my wishes and who will also instruct the people, in order that the provincial governors will be able to please and serve me.

Just as a man feels confident when he has intrusted his child to a skilled nurse, thinking, "This skilled nurse will take good care of my child," so I have appointed the provincial governors for the welfare and happiness of my provincial people.

In order that they may perform their duties fearlessly, confidently and cheerfully, they have been given discretion in the distribution of honors and the infliction of punishments.

Impartiality is desirable in legal procedures and in punishments. I have therefore decreed that henceforth prisoners who have been convicted and sentenced to death shall be granted a respite of three days. [During this period their] relatives may appeal to the officials for the prisoners' lives; or, if no one makes an appeal, the prisoners may prepare for the other world by distributing gifts or by fasting.

For I desire that, when the period of respite has expired, they may attain happiness in the next world, and that various ways of practicing Dharma by self-control and the distribution of gifts may be increased among the people.

LAND GRANT, 23 B.C.*

Of the many early edicts and formal legal documents many were lost because they were usually made of strips of birch bark or palm leaves, were inscribed with a sharp instrument and bound in wooden or silk containers. The earliest legal document found intact and in pure Sanskrit is a royal land grant inscribed upon or on copper and using phraseology not too uncommon to modern law.

[After a preamble reciting the virtues and conquests of the grantor-prince,] To all the inhabitants of the town of Mesika . . . [naming other districts]; to the keeper of the elephants, horses and camels, to the keeper of the mares, colts, cows, buffaloes, sheep, and goats; . . . to the different tribes [naming them], to all our other subjects not here mentioned; and to the inhabitants of the neighboring villages, . . .

Be it known that I have given the above-mentioned town of Mesika, whose limits include the fields where the cattle graze, above and below the surface, with all the lands belonging to it, together with the mango and modhoo trees, all its waters, and all their banks and verdure, all its rents and tolls, with all fines for crimes and rewards for catching thieves. In it there shall be no molestation, no passage for troops, nor shall any one take from it the smallest part. I give likewise everything that has been possessed by the servants of the Rajah. I give the Earth and Sky, as long as the Sun and Moon shall last. Except, however, such lands as have been given to God, and to the Brahmans, which they have long possessed

*Translated by Charles Wilkins, *Asiatic Researches,* Vol. I., London, 1806.

and now enjoy. And that the glory of my father and mother, and my own fame, may be increased, I have caused this edict to be engraved, and granted unto the great Botho Bekorato Misro, who has acquired all the wisdom of books, and has studied the Vedas under Oslayono, who is descended from Opomonyobo, who is the son of the learned and immaculate Botho Borahorato, and whose grandfather was Botho Besworato, learned in the Vedas and expert in performing the sacrifice.

Know all the aforesaid, that as bestowing is meritorious, so taking away deserves punishment; wherefore, leave it as I have granted it. Let all his neighbors, and those who till the land, be obedient to my commands. What you have formerly been accustomed to perform and pay, do it unto him in all things. Dated in the 33rd year of the era and 21st day of the month of Margo.

Thus speak the following stanzas from the book of Justice:

1. "Ram hath required, from time to time, of all the Rajahs that may reign, that the bridge of their beneficence be the same, and that they do continually repair it.

2. "Lands have been granted by Sogor, and many other Rajahs, and the fame of their deeds devolves to their successors.

3. "He who dispossesses any one of his property, which I myself, or others, have given, may he, becoming a worm, grow rotten in ordure with his forefathers!"

THE JUDGMENT OF OKA TADASUKE*

Considered the ideal judge of Japanese justice in the early 1700's Oka Tadasuke, Baron Echizen is presented as having the wisdom and fame of Solomon. There is still in existence a popular book containing stories showing his excellent insight and shrewd justice. The following anecdote is almost a duplicate of that of Solomon's judgment upon two women who claim the same child.

About a century and a half ago, a woman who was acting as a servant in the house of a certain Baron had a little girl born to her. Finding it difficult to attend to the child properly while in service, she put it out to nurse in a neighboring village, and paid a fixed sum per month for its maintenance.

When the child reached the age of ten, the mother, having finished the term of her service, left the Baron's mansion. Being now her own mistress, and naturally wishing to have the child with her, she informed the woman who had it that she wanted the child. But the woman was reluctant to part with her. The child was very intelligent, and the foster-mother thought that she might get some money by hiring her out. So she refused to give her up to the mother. This of course led to a quarrel. The disputants went to law about it; and the case came up before Oka Tadasuke, then Magistrate of Yedo.

The woman to whom the child had been intrusted asserted that it was her own offspring, and that the other woman was a pretender. Oka saw that the dispute was a difficult one to

*From J. H. Wigmore, *Legal Systems of Old Japan*.

decide by ordinary methods. So he commanded the women to place the child between them, one to take hold of its right hand and the other of its left, and each to pull with all her might. "The one who is victorious," said the Magistrate, "shall be declared the true mother." The real mother did not relish this mode of settling the dispute; and though she did as she was bidden and took hold of the child's hand, she did what she could to prevent the child from being hurt, and slackened her hold as soon as the foster-mother began to pull, thus giving her an easy victory. "There!" said the foster mother, "the child, you see, is mine."

But Oka interposed: "You are a deceiver. The real mother, I perceive, is the one who relaxed her grasp on the child, fearing to hurt her. But you thought only of winning in the struggle, and cared nothing for the feelings of the child. You are not the true mother"; and he ordered her to be bound. She immediately confessed her attempt to deceive. and begged for pardon. And the people who looked on said, "The judgment is indeed founded on a knowledge of human nature."

KING THUTMOSE III'S INSTRUCTIONS TO CHIEF JUSTICE REKHMIRE*

One of the most impressive passages in the history of world justice is a speech of instruction purported to have been announced by King Thutmose III, who ruled Egypt around 1500 B.C. and at the height of Egypt's power. These instructions were found recorded on the tomb of Chief Justice Rekhmire and were supposedly uttered when he was appointed by Thutmose to the post of Chief Judge of the kingdom.

Regulation laid upon the chief judge, Rekhmire. The officials were brought to the audience-hall; his majesty commanded that the chief judge, Rekhmire, be presented for appointment for the first time.

His majesty spake before him: "Take heed to thyself for the hall of the chief judge; be watchful over all that is done therein. Behold, it is a support of the whole land; behold, as for the chief judge, behold, he is not sweet, behold, bitter is he, when he speaks. . . . Behold, he is not one setting his face toward the officials and councilors neither one making brethren of all the people. . . . Mayest thou see to it for thyself, to do everything after that which is in accordance with law; to do everything according to the right thereof . . . lo, it is the safety of an official to do things according to the law, by doing that which is spoken by the petitioner. . . .

"It is an abomination of the god to show partiality. This is the teaching: thou shalt act alike to all, shalt regard him who is known to thee like him who is unknown to thee, and him who is near to . . . like him who is far. . . . An official who does this, then shall he flourish greatly in the place.

*From the translation in Breasted, *Ancient Records*, II, 666-670.

"Do not avoid a petitioner, nor yet nod thy head when he speaks. As for him who draws near, who will approach to thee, do not . . . the things which he saith in speaking. Thou shalt punish him when thou hast let him hear that on account of which thou punishest him.

"Be not enraged toward a man unjustly, but be thou enraged concerning that about which one should be enraged.

"Show forth the fear of thee; let one be afraid of thee, for a prince is a prince of whom one is afraid. Lo, the true dread of a prince is not to do justice.

". . . Thou shalt do thy office, as thou doest justice. Lo, one shall desire to do justice. . . . Lo, one shall say of the chief scribe of the chief judge: 'A scribe of justice,' shall one say of him."

THE KORAN*

Like Judaism, the legal system of Islam is founded on the Word of God or Koran. This "law" is part of the religion and not a separate thing. The sources of Islamic law are three, consisting of, first, the Koran or Word of God as written by Mohammed; second, the sayings of Mohammed, and, last, the decisions and treatises developed from the above two by jurists. The Koran was originally written in an Arabic style known as Kufic. It was later written in the so-called Neskhi script which is now the most common style. Some six hundred thousand sayings or anecdotes have been attributed to Mohammed but only seven thousand currently are accepted as authentic.

[*The Koran, Sect. IV, Verse 12.*] God bids that, in distributing an estate, a son receive as much as two daughters; if only daughters remain, and more than two, they receive two thirds of the estate; if only one, the half. Father and mother shall have each one sixth, if there is a child; if none, and parents take, the mother has one third; if brothers survive, the mother takes one sixth; provided that legacies and debts be first paid.

[*Al Bukhari, "Wills," Ch. III, Sect. 2.*] Sahad tells: I was ill. The Prophet came to visit me. "O Messenger of God, pray God that I get home before I die." The Prophet said: "Mayhap God will cure thee, to be useful among men." I said: "I would make a will and I have only a daughter. I would will away half my estate." Said the Prophet, "The half is too much." "Then a third?" I asked. "Yes, a third, but even a third is much." Since then people have willed away as much as a third; for it is allowed.

*From *Al-Bukhari,* translated from the French in Frédéric Peltier, *Le Livre des Testaments du Sahih d'El-Bokhari,* Algiers, Jourdan, 1909.

[*Al Bukhari, Ch. X.*] In the passage of Holy Writ "if one declares a trust or makes a legacy in favor of one's kindred," what is to be understood by "kindred?" Tsabit, as recorded by Anas, relates that the Prophet said to Abu Talha: "Make that land an alms for the benefit of the poor among thy kindred;" and Abu Talha did so in favor of Hasan and of Obayi ben Kab. El-Ansari said: "My father told me that he heard from Tsumama, who heard it from Anas, a saying similar to that of Tsabit; the Prophet said, 'Make the alms in favor of the poor of thy family.'"

[*Al Bukhari, Ch. XXII.*] Ibn Omar relates that Omar, in the lifetime of the Messenger of God, made an alms of one of his properties called Tsamgh, which consisted of a palm-grove. Omar said: "O Messenger of God, I possess a property which is precious to me, and I would make alms with it." The Prophet replied: "Give it in alms, but provide that it shall never be sold nor given away nor divided among heirs, but the fruits of it shall be used." So Omar made alms with the property, dedicating it to the use of the holy war, the ransom of slaves, and the support of the poor, of guests, of travelers, and of kindred. It was provided that the trustee might not unlawfully draw therefrom a moderate subsistence either for himself or for a friend, but that he should not enrich himself.

A woman belonging to the tribe of Makhzum was found guilty of theft; and her relations requested Usama-bin-Zaid, for whom the Prophet had much regard, to intervene and entreat the Prophet to release her. The Prophet said, "O Usama, do you mean to come to me and intercede against the laws of God?" then the Prophet convened a meeting, and thus addressed them: "Nations which have preceded you have been wiped off the face of the earth, for the one reason only, that they imposed punishment upon the poor and relaxed the laws in favor of the rich. I swear by God that if Fatima my daughter were to be found guilty of theft, then I would have her hands cut off."*

* From *Kwaja Kamal-ud-Din.*

48

THE TORAH

After the Israelites arrived in the wilderness of Sinai, three years after their departure from Egypt, the Lord revealed to Moses the law which he transmitted to the Jewish people. Found in the Pentateuch, or first five books of the Old Testament, the *Torah* is the "constitution" of the Jewish people. The word *Torah* literally means "the law" or "direction" or "guidance." All other sources of Jewish law are an outgrowth or dependent on the early teachings of the *Torah*.

FROM *LEVITICUS*

And when ye reap the harvest of your land, thou shalt not wholly reap the corners of thy field, neither shalt thou gather the gleanings of thy harvest.

And thou shalt not glean thy vineyard, neither shalt thou gather *every* grape of thy vineyard; thou shalt leave them for the poor and stranger: I *am* the LORD your God.

Ye shall not steal, neither deal falsely, neither lie one to another.

And ye shall not swear by my name falsely, neither shalt thou profane the name of thy God: I *am* the LORD.

Thou shalt not defraud thy neighbour, neither rob *him:* the wages of him that is hired shall not abide with thee all night until the morning.

Thou shalt not curse the deaf, nor put a stumbling-block before the blind, but shalt fear thy God: I *am* the LORD.

Ye shall do no unrighteousness in judgment; thou shalt not respect the person of the poor, nor honour the person of the mighty: *but* in righteousness shalt thou judge thy neighbour.

Thou shalt not go up and down *as* a tale-bearer among thy people; neither shalt thou stand against the blood of thy neighbour; I *am* the LORD.

Thou shalt not hate thy brother in thy heart: thou shalt not in any wise rebuke thy neighbour, and not suffer sin upon him.

Thou shalt not avenge, nor bear any grudge against the children of thy people, but thou shalt love thy neighbour as thyself: I *am* the LORD.

Ye shall not eat *any thing* with the blood: neither shall ye use enchantment, nor observe times.

Regard not them that have familiar spirits, neither seek after wizards, to be defiled by them: I *am* the LORD your God.

Thou shalt rise up before the hoary head, and honour the face of the old man, and fear thy God: I *am* the LORD.

And if a stranger sojourn with thee in your land, ye shall not vex him.

But the stranger that dwelleth with you shall be unto you as one born among you, and thou shalt love him as thyself; for ye were strangers in the land of Egypt; I *am* the LORD your God.

Ye shall do no unrighteousness in judgment, in meteyard, in weight, or in measure.

Just balances, just weights, a just ephah, and a just hin shall ye have: I *am* the LORD your God, which brought you out of the land of Egypt.

Therefore shall ye observe all my statutes, and all my judgments, and do them: I *am* the LORD.

XIX

And the LORD spake unto Moses in mount Sinai saying, Speak unto the children of Israel, and say unto them, When ye come into the land which I give you then shall the land keep a sabbath unto the LORD.

Six years thou shalt sow thy field, and six years thou shalt prune thy vineyard, and gather in the fruit thereof;

But in the seventh year shall be a sabbath of rest unto the

land, a sabbath for the LORD; thou shalt neither sow thy field, nor prune thy vineyard.

That which groweth of its own accord of thy harvest, thou shalt not reap, neither gather the grapes of thy vine undressed: *for* it is a year of rest unto the land.

And the sabbath of the land shall be meat for you; for thee, and for thy servant, and for thy maid, and for thy hired servant, and for thy stranger that sojourneth with thee.

And for thy cattle, and for the beasts that *are* in thy land, shall all the increase thereof be meat.

And thou shalt number seven sabbaths of years unto thee, seven times seven years; and the space of the seven sabbaths of years shall be unto thee forty and nine years.

Then shalt thou cause the trumpet of the jubilee to sound on the tenth *day* of the seventh month, in the day of atonement shall ye make the trumpet sound throughout all your land.

And ye shall hallow the fiftieth year, and proclaim liberty throughout *all* the land unto all the inhabitants thereof: it shall be a jubilee unto you; and you shall return every man unto his possession, and ye shall return every man unto his family.

A jubilee shall that fiftieth year be unto you: ye shall not sow, neither reap that which groweth of itself in it, nor gather *the grapes* in it of thy vine undressed.

For it *is* the jubilee; it shall be holy unto you: ye shall eat the increase thereof out of the field.

In the year of this jubilee ye shall return every man unto his possession.

And if thou sell aught unto thy neighbour, or buyest *aught* of thy neighbour's hand, ye shall not oppress one another:

According to the number of years after the jubilee, thou shalt buy of thy neighbour, *and* according unto the number of years of the fruits he shall sell unto thee:

According to the multitude of years thou shalt increase the price thereof, and according to the fewness of years thou shalt diminish the price of it: for *according* to the number *of the years* of the fruits doth he sell unto thee.

Ye shall not therefore oppress one another; but thou shalt fear thy God: for I *am* the LORD your God.

Wherefore ye shall do my statutes, and keep my judgments, and do them; and ye shall dwell in the land in safety.

And the land shall yield her fruit, and ye shall eat your fill, and dwell therein in safety.

And if ye shall say, What shall we eat the seventh year? behold, we shall not sow nor gather in our increase:

Then I will command my blessing upon you in the sixth year, and it shall bring forth fruit for three years.

And ye shall sow the eighth year, and eat *yet* of old fruit until the ninth year; until her fruits come in ye shall eat *of* the old *store*.

The land shall not be sold for ever; for the land *is* mine, for ye *are* strangers and sojourners with me.

And in all the land of your possession ye shall grant a redemption for the land.

If thy brother be waxen poor, and hath sold away *some* of his possession, and if any of his kin come to redeem it, then shall he redeem that which his brother sold.

And if the man have none to redeem it, and himself be able to redeem it;

Then let him count the years of the sale thereof, and restore the overplus unto the man to whom he sold it; that he may return unto his possession.

But if he be not able to restore *it* to him, then that which is sold shall remain in the hand of him that hath bought it until the year of jubilee: and in the jubilee it shall go out, and he shall return unto his possession.

And if a man sell a dwelling-house in a walled city, then he may redeem it within a whole year after it is sold: *within* a full year may he redeem it.

And if it be not redeemed within the space of a full year, then the house that *is* in the walled city shall be established for ever to him that bought it, throughout his generations: it shall not go out in the jubilee.

But the houses of the villages which have no walls round about them, shall be counted as the fields of the country: they may be redeemed, and they shall got out in the jubilee.

Notwithstanding the cities of the Levites, *and* the houses of the cities of their possession, may the Levites redeem at any time.

And if a man purchase of the Levites, then the house that was sold, and the city of his possession shall go out in *the year of* jubilee; for the houses of the cities of the Levites *are their possession among the children of Israel.*

But the field of the suburbs of their cities may not be sold, for it *is* their perpetual possession.

And if thy brother be waxen poor, and fallen in decay with thee; then thou shalt relieve him: *yea, though he be* a stranger, or a sojourner; that he may live with thee.

Take thou no usury of him, or increase; but fear thy God; that thy brother may live with thee.

Thou shalt not give him thy money upon usury, nor lend him thy victuals for increase.

I *am* the LORD your God, which brought you forth out of the land of Egypt, to give you the land of Canaan, *and* to be your God.

And if thy brother *that dwelleth* by thee be waxen poor, and be sold unto thee; thou shalt not compel him to serve as a bond-servant:

But as a hired servant, and as a sojourner he shall be with thee, *and* shall serve thee unto the year of jubilee:

And *then* shall he depart from thee, *both* he and his children with him, and shall return unto his own family, and unto the possession of his fathers shall he return.

For they *are* my servants which I brought forth out of the land of Egypt; they shall not be sold as bond-men.

Thou shalt not rule over him with rigour, but shalt fear thy God.

THE TEN COMMANDMENTS

Although there is some disagreement as to just which commandments should be considered the "Ten Commandments," there
can be little doubt that their influence has been part of the basic
foundation of modern law in the so-called Christian world. They
are found, in somewhat different language, in both Exodus XX
and Deuteronomy V in the Old Testament of the Bible. The
first four Commandments are purely religious, but the rest have
secular significance. Like modern law the Ten Commandments
illustrate the need of lawyers and judges to interpret the law.
Thus the Jewish jurists have been required to interpret, clarify,
and make exceptions not only in the Ten Commandments but
in the general area of Mosaic law. The number of Commandments, which are not numbered in any way, probably came with
the ease of counting off on the fingers the separate Commandments.

EXODUS 20

1. And God spake all these words, saying,
2. I am the Lord thy God, which have brought thee out of
the land of Egypt, out of the house of bondage.
3. Thou shalt have no other gods before me.
4. Thou shalt not make unto thee any graven image, or any
likeness of anything that is in heaven above, or that is in
the earth beneath, or that is in the water under the earth;
5. Thou shalt not bow down thyself to them, nor serve

them: for I the Lord thy God am a jealous God, visiting the iniquity of the fathers upon the children unto the third and fourth generation of them that hate me;

6. And shewing mercy unto thousands of them that love me, and keep my commandments.

7. Thou shalt not take the name of the Lord thy God in vain; for the Lord will not hold him guiltless that taketh his name in vain.

8. Remember the sabbath day, to keep it holy.

9. Six days shalt thou labour, and do all thy work:

10. But the seventh day is the sabbath of the Lord thy God: in it thou shalt not do any work, thou, nor thy son, nor thy daughter, thy manservant, nor thy maidservant, nor thy cattle, nor thy stranger that is within thy gates:

11. For in six days the Lord made heaven and earth, the sea, and all that in them is, and rested the seventh day: wherefore the Lord blessed the sabbath day, and hallowed it.

12. Honour thy father and thy mother: that thy days may be long upon the land which the Lord thy God giveth thee.

13. Thou shalt not kill.

14. Thou shalt not commit adultery.

15. Thou shalt not steal.

16. Thou shalt not bear false witness against thy neighbour.

17. Thou shalt not covet thy neighbour's house, thou shalt not covet thy neighbour's wife, nor his manservant, nor his maidservant, nor his ox, nor his ass, nor any thing that is thy neighbour's.

THE TALMUD*

The *Talmud* is divided into two divisions, the Mishna or He-
brew oral law, and the Gemara which is in Aramaic and is a sort
of commentary and supplement to the Mishna. The Gemara was
the outgrowth of scholarly work which served to expound upon
and interpret the Mishna. The Mishna is divided into six orders
and comprises sixty-three tractates of which only thirty-six and
a half have a Gemara. The Mishna is practically the sole work of
Judah I, who collected and organized the legal material which
had been accumulated through the exposition of the law by the
Soferim. The legal section of the Gemara illustrates the application of ethical and religious principles through legends, parables
and anecdotes, and is called the Halakah. There are two *Tal-
muds,* the first finished in Palestine in the fifth century and the
second more complete *Talmud* produced in the sixth century in
Babylonia.

Mishna, V: All special artificers are considered bailees
for hire. If, however, they have notified the owners that the
work is ready and they may take it, and the payment should
be made thereafter, they are considered from that time
gratuitous bailees. If one says: "Guard for me this article,
and I will guard yours," the depositary is considered a bailee
for hire. If one says: "Guard for me this article," and the
depositary answers: "Leave it with me," he is a gratuitous
bailee. If one has lent money on a pledge, he is considered
a bailee for hire. R. Jehudah, however, said that if he has
lent him money on a pledge (without interest) he is con-

*From Baba Melzia, II, 6, Translated by Rodkinson.

sidered a gratuitous bailee; if, however, he has lent fruit on the pledge, he is considered a bailee for hire . . .

Gemara: . . . *"If, however, they have notified,"* etc. There is a Mishna (in Chapter VIII of this tract): "If the borrower told the lender to send through a messenger, and he did so, he is responsible for an accident; and the same is the case when he returns it in that way." . . .

Huna Mar b. Mrimar, in the presence of Rabina, raised a contradiction between the two Mishnas mentioned above, and afterwards explained them as follows: In our Mishna it is stated: If they said, "Take yours," etc., they are considered from that time bailees for hire; and the same is the case if they have notified the owners that the work is ready for them. Is it not a contradiction from the above-cited Mishna that if the borrower told him to send, etc., he is responsible? (Hence we see that it is considered under the control of the borrower even when he returned it, and this contradicts the statement in our Mishna, which is, that as soon as the specialist has notified the owner of the article that it is ready for delivery it is considered under the control of the owner.) And he himself answered that Raphram b. Papa said, in the name of R. Hisda, that the cited Mishna treats of when the borrower has returned the loan through his messenger before the agreed time has elapsed (consequently it was under his control unquestionably); but if he did so after the elapse of the agreed time, he is free.

The schoolmen propounded a question: What is meant by the expression "free"? Is it meant free of the responsibility of a borrower (who is responsible for an accident also), but that he is still responsible as a bailee for hire (who must pay for theft and loss), or does it mean entirely free from any charge? Said Amimar: It seems that he is free only from the responsibility of a borrower, but not from the responsibility of a bailee for hire; as he has derived benefit from it, he is considered such . . .

"Guard for me," etc. Why so? Is this not to be considered a guard in the presence of the owner? . . .

The rabbis taught: if one says: "Guard for me this article, and I will guard yours to-morrow; or, lend me, and I will lend you;" "guard for me, and I will lend you," or vice versa, all are considered bailees for hire, one to the other.

There were sellers of spices who agreed that each one of them should be engaged one day in each week in preparing food for the whole company. One day they said to one of their number: "Go and bake bread for us," and he replied: "Then guard for me my garment." They, however, neglected to do so, and the garment was stolen; and when the case came before R. Papa, he made them responsible. Said the rabbis to R. Papa: Why should they be responsible? Was not the neglect in the presence of the owner? And he was embarrassed. Finally it was learned that at the time the garment was stolen its owner was not occupied in baking, but was drinking beer (consequently the decision of R. Papa was a just one). But why was R. Papa embarrassed? There is a different opinion between the Tanaim in such a case. According to one, he is free; and according to the other, he is not. Could not R. Papa say that he agreed with the latter? The case was, the day on which he was told to bake for the company was not the day appointed for him, and he was asked to do this as a favor. He, however says: "For this favor you will favor me by guarding my garment," and it was not owing to wilful neglect that it was stolen. And R. Papa made them responsible according to the law of a bailee for hire; and the rabbis told him that the company ought not to be held responsible, because of the law concerning a guard in the presence of the owner, to which all agree that there is no responsibility, and therefore he was embarrassed; but finally it was learned that his decision was correct as stated above.

There were two men on the road; one was tall and the other was short. The tall man was riding an ass, and with him an ironed sheet for a covering, and the short one was covered with a cloak (a woolen one). When they came to cross a stream, the short man placed his cloak upon the ass, and instead of it took the sheet of the tall man and wrapped himself up in it, and the water carried it away. When the case came before Rabha he made him responsible. Said the rabbis to Rabha: Why should he be responsible? Was it not in the presence of his owner (i.e., at the same time the sheet was lost, the lender was crossing the stream with the borrower's cloak; is this not equal to the case, "guard my article, and I will do so with yours," of which it is said above that if it was at the same time there is no responsibility)? And Rabha was embarrassed. Finally, it was learned that the short man took it without the consent of his comrade, and he also placed his cloak upon the ass without consent. . . .

"On a pledge, he is a bailee for hire," etc. Our Mishna is not in accordance with R. Eliezer of the following Boraitha: "If one lends money on a pledge, and the pledge was lost, he may take an oath that there was no wilful neglect in guarding it, and collect his money from the borrower; so is the decree of R. Eliezer." R. Aqiba, however, maintains the defendant may claim, "You have lent me the money only on this pledge, and as the pledge is lost, so is your money." But if he lends a thousand zuz on a note, and also added a pledge, then all agree that he loses his money in case the pledge is lost (as then the pledge is not for any other purpose than to collect the money from it in case of default; otherwise the note would be sufficient even from an encumbered estate. Hence we see that R. Eliezer considers the possessor of the pledge a gratuitous bailee, contrary to our Mishna).

Shall we assume that the above-mentioned older masters [of the Mishna period] speak of a case in which the pledge was not worth the amount lent upon it, and their point of differing is in a case which is similar to Samuel's following theory: If one lends to his neighbor a thousand zuz, and pledges for them the handle of a scythe only, if the handle is lost, the thousand zuz are lost (as he accepted it as a pledge for his money, he intends to collect his money only from it)? Nay, when the pledge was not worth the amount lent, none of them agrees with Samuel, as they speak of a pledge worth the amount lent. . . .

But is it to be assumed that as to the above decision of R. Joseph the older masters differ? Nay; all agree with his decision. Here, however, they differ in case the lender uses this pledge for the purpose of deducting from the debt. According to one, a meritorious deed was done by him by lending the money (for which he will be rewarded), and he is therefore considered a bailee for hire; and according to the other, the using of the pledge is for his own sake, and there is no meritorious deed, and therefore he is considered a gratuitous bailee.

III.

ANCIENT GREECE

CITY LAWS OF GORTYNA*

While none of the law records of Minos, the first Greek lawgiver, who lived perhaps 1600 B.C., have survived, the oldest law now existing belongs in Crete about 1000 years later than laws of the City of Gortyna, dating from perhaps 400 B.C. and was found chiseled into stone that in its original form was perhaps 30 feet long. The first paragraphs of these legal documents prescribe the method of trying an issue of individual freedom or slavery while later paragraphs deal mainly with the inheritance of property.

[1] Whoever claims for his own another person, whether free or slave, shall not distrain him before suit. If he does, he shall be adjudged to pay for such distraint 10 staters to the freeman or 5 staters to the slave, and to release him within 3 days. If he does not release him, he shall be adjudged to pay, for each day of delay, 1 stater to the free man or 1 drachma to the slave. The time shall be determined by the judge's oath. If he denies the distraint, the judge's oath shall determine, if there is no witness. . . .

[25] To the father belongs the power over the children and the property, and he may make partition of the property; and the mother likewise as to her own property; but while they live partition is not demandable. But if one child is adjudged liable to pay to some one, the prescribed share may be allotted to the child so adjudged.

[26] If a man dies, his town houses, and all therein, ex-

*From the French translation in R. Dareste, etc., *Recueil des Inscriptions Juridiques Grecques,* I Paris, 1891.

cept such houses as occupied by serfs attached to the rural lands, and the sheep and large cattle, except those in a serf's possession, shall go to the sons. All the rest of the property shall be divided, as fairly as may be, two parts to each son however many there are, and one part to each daughter, however many there are.

[27] The mother's goods also shall be divided, if she dies, in the same manner as the father's. . . .

[31] If a man or a woman dies, and if there exist children, or children's children, or the latter's children, this group shall have the property. And if none of these exist, then the deceased's brothers and their children and the latter's children, this group shall have the property. And if none of these exist, the sisters of the deceased and their children and the latter's children, this group shall have the property. And if none of these exist, then the other relatives whoever they are, this group shall have the property. And if no other relatives exist, all those who are the household's serfs, these shall have the property. . . .

[36] While the father lives, the father's property shall not be sold nor mortgaged by the son; but what the son has himself earned or received by partition he may dispose of as he pleases. Nor shall the father dispose of property earned by the children or partitioned to them, nor the husband dispose of nor bind the wife's property, nor the son the mother's.

[37] If any one buys or takes in mortgage or receives an obligation on property other than as prescribed herein, the property shall remain in the mother or wife, and he who has [fraudulently] sold, mortgaged, or promised it shall pay double to the vendee, mortgagee, or promisee, and the full amount of any other loss caused; but transactions prior to this law shall not be adjudged by it. If the opponent [in a proceeding under this law] disputes that the property belongs to the mother or wife, the claim shall be adjudicated before the court having jurisdiction.

[38] If a mother dies leaving children, to the father belongs the power over the mother's property, but he shall not

dispose of or mortgage it, unless the children consent, being of age. And if any one buys or takes a mortgage contrary hereto, the property shall remain in the children, and to the buyer or mortgagee he who has [fraudulently] disposed or mortgaged shall pay double the sum and also the full amount of any loss caused.

[39] If the father marries another woman [after the first wife's death], the children shall have the power over their mother's property.

IV.

THE LAW THAT WAS ROME

LAWS OF THE TWELVE TABLES*

The Twelve Tables constitute the earliest Roman code of laws. They were drawn up by a special commission in 451-450 B.C., and published in the Roman Forum on tablets of bronze or wood.

The original Tables were destroyed when the Gauls sacked Rome, but possibly a third of the original text has survived. Some passages, however, in archaic language, are not always clear.

LAW I

Sons shall be under the jurisdiction of the father.

This implies, in the early Roman state, the patria potestas, the sovereign authority of the Roman father over all members of the family, and included the power of life and death over his children.

LAW II

Sons shall not possess any property while the father is alive.

The father's authority was such that the son had no personal possessions. Whatever he did possess reverted to the father and was within the father's jurisdiction. Later laws modified the harshness of this law, as for laws associated with Ulpian, Theodosius, Justinian.

LAW III

Parents shall have the right to sell their children thrice, and that shall be their authority.

*Translated by H. E. Wedeck.

The sale of children was, according to some jurists, necessitated by domestic scarcities of food: *ob nimiam egestatem victus.*

LAW IV
Those who are free by statute may be sold as slaves.

Ulpian the purist expounds this law as meaning: A slave ordered to be freed in accordance with a will is called free by statute.

LAW V
It is ordered that a man be free, who gives the heir 10,000 sesterces and is sold by him; by giving a sum of money to the buyer, he shall secure his freedom.

Ulpian the purist asserts: if one who is free by statute is sold by the heir, he carries with him the status of a free man.

The nominal value of a Roman sestertius was approximately 4.1 cents.

LAW VI
Patricians shall not contract marriages with the commons.

In accordance with the Julian Law, the sons of senators as well were forbidden marriage with freedwomen and professional prostitutes.

LAW VII
If a father sells his son thrice, the son shall be free of his father.

Ulpian cites this law in listing methods of manumitting children: by emancipation, death, banishment, captivity.

LAW IX
Private statutes shall not be proposed, except in the comitia centuriata.

According to Ulpian, since a law is a common decree, it does not exclude individual persons.

LAW X

Whoever sets a hedge around his land shall not exceed the boundary; in the case of a wall, he shall leave one foot; in the case of a house, two feet. If a grave or pit, the required depth. If a well, a path, an olive or fig tree, nine feet. Finally, whoever plants other trees shall leave a space of five feet between property and his neighbor's. If there is litigation about boundaries, five feet.

LAW XIII

No one shall exact interest at more than a twelfth of the principal yearly.

This rate of interest, which was 8⅓ per cent, was often exceeded in later Roman times.

LAW XIV

If the people, or worshippers of the same religion, or priests of the mystery cults, or mariners, or guild members, or those who have a common burial ground, or tax collectors, or those who belong to a club for buying cattle, or for transacting business, or those who meet for any other purpose, make an agreement among themselves, it shall be valid, provided the public records do not forbid it.

LAW XV

In contracts, what is orally promised shall be valid.

LAW XVI

Things sold and given shall be possessed by the buyer as if he paid the price to the vendor or satisfied him in any other manner.

LAW XVII

The use and prescriptive title of any property shall be for a period of two years; in other cases, it shall be for one year.

LAW XVIII
Against a foreigner there shall be prescriptive title to property in perpetuity.

LAW XIX
In the case of a stolen object there shall be prescriptive title in perpetuity.

LAW XX
If timber is attached to your house or your vines, you shall not remove it, but give double the price to the offender.

LAW XXII
If a neighbor's cattle graze in your field, legal action shall be taken over the question of grazing.

LAW XXIII
If a four-footed animal causes damage, there shall be an action at law against the owner of the animal.

LAW XXIV
If a man leaves a legacy in respect of money or the guardianship of his property, it shall be valid by law.

LAW XXVI
Those to whom a guardian has not been assigned by a will shall be legal guardians.

LAW XXVII
If a person is insane, there shall be jurisdiction over him and his finances by his relatives and kinsmen.

LAW XXVIII
A spendthrift shall have no jurisdiction over property, and he shall be in the charge of his relatives.

LAW XXX
If a guardian is under suspicion, there shall be a court action.

LAW XXXIII

Inheritances of those who die intestate shall automatically go to the first of the heirs; and the grandsons shall succeed to the sons.

LAW XXXVII

Daughters shall have the same rights as sons in the matter of the property of a freedman father.

LAW XL

The dead shall not be buried or cremated within the city.

LAW XLII

Funerals shall not involve expense; the funeral pile shall not be smoothed with the axe.

LAW XLIII

Women shall not lacerate their cheeks; nor shall they lament at a funeral.

LAW XLVIII

If a patron commits a fraud, he shall be accursed; he shall be bound to silence; and throughout his life he shall be unworthy to hold any office or magistracy.

LAW LI

If a judge, or one of the litigants, is prevented from appearance by a serious illness, the day of trial shall be adjourned.

LAW LIV

In the presence of witnesses, claims shall be lodged by those who are entertaining litigation.

LAW LIX

There shall be no assemblies at night.

The jurist makes a comment on this law: that it is a proper

regulation, as, according to the poet Menander, the night-time is associated with evil activities, involving attacks of armed men, looting, burning, pillaging of all kinds.

LAW LXI
The death penalty of a citizen shall not be determined except in the comitia centuriata.

LAW LXII
If a person encourages an enemy or betrays a citizen to an enemy, he shall suffer the death penalty.

LAW LXIII
The charge of treason is punishable by death.
According to Ulpian's definition, a man may be charged with treason if he acts with hostile intentions against the State or against the Emperor.

LAW LXIV
There shall be the same law for those who have defected as for those who have remained loyal.

LAW LXV
If a man swears false testimony, he shall be thrown from the tarpeian rock.
The harshness of the punishment was thought to be in the nature of a deterrent, a measure of prevention rather than a consequent penalty.

LAW LXVI
If a man is assigned by law as a judge or arbiter, and is convicted of having received monies for deciding a case, he shall suffer the death penalty.

LAW LXVII
Whoever performs a spell or composes one that invokes infamy and outrage upon another shall suffer the death penalty.

74

LAW LXVIII

Whoever casts an evil spell or puts a spell upon crops shall be restrained.

LAW LXIX

You shall not lure away by incantation your neighbor's harvest.

LAW LXX

If a man unjustly cuts down his neighbor's trees, he shall pay twenty-five pieces of money for each tree.

LAW LXXII

If a thief is caught red-handed and committed the theft when it was dark, or was caught armed in the daytime, he shall be put to death. If others caught in the act are free men, they shall receive lashes. If a man commits a theft in the open daylight and is not armed, he shall be sentenced. Slaves, after receiving lashes, shall be thrown from the tarpeian rock.

LAW LXXIV

In the case of a theft it shall be lawful to effect an agreement.

LAW LXXV

If a man breaks my limb, there shall be retribution according to agreement.

LAW LXXVI

If a man does a wrong to another, the penalty shall be twenty-five pieces of money.

CATO THE ELDER* (234-149 B.C.)

IN SUPPORT OF THE OPPIAN LAW

Renowned for his devotion to the old Roman ideals, simplicity of life, courage, honesty, morality and loyalty to family and Rome, Cato the Elder or Cato the Censor, to distinguish him from his grandson, sought to limit luxury, restrict seats in the senate and undertook much building and repair of the city. After being sent on an official visit to Carthage Cato returned with strong disapproval of Carthaginian ways and thereafter ended every speech he made in the senate with the words "Carthage much be destroyed." In this way he helped to bring on the Third Punic War in which Carthage was destroyed. Cato exemplified many of the old Roman virtues and some of the Roman shortcomings. His acceptance of class division prompted harshness toward his servants and his dislike for extravagance made him miserly. Of his many written works most are now lost. The most influential single work was his history of early Rome, which may be considered the first real Roman historical work. The present excerpt was from an address in which he supported a repressive measure against women.

If, Romans, every individual among us had made it a rule to maintain the prerogative and authority of a husband with respect to his own wife, we should have less trouble with the whole sex. But now our privileges, overpowered at home by female contumacy, are, even here in the Forum, spurned and trodden under foot; and because we are unable to with-

*From *The World's Great Speeches,* edited by Lewis Copeland and Lawrence W. Lamm, New York, Dover Publications, Inc., 1958.

stand each separately we now dread their collective body. I was accustomed to think it a fabulous and fictitious tale that in a certain island the whole race of males was utterly extirpated by a conspiracy of the women.

But the utmost danger may be apprehended equally from either sex if you suffer cabals and secret consultations to be held; scarcely indeed can I determine, in my own mind, whether the act itself, or the precedent that it accords, is of more pernicious tendency. The latter of these more particularly concerns us consuls and the other magistrates; the former, you, my fellow citizens: for, whether the measure proposed to your consideration be profitable to the state or not, is to be determined by you, who are to vote on the occasion.

As to the outrageous behavior of these women, whether it be merely an act of their own, or owing to your instigations, Marcus Fundanius and Lucius Valerius, it unquestionably implies culpable conduct in magistrates. I know not whether it reflects greater disgrace on you, tribunes, or on the consuls: on you certainly, if you have brought these women hither for raising tribunitian seditions; on us, if we suffer laws to be imposed on us by a secession of women, as was done formerly by that of the common people. It was not without painful emotions of shame that I, just now, made my way into the Forum through the midst of a band of women.

Had I not been restrained by respect for the modesty and dignity of some individuals among them, rather than of the whole number, and been unwilling that they should be seen rebuked by a consul, I should not have refrained from saying to them, "What sort of practice is this, of running out into public, besetting the streets, and addressing other women's husbands? Could not each have made the same request to her husband at home? Are your blandishments more seducing in public than in private, and with other women's husbands than with your own? Although if females would let their modesty confine them within the limits of their own rights, it did not become you, even at home, to concern yourselves about any laws that might be passed or repealed here." Our ancestors thought it not proper that women should perform any, even private business, without a director; but that they should be ever under the control of parents, brothers, or husbands. We, it seems, suffer them, now, to interfere in the management of state affairs, and to thrust themselves into the Forum, into general assemblies, and into assemblies of election: for what are they doing at this moment in your streets and lanes? What but arguing, some in support of the motion of tribunes; others contending for the repeal of the law?

Will you give the reins to their intractable nature, and then expect that themselves should set bounds to their licentiousness, and without your interference? This is the smallest of the injunctions laid on them by usage of the law, all which women bear with impatience: they long for entire liberty; nay, to speak the truth, not for liberty, but for unbounded freedom in every particular: for what will they not attempt if they now come off victorious? Recollect all the institutions respecting the sex, by which our forefathers restrained their profligacy and subjected them to their husbands; and yet, even with the help of all these restrictions, they can scarcely be kept within bounds. If, then, you suffer them to throw these off one by one, to tear them all asunder, and, at last, to be set on an equal footing with yourselves, can you imagine that they will be any longer tolerable? Suffer them once to arrive at an equality with you, and they will from that moment become your superiors.

But, indeed, they only object to any new law being made against them; they mean to deprecate, not justice, but severity. Nay, their wish is that a law which you have admitted, established by your suffrages, and found in the practice and experience of so many years to be beneficial, should now be repealed; and that by abolishing one law you should weaken all the rest. No law perfectly suits the convenience of every member of the community; the only consideration is, whether, on the whole, it be profitable to the greater part. If,

because a law proves obnoxious to a private individual, it must therefore be canceled and annulled, to what purpose is it for the community to enact laws, which those, whom they were particularly intended to comprehend, could presently repeal? Let us, however, inquire what this important affair is which has induced the matrons thus to run out into public in this indecorous manner, scarcely restraining from pushing into the Forum and the assembly of the people.

Is it to solicit that their parents, their husbands, children, and brothers may be ransomed from captivity under Hannibal?

By no means: and far be ever from the commonwealth so unfortunate a situation. Yet, when such was the case, you refused this to the prayers which, on that occasion, their duty dictated. But it is not duty, nor solicitude for their friends; it is religion that has collected them together. They are about to receive the Idæan Mother, coming out of Phrygia from Pessinus.

What motive, that even common decency will not allow to be mentioned, is pretended for this female insurrection? Hear the answer:

That we may shine in gold and purple; that, both on festival and common days, we may ride through the city in our chariots, triumphing over vanquished and abrogated law, after having captured and wrested from you your suffrages; and that there may be no bounds to our expenses and our luxury.

Often have you heard me complain of the profuse expenses of the women—often of those of the men; and that not only of men in private stations, but of the magistrates; and that the state was endangered by two opposite vices, luxury and avarice; those pests which have ever been the ruin of every great state. These I dread the more, as the circumstances of the commonwealth grow daily more prosperous and happy; as the empire increases; as we have passed over into Greece and Asia, places abounding with every kind of temptation that can inflame the passions; and as we have begun to handle even royal treasures: for I greatly fear that these matters will rather bring us into captivity than we them.

Believe me, those statues from Syracuse made their way into this city with hostile effect. I already hear too many commending and admiring the decorations of Athens and Corinth, and ridiculing the earthen images of our Roman gods that stand on the fronts of their temples. For my part, I prefer these gods,—propitious as they are, and I hope will continue, if we allow them to remain in their own mansions.

In the memory of our fathers, Pyrrhus, by his ambassador Cineas, made trial of the dispositions, not only of our men, but of our women also, by offers of presents: at that time the Oppian law, for restraining female luxury, had not been made; and yet not one woman accepted a present. What, think you, was the reason? That for which our ancestors made no provision by law on this subject: there was no luxury existing which might be restrained.

As diseases must necessarily be known before their remedies, so passions come into being before the laws which prescribe limits to them. What called forth the Licinian law, restricting estates to five hundred acres, but the unbounded desire for enlarging estates? What the Cineian law, concerning gifts and presents, but that the plebeians had become vassals and tributaries to the senate? It is not, therefore, in any degree surprising that no want of the Oppian law, or of any other, to limit the expenses of the women, was felt at that time, when they refused to receive gold and purple that was thrown in their way and offered to their acceptance. If Cineas were now to go round the city with his presents, he would find numbers of women standing in the public streets ready to receive them.

There are some passions the causes or motives of which I can no way account for. To be debarred of a liberty in which another is indulged may perhaps naturally excite some degree of shame or indignation; yet, when the dress of all is alike, what inferiority in appearance can any one be ashamed of? Of all kinds of shame, the worst, surely, is the being ashamed of frugality or of poverty; but the law relieves you with regard to both; you want only that which it is unlawful for you to have.

This equalization, says the rich matron, is the very thing that I cannot endure. Why do not I make a figure, distinguished with gold and purple? Why is the poverty of others concealed under this cover of a law, so that it should be thought that, if the law permitted, they would have such things as they are not now able to procure? Romans, do you wish to excite among your wives an emulation of this sort, that the rich should wish to have what no other can have; and that the poor, lest they should be despised as such, should extend their expenses beyond their abilities? Be assured that when a woman once begins to be ashamed of what she ought not to be ashamed of, she will not be ashamed of what she ought. She who can, will purchase out of her own purse; she who cannot, will ask her husband.

Unhappy is the husband, both he who complies with the request, and he who does not; for what he will not give himself, another will. Now they openly solicit favors from other women's husbands; and, what is more, solicit a law and votes. From some they obtain them; although, with regard to you, your property, or your children, you would find it hard to obtain anything from them. If the law ceases to limit the expenses of your wife, you yourself will never be able to limit them. Do not suppose that the matter will hereafter be in the same state in which it was before the law was made on the subject. It is safer that a wicked man should never be accused than that he should be acquitted; and luxury, if it had never been meddled with, would be more tolerable than it will be, now, like a wild beast, irritated by having been chained and then let loose. My opinion is that the Oppian law ought on no account to be repealed. Whatever determination you may come to, I pray all the gods to prosper it.

THE CONSTITUTION AND EDICTS OF AUGUSTUS*

Augustus was the first Roman Emperor and the grandson of a sister of Julius Caesar. He is well known for his reforms of the Roman Senate, the city and provinces. He fostered a revival of Roman tradition and considered himself not the ruler of Rome but the first citizen of the republic. His reforms have had far-reaching effects in many areas, including civil and criminal law. He divided the provinces into two classes, the senatorial, ruled by a proconsul, selected by the Senate for a term of one year and an imperial in charge of a governor who served a definite term and was solely responsible to Augustus. Perhaps his greatest achievement was his establishment of the Pax Romana or Roman Peace, which is said to have made possible the civilization of the Roman Empire. The edicts of Augustus are engraved one after the other on a stele found in the agora of Cyrene. There are five edicts, the first four dated 7-6 B.C. These four concern Cyrenaica alone and consist of three regulations, two judicial and one financial, together with the decisions of Augustus in two particular cases. The fifth edict is dated 4 B.C. and applies to the entire Roman Empire, which presents to the provincials a decree of the Senate on the initiative of Augustus himself.

BOOK I

TITLE 1: CONSTITUTIONS AND EDICTS OF THE EMPERORS (DE CONSTITUTIONIBUS PRINCIPUM ET EDICTIS)

1. Emperor Constantine Augustus to the Lusitanians.

If any edicts or constitutions without the day and the year

*From *The Augustan Edicts from Cyrene*, by J. G. C. Anderson.

of the consulship should hereafter be discovered, they shall lack authority.

Given on the seventh day before the kalends of August at Szombathely (Savaria) in the year of the consulship of Probianus and Julianus.—July 26, 322.

INTERPRETATION: If any laws without the day and the year of the consulship should be produced, they shall not be valid.

2. The same Augustuses to Flavianus, Praetorian Prefect of Illyricum and Italy.

We do not permit any person either to be ignorant of or to pretend ignorance of the constitutions which have been carefully weighed with long deliberation by Our Serenity.

Given on the sixth day before the kalends of June at Vincentia in the year of the consulship of the Most Noble Tatianus and Symmachus.—May 27, 391.

INTERPRETATION: No person shall be permitted to be ignorant of the laws or scornful of the statutes.

3. The same Augustuses to Aurelianus, Prefect of the City.

No constitution produces any calumny for past deeds, but all constitutions establish regulations for the future.

Given on the third day before the kalends of March at Constantinople in the year of the third consulship of Our Lord Theodosius Augustus and the consulship of the Most Noble Abundantius.—February 27, 393.

INTERPRETATION: No laws condemn the deeds which have been done at a previous time, but they establish the regulations which must be observed in the future.

4. The same Augustuses to Victorius, Proconsul of Asia.

A general regulation must be preferred to a special grant of imperial favor.

Given on the eleventh day before the kalends of September at Constantinople in the year of the third consulship of Theodosius Augustus and the consulship of the Most Noble Abundantius.—August 22, 393.

INTERPRETATION: A single person or a single case shall not nullify a law which binds all persons in common. . . .

BOOK II

TITLE 1: JURISDICTION; THE PLACE WHERE A PERSON MUST BE SUED (DE JURISDICTIONE ET UBI QUIS CONVENIRI DEBEAT)

1. Emperor Constantius Augustus to Eustathius, Praetorian Prefect.

It is Our will that the judges of the provinces shall assume the power of due authority, so that the same discipline which governs the provincials shall govern the overseers and all other persons of Our imperial estates. Prisons shall hold the scoundrels when they are convicted, tortures shall tear them in pieces, the avenging sword shall destroy them. For in this way the license of the inveterate lawlessness of desperadoes is restrained, if they understand that they must live with one and the same aspiration as do all others. (Etc.)

Given on the eighth day before the ides of March in the year of the consulship of Limenius and Catullinus.—March 8, 349.

INTERPRETATION: Those persons who have been appointed as judges in the provinces shall know that they are permitted to have unrestrained power, if any of the slaves or coloni of the Emperor's private domain should be involved in any criminality, to arrest and punish them, just as their guilt demands, as though they were private persons, and no administrator of Our patrimony shall object.

2. The same Augustus to Taurus, Praetorian Prefect.

It has been decided that the governors of the provinces shall terminate litigation in civil cases, even if men in the imperial service should defend or institute suit. 1. In order, therefore, that no usurpation may confound the courts and the law or rob judges ordinary of their proper jurisdiction, the trials of civil suits shall be transferred to the governors of the provinces. 2. In criminal cases also, if any person in the imperial service should prosecute an accused person, the governor of the province shall try the case. If it should be affirmed that any military man has committed any crime, it shall be tried by the person to whom the direction of military affairs has been entrusted.

Given on the eighth day before the kalends of August at Milan in the year of the consulship of Arbito and Lollianus. —July 25, 355.

INTERPRETATION: Although We order that the governors of the provinces shall have jurisdiction over civil cases, nevertheless, wherever a criminal action arises between those persons who serve with Our arms, and private citizens, the governor of the province shall have the power to hear and judge if a soldier should summon a private citizen into court. But if by chance a private citizen should bring suit against one serving Us in arms, or one in the imperial service, that person shall hear the case under whose command the one in the imperial service or the bearer of arms serves.

3. The same Augustus and Julian Caesar to Taurus, Praetorian Prefect.

Not only against the members of the secret service but also against other men of whatever status, punishment of adequate vigor shall be inflicted if only it should be proved that they are guilty of wrongdoing. If any person, therefore, should commit any wicked or shameful act or by chance should violate the chastity of anyone with the stain of lust, vengeance of appropriate severity must be extended against him. When, however, persons testify that grave wrongs have been committed and appear to have brought a complaint against rapine, the guilty persons shall be compelled to restore twofold that property which they appear to have entered and seized by force.

Given and received on the eighth day before the kalends of October in the year of the ninth consulship of Constantius

Augustus and the second consulship of Julian Caesar.—September 24, 357.

INTERPRETATION: In the case of all persons, even those who are attended by the dignity of Our presence, it is Our will that this decree shall be observed: namely, that if a person should violate the chastity of anyone, he shall receive the punishment established by law, and if any person should commit a robbery, he shall repay twofold that which he has violently seized.

4. Emperors Valentinian and Valens Augustuses to Terentius, Governor of Tuscany.

The plaintiff shall follow the forum of the defendant, so that if Senators should sue provincials for anything, they shall litigate before the governor of the province as their judge. If on the other hand a provincial should not defend, but should bring, an action, he shall litigate before the prefect of the City as judge.

Given on the kalends of December at Milan in the year of the consulship of the sainted Jovian and of Varronianus.— December 1, 364.

INTERPRETATION: If any person should suppose that suit should be brought against another, he shall know that his case must be presented before the judge of that province in which the defendant resides. . . .

BOOK III

TITLE 1: CONTRACTS OF PURCHASE (DE CONTRA-HENDA EMPTIONE).

1. Emperor Constantine Augustus to Profuturus, Prefect of the Annona.

It is not at all fitting that the good faith of sale and purchase should be broken, when no duress was exerted through fraud. For a contract that has been executed without any flaw must not be disturbed by a litigious controversy because of the sole complaint that the price was too cheap.

Posted on the ides of August in the year of the fifth consulship of Constantine Augustus and the consulship of Licinius Caesar.—August 13, 319.

INTERPRETATION: When a thing has been purchased for a definite price that is agreed upon between the buyer and seller, although it is worth more than it is sold for at the present, this only must be investigated, whether the person who is proved to have purchased it has committed no fraud or violence. If the seller should wish to revoke the sale, by no means shall he be permitted to do so.

2. The same Augustus to Gregorius.

The purchaser shall assume the tax assessment of property that is purchased, and no person shall be permitted either to buy or sell property without its tax assessment.

1. Moreover, in accordance with this law, there must henceforth be a public or fiscal inspection, so that if any property should be sold without its tax assessment and this fact should be reported by another, the seller, indeed, shall lose the landholding, and the purchaser for his part shall lose the price that he has paid, since the fisc shall vindicate both.

1a. It is also Our pleasure that no person shall engage in the sale of anything whatsoever unless at the time when the contract between the seller and the buyer is formally executed, a certain and true ownership is proved by the neighbors. To such an extent shall the precaution prescribed by this law be observed that even if "benches," or strips of land, as they are commonly called, are sold, the proof of showing ownership shall be fulfilled.

2. Nor shall the formalities between the buyer and the seller be solemnized in hidden corners, but fraudulent sales shall be completely buried and shall perish.

Given on the day before the nones of February at Constantinople in the year of the consulship of Felicianus and Titianus.—February 4, 337.

INTERPRETATION: If any person should purchase a villa, he shall know that he has purchased the obligation of the tribute

87

of the thing itself as well as the right to the landholding, because no person is permitted either to buy or sell a farm without the tribute or fiscal payment. But if any person should dare to sell or presume to purchase anything when the fiscal payment had been concealed, those between whom such a contract has been made by a secret transaction shall know that both the purchaser shall lose the price and the seller shall lose the landholding, because it is ordered that the neighbors of the property which is sold must be witnesses and present, to the extent that even in the case of things of slight value, if anything is sold for use, it is Our pleasure that it shall be shown to the neighbors and thus purchased, in order that the property of others may not be sold.

3. Emperor Julian Augustus to Julianus, Count of the Orient.

We order that the constitution of My paternal uncle, Constantine, shall be repealed, in which he commanded that minor women who were united with husbands in marriage should be able to negotiate sales without the interposition of a decree, if their husbands should suppose that they ought to give their consent as well as provide their subscription to the documents. For it is absurd that husbands who are at times needy men should be obligated for their wives, because when the right itself of the sale is not valid, these women are able to recover their own property from those persons who have participated in the illicit contracts. 1. Therefore We revive the old law, that on no account shall any sale whatsoever be valid when it has been contracted by a minor, whether a man or woman, without the interposition of a decree.

Given on the eighth day before the ides of December at Antioch in the year of the consulship of the Most Noble Mamertinus and Nevitta.—December 6, 362.

INTERPRETATION: It had been ordained by a law of the Emperor Constantine that minor women who had husbands could sell anything from their own resources with the consent of their husbands. But this ordinance is abrogated by the present law, and the following rule must be observed, namely, that if under the compulsion of necessity men or women who are minors should wish to sell anything, whoever should wish to buy it shall be protected by the authorization of the judge or by the consent of the municipal council; for otherwise a sale made by minors will not be valid. . . .

BOOK IV

TITLE 1: CRETION AND THE POSSESSION OF GOODS (DE CRETIONE VEL BONORUM POSSESSIONE)

1. Emperors Theodosius and Valentinian Augustuses to the Senate.

(After other matters.) We shall not allow fathers to be legally inferior to mothers in any particular. For since a mother obtains as a solace the goods of a deceased child, even though it should be an infant, We do not see why a father should suffer the snares of grievous legal technicalities with respect to the age of such child. Since in the case of statutory succession, neither the mother nor even successors farther removed are compelled to observe either the requirements of a petition for the possession of the goods or the formalities of cretion, because the requirements of the statute are satisfied by any indication whatsoever that the heir has entered upon or intends to enter upon the inheritance, how much more should fathers be freed from such constraints?

1. Therefore by this oration We sanction that without any question the father shall succeed to the inheritance of a child even though the child should be an infant and even though at death such infant should be of any age whatever, whether the father of such a child, on the death of the child's mother, has observed the formalities of entering upon the inheritance or of filing the petition for the possession of the goods or has neglected these formalities.

Given on the seventh day before the ides of November at Ravenna in the year of the twelfth consulship of Our Lord

Theodosius Augustus and the second consulship of Our Lord Valentinian Augustus.—November 7, 426.

INTERPRETATION: According to the ancient law, cretion and the possession of the goods were formerly obtained by petition from the praetors. It is not necessary to explain this procedure, since both formalities have been abolished by statute. Therefore an infant child, even though unable to speak, yet takes the inheritance due to him, and on the death of such infant child, his father or nearest kinsman succeeds to his inheritance, according to the law.

TITLE 2: "ON WHAT GROUNDS CHILDREN . . ." ("UNDE LIBERI . . .")

1. Emperors Arcadius and Honorius Augustuses to Aurelianus, Praetorian Prefect.

If a daughter should receive a dowry from her father and should thus be united in marriage, and if her father should die intestate and she should wish to enter upon the inheritance along with her brothers, she shall be required to bring such dowry into a common fund with the estate of her father, and thus she may become a co-heir with her brothers in sharing the inheritance.

Given on the day before the nones of October at Constantinople in the year of the fourth consulship of Arcadius Augustus and the third consulship of Honorius Augustus.— October 6, 396; 402.

INTERPRETATION: If a daughter has been dowered by her father at the time of her marriage and her father afterward dies intestate, and if she should wish to participate as an equal along with her brothers in the remainder of her father's estate, such dowry or whatever she received at the time of her marriage shall be brought by her into a common fund with the paternal inheritance, to be divided with her brothers. But if she should be unwilling to do this, she shall be content with the portion that she received as her share.

TITLE 3: THE CARBONIAN EDICT (DE CARBONI-ANO EDICTO)

1. Emperors Valentinian, Theodosius, and Arcadius Augustuses to Rufinus, Praetorian Prefect.

The benefit of the Carbonian Edict is granted at the request of legally qualified persons when the marriage is undoubted, the birth of the child is guarded, and the statutory right to the succession is proved, so that, of course, the new heir, established in possession of the inheritance until the years of puberty, may without molestation enjoy what at times may prove to be the property of others.

Given on the fourth day before the kalends of October at Constantinople in the year of the third consulship of Theodosius Augustus and the consulship of Abundantius.—September 28, 393.

INTERPRETATION: If any man at his death should leave his lawfully wedded wife pregnant, the law ordains that the wife shall be guarded by the near kinsmen until she arrives at the time of the birth. If she should bear a child within the statutory time limit, the child that is born shall succeed to his portion of the inheritance of his father, and until the fifteenth year of his age he shall possess the estate left by his father, without any person having the right to recover the inheritance, and later the child may defend or prosecute his own suits through a curator. . . .

BOOK V

TITLE 1: STATUTORY INHERITANCES (DE LEGITIMIS HEREDITATIBUS)

1. Emperor Constantine Augustus to Bassus, Prefect of the **City.**

It is Our pleasure that although a mother should not have the rights that accrue to parents on account of their children, a third portion of the entire estate of a child shall devolve upon her whenever she comes to the inheritance on intestacy, even though there should come between a paternal uncle of the decedent or the others to whom unimpaired rights of agnation are extended successively, and who will be the next following agnates by whom the mother could have been formerly excluded from the inheritance by right of consanguinity. Also by a like benefit, although a mother should have the rights that accrue to parents on account of their children, a third portion of such estate shall devolve upon a paternal uncle of the decedent or upon the uncle's son or finally his grandson, even when the tie of agnation is broken, as if, perchance, the right of consanguinity has been destroyed by the emancipation of anyone. Not without cause is it Our pleasure that when the mother is supported by the aforementioned privilege and the ties of agnation have been destroyed, Our benefit shall not be extended beyond the degree of grandson, for otherwise, if many persons were called to the inheritance, too much would appear to be taken from the mother and too little bestowed. 1. Therefore, whether one or several paternal uncles survive, or one or more sons of such paternal uncles, or even grandsons or granddaughters, no more than one third of all the goods shall devolve upon all of them together or upon individuals, in each case according to their degree of kinship. 2. In like manner, if there should be several persons by whom the mother can be excluded, no more than one third of the goods shall accrue to the mother as against them all. 3. Therefore, We decree that if persons of the aforesaid kinship should survive as agnates in unlimited number, the mother's interests shall be supported against them all, although such aid shall not be granted against the mother to all such kinsmen, but only to certain persons included above. Without a petition for possession of the goods—for the benefit rests upon this law and not upon action of the praetor—they shall immediately obtain the full ownership of the portion accruing to them, when the day for the accrual of such portion has arrived, by simple entry, that is, by the appropriation of any piece of property whatsoever, or by the disclosure of their intention. As long as they live they shall have the perpetual right of entry upon the portion of the inheritance granted to them.

4. Indeed, if the inheritance should not be first acquired thus by those persons whom the plan of Our indulgence embraces, We order that nothing shall pass to their successors, but the property shall remain in the possession of those persons who would have been able to retain it before the issuance of this law.

Given on the fourteenth day before the kalends of January at Rome in the year of the second consulship of Crispus and Constantine Caesars.—December (May) 19, 321; 317-319.

INTERPRETATION: If a mother should not have the rights that accrue to parents on account of their children, that is, if a freeborn woman has not borne three, or a freedwoman four, living children, and if perchance such woman should lose an only child who dies intestate and the child at death should leave, together with the mother, one or more paternal uncles, or at least several children or grandchildren of the uncle or uncles, who, however, have not been emancipated, the mother shall succeed to one third of the inheritance of her intestate child, and the uncle or uncles, if there should be more than one, or their children or grandchildren, shall vindicate to themselves two thirds of the inheritance. But if the mother should have the rights that accrue to parents on account of their children, and if, in addition to the mother, a paternal uncle or uncles should survive, even when such uncles have been emancipated, the mother who has the rights that accrue to parents on account of their children shall receive two thirds of the property of her child who dies intestate, and the paternal uncle or uncles shall receive one third. If there should be no paternal uncles surviving, the children of such uncles, however many they may be, shall divide for themselves in equal portions share and share alike. But if there should be no children of paternal uncles, the grandchildren of such uncles shall succeed, with a similar apportionment. In the case of this succession, the present constitution

93

alone is sufficient authorization that, between them, the mother and the paternal uncles or their children or grandchildren shall take exclusive possession of the goods, if, perchance, no person should enter upon this inheritance and those who ought to have entered should die, this constitution excludes their heirs from succession to the inheritance which had not been entered upon, since this law manifestly establishes that an inheritance which a person has not entered upon shall not pass to his heirs. (Here an addition must be made from the law.) . . .

BOOK VI

TITLE 1: OFFICIAL RANKS (DE DIGNITATIBUS)

TITLE 2: SENATORIAL RANK (DE SENATORIA DIGNITATE)

12 (7). Emperors Valens, Gratian, and Valentinian Augustuses to Procopius.

. . . the necessity for the payment of the glebal tax shall be removed. It is recognized that this provision is not only established with reference to grown sons, but it shall also be observed in like manner with respect to daughters.

Given on the eighteenth day before the kalends . . . at Hierapolis in the year of the fourth consulship of Gratian Augustus and the consulship of Merobaudes.—Summer, 377.

13 (8). Emperors Gratian, Valentinian, and Theodosius Augustuses to Hypatius.

If any person by Our bounty should attain the most exalted rank of Senator or if this high dignity should fall to his lot by the felicity of his birth and he should suppose that he should conceal the tax declaration of any landholding, he shall know that such landed estate will be vindicated to the fisc, whatsoever the property may be that was stealthily withdrawn from the resources that rightfully belong to the State.

1. . . . if any person should attain the insignia of consular, he shall not have the privilege of assuming this rank or of exercising this administration, unless by his own written statement he should declare that he acknowledges the title of Senator, that he has established his lares and his domicile or fixed residence in a province and town, and that within the various provinces he possesses nothing more than the definite amount specified in his tax declaration. When this information has been obtained by the palatine bureaus, as soon as possible the complete statement shall make readily clear what titles and how important are the ones that have increased the resources of Our immortal treasury, and to what extent.

2. But the tax declaration of two folles shall remain fixed for all Senators alike, even though perchance they may not have any landholding, provided that they have been advanced to the consular rank or to any very distinguished and lofty position of authority. No person shall be admitted to the insignia of authority unless he has duly affirmed his tax declaration, and from such necessity, only those shall be exempted who have been approved by the honor and their terms of service in the imperial palatine service, whence in accordance with their due, rather than by their request, they are called to the fellowship of the Senatorial order.

Given on the fourth day before the ides of January in the year of the second consulship of Merobaudes and the consulship of Saturninus.—January 10, 383.

14. (9). The same Augustuses to Clearchus, Prefect of the City.

We order that exemption from the payment of the glebal tax shall be granted to all those persons from Macedonia . . . who have been added to the Most August Order of the City of Constantinople, according to the precedent of the Senators who were chosen from Thrace.

Given . . . September at Constantinople in the year of the consulship of Richomer and Clearchus.—August 14-September 13, 384.

15 (10). Emperors Valentinian, Theodosius, and Arcadius Augustuses to Aurelianus, Prefect of the City.

In reply to the complaints of those persons who testify that they are not able to bear the burden of the glebal tax, it has been decreed by the Council of the Most August that seven solidi shall be paid annually for his portion by each man who is not able to fulfill the payment of the folles. By this law We confirm this decree of the aforesaid council to the extent that if the property of any man should be meager and if this tax payment is not displeasing to him, he shall have the free choice, in contemplation of the resources of his patrimony, and he shall not withdraw from his fellowship in this Most August Order, but if the tax payment seems burdensome, that is, ruinous, he shall not seek to retain the Senatorial rank.

Given on the day before the kalends of September at Constantinople in the year of the third consulship of Theodosius Augustus and the consulship of the Most Noble Abundantius. —August 31, 393. . . .

BOOK VII

TITLE 1: MILITARY AFFAIRS (DE RE MILITARI)

1. Emperor Constantine Augustus and the Caesar.

If any man by an infamous conspiracy should give to barbarians an opportunity to plunder Romans, or if any man should share the spoils acquired in any other way, he shall be burned alive.

Given on the fourth day before the kalends of May in the year of the consulship of Severus and Rufinus.—April 28, 323.

INTERPRETATION: If any man in collaboration with any public enemy whatsoever should take plunder or if a person should share booty with brigands, he shall be consumed by fire.

2. Emperor Constantius Augustus to Silvanus, Count and Master of the Horse and Foot.

If any soldier should be permitted to be absent on a leave of absence granted by a tribute or a provost, or if, without consulting the aforementioned officers, he should depart from his military service and standards, for each such soldier the tribunes and provosts shall pay five pounds of gold each to the fisc.

Given on the sixth day before the kalends of June at Sirmium in the year of the consulship of Limenius and Catullinus.—May 27, 349; 352.

3. The same Augustus to Titianus, Praetorian Prefect.

If any soldiers in accordance with Our authority should attain the right for their households to come to them, Your Excellency shall cause to be dispatched to the aforesaid soldiers only their wives, children, and slaves bought with their military peculium, but not those enrolled on the tax lists.

Given on the third day before the kalends of June in the year of the consulship of Limenius and Catullinus.—May 30, 349.

4. The same Augustus to the Most Noble Cretio, Count.

Although at all times care must be taken that discharges from the oaths of military service shall not be granted to any persons unless they ought to enjoy leisure because of their number of terms of service or because of poor health, nevertheless We accept the recommendation of Your Prudence which was made verbally before Us, and therefore We command that those persons who have been released to the leisure of civilian life before the completion of their terms of service and while their health was unimpaired shall be restored to their original service units.

Given on the fifth day before the kalends of July in the year of the consulship of Sergius and Nigrinianus.—June 27, 350; 349. . . .

BOOK VIII

TITLE 1: CIVIL ACCOUNTANTS, MILITARY ACCOUNTANTS, BUREAU CLERKS, AND SECRETARIES (DE NUMERARIIS, ACTUARIIS, SCRINIARIIS, ET EXCEPTORIBUS)

1. Emperor Constantine Augustus to Leontius.

We formerly sanctioned that no person by corrupt solicitation should attain the administration of any office staff, especially that of the office of registrars, but such person must be from the main body and the high ranking members of the office staff concerned. We also command that those persons upon whom such administrative duties have been enjoined shall continue to perform such services as long as it is evident that they are qualified or as long as it is proved that their age does not hinder them in their ability to fulfill their tasks. Thus if the administration remains continually under the control of one person, his loyalty also becomes apparent. Therefore, if any person by the support of corrupt solicitation should attain an office responsible to the fisc, he shall be compelled to pay ten pounds of gold as a fine.

Posted on the fifth day before the ides of June at Hierapolis in the year of the fifth consulship of Constantine Augustus and the consulship of Licinius Caesar.—June 9, 319.

2. The same Augustus.

In order that those persons who are far removed from the office of Your Sublimity and who adduce no evidence of merit through industry and services rendered may not be able to steal into positions that are due to those persons who toil, it is Our pleasure that the secretaries, in accordance with their rank and order of service, shall attain the administration of the office records and be chosen as substitutes for the management thereof and that all other persons shall be rejected. Thus among such secretaries, each one shall obtain his place in accordance with his order in the service and his merit, just as he has deserved to obtain such place by length of time.

Given on the kalends of July at Trier in the year of the consulship of Bassus and Ablavius.—July 1, 331.

3. The same Augustus to Maximus, Praetorian Prefect.

In the interests of the public welfare We command that assistant military accountants and military accountants shall be of ignoble status, that they shall also be sustained by subsistence allowances, and that those of them who are enrolled on the tax lists shall be exempt from the capitation tax.

1. Therefore Your Wisdom shall admonish the competent officers to pay forthwith two subsistence allowances to each military accountant and one allowance to each assistant military accountant. Of the aforesaid persons, you shall provide that only those who are enrolled on the tax lists shall be exempt from the capitation tax as long as they are engaged in actual service; for afterward they shall either be honored by glory and dignity, or else attended with punishment if they should be apprehended in wrongdoing.

Issued on the third day before the nones of May in the year of the consulship of Dalmatius and Zenophilus.—May 5, 333.

4. The same Augustus to Veronicianus, Vicar of Asia.

The rapacious and fraudulent conduct of the accountants who serve the various governors must be so restrained that, as We formerly sanctioned and as We now sanction again, they shall be made subject to the ignoble status of those persons who may be tortured, they shall be subject to the punishment of torture horses and to lacerations, and they shall not perform the duties of this office for more than two years. (Etc.)

Given on the fourteenth day before the kalends of June in the year of the consulship of Optatus and Paulinus.—May 19, 334.

5. Emperor Constantius Augustus to Taurus, Praetorian Prefect.

Military accountants shall be of ignoble status, they shall diligently perform their own duties, and they shall not steal into any positions of dignity, from the enjoyment of which they are prohibited by the divine imperial statutes. To correct this vice, We also command that the salutary regulations of Our father shall be observed, and by the issuance of letters to the masters of the foot and horse, We have instructed them to give effect to this order.

Given on the day before the nones of May at Rome in the year of the ninth consulship of Constantius Augustus and the second consulship of Julian Caesar.—May 6, 357. . . .

BOOK IX

TITLE 1: ACCUSATIONS AND INSCRIPTIONS (DE ACCUSATIONIBUS ET INSCRIPTIONIBUS)

1. Emperor Constantine Augustus to Octavianus, Count of Spain.

If any person of Most Noble rank should rape a maiden or invade the boundaries of another or be apprehended in any wrongdoing or crime, he shall immediately be subjected to the public laws, within the province wherein he perpetrated the offense. Neither shall his name be referred to Our knowledge nor shall he make use of any prescription of forum; for an accusation excludes all prerogatives of rank when a criminal case, not a civil or pecuniary suit, is brought.

Given on the day before the nones of December at Sofia (Serdica)—December 4, (316). Received on the fifth day before the nones of March at Cordoba in the year of the consulship of Gallicanus and Bassius.—March 3, 317.

INTERPRETATION: If any person should commit a crime damnable and punishable by law, he shall not assert that he ought to be prosecuted in his own forum, that is, in the place where he lives, but he shall be punished by the judges of the district in which the crime was committed; and there shall be no reference to the Emperor concerning such person.

2. The same Augustus to Januarinus.

If any person should be unwilling to appear in court within a period of a year from the day on which he was prosecuted as a defendant in court, his property shall be vindicated to the fisc, and if afterwards he should be found and convicted as guilty, he shall be subjected to a more severe sentence. But even if he should be able to establish his innocence by manifest evidence and clear proof, nonetheless his property shall remain in the possession of the fisc.

Given on the ides of January.—January 13. Received on the fifth day before the kalends of August at Corinth in the year of the fifth consulship of Constantine Augustus and the consulship of Licinius Caesar.—July 28, 319.

3. The same Augustus to Agricolanus.

Since it is clear and manifest law that women do not have the right to prosecute public criminal suits, except in certain cases, that is, when prosecuting a case of outrage to themselves or to members of their families, the ancient statutes must be observed. For it is not right that the power to make an accusation should be entrusted generally to women. On the other hand, in public criminal trials at times their testimony or their authority as accusers has been admitted. Advocates also must be warned that they must not, in the interest of gain, rashly accept women as clients, who depend on the security of their sex and perhaps rush into unlawful action.

Posted on the fifth day before the ides of February in the year of the consulship of Probianus and Julianus.—February 9, 322.

INTERPRETATION: Women shall not be permitted, except in their own causes or in those of their families, to accuse any person, since they are prevented by law from undertaking the causes of others. Advocates also must be warned that they shall not, contrary to law, accept as clients women who wish to litigate in the causes of others.

4. The same Augustus to all Provincials.

If there is any person of any position, rank, or dignity whatever who believes that he is able to prove anything truthfully and clearly against any judge, count, or any of My retainers or palatines, in that any of these persons has committed some act which appears to have been done without integrity and justice, let him approach Me and appeal to Me unafraid and secure. I Myself will hear everything; I Myself will conduct an investigation; and if the charge should be proved, I Myself will avenge Myself. Let him speak with safety, and let him speak with a clear conscience. If he should prove the case, as I have said, I Myself will avenge Myself on that person who has deceived Me up to this time with feigned integrity. The person, moreover, who has revealed and proved the offense I will enrich with honors as well as with material rewards. Thus may the Highest Divinity always be propitious to Me and keep Me unharmed, as I hope, with the State most happy and flourishing.

Posted on the fifteenth day before the kalends of October at Nicomedia in the year of the consulship of Paulinus and Julianus.—September 17, 325....

BOOK X

TITLE 1: FISCAL LAW (DE JURE FISCI)

1. Emperor Constantine Augustus and the Caesar to the People.

Henceforth if any property must be seized by the fisc and either is about to be presented by Us to any individual on account of his merits and services, or is about to be sold by the fisc, for the space of a year all persons shall abstain both from petitioning for this property and from purchasing it, while those who consider that their own property has been unjustly acquired by the fisc shall hasten to bring suit against the fisc. Such dispossessed owners shall know and be grateful that the space of a year has been graciously granted to them within which they shall have the right to recover their own property, and if they should prove that their petition is founded on justice, they shall recover and hold their property which will be restored by Our grant of special favor.

Given on the ides of September at Rome in the year of the fourth consulship of Constantine Augustus and of Licinius. September 13, 315.

2. The same Augustus to Severus, Fiscal Representative of Africa.

(After other matters.) From the patrimony of the fisc We have taken out certain landholdings and slaves and presented them to certain individuals. It is Our will that this property shall be held by direct and permanent title and without any question. Punishment is threatened against the fiscal representatives and the masters of Our privy purse and against the apparitors, if they should attempt anything to the contrary. (Etc.)

Posted on the sixteenth day before the kalends of June at Rome in the Forum of Trajan in the year of the fifth consulship of Constantine Augustus and the consulship of Licinius Caesar.—May 17, 319; 357.

INTERPRETATION: It is Our will that if any fields and slaves from the property of Our fisc should be granted to any person, they shall remain in the possession of such person without any mistrust, and a penalty is threatened against the administrators of the property of the imperial household, if it should be learned that they are acting contrary to this regulation.

3. The same Augustus to the Provincials.

We command that even just and well-founded fiscal actions shall be barred, for the sole reason that they were not brought at the proper time. Thus now vexatious suits of private individuals shall be prevented at least by this example, whereby

We command that just fiscal actions shall be barred.

Given on the third day before the kalends of June in the year of the fifth consulship of Constantine Augustus and the consulship of Licinius Caesar.—May 30, 319.

4. The same Augustus to Dometius Dracontius, Master of the Privy Purse in Africa.

Whenever the fisc is either sued or brings suit, it is necessary to await only the space of a year for the determination of the case, because this length of time is sufficient for the preparation of the case, and the interests of either private individuals or of the fisc must not be disturbed for a longer time.

Given on the fourteenth day before the kalends of June at Sofia (Serdica) in the year of the sixth consulship of Constantine Augustus and the consulship of Constans Caesar.—May 19, 320.

5. The same Augustus.

Opportunity for defense must be given to persons disquieted in any way by the fisc, since it is not just that their property be disturbed or an inventory thereof be made while the controversy is still pending. Whenever, therefore, a controversy arises through the fisc undertaking to vindicate the patrimony of any person, all the property shall remain firmly in his possession while the judicial investigation is being conducted. Only if the outcome of the matter should prove that said property should be vindicated by the fisc, then finally shall it be permitted to pursue the property and to institute an inquiry as to the amount of property and goods. This inquiry shall be conducted through an examination of slaves who are of ignoble status, so that if any of the property should be secretly removed, it may be recovered and in addition thereto in the name of a fine an amount equal to the value of the property that was fraudulently carried away.

1. Of course, if the name of any Caesarian should be involved in an inquiry of this sort, he must not be allowed to usurp the benefits of this constitution, since the customary

fraud with which the aforesaid persons ordinarily violate all regulations deserves that an exception be made in their case.

Given on the day before the kalends of January at Sirmium in the year of the seventh consulship of Constantine Augustus and the consulship of Constantius Caesar.—December 31, 326. . . .

BOOK XI

TITLE 1: TAXES IN KIND AND TRIBUTE (DE ANNONA ET TRIBUTIS)

1. Emperor Constantine Augustus to Proclianus.

With the exception of the property of Our private domain and the Catholic churches and the household of Eusebius, of Most Noble memory, Ex-Consul and Ex-Master of the Horse and Foot, and the household of Arsaces, King of Armenia, no person in accordance with Our order shall be assisted by especial advantages for his family property. For the Most Noble Datianus, a patrician, who formerly obtained this special favor, besought that it should be taken from him, with as much insistence as other men have been accustomed to request it. Therefore all men must pay whatever is ascribed by Our hand in the tax levies, but nothing more shall be exacted of them. For if any vicar or any governor of a province should suppose that he may remit anything for any person, he shall be compelled to compensate from his own resources whatever he remitted for others.

Given on the fifteenth day before the kalends of July at Constantinople in the year of the fourth consulship of Constantine Augustus and of Licinius.—June 17, 315; January 18, 360.

2. The same Augustus to Aelianus, Proconsul of Africa.

When landholders have satisfied the public tax payment, they shall deposit their tax receipts with the public registrars so that the registrars or the sexagenarii, mindful of their own risk, shall receive these receipts from the taxpayers, and the taxpayers shall deliver to the several municipalities each month from their own storehouses the actual supplies that are due. This shall be done so that the payment of tribute may not be acknowledged solely from forged or imaginary tax receipts. (Etc.)

Given on the kalends of November at Trier in the year of the fourth consulship of Constantine Augustus and of Licinius.—November 1, 315; November 8, 313.

3. The same Augustus to Gregorius, Praetorian Prefect.

By their own hand and at their own risk all judges shall designate the supplies in kind and all other payments that are made for the year of the indiction, by defining the amount and including the measure in the assessments which are made. This method of procedure will have the advantage that after each judge has been succeeded in office, it may be easy to learn whether the tax collectors wished to extort from the fortunes of the provincials more than they should.

Given on the seventh day before the ides of October in the year of the consulship of Nepotianus and Facundus.—October 9, 336.

4. Emperor Constantius Augustus.

If any person should purchase anything under the private ownership of an emphyteuticary or patrimonial landholder, by the substance of which property the emphyteuticary or patrimonial landholder had been accustomed to support other landholdings, and if by such sale the rest of the property should collapse as though the sinews of its strength had been cut out, so to speak, the purchaser must assume the burdens of the landholdings which remain as useless in the possession of the seller.

Given on the eighth day before the ides of December at Thessalonica in the year of the consulship of Felicianus and Titianus.—December 6, 337.

5. The same Augustus to Uranius.

Absolutely everyone must be compelled to make the tax payments in money. For it is indicated by Our law that the taxes which must be specifically paid by Our most devoted provincials are not extraordinary and they must not be so called.

Given on the third day before the nones of February in the year of the second consulship of Constantius Augustus and the consulship of Constans.—February 3, 339.

6. Emperors Constantius and Constans to the Senate of Caesena.

In accordance with the statute of My brother Constantius, all the landholders of Italy shall provide the wine which is customarily furnished for use as cellar supplies. In order that this may be done the more easily, that quantity of money shall be contributed by all Our Italians which the regulation of the Most Noble and Illustrious Praetorian Prefect, Rufinus, Our Father and Retainer, decreed must be given. . . .

BOOK XII

TITLE 1: DECURIONS (DE DECURIONIBUS)

1. Emperor Constantine Augustus to Evagrius.

No judge shall attempt to grant exemption from compulsory municipal services to any decurion, nor shall he free anyone from the municipal council by his own judgment. For if any man should be impoverished by a misfortune of such kind that he needs to be assisted, his name must be referred to Our Wisdom, so that an exemption from compulsory municipal services may be granted to him for a limited space of time.

Posted on the ides of March in the year of the third consulship of Constantine Augustus and of Licinius.—March 15, 313; 315; 326.

INTERPRETATION: No judge shall grant an undue exemption to a decurion, nor shall he desire to free him from his duties. For if the property of any decurion is so impoverished and exhausted that the compulsion to bear the burden of public service should not be entrusted to him, the law commands that the case shall be referred to the attention of the Emperor.

2. The same Augustus to Crispinus.

Since you are in doubt as to whether the periods of two months should be computed according to the number of days or from the date of the kalends, the general rule of public law must be observed which manifestly declares what it has commanded to be comprehended by the different methods of computing dates.

Given on the kalends of October in the year of the fourth consulship of Constantine Augustus and of Licinius.—October 1, 315; 353.

3. The same Augustus to Mecilius Hilarianus, Governor of Lucania and Bruttium.

It is Our will that all decurions shall refrain from administering the duties of notaries. No man, moreover, if he should be called to the decurionate, shall be able to excuse himself from this duty because he has been a notary, since even men of this class, if they are financially responsible, must be called to the decurionate. For the law which wished decurions to be removed from the duties of notaries does not prohibit notaries from being called to the decurionate.

Given on the third day before the kalends of February in the year of the consulship of Sabinus and Rufinus.—January 30, 316.

4. The same Augustus to Octavianus, Count of Spain.

Persons who have presumed to appropriate the insignia of an undue honor shall stand, when the chief decurions of the municipalities and the decurions are gathered together in council, and those persons shall remain seated to whom every honor is legally and rightfully due because they have actually served in office. Therefore, Your Sublimity shall provide that no person at all shall enjoy the prerogative of the governorship except a person who has passed through each step of rank in his municipality and has attained the foremost rank in due order. Thus persons also who have obtained the governorship before the proper time shall obtain these distinguished marks of honor that shall be granted them, after they have fulfilled the honorable duties of their own municipalities.

Posted on the fourteenth day before the kalends of February in the year of the consulship of Gallicanus and Bassus.— January 19, 317.

5. The same Augustus to the Bithynians.

Persons who have performed imperial service in the palace and those to whom provinces have been entrusted and those who have deservedly obtained the rank of Most Perfect or of Egregious by merit of service in the Most August administrative offices, and also those persons who have been established as decurions or chief decurions and have performed all the compulsory public services of their municipality shall enjoy the dignity that is granted them. But if a decurion should obtain the rank of Most Perfect, of ducenarius, of centenarius, or of Egregious by use of venal patronage, because he desires to evade the duties of his own municipal council, he shall surrender the imperial letters patent and shall be returned to his own status. Thus after he has undergone an investigation of all his honors and compulsory municipal services, he may obtain some prerogative according to municipal law. Also, the rank of Most Perfect, if impetrated by patronage, does not defend a man who is called to the duties of the municipal council on account of birth status, legal residence, or status as a landholder. Rank so obtained shall be surrendered and he shall be delivered to his municipal council.

Given on the twelfth day before the kalends of August in the year of the consulship of Gallicanus and Bassus.—July 21, 317....

BOOK XIII

TITLE 1: THE LUSTRAL TAX PAYMENT (DE LUSTRALI COLLATIONE)

1. Emperors Constantius Augustus and Julian Caesar to Taurus, Praetorian Prefect.

All tradesmen must pay immediately the tax payable in gold and silver, and only clerics who are called gravediggers shall be excepted, nor shall anyone else be exempt from the performance of the duty of this tax payment.

Given on the fourth day before the nones of December.—December 2, (356). Received at Rome on the eighth day before the ides of February in the year of the ninth consulship of Constantius Augustus and the second consulship of Julian Caesar.—February 6, 357.

2. The same Augustus and Caesar to Taurus, Praetorian Prefect.

All persons who appear to practice the business of merchandising shall be constrained to the burden of the tax payment, except those who are demonstrated by manifest proof to have sustained terms of imperial service under arms, and who, when they have attained their leisure, are proved to have obtained exemption up to a fixed sum of money.

Received on the sixth day before the ides of July at Carthage in the year of the tenth consulship of Constantius Augustus and the third consulship of Julian Caesar.—July 10, 360; 357.

3. The same Augustus to the Senate.

Of course, if your rustics and coloni do not engage at all in the business of commerce, they must not be assessed for taxes as tradesmen. Indeed, it must not be reckoned as business and merchandising if your men and also the rustics dwelling on your landholdings should sell those products yielded by the lands which they are cultivating and on the same farm.

Given on the fifth day before the nones of May in the year of the consulship of Taurus and Florentius.—May 3, 361.

4. **Emperor Julian Augustus to Secundus, Praetorian Prefect.**

(After other matters.) Decurions who evade their compulsory public services on the ground that they are Christians shall be recalled.

1. The municipal councils shall be exempt from payment of the tax payable in gold and silver which is levied upon tradesmen, unless perchance it should be proved that a decurion is engaged in merchandising to any extent. Thus the senates of the municipalities shall be exempt from the arrears of such burdens, as We have already said.

Posted on the third day before the ides of March at Constantinople in the year of the consulship of Momertinus and Nevitta.—March 13, 362.

5. **Emperors Valentinian and Valens Augustuses to Secundus, Praetorian Prefect.**

You shall compel to the necessity of the tax payment any tradesmen who belong to Our imperial household, provided only that they appear to practice the business of commerce, and Christians who, if they have the true religion, wish to assist the poor and those situated in need, and also those men under the control of the more powerful classes and the more powerful men themselves, if, indeed, their occupation is buying and selling, especially since any person of the more powerful classes either must not engage in business himself or must pay the tax and rather be the first to assume the tax as honor demands.

Given on the fifteenth day before the kalends of May at Constantinople in the year of the consulship of the sainted Jovian and of Varronianus.—April 17 (20), 364.

6. **The same Augustuses to Florentius, Count of the Sacred Imperial Largesses.**

We levy upon merchants a tax payment in gold and silver, whereby public expenditures may be assisted. No man, therefore, shall employ a special plea of exemption. For We command such men of all religions and all ranks to sustain this equal share in assisting the State without the indulgence of any special privilege. Furthermore, in this situation that is common to almost all persons, a special plea shall defend only those persons who are very evidently recognized as engaged in business on their own land, through themselves or through their men, and such persons must not be considered so much in the category of merchants as of skilled and zealous masters.

Given on the sixth day before the ides of September in the year of the consulship of the sainted Jovian and of Varronianus.—September 8, 364....

BOOK XIV

TITLE 1: THE DECURIES OF THE CITY OF ROME (DE DECURIIS URBIS ROMAE)

1. Emperor Constantius Augustus and Julian Caesar to Julianus.

In the distinguished order of the decuries which bears the name of either copyists or fiscal clerks or tax assessment clerks, by no means shall any person obtain a place of the first order, unless it is established that he excels in the practice and training of the liberal studies and that he is so polished in the use of letters that words proceed from him without the offense of imperfections, and it is Our will that all men shall be so informed. Moreover, in order that its rewards may not be denied to literature, which is the greatest of all the virtues, if any man should appear to be worthy of the first place on account of his studies and his skill in the use of words, Our provision shall make him of more honorable rank . . . or Your Sublimity shall report his name to Us, so that We may deliberate as to the kind of high rank that should be conferred upon him.

Given on the sixth day before the kalends of March at Constantinople: February 24 (25). Received on the ides of May at Rome in the year of the ninth consulship of Constantius Augustus and the second consulship of Julian Caesar.—May 15, 357; 360.

2. Emperors Valentinian, Theodosius, and Arcadius Augustuses to Sallustius, Prefect of the City.

It is Our will and Our duty to provide that the stability of the privileges formerly granted to the decurials shall not be changed. Furthermore, by the sanction of Our Clemency, those privileges shall remain fixed that are proved to have been originally established.

Given on the third day before the ides of June at Milan in the year of the consulship of Emperor Designate Honorius and of Evodius.—June 11, 386; 384.

3. The same Augustuses to Trifolius, Praetorian Prefect.

It is Our will that if any privileges appear to have been granted to the Eternal City, they shall not perish, and to such an extent do We preserve its ancient privileges that We wish to grant new imperial favors so far as reason permits. Wherefore, in defending the decurials whose number was decreed by venerable antiquity to be two from each city of every province, you must observe those regulations which you understand to have been defined by the constitutions of ancient Emperors or by Our Own sanctions. But if any person should suppose that he should sue decurials for the purpose of depriving them of their privileges, he must understand that he shall apply to the judge of the decury.

Given on the fourteenth day before the kalends of February at Milan in the year of the consulship of Timasius and Promotus.—January 19, 389.

4. Emperors Arcadius, Honorius, and Theodosius Augustuses

to Exsuperantius, Julius, and the other Decurials.

We confirm by Our authority the laws established by former Emperors as well as those of Our sainted father. Therefore, it is Our will that all judges shall know that no person shall attempt to inflict a brand of disgrace upon members of this guild by means of corporal injuries, nor shall he dare to deprive them of those advantages which are approved by reason. For it is Our will that their ancient prerogative of privileges shall be preserved for members of this guild.

Given on the eighth day before the ides of July at Rome in the year of the sixth consulship of Honorius Augustus and the consulship of Aristaenetus.—July 8, 404.

5. The same Augustuses to Curtius, Praetorian Prefect.

Although the privileges of the decury of Our most sacred City have been confirmed by so many and by such manifest sacred imperial regulations of ancient Emperors, as well as by Our own rescripts, nevertheless, by this law also We confirm those privileges which have very often been established. (Etc.)

Given on the seventh day before the ides of April at Ravenna in the year of the seventh consulship of Honorius Augustus and the second consulship of Theodosius Augustus.— April(?) 7, 407.

6. Emperors Honorius and Theodosius Augustuses to Bonosianus, Prefect of the City.

It would be Our desire to increase the privileges of the decury, were it not a kind of outrage to add anything to antiquity. Therefore, all men shall know that five pounds of gold are established as a fine if any person in any place should perchance surreptitiously attempt to take part in their official acts. We decree that all emoluments wrested from them by various persons shall be restored. Of course, if any person should be said to contravene the sacred imperial statutes, the Respectable Vicar of Africa will provide that vengeance shall be inflicted upon him.

Given on the seventh day before the kalends of October at

Ravenna in the year of the eighth consulship of Honorius Augustus and the third consulship of Theodosius Augustus. —September 25, 409; 410. . . .

BOOK XV

TITLE 1: PUBLIC WORKS (DE OPERIBUS PUBLICIS)

1. Emperor Constantine Augustus to Flavianus, Proconsul of Africa.

No man shall suppose that municipalities may be deprived of their own ornaments, since indeed it was not considered right by the ancients that a municipality should lose its embellishments, as though they should be transferred to the buildings of another city.

Given on the fourth day before the nones of February at Milan.—February 2. Received on the eighth day before the ides of July in the year of the consulship of Constantine Augustus and the Caesar.—July 8, 357.

2. The same Augustus to Menander.

On account of the remissness of the judges who delay the execution of the imperial orders, We have dispatched various men to the different provinces to report to Our knowledge the matters which they see have been promoted by diligence and those that they blame on the ground that they are ruined by sloth.

Judges, moreover, who must restore public works, shall be admonished to report to Our knowledge works that have been completed rather than those that have been commenced, unless, perhaps, upon just ground, a petition must be presented that provision should be made for the accounts of certain expenditures, if perchance the funds for such expenditures should be lacking. Furthermore, the judges must call on Our advice in connection with the most important and largest works, not in connection with every trivial work.

Given on the third day before the ides of April at Sirmium in the year of the second consulship of Crispus and Constantine Caesars.—April 11, 321.

3. The same Augustus to Secundus, Praetorian Prefect.

We direct that judges of the provinces shall be admonished that they must know that they shall not arrange for any new work until they have completed those works which were commenced by their predecessors, excepting only the construction of temples.

Given on the third day before the kalends of July in the year of the seventh consulship of Constantine Augustus and the consulship of Constantius Caesar.—June 29, 326; 362.

4. The same Augustus to His Very Dear Friend Felix, Greetings.

The whole space of one hundred feet adjacent to State storehouses shall be kept vacant, and if anything should be constructed therein, it shall be torn down, since it has been shown by very recent experience that fiscal supplies have suffered from the burning of buildings which are adjacent to State storehouses. But if any person through love of building should disregard public damage, We direct that not only what he constructed, but all his property and whatever he had in his own right, shall be adjudged to the fisc.

Given on the eleventh day before the kalends of August at Sirmium in the year of the fourth consulship of Constantine Augustus and the consulship of Constantius Caesar.—July 22, 326; 320.

5. Emperors Constantius and Constans Augustuses to Their Very Dear Friend, Catullinus, Greetings.

Very many persons, by the concessions of judges, have received exemption in connection with the construction of public works. We therefore order that inquiry shall be made as to all such persons, so that Our Clemency may know their names, and also such private grants of exemption.

(And below.) We now order, however, that if it should be

learned that exemptions have been elicited contrary to justice and to the detriment of the public, the recipients shall cease to have such exemptions as gain. Hereafter access shall be denied to those persons who seek similar privileges.

Given on the sixth day before the kalends of August at Sirmium in the year of the consulship of Ursus and Polemius.— July 27, 338.

6. The same Augustuses to Marcellinus, Count of the Orient.

You shall know that the amounts that are proved to have been expended on public works must be credited.

Given on the fifth day before the nones of October at Constantinople in the year of the consulship of Limenius and Catullinus.—October 3, 349. . . .

BOOK XVI

TITLE 1: THE CATHOLIC FAITH (DE FIDE CATHOLICA)

1. Emperors Valentinian and Valens Augustuses to Symmachus, Prefect of the City.

If any judge or apparitor should appoint men of the Christian religion as custodians of temples, he shall know that neither his life nor his fortunes will be spared.

Given on the fifteenth day before the kalends of December at Milan in the year of the consulship of Valentinian and Valens Augustuses.—November 17, 365; 364.

2. Emperors Gratian, Valentinian, and Theodosius Augustuses: An Edict to the People of the City of Constantinople.

It is Our will that all the peoples who are ruled by the administration of Our Clemency shall practice that religion which the divine Peter the Apostle transmitted to the Romans, as the religion which he introduced makes clear even unto this day. It is evident that this is the religion that is followed by the Pontiff Damascus and by Peter, Bishop of Alexandria, a man of apostolic sanctity; that is, according to the apostolic discipline and the evangelic doctrine, we shall believe in the single Deity of the Father, the Son, and the Holy Spirit, under the concept of equal majesty and of the Holy Trinity.

1. We command that those persons who follow this rule shall embrace the name of Catholic Christians. The rest, however, whom We adjudge demented and insane, shall sustain the infamy of heretical dogmas, their meeting places shall not receive the name of churches, and they shall be smitten first by divine vengeance and secondly by the retribution of Our own initiative, which We shall assume in accordance with the divine judgment.

Given on the third day before the kalends of March at Thessalonica in the year of the fifth consulship of Gratian Augustus and the first consulship of Theodosius Augustus.— February 28, 380.

3. The same Augustuses to Auxonius, Proconsul of Asia.

We command that all churches shall immediately be surrendered to those bishops who confess that the Father, the Son, and the Holy Spirit are of one majesty and virtue, of the same glory, and of one splendor; to those bishops who produce no dissonance by unholy distinction, but who affirm the concept of the Trinity by the assertion of three Persons and the unity of the Divinity; to those bishops who appear to have been associated in the communion of Nectarius, Bishop of the Church of Constantinople, and of Timotheus, Bishop of the City of Alexandria in Egypt; to those bishops also who, in the regions of the Orient, appear to be communicants with Pelagus, Bishop of Laodicea, and with Diodorus, Bishop of Tarsus; also, in the Proconsular Province of Asia and in the Diocese of Asia, with Amphilochius, Bishop of Iconium, and with Optimus, Bishop of Antioch; in the Diocese of Pontus, with Helladius, Bishop of Caesarea, and with Otreius of Melitene, and with Gregorius, Bishop of Nyssa; with Terennius, Bishop of Scythia, and with Marmarius, Bishop of Martianopolis. Those bishops who are of the communion and fellowship of such acceptable priests must be permitted to obtain the Catholic churches. All, however, who dissent from the communion of the faith of those who have been expressly mentioned in this special enumeration shall be expelled from their churches as manifest heretics and hereafter shall be altogether denied the right and power to obtain churches, in order that the priesthood of the true Nicene faith may remain pure, and after the clear regulations of Our law, there shall be no opportunity for malicious subtlety.

Given on the third day before the kalends of August at Heraclea in the year of the consulship of Eucherius and Syagrius.—July 30, 381.

4. Emperors Valentinian, Theodosius, and Arcadius Augustuses to Eusignius, Praetorian Prefect.

We bestow the right of assembly upon those persons who believe according to the doctrines which in the times of Constantius of sainted memory were decreed as those that would endure forever, when the priests had been called together from all the Roman world and the faith was set forth at the Council of Ariminum by these very persons who are now known to dissent, a faith which was also confirmed by the Council of Constantinople. The right of voluntary assembly shall also be open to those persons for whom We have so ordered. If those persons who suppose that the right of assembly has been granted to them alone should attempt to provoke any agitation against the regulation of Our Tranquillity, they shall know that, as authors of sedition and as disturbers of the peace of the Church, they shall also pay the penalty of high treason with their life and blood. Punishment shall no less await those persons who may attempt to supplicate Us surreptitiously and secretly, contrary to this Our regulation.

Given on the tenth day before the kalends of February at Milan in the year of the consulship of Emperor Designate Honorius and of Evodius.—January 23, 386. . . .

THE SIRMONDIAN CONSTITUTIONS (CONSTITUTIONES SIRMONDIANAE)

TITLE 1: THE CONFIRMATION OF EPISCOPAL DECISIONS EVEN AMONG MINORS; THE UNSUPPORTED TESTIMONY OF A BISHOP SHALL BE GIVEN FULL CREDIT (DE CONFIRMANDO ETIAM INTER MINORES AETATES JUDICIO EPISCOPORUM ET TESTIMONIUM UNIUS EPISCOPI ACCEPTO FERRI)

Emperor Constantine Augustus to Ablavius, Praetorian Prefect.

We are much surprised that Your Gravity which is replete with justice and the approved religion should have wished to inquire of Our Clemency what Our Sovereignty has either previously ordained or what We now wish to be observed as to the judicial decisions of bishops, O Ablavius, dearest and most beloved Father.

Therefore, because you wished to be instructed by Us, We again, by means of Our salutary power do hereby spread abroad the ordinance of Our previously promulgated law.

For We previously sanctioned, just as the official statement of Our edict makes clear, that the judicial decisions, of whatsoever nature, rendered by the bishops, without any distinction as to age, must be observed as forever inviolate and unimpaired, namely, that whatever has been settled by the judicial decisions of the bishops shall be considered as forever holy and revered.

Whether, therefore, a bishop has decided a case between minors or between adults, it is Our will that the obligation for its enforcement shall rest upon you, who hold the highest judicial authority, and upon all other judges.

Therefore, if any man, either as defendant or as plaintiff, should have a suit at law, and either at the beginning of the suit, or after the statutory time limits have elapsed, or when the final pleadings are being made, or when the judge has already begun to pronounce sentence, and if such litigant should choose the court of a bishop of the sacrosanct law, even though the other party to the suit should oppose it, immediately, without any question, the principals in the litigation shall be dispatched to the bishop.

For the authority of sacrosanct religion searches out and reveals many things which the captious restrictions of legal technicality do not allow to be produced in court.

Therefore, all cases which are tried either by praetorian or by civil law, when settled by the decisions of bishops, shall be affirmed by the eternal law of permanence; nor shall any case be subject to review which the judgment of a bishop has decided.

Furthermore the testimony given by a bishop, even though he may be the only witness, shall be unhesitatingly accepted by every judge, nor shall any other witness be heard when the testimony of a bishop has been promised by any party whatsoever.

For that is established with the authority of truth, that is incorruptible, which the consciousness of an undefiled mind has produced from a sacrosanct man.

This We formerly decreed by Our salutary edict, this We confirm by Our eternal law, thus crushing out the mischievous seeds of litigation, so that wretched men, entangled in the long and almost endless toils of litigation, may at length, with timely settlement, escape from unscrupulous legal attacks and from an unreasonable avarice.

Therefore Your Gravity and all others shall forever observe whatever Our Clemency formerly decreed as to the judicial decisions of bishops and whatever We have now embodied in this law which has been issued for the general good.

Given on the third day before the nones of May at Constantinople in the year of the consulship of Dalmatius and Zenophilus.—May 5, 333. . . .

121

THE NOVELS OF THE SAINTED
THEODOSIUS AUGUSTUS

TITLE 1: THE VALIDATION OF THE THEODOSIAN CODE (DE THEODOSIANI CODICIS AUCTORITATE)

1. Emperors Theodosius and Valentinian Augustuses to Florentius, Praetorian Prefect of the Orient.

Our Clemency has often been perplexed as to the cause that has brought it about that, although so great rewards have been established whereby the arts and scholarly pursuits are fostered, so few and infrequent persons have existed who were fully enriched by a knowledge of the Civil Law, and in such a great and somber pallor that is produced by their nocturnal studies, scarcely one or two have attained the completeness of perfected learning.

1. In order that this matter may not be further discussed by anyone with zealous ambiguity, as there occurs to Our minds the boundless multitude of books, the diversity of actions and the difficulty of cases, and finally the mass of imperial constitutions which shut off from human ingenuity a knowledge of themselves by a wall, as though they were submerged in a thick cloud of obscurity, We have completed a true undertaking of Our time; We have dispelled the darkness and given the light of brevity to the laws by means of a compendium. We have selected noble men of proved fidelity and renowned learning, to whom had been delegated the responsibilities of civil office. The decrees of previous Emperors have been purged of interpretations and published by Us, in order that no further may the jurisconsults dissimulate their ignorance by a pretended severity, while their formidable responses are awaited as though they proceed from the very innermost shrines, since it is now clearly evident with what validity a gift may be bestowed, by what action an inheritance may be claimed, and by what words a stipulation may be drawn up, in order that a definite or indefinite debt

may be collected. Each of these matters has been revealed by the vigilance of Our jurists and brought forth into the open and into clear light by the radiant splendor of Our name.

2. These jurists, to whom We have entrusted the divine thoughts of Our heart, shall suppose that no small reward has been conferred upon them. For if We rightly foresee the future with the keenness of Our mind, they will come down to posterity because of their association with Our labors.

3. Wherefore, We have cleared away the cloud of volumes on which have been wasted away the lives of many persons who explain nothing; We confirm this compendious body of knowledge of the divine imperial constitutions from the times of the sainted Constantine, and after the kalends of next January, to no man is granted the right to cite an imperial law in court and in daily legal practice or to compose the instruments of litigation, except, of course, from these books that have come to be under Our name and are kept in the sacred imperial bureaus. However, their own immortality has not been taken away from any of the previous Emperors, the name of no lawgiver has perished; rather, their laws have been changed by the clarification of Our jurisconsults for the sake of lucidity, and they are joined with Us in an august fellowship. The consummate glory of the founders of the laws, therefore, remains and will forever remain, and to Our account has passed nothing except the light of brevity. . . .

GAIUS (SECOND CENTURY)

As a Roman jurist Gaius is best known for his *Institutes,* which was a legal test book which has contributed materially to our knowledge of early Roman law. The *Institutes* were used extensively in the compilation of the Roman *Corpus Juris Civilis.*

THE FOUR COMMENTARIES OF GAIUS ON THE INSTITUTES OF THE CIVIL LAW*

FIRST COMMENTARY

I. CONCERNING CIVIL AND NATURAL LAW

(1) All peoples who are ruled by laws and customs partly make use of their own laws, and partly have recourse to those which are common to all men; for what every people establishes as law for itself is peculiar to itself, and is called the Civil Law, as being that peculiar to the State; and what natural reason establishes among all men and is observed by all peoples alike, is called the Law of Nations, as being the law which all nations employ. Therefore the Roman people partly make use of their own law, and partly avail themselves of that common to all men, which matters we shall explain separately in their proper place.

(2) The Civil Law of the Roman people consists of statutes, plebiscites, Decrees of the Senate, Constitutions of the Emperors, the Edicts of those who have the right to promulgate them, and the opinions of jurists.

(3) A statute is what the people order and establish. A plebiscite is what the commonalty order and establish. Moreover, the commonalty is distinguished from the people by

*Translated by H. E. Wedeck.

the fact that the entire body of citizens including the patricians, is designated by the appellation, "the people"; but the other citizens, exclusive of the patricians, are indicated by the term commonalty; for which reason the patricians formerly declared that they were not bound by plebiscites, as they were enacted without their sanction; but subsequently the *Lex Hortensia* was passed, by which it was provided that plebiscites should bind the entire people; and hence, in this way, they were placed on the same footing as laws.

(4) A Decree of the Senate is what the Senate orders and establishes, and therefore it obtains the force of law, although this formerly was disputed.

(5) An Imperial Constitution is what the Emperor establishes by a decree, an edict, or a letter, and there was never any doubt that it had the force of a law, as the Emperor himself derives his authority from a statute.

(6) The magistrates of the Roman people have the power of promulgating edicts, but the highest authority attaches to the edicts of the two prætors, the urban and the foreign, whose jurisdiction is vested in the governors of the provinces; as well as to the edicts of the curule Ædiles, whose jurisdiction the quæstors administer in the provinces of the Roman people, for quæstors are not appointed in the provinces of the Emperor and, therefore, the latter edict is not published in these provinces.

(7) The answers of jurists are the decisions and opinions of those who are authorized to define the law. If the opinions of all of them concur, what they agree upon obtains the force of law; if, however, they disagree, the judge has a right to follow whichever opinion he may wish, and this is set forth in a rescript of the Divine Hadrian.

II. Concerning the Divisions of the Law

(8) All the law which we make use of has reference either to persons, to things, or to actions. Let us first consider persons.

III. Concerning the Different Conditions of Men

(9) The principal division of the law of persons is the following, namely, that all men are either free or slaves.

(10) Again, men who are free are either freeborn or freedmen.

(11) Freeborn are those who are free by birth, freedmen are those who have been manumitted from legal slavery.

(12) Moreover, there are three classes of freedmen, namely, Roman citizens, Latins, and *dediticii*. Let us consider each of these separately, and, in the first place, *dediticii*.

IV. Concerning Dediticii and the Provisions of the Lex Ælia Sentia

(13) It is provided by the *Lex Ælia Sentia* that slaves who have been placed in chains by their masters, or have been branded, or have been subjected to torture for some offence and convicted, or have been delivered up to fight with others or with wild beasts, or to contend with gladiators, or have been thrown into prison and have afterwards been manumitted by the same, or by another master, shall become free, and belong to the same class as that of enemies who have surrendered at discretion.

V. Concerning Enemies Who Have Surrendered at Discretion

(14) Those enemies are called *dediticii* who, having formerly taken up arms and fought against the Roman people afterwards have been conquered and have surrendered at discretion.

(15) From this it is evident that slaves who have been guilty of criminal acts of this kind, no matter in what way, or at what age they may have been manumitted, and even though their masters had complete authority over them, can never become either Roman citizens or Latins, but must always be classed among enemies who have surrendered at discretion.

(16) If, however, a slave has not been guilty of such

criminality, we declare that by manumission he sometimes becomes a Roman citizen, and sometimes a Latin.

(17) Where the following three requisites are combined in the person of a slave, that is to say where he is over thirty years of age, where his master is invested with full civil rights, and he is set free by proper and lawful manumission through the intervention of the prætor, by enrollment on the register of the census, or by will, he becomes a Roman citizen; if, however, one of these requisites should be lacking, he will become a Latin.

VI. CONCERNING MANUMISSION, AND PROOF OF THE REASON FOR IT

(18) The requisite of the age of the slave was introduced by the *Lex Ælia Sentia,* for this law did not permit slaves under the age of thirty years, who had been manumitted, to become Roman citizens unless they were set free by the wand of the prætor, after proof of good reason for the manumission had been established in the presence of the Council.

(19) A good reason for manumission exists where, for instance, anyone offers for manumission before the Council a natural son or daughter, or brother or sister, or foster-child or teacher, or a slave with the intention of appointing him a steward, or a female slave on account of prospective marriage.

VII. CONCERNING THE CONSTITUTION OF THE COUNCIL

(20) The council in the City of Rome consists of five senators and five Roman knights of the age of puberty. In the provinces it consists of twenty magistrates who are Roman citizens, and who are convoked on the last day of the term. At Rome, however, manumissions take place in the presence of the Council upon certain days. Slaves who are more than thirty years of age can be manumitted at any time, and the ceremony can be performed even while walking in the streets, as for instance, when the prætor or the proconsul is on his way to the bath or the theatre.

127

(21) A slave, who was under the age of thirty years when manumitted, can become a Roman citizen if he was granted his freedom and appointed heir by the will of his master who died insolvent.

(22) Slaves manumitted in certain ways are called *Latini Juniani; Latini* for the reason that they are classed with Latin colonists, *Juniani* because they received their freedom under the terms of the *Lex Junia,* as before it was passed they were considered slaves.

(23) The *Lex Junia* does not, however, permit them either to make a will, or to take under the will of another, or to be appointed testamentary guardians.

(24) What we have said with reference to their being unable to take under a will must be understood to mean that they cannot take anything directly as heirs, or legatees, but, on the other hand, they have a right to take under the terms of a trust.

(25) Those, however, who belong to the class of *dediticii* can, under no circumstances, take under a will, any more than a foreigner; nor can they, in accordance with a majority of the decisions, themselves make a will.

(26) Hence, only the lowest degree of freedom is possessed by those who belong to the class of *dediticii* nor is any way afforded them of obtaining Roman citizenship either by a law, by a Decree of the Senate, or by an Imperial Constitution.

(27) Moreover, they are forbidden to dwell in the City of Rome or within the hundredth mile-stone of the Capitol; and if they should disobey, they and their property are ordered to be publicly sold under the condition that they shall remain slaves beyond the hundredth milestone of the City of Rome, and that they shall never be manumitted; and if they should be manumitted, they are ordered to become the slaves of the Roman people; and these things are included in the *Lex Ælia Sentia.*

In What Way Latins May Obtain Roman Citizenship

(28) Latins obtain Roman citizenship in many ways.

(29) For, by the *Lex Ælia Sentia,* where slaves under the age of thirty years are manumitted and become Latins, if they marry either women who are Roman citizens or Latin colonists, or those who belong to the same condition as themselves, and prove this by the testimony of not less than seven Roman citizens who have arrived at the age of puberty; and they have sons, and the latter are a year old, authority is granted them by this law to appear before the prætor—or, in the provinces before the governor—and prove that they have married wives in accordance with the terms of the *Lex Ælia Sentia,* and have sons by them who are a year old; and if the magistrate before whom this proof is adduced should declare it to be true, then the Latin and his wife, provided she and her son are of the same condition, are ordered to become Roman citizens.

(30) I added the clause, "If the son is of the same condition," for the reason that if the wife of the Latin aforesaid is a Roman citizen, her son is a Roman citizen by birth under the terms of the recent Decree of the Senate promulgated by the Divine Hadrian.

(31) This right of acquiring Roman citizenship, though at first only conferred upon those who had been manumitted under thirty years of age and had become Latins by the *Lex Ælia Sentia,* was afterwards, by a Decree of the Senate issued under the consulship of Pegasus and Pusio, granted to all Latins, even though they were more than thirty years of age at the time when they were manumitted.

(32) However, even if the Latin should die before he was able to prove that his son was a year old, the mother of the latter can prove his condition, and hence both she and her son (if she is a Latin) will become Roman citizens. If the mother should not be able to prove this, the son himself can do so when he reaches the age of puberty. If the son himself is a Roman citizen, for the reason that he is born of a mother

who is a Roman citizen, he must still prove his condition in order to become the heir of his father.

(32a) What we have stated with reference to a son being a year old we also understood to apply to a daughter of the same age.

(32b) Moreover, by the *Lex Visellia,* persons become Roman citizens, where by manumission they have become Latins, when either under or over thirty years of age, if they have served for six years in the guards at Rome. A Decree of the Senate is said to have been subsequently enacted by which Roman citizenship was bestowed on Latins if they had served for three years in the army.

(32c) Likewise, by an Edict of the Divine Claudius, Latins obtain the rights of Roman citizens if they build a ship with a capacity not less than ten thousand measures of grain, and the said ship, or one substituted for it, should transport grain to Rome for the term of six years.

(33) Moreover, it was established in an Edict published by Nero that if a Latin who had property worth two hundred thousand sesterces, or more, should build a house in the City of Rome on which he expended not less than half his estate, he should obtain the right of Roman citizenship.

(34) Finally, the Divine Trajan decreed that if a Latin should exercise the calling of a miller in the City of Rome for the term of three years, and should grind each day not less than a hundred measures of grain, he could acquire Roman citizenship.

(35) Slaves who become Latins either because they are under thirty years of age when manumitted, or being over that age, have been informally manumitted, may become Roman citizens by being again manumitted either by the wand of the prætor, or by inscription on the register of the census, or by will; and in either of these cases they become the freedmen of the party who manumitted them a second time. Therefore, if a slave forms part of your property by bonitarian right and belongs to me by quiritarian right, he can be made a Latin solely by you, and he can be manumitted

a second time by me but not by you, and in this way he will
become my freedman; and if he obtains the right of citizenship in other ways he still will be my freedman. The possession of his estate at the time of his death is however granted
to you, no matter in what way he may have obtained Roman
citizenship. But, if he is manumitted by one who has in him
both bonitarian and quiritarian rights he can be manumitted
by the said party, and become both a Latin and a Roman
citizen.

(36) Every one who desires to manumit a slave is not
permitted to do so.

(37) For he who manumits a slave for the purposes of
defrauding his creditors or his patron, commits an act which
is void, for the reason that the *Lex Ælia Sentia* prevents the
grant of freedom.

(38) Likewise, by the same law a minor owner under the
age of twenty years is not permitted to manumit a slave,
except by the intervention of the prætor, after proper cause
has been shown for the manumission in the presence of the
Council.

(39) The following are proper causes for manumission,
for instance, where anyone manumits his father, his mother,
his teacher, or his foster-brother. Moreover, the reasons which
we have designated above with reference to a slave under
thirty years of age may be adduced also in the case of which
we speak; and likewise, on the other hand, the same reasons
which we stated with reference to an owner under the age of
twenty years may be advanced where the slave is less than
thirty years old.

(40) Therefore, as a certain restriction on the manumission of slaves is imposed upon owners under the age of
twenty years by the *Lex Ælia Sentia,* the result is that anyone
who has completed his fourteenth year, although he can make
a will, appoint an heir to his estate, and bequeath legacies,
still, if he is under the age of twenty years, he cannot grant
freedom to his slave.

(41) And even though an owner under the age of twenty

years may desire to constitute a slave a Latin, he must, nevertheless, prove before the Council, that he has a good reason for doing so, and afterwards manumit the said slave in the presence of friends.

(42) Moreover, by the *Lex Fufia Caninia* a certain limit is established with reference to the manumission of slaves by a will.

(43) Hence, he who has more than two slaves and not more than ten, is permitted to manumit as many as half of that number. He, however, who has more than ten and not more than thirty slaves, is permitted to manumit a third of that number; and he who has more than thirty slaves and not more than a hundred, is granted authority to manumit one fourth of his slaves. Finally, he who has more than one hundred and not more than five hundred, is not permitted to manumit more than a fifth; and, no matter how many slaves a man may have, he is not permitted to manumit more than this, as the law prescribes that no one shall have the right to manumit more than a hundred. Still, where anyone has only one or two slaves, his case does not come under this law, and therefore he has free power of manumission.

(44) Nor does this law have any reference whatever to persons who manumit in any way except by will, and therefore those who do so either in the tribunal of the Prætor, or by enrollment on the registers of the census, or in the presence of friends, are permitted to liberate their entire bodies of slaves; provided however, that no other reason prevents their receiving their freedom.

(45) What we have stated with reference to the number of slaves which can be manumitted by will should be understood to mean that where a man has a right to liberate the half, the third, the fourth, or the fifth part of his entire body of slaves, he shall in no case be restricted to a smaller number than he would have been permitted to manumit had the estimate been made according to the next preceding scale. This provision is in accordance with reason, for it certainly would be absurd for any one to be permitted to liberate five

132

out of his ten slaves, because he is granted authority to manumit half of that number; while another, having twelve slaves, would not be permitted to manumit more than four; and anyone who has more than ten and not more than thirty, under the same rule should be permitted also to manumit five, the same number which he who has ten is allowed to liberate.

(46) If freedom should be granted by a testator in his will to a greater number of slaves than is above mentioned, and the names are written in a circle so that no order of manumission can be ascertained, none of the said slaves shall become free; because the *Lex Fufia Caninia,* as well as other special Decrees of the Senate, have declared all testamentary provisions devised for the purpose of evading the law to be void.

(47) In conclusion, it should be noted that, as it is provided by the *Lex Ælia Sentia* that slaves who have been manumitted for the purpose of defrauding a patron, or creditors, do not become free; for the Senate, at the suggestion of the Divine Hadrian, decreed that this rule should also apply to foreigners, while the other provisions of the same law do not apply to them.

(48) There is another division with reference to the law of persons, for some persons are their own masters, and some are subject to the authority of others.

(49) Again, of those persons who are subject to the authority of another, some are in his power, others are in his hand, and others are considered his property.

(50) Let us now consider those that are subject to the authority of another, for, when we ascertain who they are, we shall then understand what persons are their own masters.

(51) In the first place, let us examine those who are in the power of another.

(52) Slaves are in the power of their masters, and this power is acknowledged by the Law of Nations, for we know that among all nations alike the master has the power of life and death over his slaves, and whatever property is acquired

by a slave is acquired by his master.

(53) At the present time, however, neither Roman citizens nor any other persons who are under the empire of the Roman people are permitted to employ excessive or causeless severity against their slaves; for by a constitution of the Most Holy Emperor Antoninus anyone who kills his slave, without good reason, is not less liable than one who kills the slave of another; and the excessive harshness of masters is restrained by another constitution of the same Emperor; for he, having been consulted by certain governors of provinces with reference to slaves who flee for refuge to the temples of the Gods or the statues of the Emperor, ordered that if the cruelty of masters appeared to be intolerable, they should be compelled to sell their slaves; and in both cases he acted justly, for we should not make a bad use of our rights, in accordance with which principle the administration of their own property is forbidden to spendthrifts.

(54) But, as among Roman citizens, a double ownership may exist (for a slave is understood to be subject to bonitarian or quiritarian right or to belong to both these classes) so we merely say that a slave is in the power of his owner if he forms part of his property by bonitarian right, even if at the same time he may not belong to him by quiritarian right; for anyone who has the bare quiritarian right in a slave is not understood to have him in his power.

(55) In like manner, our children whom we have begotten in lawful marriage are under our control. This right is peculiar to Roman citizens, for there are hardly any other men who have such authority over their children as we have, and this the Divine Hadrian stated in the Edict which he published with reference to persons who petitioned for Roman citizenship for themselves and for their children, for he said: "It does not escape my knowledge that the Galatians hold that children are in the power of their parents."

(56) Roman citizens are understood to have contracted marriage according to the Civil Law and to have the children

begotten by them in their power if they marry Roman citizens, or even Latins or foreigners whom they have the right to marry; for the result of legal marriage is that the children follow the condition of the father and not only are Roman citizens by birth, but also become subject to paternal authority.

(57) Therefore, certain veterans are usually granted permission by the Imperial Constitutions to contract civil marriage with those Latin or foreign women whom they first marry after their discharge, and the children born of such unions become Roman citizens by birth, and are subject to the authority of their fathers.

(57a) Marriage, however, cannot take place with persons of servile condition.

(58) Nor are we permitted to marry any free woman, as we should refrain from contracting matrimony with certain ones of this class.

(59) For marriage cannot be contracted between persons who sustain to one another the relation of ascendants and descendants, nor can legal matrimony exist between them; for instance, between father and daughter, mother and son, or grandfather and granddaughter; and if such persons form unions they are said to have contracted nefarious and incestuous marriages.

To such an extent does this rule apply that, although the relationship of parents and children may have been established by adoption, they cannot contract matrimony with one another, and even if the adoption has been dissolved, the same rule of law will continue to apply; so that I could not take as a wife a woman who sustains to me the relationship of daughter or granddaughter by adoption, even if I have emancipated her.

(60) This rule also applies to persons related in the collateral degree, but not to the same extent.

(61) Marriage is indeed prohibited between brother and sister, whether they are born of the same father or mother or merely of one of these parents in common; but although

legal marriage cannot take place between me and my sister by adoption as long as the adoption continues to exist, still if the adoption is dissolved by emancipation I can marry her, and if I should be emancipated no impediment to the marriage will exist.

(62) It is lawful for a man to marry the daughter of his brother, and this first became customary when the Divine Claudius married Agrippina, his brother's daughter, but it is not lawful for anyone to marry his sister's daughter, and this rule is stated in the Imperial Constitutions. It is likewise illegal for a man to take as his wife his paternal or maternal aunt.

(63) Moreover, I cannot marry my former mother-in-law or daughter-in-law, or my step-daughter or step-mother. We make use of the word "former," because if the marriage by which affinity of this kind was established is still in existence, there is another reason why I cannot marry her, for a woman cannot marry two men, nor can a man have two wives.

(64) Therefore, if anyone should contract a nefarious and incestuous marriage he is considered to have neither a wife nor children, hence the issue of such a union are considered to have a mother but no father, and for this reason are not subject to paternal authority, but resemble children whom the mother has conceived through promiscuous intercourse; and they, in like manner, are understood to have no father, as he also is uncertain; therefore they are ordinarily called illegitimate children, either from the Greek word meaning conceived indiscriminately, or because they are children without any father.

(65) It sometimes happens that children when born are not under the control of their fathers but are afterwards subjected to their authority.

(66) For instance, under the Lex Ælia Sentia, if a Latin, after having married, should have a son who is a Latin by a Latin mother, or who is a Roman citizen by a Roman mother, he will not have him under his control; but if he should afterwards obtain the right of Roman citizenship by

the evidence required by law, his son will, at the same time, be brought under his power.

(67) Likewise, if a Roman citizen should marry a Latin or a foreign woman through ignorance, believing that she was a Roman citizen, and should have a son, the latter will not be under his control because he will not be a Roman citizen, but either a Latin or a foreigner; that is to say, he will belong to the same condition as his mother, as no child follows the condition of its father unless the right to legal marriage existed between its parents; but by a Decree of the Senate it is permitted to prove the cause of error, and in this way the wife and the son will both obtain Roman citizenship, and the son will, from that time, begin to be under the control of his father. The same rule applies where a Roman citizen marries a woman belonging to the class of the *dediticii*, except that the wife does not become a Roman citizen.

(68) Moreover, if a female Roman citizen should, through mistake, marry a foreigner under the impression that he was a Roman citizen, she will be permitted to prove the cause of error, and in this way both her son and her husband will obtain Roman citizenship, and, at the same time, the son will begin to be subject to the authority of the father. The same rule also applies if the woman marries a foreigner as a Latin under the terms of the *Lex Ælia Sentia*, as provision for a case of this kind is specially made by the Decree of the Senate. Again, the same rule applies to a certain extent if she should marry a man belonging to the class of the *dediticii*, as being either a Roman citizen or a Latin under the provisions of the *Lex Ælia Sentia*, except that her husband belonging to the class of the *dediticii* remains in the condition, and therefore his son, although he becomes a Roman citizen, is not subjected to the authority of his father.

(69) Likewise, if a Latin woman should marry a foreigner believing him to be a Latin in accordance with the *Lex Ælia Sentia*, on the birth of a son she can, under the Decree of the Senate, prove the cause of her error, and then all the

parties will become Roman citizens, and the son will pass under the control of his father.

(70) The same rule has been established where a Latin man marries a woman who is a foreigner under the impression that she is either a Latin or a Roman citizen, with a view to taking advantage of the *Lex Ælia Sentia.*

(71) Moreover, a Roman citizen who thinks that he is a Latin, and for this reason marries a Latin woman, will be permitted to prove the cause of his error in case of the birth of a son, just as if he had married his wife under the provisions of the *Lex Ælia Sentia.* Likewise, those who being Roman citizens think that they are foreigners and marry foreign women, are permitted by the Decree of the Senate, on the birth of a son, to prove the cause of their error; and this having been done, the wife becomes a Roman citizen, and the son not only obtains to Roman citizenship but also is brought under the authority of his father.

(72) Whatever we have said with reference to a son is also understood to apply to a daughter.

(73) And, so far as proving the cause of the error is concerned, as nothing with reference to this was provided by the Decree of the Senate, it makes no difference how old the son or daughter may be unless he or she should be a Latin; because it was also declared by the *Lex Ælia Sentia* that in this case if the son or daughter is less than a year old the cause cannot be proved. It has not escaped my observation that it was stated in a rescript of the Divine Hadrian, with reference to the proof of the cause of the error, that the child must be a year old, but the right did not seem to be of general application, as the Emperor issued the rescript under peculiar circumstances.

(74) If a foreigner, believing himself to be a Roman citizen, married a woman who is a Roman citizen, the question arises whether he could prove the cause of error under the Decree of the Senate. He could not do so, however, as this privilege is not granted by the Decree of the Senate to a foreigner, even though he, being mistaken, should have

married a Roman citizen, unless this right was especially conferred upon him. But, when a foreigner married a woman who is a Roman citizen, and after a son was born, he obtained Roman citizenship in some other way, then when the question arose whether he could prove the cause of error, the Emperor Antoninus stated in a rescript that he could do so, just as if he had remained a foreigner; from which we gather that even a foreigner can prove the cause of error.

(75) From what we have said, it is apparent that where either a Roman citizen marries a foreign woman or a foreigner marries a woman who is a Roman citizen, the child born of the union is a foreigner. If, however, a marriage of this kind should have been contracted through mistake, the defect can be remedied in the manner which we explained above. But if no error took place, and the parties, aware of their condition, contracted marriage, the defect of an union of this kind can, under no circumstances, be remedied.

(76) We, however, are speaking of persons who have not the right to contract legal marriage; for, otherwise, if a Roman citizen should marry a foreign woman with whom civil marriage can be contracted as is stated above, a legal marriage takes place, and a son born to the parties is a Roman citizen, and will become subject to the authority of his father.

(77) Likewise, if a female Roman citizen should marry a foreigner who is entitled to contract a legal marriage, and a son is born, he will be an alien, and the lawful son of his father, just as if he had begotten him with a foreign woman. At the present time, however, by a Decree of the Senate enacted at the instance of the Divine Hadrian, even if the right of civil marriage did not exist between a woman who is a Roman citizen and a foreigner, the child born of the union is the lawful son of his father.

(78) What we have stated, however, with reference to a female Roman citizen marrying a foreigner, and their issue being an alien, is derived from the *Lex Minicia,* by which it is provided that where a child is born of an unequal marriage

139

it follows the condition of the parent of inferior rank. On the other hand, it is provided by the same law that if a Roman citizen should marry a foreign woman with whom the right of legal marriage did not exist, the child born of this union will be a foreigner. The *Lex Minicia* was not especially necessary in a case of this kind, for, without this law, the child would have followed the condition of its mother, as this is the rule by the Law of Nations, among those between whom the right of civil marriage does not exist. This provision of the law which directs that the issue of a Roman citizen and a foreign woman shall be a foreigner seems to be superfluous, for even without this law this would be the case under the Law of Nations.

(79) Moreover, to such an extent does this rule apply that the issue of the marriage between a Roman citizen and a Latin woman follows the condition of its mother, for in the *Lex Minicia* not only are alien nations and peoples designated as "foreigners," but also those who are called Latins; and it also refers to other Latins who had their own peoples and states, and were included under the head of foreigners.

(80) On the other hand, by the same rule, the son of a Latin father and a mother who was a Roman citizen, whether the marriage was contracted under the provisions of the *Lex Ælia Sentia* or not, is born a Roman citizen. There were some authorities, however, who held that where a marriage was contracted under the *Lex Ælia Sentia* the child was born a Latin; for the reason that in this instance the right of legal marriage was conferred upon the parties by the *Lex Ælia Sentia et Junia,* and legal marriage always has the effect of giving the child the same condition as its father; for, if the marriage were otherwise contracted, the child, by the Law of Nations, would follow the condition of its mother, and for this reason would be a Roman citizen. We, however, make use of the rule established by the Decree of the Senate at the instance of the Divine Hadrian, by which it is declared that, under all circumstances, the child of a Latin

man and a woman who is a Roman citizen is born a Roman citizen.

(81) In conformity with these provisions, the said Decree of the Senate, enacted at the instance of the Divine Hadrian, also prescribes that the issue of a Latin man and a foreign woman, as well as that of a foreign man and a Latin woman, follows the condition of the mother.

(82) The result of this is that the child of a female slave and a freeman is, by the Law of Nations, born a slave; and, on the other hand, the child of a free woman and a male slave is free by birth.

(83) We should note, however, whether any law or enactment having the force of the law, in any case changes the rule of the Law of Nations.

(84) For example, under the Claudian Decree of the Senate, a woman who is a Roman citizen and has sexual intercourse with a slave belonging to another with the consent of his master will, in accordance with the agreement, remain free herself while she gives birth to a slave; for the contract entered into between her and the owner of the slave is declared to be valid by the Decree of the Senate. Afterwards, however, the Divine Hadrian, influenced by the injustice and impropriety of the law, restored the rule of the Law of Nations, so that as the woman herself remains free, her child is also born free.

(85) Likewise, by another law, children born of a female slave and a freeman could be born free; for it is provided by the said law that if anyone should have sexual intercourse with a female slave belonging to another and whom he believed to be free, and any male children should be born, they will be free; but any female children would be the property of him to whom their mother, the female slave, belonged. In this case, however, the Divine Vespasian, influenced by the impropriety of the law, restored the rule of the Law of Nations, so that, in every instance, even if female children should be born, they will become the slaves of the person who owned their mother.

(86) Another section of the same law remains in force, namely, that any children born to a free woman and a slave who is the property of another, and whom she knew to be a slave, are born slaves; hence among those who are not subject to this law, the child follows the condition of its mother by the Law of Nations, and on this account is free.

(87) In those cases, however, where the child follows the condition of the mother and not that of the father, it is perfectly clear that it is not subject to the authority of his father, even though the latter may be a Roman citizen; and therefore we stated above that in certain instances where a marriage which was not lawful was contracted through a mistake, the Senate could intervene and remedy the defect of the marriage, and in this way generally bring it about that the son should be subjected to the authority of his father.

(88) If a female slave should conceive by a Roman citizen and afterwards, having been manumitted, should become a Roman citizen and a child should be born, although the latter would be a Roman citizen like its father, it would still not be under the control of the latter, for the reason that it was not conceived in lawful marriage, and because an union of this kind is not declared to be legal by any decree of the Senate.

(89) The decision which was made that if a slave should conceive by a Roman citizen and then, after having been manumitted, her child should be born free, is in accordance with natural law, for children who are illegitimately conceived assume their status at the time when they are born, and therefore, if they are born of a free woman, they will be free, nor does it make any difference by whom their mother conceived them while she was a female slave; but those who are lawfully conceived assume their status at the time of conception.

(90) Therefore, where a female citizen at Rome, who is pregnant at the time, is interdicted from fire and water, and for this reason having become a foreigner, gives birth to a child; many authorities make a distinction, and are of the

opinion that, as she conceived in lawful marriage, her child is born a Roman citizen, but if she conceived as the result of promiscuous intercourse, her child will be an alien.

(91) Likewise, where a woman who is a Roman citizen while pregnant, becomes a slave under the Claudian Decree of the Senate, for the reason that she had intercourse with a slave belonging to another, against the consent and protest of his master, many authorities make a distinction and hold that as the child was conceived in lawful marriage, it will be born a Roman citizen, but if it was conceived as the result of promiscuous intercourse, it will be born the slave of the person to whom his mother belongs.

(92) Again, if an alien woman should conceive as the result of promiscuous intercourse, and afterwards become a Roman citizen and bring forth a child, the latter will be a Roman citizen. If, however, she should conceive by an alien whom she married in accordance with foreign laws and customs, she will, under the terms of the Decree of the Senate enacted at the instance of the Divine Hadrian, be held to give birth to a Roman citizen, provided Roman citizenship has also been conferred upon the father.

(93) Where an alien has acquired Roman citizenship for himself and his children, the latter do not pass under the control of their father unless the Emperor should expressly cause them to do so; and this he only does when, after the case has been examined, he thinks that this would be advantageous to the children. He, moreover, makes a more diligent and minute investigation with reference to children who are under the age of puberty and absent; and this rule is set forth in an Edict of the Divine Hadrian.

(94) Likewise, where anyone with his wife, during her pregnancy, is presented with Roman citizenship, although the child, as we have mentioned above, is born a Roman citizen, he still does not pass under the control of his father; and this is stated in a rescript of the Divine Hadrian. For this reason if he knows that his wife is pregnant, and he petitions the Emperor for citizenship for himself and his wife,

he should, at the same time, ask that his child shall be subjected to his authority.

(95) The rule is otherwise in the case of those who, together with their children, attain to Roman citizenship by the right of being Latins, for their children pass under their control.

(96) This right has been granted to certain foreign States, either by the Roman people, or by the Senate, or by the Emperor.

The right of Latinity is either greater or less. Greater Latinity is that of those who are elected decurions or administer any honorable office or magistracy, and by this means obtain Roman citizenship. The lesser right of Latinity is where only those who administer the office of magistrate or any other honorable employment attain to Roman citizenship; and this difference is referred to in many Imperial rescripts.

(97) Not only as we have stated are natural children in our power, but also those whom we adopt.

(98) Adoption takes place in two ways; either by the authority of the people, or by the command of the magistrate, as for instance, of the Prætor.

(99) We adopt, by the authority of the people, those who are their own masters, which kind of adoption is called arrogation, for the reason that he who adopts is asked, that is to say, interrogated, whether he desires to have the person whom he intends to adopt as his lawful son; and he who is adopted is asked whether he is willing to have this done; and the assembled people are asked whether they direct this to take place. By the command of the magistrate we adopt those who are under the control of their parents, whether they are in the first degree of descendants, as a son or a daughter, or whether they belong to an inferior degree, as a grandson or a granddaughter, a great-grandson or a great-granddaughter.

(100) Adoption by the people can only take place at Rome; and the other usually takes place in the provinces

before the governors of the same.

(101) The better opinion is that women cannot be adopted by the voice of the people; but women may be adopted in the tribunal of the Prætor at Rome, or in the provinces in the tribunal of the proconsul or the lieutenant.

(102) The adoption of a child under the age of puberty by the vote of the people was at one time forbidden, and at another permitted; but at present, by the Epistle of the Emperor Antoninus addressed to the pontiffs, it is allowed under certain conditions, if there seems to be good cause for the adoption. We can, however, adopt persons of any age in the tribunal of the Prætor at Rome, or in the provinces in that of the proconsul, or the lieutenant.

(103) It is a rule common to both kinds of adoption that persons who are incapable of begetting children, such as eunuchs, can adopt.

(104) Women, however, cannot in any way adopt other persons, for the reason that they cannot exercise authority even over their natural children.

(105) Likewise, if anyone adopts another, either by the vote of the people, or by the consent of the Prætor or the governor of a province, he can give the son whom he has adopted in adoption to another.

(106) It is a question, however, with reference to both forms of adoption, whether a person can adopt another who is older than himself.

(107) It is peculiar to that kind of adoption which takes place by the vote of the people, that if he who gives himself to be arrogated has children under his control, he will not only himself be subject to the authority of the arrogator, but his children will also be under the control of the latter, as grandchildren.

(108) Now let us consider those persons who are in our hand, which right is also peculiar to Roman citizens.

(109) Both males and females are under the authority of another, but females alone are placed in the hands.

(110) Formerly this ceremony was performed in three

different ways, namely, by use, by confarreation, and by coemption.

(111) A woman came into the hand of her husband by use when she had lived with him continuously for a year after marriage; for the reason that she was obtained by usucaption, as it were, through possession for the term of a year, and passed into the family of her husband where she occupied the position of a daughter. Hence it is provided by the Law of the Twelve Tables that if a woman was unwilling to be placed in the hand of her husband in this way, she should every year absent herself for three nights, and in this manner interrupt the use during the said year; but all of this law has been partly repealed by legal enactments, and partly abolished by disuse.

(112) Women are placed in the hand of their husbands by confarreation, through a kind of sacrifice made to Jupiter Farreus, in which a cake is employed, from whence the ceremony obtains its name; and in addition to this, for the purpose of performing the ceremony, many other things are done and take place, accompanied with certain solemn words, in the presence of ten witnesses. This law is still in force in our time, for the principal flamens, that is to say, those of Jupiter, Mars, and Quirinus, as well as the chief of the sacred rites, are exclusively selected from persons born of marriages celebrated by confarreation. Nor can these persons themselves serve as priests without marriage by confarreation.

(113) In marriage by coemption, women become subject to their husbands by mancipation, that is to say by a kind of fictitious sale; for the man purchases the woman who comes into his hand in the presence of not less than five witnesses, who must be Roman citizens over the age of puberty, and also of a balance-holder.

(114) By this act of sale a woman can not only make a coemption to her husband but also to a stranger, that is to say, the sale takes place either on account of marriage or by way of trust; for a woman who disposes of herself in this way

to her husband for the purpose of occupying the place of his daughter is said to have done so on account of matrimony; but where she does this for some other purpose, either to a husband or to a stranger, as for instance in order to avoid a guardianship, she is said to have made a coemption by way of trust.

(115) The method by which this is done is as follows: if a woman wishes to get rid of her present guardians and obtain another in their stead, she makes this disposal of herself with their consent; and then the other party to the sale sells her again to him to whom she wishes to be her guardian, and he manumits her by the ceremony of the wand of the Prætor, and by this means becomes her guardian, and is designated a fiduciary guardian, as will hereafter appear.

(115a) Formerly a fiduciary coemption took place for the purpose of acquiring power to make a will, for women, with some exceptions, did not then have testamentary capacity unless they had made fictitious sales of this kind, and after having been resold, were manumitted; but the Senate, at the suggestion of the Divine Hadrian, abolished this necessity of making a fictitious sale.

(115b) Even if the woman makes a fiduciary sale of herself to her husband, she nevertheless occupies the place of his daughter; for if a wife comes into the hand of her husband for any reason whatsoever, it has been decided that she enjoys the rights of a daughter.

(116) It remains for us to explain what persons are subject to mancipation.

(117) All children of either the male or female sex who are under the control of their father can be mancipated by him in the same way as that in which slaves can be mancipated.

(118) The same rule of law applies to those persons who are in the hand of others, and they can be mancipated in the same way by those to whom they have been sold, just as children may be mancipated by their father; and while she who is married to the purchaser may only occupy the

place of his daughter; still, though she may not be married to him, nor occupy the place of his daughter, she can still be mancipated by him.

(118a) Generally speaking, mancipation takes place either by parents or by those who obtain possession by coemption, when the parents and the so-called purchasers desire to release the persons from their authority, as will appear more clearly hereafter.

(119) Mancipation, as we have mentioned above, is a kind of fictitious sale, and the law governing it is peculiar to Roman citizens. The ceremony is as follows: After not less than five witnesses (who must be Roman citizens above the age of puberty) have been called together, as well as another person of the same condition who holds a brazen balance in his hand and is styled the "balance holder," the so-called purchaser, holding a piece of bronze in his hands, says: "I declare that this man belongs to me by my right as a Roman citizen, and let him be purchased by me with this piece of bronze, and bronze balance." Then he strikes the scales with the piece of bronze, and gives it to the so-called vendor as purchase money.

(120) In this manner both slaves and free persons are mancipated, as well as such animals as are subject to sale, among which are included oxen, horses, mules, and asses, as well as urban and rustic estates; for instance, Italian lands are usually disposed of in the same manner.

(121) The sale of land differs from the mancipation of other things, in that both slaves and free persons, as well as animals subject to mancipation cannot be disposed of in this way unless they are present; as it is necessary for him who acquires the object by mancipation to be able to grasp it with his hands, and the ceremony is designated mancipation because the property is seized with the hands. Lands, however, are usually mancipated at a distance.

(122) A piece of brass and a balance are employed for the reason that in former times only brazen money was in circulation, and this consisted of asses, double asses, half asses,

and quarter asses; nor was any gold or silver coin in circulation, as we learn by the Law of the Twelve Tables. The value of the purchasing power of these coins was not estimated by their number, but by their weight; hence an as consisted of a pound of bronze, a double as of two pounds (whence it derived its name, which is still retained), while the half-asses and quarter-asses were estimated by their respective parts of a pound. Therefore, in former times, those who paid out money to anyone did not count it but weighted it, and the slaves who were permitted to disburse money were called "weighers."

(123) If anyone should ask what is the difference between coemption and mancipation, the reply is that the first ceremony does not reduce the party to a servile condition; but persons of either sex mancipated by parents or others are reduced to the condition of slaves, to such an extent that they cannot take either an estate or a legacy under the will of the party by whom they have been mancipated, unless they have been ordered to be free by the terms of the same will; just as the law is with reference to the persons of slaves. The reason for this distinction is clear, as the words used by parents and so-called purchasers are the same as those employed in the mancipation of slaves, but in the coemption of women this is not the case.

(124) Let us now consider in what ways those who are subject to the authority of another are released from it.

(125) And, in the first place, let us examine those who are under the power of others.

(126) We can understand from what has been stated above with reference to the manumission of slaves, how they are freed from the power of their masters.

(127) Children who are under the authority of their father become their own masters at his death. The following distinction, however, must be made, namely: When a father dies, his sons and his daughters always become independent; but when a grandfather dies, his grandsons and granddaughters do not, under all circumstances, become independ-

ent, but only where, after the death of their grandfather, they do not again pass under the control of their father. Therefore, if at the time of the death of their grandfather their father was living and was under the control of his father, they pass under the control of their father after the death of their grandfather; but if, at the time of the death of their grandfather, their father was either dead or had been released from the control of his father, then the grandchildren, for the reason that they cannot pass under his control, will become their own masters.

(128) As a person who, on account of the commission of some crime, has been interdicted from water and fire under the *Lex Cornelia,* loses his Roman citizenship, and for this reason is excluded from the number of Roman citizens, his children cease to be under his control, just as if he were dead; for reason does not permit that a person of the condition of an alien should have a Roman citizen subject to this authority. In like manner, if anyone who is in the power of his father is interdicted from water and fire, he ceases to be under his control, as it is not reasonable that a man of the condition of an alien should be under the parental authority of a Roman citizen.

(129) Even if the father should be taken captive by the enemy and thereby become the enemy's slave, nevertheless, his authority over his children remains in abeyance under the law of *postliminium,* by which those who were captured by the enemy and return, recover all their former rights; and, therefore, if he should return, he will have his children in his power. If, however, he should die while in captivity, his children will become their own masters; but it may be doubted whether this took place at the time when the father died in the hands of the enemy, or at the time when he was captured. Likewise, if the son himself, or a grandson, should be taken captive by the enemy, we say that the authority of the father remains in abeyance on account of the law of *postliminium.*

(130) Moreover, male children are released from paternal

authority if they are installed priests of Jupiter; and females, if they are chosen Vestal Virgins.

(131) In former times also, when the Roman people were accustomed to establish colonies in Latin territory, sons, who, by the order of their father, placed their names upon the roll of the Latin colony, ceased to be under the control of their father, because they became citizens of another State.

(132) Again, children cease to be under parental authority by means of mancipation. A son, however, by three mancipations, and other children either of the male or female sex by a single mancipation, are released from parental authority; for the Law of the Twelve Tables only mentions three mancipations with reference to a son, as follows: "If a father sells his son three times, let him be free from the control of his father." This ceremony takes place in the following manner. The father sells his son to a third party, and the latter manumits him by the wand of the prætor, and by doing so, he is restored to the control of his father; and the latter then sells him a second time, either to the same person or to another (but it is customary to sell him to the same person); and he again manumits him in the same way, and by this act the son is again placed in the power of his father; and the father then sells him a third time, either to the same person or to another (it is customary, however, for him to be sold to the same person), and by virtue of this sale he ceases to be under the control of his father, even though he has not yet been manumitted, but still remains in the condition of one who has been sold.

(133) It should, however, be noted that one who has a son, and by him a grandson under his control, has full power to release his son from his control, and still to retain authority over his grandson; or, on the other hand, he has the right to manumit his grandson, or to render both parties their own masters. We understand that this rule also applies to great-grandsons.

(134) Again, parents also lose their authority over their children by giving them in adoption. Where a son is given

in adoption, three sales are required, and two intervening manumissions must take place, as is customary when the father releases a son from his authority, in order that he may become his own master. Then, the son is either resold to the father and he who adopts him claims him as his son before the prætor; and, if his natural father does not claim him, he is given by the prætor to the party who claims him by adoption; or, if he is not sold again to his father, he who adopts him claims him from him to whom he was sold for the third time. It is, however, more convenient for him to be resold to his natural father. In the case of other offspring of either sex, one sale is sufficient, whether a resale is made to the natural father or not. The same ceremony ordinarily takes place in the provinces, in the presence of the governor.

(135) When a grandson is conceived after the first or second sale of a son, although he may not be born until after the third sale of his father, he, nevertheless, remains under the control of his grandfather, and may be emancipated, or given in adoption by him. A grandson, however, who is begotten after the third sale of a son, is not born under the control of his grandfather; but Labeo holds that he is born under the control of him to whom his father was sold. We, however, make use of the following rule, that as long as its father is in mancipation the right of the child remains in suspense; and if the father should be manumitted, the child will pass under his authority; but if he should die before the ceremony of mancipation has been completed, the child will become its own master.

(135a) We understand that the same rule applies to the case of a grandson who has been mancipated once, as it does to that of a son who has been mancipated three times, for, as we stated above, what three sales accomplished with reference to a son, one accomplishes in the case of a grandson.

(136) A woman placed in the hand of her husband by confarreation is not, for this reason, at present, released from paternal authority unless the ceremony of coemption has been performed; for it is provided by the *Lex Asinia Antistia*

152

enacted during the Consulate of Cornelius Maximus and Tubero, with reference to priestesses of Jupiter being in the hand of their husbands as far as relates to the sacred rites; but in all other respects they are considered as not being under such restraint. Where, however, women are placed in the hand of their husbands by coemption, they are released from parental control; and it makes no difference whether they are placed in the hand of their husbands, or in that of strangers; although those alone are considered to occupy the place of daughters who are placed in the hand of their husbands.

(137) Women placed in the hand of their husbands by coemption cease to be subject to this authority in the same way as daughters under the control of their father; that is to say, either by the death of him in whose power they are, or because he has been interdicted from water and fire.

(137a) They also cease to be in the hand of their husbands by remancipation; and if emancipated after a single sale they become their own mistresses. A woman who has concluded a coemption with a stranger by way of trust, can compel him to sell her again to anyone whom she may select; but one who has been sold to her husband, in whose hand she is, cannot compel him to do so, any more than a daughter can compel her father, even though she may be an adopted daughter. A woman, however, can, by serving notice of repudiation, force her husband to release her, just as if she had never been married.

(138) As persons who have been sold in this way are considered to occupy the position of slaves, if they should be manumitted either by the prætor, or by enrollment in the census, or by will, they become their own masters.

(139) In this instance, however, the *Lex Ælia Sentia* does not apply. Therefore, we do not require the party who manumits, or the one who is manumitted, to be of any particular age; and no attention is paid to whether the party granting the manumission has either a patron or a creditor; and not even the number prescribed by the *Lex Fufia Can-*

inia is considered with reference to persons of this description.

(140) But even if the party having possession of the one who is sold should be unwilling, the latter can obtain his freedom by being enrolled on the register of the census; except in the case of one whom his father has mancipated under the condition that he should be again sold to him; for, in this instance, the father is considered to have reserved, to a certain extent, his own power for himself which he received by mancipation. And, indeed, he is not said to have received his freedom by enrollment on the register of the census, against the consent of the party who holds him in mancipation, if his father gave him up as the result of a noxal action; for instance, where his father has been condemned on account of a theft committed by his son and has surrendered him by mancipation to the plaintiff, for then the plaintiff holds him instead of the payment of a sum of money.

(141) In conclusion, we observe that no insulting act should be committed by us against persons whom we hold in mancipation; otherwise, we shall be liable to a suit for injury committed. And, indeed, men should not be retained for any length of time in this condition, but, for the most part, as a matter of form, and only for an instant, unless the parties are mancipated on account of a noxal action.

(142) Let us now pass to another division. For persons who are neither subject to paternal authority, nor are in the hand, nor are held in mancipation by another, may still be under guardianship or curatorship, or may be free from either of these restrictions. Let us first consider those who may be under guardianship and curatorship; for then we shall understand who the other persons are who are subject to neither of these restraints.

(143) And, first, let us examine those who are under guardianship.

(144) Parents are permitted to appoint testamentary guardians for their children who are subject to their authority, who are under the age of puberty, and of the male

sex; and for those of the female sex, no matter what their age may be, and even if they are married; for the ancients required women, even if they were of full age, to remain under guardianship on account of the levity of their disposition.

(145) Therefore, if anyone appoints a guardian for his son and daughter by will, and both should arrive at the age of puberty, the son will cease to have a guardian, but the daughter will nevertheless remain subject to guardianship; for it is only under the *Lex Julia et Papia* that women are released from guardianship by the birth of children. Those whom we speak of do not include Vestal Virgins, whom the ancients desired to be free on account of the honor of the priesthood; hence this was provided by the Law of the Twelve Tables.

(146) We can, however, only appoint testamentary guardians for grandsons and granddaughters, if after our death they do not again pass under the control of their father. Therefore, if my son was under my control at the time of my death, my grandsons by him cannot have a guardian appointed by my will, although they were under my control at the time; for the reason that by my death they were placed under the control of their father.

(147) As in many other instances posthumous children are considered as already born, in this case also it has been decided that testamentary guardians can be appointed for posthumous children, as well as for those previously born; provided, however, that if born during our lifetime, they would have been subject to our authority. We can also appoint them our heirs, but it is not permitted to appoint posthumous strangers heirs.

(148) A testamentary guardian can be appointed for a wife who is in the hand of the testator; just as if she were a daughter; and, likewise, one may be appointed for a daughter-in-law who is in the hand of a son, just as if she were a granddaughter.

(149) A guardian can most properly be appointed in the

following manner, namely: "I appoint Lucius Titius guardian of my children." If, however, the appointment was made as follows: "Let Lucius Titius be the guardian of my children and my wife," it is understood to be legally made.

(150) The choice of a guardian may be left to a wife who is in the hand of the testator, that is to say, he can permit her to select any guardian whom she may choose, as follows: "I give to Titia, my wife, the selection of her guardian." In this instance, the wife is permitted to appoint a guardian either for the administration of all the property, or only of one or two things.

(151) Moreover, the choice may be granted either absolutely or with restrictions.

(152) It is ordinarily granted absolutely in the way that we have mentioned above. Where it is granted with restrictions, the following form is usually employed: "I grant to Titia, my wife, only one choice of a guardian"; or: "I only grant her the right to make two selections."

(153) These privileges of selection are very different, for she who has an unlimited right of choice, can choose a guardian twice or three times, or oftener; but she who has a limited right of choice cannot make more than one if only one is granted; and if only two are granted she has no right to make more than two selections.

(154) Guardians who are especially appointed by will are called "dative"; and those to whom the selection of a guardian is left are called "optative."

(155) By the Law of the Twelve Tables the nearest agnates become the guardians of children for whom no guardian was appointed by will, and they are styled legal guardians.

(156) Agnates are blood relatives through the male sex, for instance, through the father; as a brother having the same father, the son of a brother, or a grandson by him, and also a paternal uncle and his son and grandson. Those who are related through the female sex are not agnates, but cognates, according to natural law. Therefore, agnation does not exist

between a maternal uncle and a son or a sister, but cognation does. In like manner, the son of my maternal aunt, or the sister of my mother, is not my agnate, but my cognate; and, on the other hand, I am related to him by the same rule, because children follow the family of their father, and not that of their mother.

(157) Formerly, however, according to the Law of the Twelve Tables, females had agnates as legal guardians, but afterwards the *Lex Claudia,* which abolished the guardianship of agnates, so far as females were concerned, was enacted, and therefore a male child under the age of puberty has his brother, who is above the age of puberty, or his paternal uncle, as his guardian; but a female child cannot have a guardian of this kind.

(158) The right of agnation is extinguished by the loss of civil rights, but the right of cognation is not affected by it, for the reason that a civil law can abrogate civil rights, but cannot extinguish natural rights.

(159) The loss of civil rights is a change of former condition, and this takes place in three ways; it is either greatest, or less, which some call intermediate, or least.

(160) The greatest loss of civil rights occurs when anyone forfeits at the same time both his citizenship and his freedom, which happens to those who are not inscribed on the register of the census, and are in consequence ordered to be sold; which rule has for some time been abolished by disuse. Under the terms of the *Lex Ælia Sentia, dediticii* are liable to the same penalty for violation of its provisions if they have established their domicile in the City of Rome. It also takes place where, under the Claudian Decree of the Senate, free women become the slaves of the owners of other slaves with whom they have cohabited against the consent and protest of their masters.

(161) Less, or intermediate, loss of civil rights occurs when citizenship is forfeited but freedom is retained, which happens when anyone is interdicted from fire and water.

(162) The least loss of civil rights results when both

citizenship and freedom are retained, but a man's domestic condition is altered; which happens to those who are adopted, as well as to women subject to coemption, and also in the case of those who are given in mancipation and are afterwards manumitted; so that as often as anyone is mancipated, or remancipated, or manumitted, he suffers a loss of civil rights.

(163) The right of agnation is extinguished not only by the two greater losses of civil rights but also by the least; and therefore if a father should emancipate one of two children, neither can be the guardian of the other by the right of agnation after his death.

(164) When agnates have a right to guardianship, all of them are not entitled to that right at once, but only those in the nearest degree.

(165) By the same law of the Twelve Tables, the guardianship of freedwomen and freedmen under the age of puberty belongs to their patrons and the children of the latter. This kind of guardianship is also styled legal, not because special provision is made for it by this law, but for the reason that this has been accepted by interpretation just as if it had been expressly stated in the words of the statute; for as the law directed that the estates of freedmen and freedwomen who died intestate should belong to their patrons and the children of the latter, the ancient authorities held that the law intended that they should be entitled to their guardianship because it ordered that agnates whom it called to the succession should also be guardians.

DIOCLETIAN'S EDICT*

In 301 A.D. the Roman Emperor Diocletian issued an Edictum de Maximis Pretiis: an edict bearing on maximum prices fixed on various commodities and services throughout the Roman Empire. The intention was to combat dubious coinage, wild spending, and sudden rises in prices.

THE EDICT

The national honor and the prestige and majesty of Rome require that the fortune of our State, to which, after the immortal gods, we may, in memory of the successful wars we have waged, give thanks for the peaceful and completely settled condition of the world, be also faithfully managed and showered with the blessings of the peace for which we have striven laboriously: so that we, who by the gracious favor of the gods have, in the past, checked the unbridled depredations of barbarous tribes by destroying those very nations, may protect this peace, secured for ever, with the defences required by justice. . . .

Our decrees cannot be honored in their entirety throughout our extensive territories, and avarice cannot be restrained within the limits of a law regulating commerce. It is therefore our will that the prices of the commodities designated in the appended schedule be brought to the attention of the whole Empire so that all may know that they may not exceed them. . . .

It is our will that whoever dares to proceed against the

*Translated by H. E. Wedeck.

159

prescriptions of this decree shall thereby become liable to capital punishment. . . .

List of Commodities and Maximum Legal Prices
(The denarius is variously estimated; usually, at approximately 2/5 of a cent)

	denarii
Prime oil—one Italian sextarius	40
Second quality oil—one Italian sextarius	24
Cibarium oil—one Italian sextarius	12
Coleseed oil—one Italian sextarius	8
Vinegar—one Italian sextarius	6
First quality liquamen—one Italian sextarius	6
Second quality liquamen—one Italian sextarius	2
Salt—one modius	100
Medicated salt—one Italian sextarius	8
Best honey—one Italian sextarius	40
Second quality honey—one Italian sextarius	20
Palm honey—one Italian sextarius	8

Items of meat

Pork—one Italian pound	12
Beef—one Italian pound	8
Goat's flesh or mutton—one Italian pound	8
Sterile womb	24
Sow's udder	20
Fattened pig's liver, best—one Italian pound	16
Lard, the best—one Italian pound	16
Best bacon ham, Westphalia or Cerdagne— one Italian pound	20
Bacon ham of country of the Marsi—one Italian pound	20
Fresh fat—one Italian pound	12
Fat for greasing—one Italian pound	12
Pigs' feet	12
(intestines at the same price as the pork)	
Rissoles of pork—one ounce	2
Rissoles of beef—one Italian pound	10
Lucanian sausages—one Italian pound	16
Lucanian sausages of beef—one Italian pound	10

Fatted cock pheasant	250
Wild cock pheasant	125
Fatted hen pheasant	200
Hen pheasant, not fatted	100
Fatted goose	200
Goose, not fatted	100
Chicken	60
Partridge	30
Turtle dove	16
Turtle dove	12
Thrush	60
Wood pigeon	20
Pigeon	24
Hazel-hen	20
Duck	40
Hare	150
Quails	20
Starlings, ten	20
Wild boar's flesh—one Italian pound	16
Stag's flesh	12
Flesh of buck, doe, or roe—one Italian pound	12
Suckling pig—per pound	16
Lamb—per pound	12
Kid—per pound	12
Tallow—one Italian pound	6
Butter—one Italian pound	16
Item fish	
Fish caught near rocks or in deep water— one Italian pound	24
Second quality fish—one Italian pound	16
Best river fish—one Italian pound	12
Second quality river fish—one Italian pound	8
Salt fish—one Italian pound	6
Oysters, 100	
Sea urchins, 100	50
Sea urchins, fresh, cleaned—one Italian sextarius	50
Sea urchins, salted	100

Sea cockles, 100	50
Dry cheese—one Italian pound	12
Sardae or sardines—one Italian pound	16
Item: large artichokes, 5	10
Best quality endive, 10	10
Second quality, 10	10
Mallows, best	14
Second quality mallows	10
Lettuce, best, 5	4
Second quality, 10	4
Best cauliflower 5	4
Second quality, 10	4
Best cabbages, a bunch	4
Leeks, largest, 10	4
Second quality, 20	4
Beets, largest, 5	4
Second quality, 10	4
Radishes, largest	4
Second quality, 20	4
Turnips, largest	10
Second quality, 20	4
Dry onions, best	4
Green onions, best, 25	4
Second quality, 50	4
Garlic—one Italian modius	60
Water-cress, bunch of 20	10
Capers—one Italian modius	100
Gourds, best, ten	4
Second quality	4
Cucumbers, best, 10	4
Second quality, 20	4
Melons, large, 2	4
Second rate, 4	4
Water melons, 4	4
French beans, bunches of 25	4
Garden asparagus, bunch of 25	6
Wild asparagus, bunch of 50	4

Butchers'-broom, bunch of 60	4
Green vetches, 4 bunches	4
Green beans, shelled—one Italian sextarius	4
Fresh French beans, shelled—one Italian sextarius	4
Shoots of palm, 4	4
African bulbs, or dried bulbs, 20	12
Smaller bulbs, 40	12
Eggs, 4	4
Wages for Labor	
Farm laborer, by the day	25
Stone mason	50
Worker inside house	50
Maker of mortar	50
Worker in marble	60
Worker in mosaic	60
Wall painter	70
Figure painter	150
Coach builder	50
Iron worker	50
Baker	50
Shipwright in sea vessels	60
Shipwright in river vessels	50
Brickmaker, making small bricks	2
Brickmaker of bricks of four feet with food, except wine	2
Shepherd, with food	20
Muledriver, with food	25
Veterinarian, cutting hair and hoofs, each animal	6
Veterinarian, combing and cleaning, each animal	20
Barber, for each customer	2
Sheep-shearer, per head, with food	2

BRAZIERS' WORK

Work in hard brass—by the pound	8
Work in copper—by the pound	6
Work on vessels of various kinds—by the pound	6
Work on small images or statues	6

Work in ductile brass	6
Work on plastic figures, with food	70
Water-carrier, working all day, with food	25
Scavenger, working all day, with food	25
Armorer, repairing sword	25
Repairing helmet	25
Repairing axe	6
Repairing double-headed axe	8
Sheath of sword	100
Scribe, 100 verses written in best style	
Public scribe, 100 lines of brochure or tablet	
Breeches-maker, cutting and making up	
Making birrhus (woolen garment) of first quality	
Birrhus of second quality	40
Pedagogue, for each pupil, by the month	50
Master appointed to teach letters, for each pupil, by month	50
Arithmetician, for each pupil, by month	75
Notary, for each boy, by month	75
Librarian or antiquarian, for each pupil, by month	50
Greek or Roman grammarian and geometry teacher, for each pupil, by month	200
Orator or philosopher, for each pupil, by month	200
Advocate or lawyer, application to court	250
Hearing of a case	1000
Master architect, for each pupil, by month	100
Attendant at public baths, for each customer	2
Attendant at private bath, for each customer	2
Skins of Babylon, Tralles, or Phoenicia	
Babylonian skin of first quality	500
Of second quality	40
Trallian skin	200
Phoenician skin	100
Ox hides, unprepared, of first quality	500
Oxhide, prepared for soling boots	750
For making straps and harness	600
Oxhide unprepared, of second quality	300

164

Beaver skin	100
The same, made up	
Bear skin, largest size	
Skin of sea-calf	250
The same, made up	1500
Leopard skin	1000
The same, made up	1250
Quilt of eight goat skins	600
Lasts for boots	
Lasts of largest size	100
Second size	80
Shoes for patricians	150
Pair of woman's shoes	60
Military saddle	500
Pair of trunks or sacks, weighing thirty pounds	40
Open sack, three feet wide, for every pound, whatever the length	16
Timber	
Fir timber, 50 cubits, 4 cubits square	50,000
45 cubits, 4 cubits square	40,000
Bruised millet—one modius	100
Whole millet—one modius	50
Fine spelt—one modius	100
Second quality, called scandula—one modius	30
Bruised beans—one modius	100
Whole beans—one modius	60
Lentils—one modius	100
Bruised peas—one modius	100
Whole peas—one modius	60
Oats—one modius	30
Fenugreek—one modius	100
Crude lupines—one modius	60
Cooked lupines—one modius	4
French beans, dry—one modius	100
Linseed—one modius	150
Sesame—one modius	200
Hayseed—one modius	30

Hemp seed—one modius	50
Mustard seed—one modius	150
Items on wine	
Picene—one Italian sextarius	30
Tiburtine—one Italian sextarius	30
Sabine—one Italian sextarius	30
Aminnean—one Italian sextarius	30
Setine—one Italian sextarius	30
Sorrentine—one Italian sextarius	30
Falernian—one Italian sextarius	30
Old wine, best quality—one Italian sextarius	24
Beer—one Italian sextarius	4
Zythus (Egyptian beer)—one Italian sextarius	2

V.

LEGAL LIGHTS OF THE DARK AGES

CONSTANTINE THE GREAT (288-337)*

The son of Constantius Chlorus, Emperor of the West, Constantine was proclaimed Emperor by his soldiers on the death of his father in 306. He was responsible for making Christianity the accepted religion of the state and constructed his capital city named Constantinople on the site of ancient Byzantium.

His interest in the Christian faith was probably more political than religious although his aims were to reconcile the various sects of Christianity and establish a single Church which would be in close association with the state. In 325 he established The Council of Nicaea which was to resolve a dispute between the Arian Christians and those of the Orthodox faith. From this Council the Nicene Creed, the Orthodox statement of Christian belief, was officially formulated.

Other advances under Constantine were a centralized administrative authority throughout the country and stabilization of the currency.

EDICT OF MILAN ON THE TOLERATION OF THE CHRISTIAN RELIGION, ENACTED IN 313

We, Constantinus and Licinius, the Emperors, having met in concord at Milan and having set in order everything which pertains to the common good and public security, are of the opinion that among the various things which we perceived would profit men, or which should be set in order first, was to be found the cultivation of religion; we should therefore give both to Christians and to all others free facility to follow the religion which each may desire, so that by this means whatever divinity is enthroned in heaven may be gracious and

*From *Church and State Through the Centuries—Historical Documents* by Sidney Z. Ehler and John B. Morrall, The Newman Press, Westminster, Maryland.

favourable to us and to all who have been placed under our authority. Therefore we are of the opinion that the following decision is in accordance with sound and true reasoning: that no one who has been given his mental assent to the Christian persuasion or to any other which he feels to be suitable to him should be compelled to deny his conviction, so that the Supreme Godhead ("Summa Divinitas"), whose worship we freely observe, can assist us in all things with his wonted favour and benevolence. Wherefore it is necessary for your Excellency to know that it is our pleasure that all restrictions which were previously put forward in official pronouncements concerning the sect of the Christians should be removed, and that each one of them who freely and sincerely carries out the purpose of observing the Christian religion may endeavour to practice its precepts without any fear or danger. We believed that these points should be fully brought to your attention, so that you might know that we have given free and absolute permission to practice their religion to the Christians. Now that you perceive what we have granted to them, your Excellency must also learn that for the sake of peace in our time a similar public and free right to practise their religion or cult is granted to others, so that every man may have free opportunity to worship according to his own wish. This has been done by us to avoid any appearance of disfavour to any one religion. We have decided furthermore to decree the following in respect of the Christians: if those places at which they were accustomed in former times to hold their meetings (concerning which a definite procedure was laid down for your guidance in previous communications) have been at any previous time acquired from our treasury or from any other person, let the persons concerned be willing and swift to restore them to the Christians without financial recompense and without trying to ask a price. Let those who have received such property as a gift restore whatever they have acquired to the Christians in similar manner. If those who have bought such property or received it as a gift, seek some recompense from our benevolence, let them apply to

170

the Vicar, by whom their cases will be referred to our clemency. You are to consider it your duty that all these things shall be handed over to the Christian body immediately and without delay by your intervention. And since the aforesaid Christians are known to have possessed not only those places at which they are wont to assemble, but others also pertaining to the law of their body, that is of the churches, not of private individuals, you are to order in accordance with the law which we have described above the return of all those possessions to the aforesaid Christians, that is to their bodies and assemblies without any further hesitation or argument. Our previous statement is to be borne in mind that those who restore this property without price may, as we have said, expect some compensation from our benevolence.

You ought to bring into play your very effective intervention in all these matters concerning the aforesaid Christian body so that there may be a swift fulfilment of our Edict, in which the interests of the public quiet have been consulted by our clemency. Let all this be done, so that as we stated above, the divine favour, of which we have experienced so many instances, may continue with us to bless our successors through all time with public wellbeing. In order that the character of this our perpetual benevolence can reach the knowledge of all, it will be well for you to circulate everywhere, and to bring to the awareness of all, these points which have been written to you as above, so that the enactment of this our benevolence may not be hidden.

THE THEODOSIAN CODE, A.D. 438*

In 438 A.D. the Emperor Theodosius II published a code which was intended to reduce and systematize the complex mass of law which had been issued since the time of Constantine I and which would supplant all previous compilations of the imperial constitutions and decrees. To a large extent it was based on two compilations, the Gregorian (*Code Gregorianus*) and the Hermogenian (*Code Hermogenianus*). Once issued the *Code Theodosianus* was adopted by Valentinian III, Emperor of the West, and was used in shaping the Corpus Juris Civilis, one of the most comprehensive codes of Roman law, compiled under Justinian I and issued between 529 and 535.

TITLE 14: THE OFFICE OF AUGUSTAL PREFECT (DE OFFICIO PRAEFECTI AUGUSTALIS)

1. Emperors Valentinian, Theodosius, and Arcadius Augustuses to Florentius, Augustal Prefect.

We order your office and the offices of the competent judges to exact all tribute throughout the provinces of Thebais and Augustamnica, to receive this tribute and finally to compel its payment, provided that if there should be any military landholders in the aforesaid provinces, their tribute shall be exacted only by the military office staff. If there should now exist any of Our provincials who are audacious about making payments that are due, you shall report them to Our Clemency, in order that, when We so order, their tribute may be exacted by armed soldiers.

*Pharr, Clyde and Others, *The Theodosian Code and Novels*. Princeton: Princeton University Press, 1952.

Given on the thirteenth day before the kalends of March at Constantinople in the year of the consulship of Emperor Designate Honorius and of Evodius.—February 17, 386

2. Emperors Theodosius, Arcadius, and Honorius Augustuses to Rufinus, Praetorian Prefect.

The augustal prefect shall have the power to investigate the shameful misdeeds of the judges ordinary who are under him and to refer the cases to Us, but he shall not have the power to remove or punish them.

Given on the day before the nones of December at Constantinople in the year of the consulship of Olybrius and Probinus.—December 4, 394-395 (?) .

TITLE 15: THE OFFICE OF VICAR (DE OFFICIO VICARII)

1. Emperor Constantine Augustus to Silvius Paulus, Master of Italy.

(After other matters.) In order that Your Gravity, occupied as you are with other duties, may not be burdened with a huge mass of such rescripts, it is Our pleasure to enjoin upon Your Gravity those cases only in which a more powerful person can oppress an inferior or lesser judge or cases in which a matter arises of the kind that is not permitted to be terminated in the court of the governor, or cases which, although they have long been handled by the aforesaid governors, must now be terminated before you.

Given on the fifth day before the kalends of March at Nicomedia in the year of the consulship of Paulinus and Julianus.—February 25, 325.

2. Emperor Constantius Augustus to Caesonianus, Vicar of Africa.

Your Sublimity shall receive and quickly make known to Us the references of cases to Us by the judges who govern the provinces, and likewise such references by the fiscal representatives and by all others who desire to have any matter referred to Our Wisdom.

Given on the fourth day before the kalends of October in the year of the consulship of Philippus and Salia.—September 28, 348; December 357.

3. The same Augustus to Ilicus, Governor of Numidia.

When the governors of the provinces wish to refer any matter to Us, this matter shall be referred first to the vicar, to whom written instructions have been given that he shall receive the reports and references of the official messengers, which are to be transmitted to My imperial court, and that he shall perform that which he sees ought to be done. Indeed, in this way, in addition to other advantages, the public post will be strengthened by great relief.

Given on the third day before the nones of December at Sirmium in the year of the sixth consulship of Constantius Augustus and the consulship of Constans Caesar.—December 3, 353; 352; 357.

4. Emperor Julian Augustus to Mamertinus, Praetorian Prefect.

Your sublimity shall notify the governors of the provinces that they shall know that the vicars must participate in all things about which the governors suppose that reference ought to be made to Us and to your knowledge.

Received on the eighth day before the ides of June in the year of the consulship of Mamertinus and Nevitta.—June 6, 362.

5. Emperors Valentinian and Valens Augustuses to Dracontius, Vicar of Africa.

The office staff of the vicar of the prefecture throughout Africa shall be so limited in number that it cannot exceed three hundred, just as We have prescribed in the cases of the other vicars.

Given on the eighth day before the kalends of February at Milan in the year of the consulship of Valentinian and Valens Augustuses.—January 25, 365.

6. The same Augustuses to Crescens, Vicar of Africa.

Whenever any tax gatherer, or tax receiver, or any registar is asserted to be liable because of his accounts or because of fraud, no apparitor shall be dispatched to compel his appearance, but the investigation of the matter shall be entrusted to the governor of the province. I. However, as soon as Your Sincerity has entered a province, you shall inquire carefully how much diligence and efficiency the judge ordinary has bestowed upon the duties enjoined upon him. When anyone of them has been discovered who has not fully conducted an investigation and attended to the satisfaction of those accounts concerning which he had been instructed, it shall be fitting that he undergo a severe judgment, suitable as a warning for his neglect of the public welfare.

Given on the fourth day before the kalends of March at Trier in the year of the consulship of Modestus and Arintheus.—February 27, 372.

7. Emperors Valens, Gratian, and Valentinian Augustuses to Antonius, Praetorian Prefect.

In civil cases the vicars must be preferred to the counts of soldiers; in military cases, the counts must be preferred to the vicars, and when they happen to be associated in judging a case, the vicar shall be considered to hold the higher position, and the count shall be attached as an adjunct. Since, indeed, the honor of the prefecture takes precedence of all other dignities, the dignity of vicar by its very name indicates that it assumes a part of the prefecture, that it has the power of the sacred imperial cognizances, and that it is accustomed to represent the reverence of Our judgment.

Given on the eighth day before the ides of January in the year of the fourth consulship of Gratian Augustus and the consulship of Merobaudes.—January 6, 377.

8. The same Augustuses to Hesperius, Praetorian Prefect.

The references of cases to the Emperors by the vicars, whenever necessity occasions them, shall be conveyed to Our Clemency. For even though there are very many questions to which your illustrious judgment can also give a response without consulting Us, nevertheless We know that there are a considerable number of problems which cannot be solved except by the authority of the imperial oracle, and

We gladly hear the references of the judges, in order that the authority of the administrators may not appear to be diminished if We should repel their consultations from Our shrines as though they were supplications of the profane.

Given on the twelfth day before the kalends of February in the year of the fourth consulship of Gratian Augustus and the consulship of Merobaudes.—January 21, 377; 378; 379.

9. Emperors Valens, Gratian, and Valentinian Augustuses to Alypius.

The office staff of Your Laudability shall supervise all accounts of the largesses, with especial care and at their own risk, in accordance with the ancient custom, so that certainly after this regulation, your office shall not be able to share any blame with the office of the fiscal representative, from which they shall understand that this duty is alien.

Given on the kalends of June at Trier: June (January) I. Received on the nomes of July in the year of the sixth consulship of Valens Augustus and the second consulship of Valentinian Augustus.—July (January) 7, 378.

10. Emperors Gratian, Valentinian, and Theodosius Augustuses to Syagrius.

The right to enter the Proconsular Province shall be denied to the Vicar of Africa, and only for the purpose of holding a council shall entry into the municipality of Theveste be open to him. Moreover, the prefect of the annona shall rigorously urge the exaction of the regular tax.

1. The office of Your Sincerity shall collect the clothing due to the largesses, a duty to which the fiscal representative shall also vigorously apply himself; provided, however, that both urgency in making the exactions and the odium resulting from fraud shall primarily rest upon your apparitors.

2. Of course, the apparitors of the vicar of the prefecture shall supervise the imposts established at Carthage.

Posted at Carthage. Given on the seventh day before the kalends of September in the year of the consulship of Auxonius and Olybrius.—August 26, 379.

11. The same Augustuses to Justianus, Vicar of the Pontic Diocese.

We have learned that the secretaries of the office staff which is subject to Your Excellency have again sought appointment in the imperial service as anciently instituted, so that after the completion of their service as secretaries of the office staff, they are joined to the corps of the secret service. But such practices are opposed by the divine imperial statutes, from which We learn that the secretaries of the office staff of the Illustrious praetorian prefect also, and even those of the count of the Orient, are placed in charge of herds of camels by a regulation of that time. It appears in accordance with this regulation that the compulsory service of the various distributions in the City of Constantinople had been imposed upon the secretaries of the office staff of all the vicars.

Given on the second day before the nones of April at Thessalonica in the year of the fifth consulship of Gratian Augustus and the first consulship of Theodosius Augustus.— April 4, 380.

12. Emperors Valentinian, Theodosius, and Arcadius Augustuses to all Vicars.

Each and every vicar shall know that only three hundred men each shall be members of the imperial service throughout the dioceses which have been entrusted to them. It shall be provided that if any persons are obligated to the municipal councils by the bond of ancestry, they shall be returned to the functions of decurions, and no person shall defend himself from this service under the pretext of some privilege or by the excuse of old age.

Given on the sixth day before the kalends of November in the year of the consulship of Emperor Designate Honorius and of the Most Noble Evodius.—October 27, 386.

13. The same Augustuses to Our Dearest Tatianus, Greetings.

We prescribe that the office of the diocese of Asia, through the broad expanses of which the boundaries of eight provinces extend, shall rely upon the services of two hundred apparitors.

Given on the fourth day before the kalends of May at Milan in the year of the consulship of Timasius and Promotus.—April 28, 389.

14. Emperors Arcadius and Honorius Augustuses to Eusebius, Praetorian Prefect.

Provision must be made that no fraud shall be perpetrated in connection with the regular tribute of grain in Africa. Therefore, it is Our will that the Respectable vicar of Africa shall assume the necessary duties of exaction and transmission of this tribute in the Proconsular Province.

Given on the fourteenth day before the kalends of January at Rome in the year of the consulship of Olybrius and Probinus.—December 19, 395.

15. The same Augustuses to Vincentius, Praetorian Prefect.

We order that the Respectable Vicar of the seven provinces shall exact the delinquent tax payments for past time. But We decree that payments of the current tribute shall be expedited by the judges ordinary, over whom, however, the vicar must stand as a constant threat.

Given on the fourteenth day before the kalends of July at Milan in the year of the consulship of Stilicho and Aurelianus.—June 18, 400.

16. The same Augustuses to Vigilius, Vicar of Spain.

At public salutations absolutely no dignitary, unless he is clad in his military cloak, shall greet the vicar who is in power. If, therefore, any person should attempt to violate Our statute, the office staff shall be obligated to pay a fine of ten pounds of gold.

Given on the fourth day before the ides of September at Milan in the year of the consulship of Vincentius and Fravitus.—September 10, 401.

17. The same Augustuses to Messala, Praetorian Prefect.

It is Our will that the Respectable Vicar of Africa, who is obligated to administer the entire collection and transmission of revenues, shall act as a constant threat to the judges, that he shall inquire very carefully how much has been paid in each and every month and what has been transmitted, and that he shall inflict certain punishment on those persons whose idleness has been revealed. (Etc.)

Given on the third day before the kalends of October at Altimum in the year of the consulship of Vincentius and Fravitus.—September 29, 401; September 28, 400.

TITLE 16: THE OFFICE OF GOVERNOR OF A PROVINCE (DE OFFICIO RECTORIS PROVINCIAE)

1. Emperor Constantine Augustus to Rufinus Octavianus, Governor of Lucania and Bruttium.

If any person should obtain permission for an extraordinary trial by a prefect or vicar or if anyone has already obtained such permission, you shall not permit his adversaries and the persons necessary to the case to proceed or to pass over to the office of the prefect or of the vicar. But you yourself shall try the whole case, with all parties and persons necessary to the suit present in your court, within the statutory time limits which you shall compute from the day on which the case began to be instituted in your court, so that if your decision should be displeasing to the person who demanded an extraordinary trial, then only may an appeal, interposed in accordance with the order of the law, suspend such decision and effect a transfer to the competent judge.

Given on the third day before the nones of August at Trier in the year of the fourth consulship of Constantine Augustus and of Licinius.—August 3, 315; 313.

2. The same Augustus to Bassus.

The decrees of provincials must not be conveyed to the imperial court before each judge has examined and approved them and sealed them along with his report. If anything should be done contrary to this regulation, the statutory punishment shall be imposed.

Posted on the eighth day before the kalends of October at Cagliari in the year of the consulship of Gallicanus and Bassus.—September 24, 317; 331.

3. The same Augustus to Felix, Governor of Corsica.

When six months have elapsed, the record books of all cases shall be transcribed by your office staff and shall go to the bureau of the most eminent prefecture, so that when these records have been examined and delivered to Our bureau, it may be disclosed which of the judges have given faithful service and what cases they have thus brought to a conclusion, in order that the worthy may obtain a reward and the negligent may incur punishment. The right is granted to the provincials to appear before your court to prefer charges of negligence and avarice against members of your office staff. 1. Of course, against a person who has been corrupted by a bribe or through favoritism and has given an unjust decision, revenge shall be granted to the person whom he has harmed, not only by means of the loss of reputation, but also by the liability of the lawsuit.

Given on the ninth day before the kalends of November at Sirmium in the year of the fifth consulship of Constantine Augustus and the consulship of Licinius Caesar.—October 24, 319; 318.

4. The same Augustus to Maximus.

If any very powerful and arrogant person should arise, and the governors of the provinces are not able to punish him or to examine the case or to pronounce sentence, they must refer his name to Us, or at least to the knowledge of Your Gravity. Thus provision shall be made for consulting the interests of public discipline and the oppressed lower classes. (Etc.)

Given on the fourth day before the kalends of January at Trier in the year of the consulship of Januarinus and Justus. —December 29, 328 (?).

5. The same Augustus to Secundus, Praetorian Prefect of the Orient.

The authority of the judge ordinary, that is, the governor of a province, or that of the vicar must act as a guard to correct wrongdoing.

1. But it is Our pleasure that the apparitors of Your

Eminence and of the office of the vicar shall be removed from the duty of collecting revenues and that all accounts shall be exacted through the provincial offices and the governors. For if a collection has not been completed, the person responsible shall be produced before Our tribunal, and he shall undergo the risk of capital punishment and the loss of all his fortune.

Given on the fourteenth day before the kalends of May at Constantinople in the year of the eighth consulship of Constantine Augustus and the fourth consulship of Constantius. —April 18, 329; 362-3; 365.

6. The same Augustus to the Provincials.

The governors shall conduct public trials with their tribunals crowded by throngs of people throughout the trials, and when they are about to hear civil controversies, they shall not hide themselves in their private council chambers so that a litigant cannot impetrate an opportunity to appear before them without a price. When they have granted an audience for all cases which have been brought to them and the frequent announcements of the herald, made in the usual manner, have found no remaining person who desires to institute an action, after all public and private acts have been completed, the judges shall have the right to withdraw.

1. Moreover, We grant to all persons the privilege of praising by public acclamation the most just and vigilant judges, so that We may grant increased accessions of honor to them. On the contrary, the unjust and the evil-doers must be accused by cries of complaints, in order that the force of Our censure may destroy them. For We shall carefully investigate whether such utterances are truthful and are not poured forth effusively and wantonly by clients. The praetorian prefects and the counts who have been stationed throughout the provinces shall refer to Our Wisdom the utterances of Our provincials.

Posted on the kalends of November at Constantinople in the year of the consulship of Bassus and Ablavius—November 1, 331.

7. The same Augustus to the Provincials.

The rapacious hands of the apparitors shall immediately cease, they shall cease, I say; for if after due warning they do not cease, they shall be cut off by the sword. The chamber curtain of the judge shall not be venal; entrance shall not be gained by purchase, the private council chamber shall not be infamous on account of the bids. The appearance of the governor shall not be at a price; the ears of the judge shall be open equally to the poorest as well as to the rich. There shall be no despoiling on the occasion of escorting persons inside by the one who is called chief of the office staff. The assistants of the aforesaid chiefs of office staff shall employ no extortion on litigants; the intolerable onslaught of the centurions and other apparitors who demand small and great sums shall be crushed; and the unsated greed of those who deliver the records of a case to litigants shall be restrained. 1. Always shall the diligence of the governor guard lest anything be taken from a litigant by the aforesaid classes of men. If they should suppose that anything ought to be demanded by them from those involved in civil cases, armed punishment will be at hand, which will cut off the heads and necks of the scoundrels. Opportunity shall be granted to all persons who have suffered extortion to provide for an investigation by the governors. If they should dissemble, We hereby open to all persons the right to express complaints about such conduct before the counts of the provinces or before the praetorian prefects, if they are closer at hand, so that We may be informed by their references to Us and may provide punishment for such brigandage.

Given on the kalends of November at Constantinople in the year of the consulship of Bassus and Ablavius.—November 1, 331.

INTERPRETATION: The apparitors of no judges shall dare to be venal or to require a price either for the entrance or for the egress of those persons who come for an audience or for litigation. Litigants, both rich and poor, shall be heard without a price. But if the apparitors should wish to be

182

rapacious, they shall be punished by the sword, or at least the story of their greed shall be carried to the ears of Our Lord.

8. The same Augustus to Secundus, Praetorian Prefect.

There are certain cases in which it is unnecessary to await the governor of the province, and therefore We grant to the governors the power to appoint petty judges, that is, judges who shall decide the less important cases.

Given on the fifth day before the kalends of August at Antioch in the year of the consulship of Mamertinus and Nevitta.—July 28, 362.

9. Emperors Valentinian and Valens Augustuses to Our Dearest Artemius, Greetings.

The judge shall not doubt that there is imposed upon him an especial duty in hearing and deciding cases, namely, that he shall not pronounce in the seclusion of his home a decision concerning the status of men or of patrimonies, but he shall hear both civil and criminal suits with the doors of his private council chambers open and with everyone called inside, or he shall take his place before the tribunal, in order that he may not be restrained from the infliction of a suitable punishment.

Moreover, it shall not be proper for a judge to be so devoted to the courting of popular favor and the production of spectacles, that he bestows more attention upon amusements than upon serious legal matters.

Given on the kalends of October at Aquileia in the year of the consulship of the sainted Jovian and of Varronianus.— October 1 (September 19), 364.

INTERPRETATION: The judge shall know that he must devote especial care in the cognizance of the cases of litigants and shall always employ equity. He shall further know that he shall not pronounce a final sentence in secret parts of his house or in some corner, but the doors of his house shall be open and throngs of people admitted, so that whatever decision he has rendered in accordance with the regular procedures of the law and the requirements of truth shall be concealed from no man.

10. The same Augustuses, to Valerianus, Vicar of Spain.

We forbid written statements of claim to be presented to the judges after they have departed, lest they pronounce sentence concerning cases of others or concerning status when they have withdrawn from the sight of their office staff and from the public eye.

Prefixed on the sixth day before the ides of September at Verona in the year of the consulship of Valentinian and Valens Augustuses.—September 8, 364; 365.

INTERPRETATION: After judges have departed from a public sitting into their own homes, they shall not accept any written statements of claim from litigants nor take cognizance of anything concerning the cases of others or concerning status, without their own office staff.

11. The same Augustuses and Gratian Augustus to Probus, Praetorian Prefect.

The governors of the provinces shall journey through the villas of all persons and all the villages, unobtrusively and in the usual manner, and of their own accord they shall inquire from each and every person what any tax collector has exacted arrogantly or greedily. For the person concerning whom any complaint reaches Us shall be seized and hurried off to the extreme penalty.

Given on the kalends of April at Trier in the year of the consulship of Emperor Designate Valentinian and of the Most Noble Victor—April 1, 369.

INTERPRETATION: The judges of the provinces must attend to traversing the various estates and districts with careful inquisition, and they shall discern of themselves in what manner the landholders are treated with respect to their payments of public obligations. If they neglect to fulfill their duty in this matter, they shall not doubt that the complaints of the citizens will be most severely avenged upon them.

12. The same Augustuses to Viventius, Praetorian Prefect. Each judge shall establish his court in those places in

which the governor ought to be available to all; he shall not frequent delightful retreats.

1. Indeed, We add that if any person should receive the governor of a province on his own landholding, the farm which the aforesaid governor used as lodging place on a journey shall be vindicated to the resources of the fisc. For thus the judges will strive to build up and to restore the post stations.

Given on the kalends of April at Trier in the year of the consulship of Emperor Designate Valentinian and of Victor.— April 1, 369.

13. Emperors Valens, Gratian, and Valentinian Augustuses to Antonius, Praetorian Prefect.

No person shall undertake to enter familiarly the home of a judge ordinary in the afternoon for the purpose of a secret conference, provided that he is of the same province, whether he is known to the judge or unknown, and although he displays the authority of a high office that he has held.

Given on the fifth day before the kalends of August at Mainz in the year of the fourth consulship of Gratian Augustus and the consulship of Merobaudes.—July 28, 377.

INTERPRETATION: No person, known or unknown, if he be a man of the same province, shall see a judge in the midday hours or in secrecy.

14. Emperors Honorius and Theodosius Augustuses to Theodorus, Praetorian Prefect.

We order the governors of the provinces to assume responsibility that the procurators of the powerful do not commit any wrongful or forbidden acts.

Given on the seventh day before the kalends of December at Ravenna in the year of the consulship of Bassus and Philippus.—November 25, 408.

INTERPRETATION: Judges of the provinces must have the utmost solicitude that the overseers of the powerful shall commit no forbidden or unjust acts against persons of inferior rank.

TITLE 17 (KR. 18): THE OFFICE OF COMPTROLLER OF THE ACCOUNTS AND OF THE PRIVY PURSE (DE OFFICIO RATIONALIS SUMMARUM ET REI PRIVATAE) (KR. XVII, UT NULLI PATRIAE SUAE ADMINISTRATIO SINE SPECIALI PERMISSU PRINCIPIS PERMITTATUR, THE ADMINISTRATION OF HIS MUNICIPALITY SHALL BE ALLOWED TO NO PERSON WITHOUT THE SPECIAL PERMISSION OF THE EMPEROR)

TITLE 18 (KR. 19): THE OFFICE OF PREFECT OF THE CITY GUARDS (DE OFFICIO PRAEFECTI VIGILUM)

TITLE 19 (KR. 21): THE OFFICE OF TRIBUNE OF AMUSEMENTS (DE OFFICIO TRIBUNI VOLUPTATUM)

TITLE 20: THE OFFICE OF CIVIL JUDGES (DE OFFICIO JUDICUM CIVILIUM)

1. Emperors Arcadius, Honorius, and Theodosius Augustuses to Curtius, Praetorian Prefect.

Dignitaries who are known to have lawsuits shall not have the right to sit with the judge during those hours in which the merits or outcome of cases are in suspense, nor shall the judges be seen by litigants during the midday hours. 1. Therefore, you shall know that a fine of five pounds of gold each shall be assessed against both the judge and his office staff and an equal fine against the dignitaries, if any person should attempt to contravene a regulation of this kind.

Given on the third day before the nones of February at Rome in the year of the consulship of Bassus and Philippus.— February 3, 408.

INTERPRETATION: The dignitaries of the provinces, that is, members of the body of municipal councils, shall not sit with a judge during the time when cases are being considered by this judge, if they themselves are also involved in litigation, and litigants shall not visit a judge in the midday hours. If they should presume to act otherwise, they shall pay the fine as stated in the above written law.

TITLE 21: THE OFFICE OF MILITARY JUDGES (DE OFFICIO JUDICUM MILITARIUM)

1. Emperors Theodosius, Arcadius, and Honorius Augustuses to the Counts and Masters of Both Branches of the Military Service.

Protection or execution by a soldier shall absolutely never be granted in legal actions of private persons.

Given on the day before the ides of February at Constantinople in the year of the third consulship of Theodosius Augustus and the consulship of the Most Noble Abundantius.
—February 12, 393.

INTERPRETATION: To absolutely no persons shall military protection or execution be granted in civil cases.

TITLE 22: THE OFFICE OF ALL JUDGES (DE OFFICIO JUDICUM OMNIUM)

1. Emperor Constantine Augustus to Domitius Celsus, Vicar.

No judge shall suppose that an apparitor may be sent to that home in which a matron resides, with any order to drag forth the aforesaid matron into public, since it is certain that the debts of a woman, who may seclude herself within her home out of consideration for sex, can be preserved for the public needs by the sale of her home or of anything whatever. But if any person hereafter should suppose that a matron ought to be dragged forth into public, he shall be punished by a capital penalty, or rather he shall be done to death with exquisite tortures amidst the greatest criminals and without any pardon.

Given on the third day before the ides of January at Trier

*in the year of the consulship of Sabinus and Rufinus.—
January 11, 316.*

INTERPRETATION: No judge shall suppose that a matron
residing in her own home may be dragged forth into public
by any apparitor, but in respect to her, with reverence for
her sex, an honorable summons shall be observed; since if
it should appear that she owes anything, it can be paid by
the constraint of her sureties. If anyone should contravene
this regulation, he shall know that he will be punished with
the supreme penalty.

2. The same Augustus to Andronicus.

If against pupils, widows, or persons who are exhausted
or disabled by illness, right to a trial by Our Clemency
should be impetrated, the aforesaid defendants shall be compelled by none of Our judges to make an appearance before
Our imperial court. But, indeed, they shall try the fortune
of their suit within the province in which the litigant and
witnesses and the documentary proofs are located, and every
precaution shall be observed that the defendants shall not
be compelled to leave the boundaries of their own provinces.
1. But if pupils or widows and others made wretched by the
wrongs of fortune should pray for a trial by Our Serenity,
especially when they are in terror of the power of any person,
their adversaries shall be compelled to make an appearance
at Our inquisition.

*Given on the fifteenth day before the kalends of July at
Constantinople in the year of the consulship of Optatus and
Paulinus.—June 17, 334.*

INTERPRETATION: If any person proceeding against pupils,
widows, or invalids should obtain Our orders, We abolish
his right to remove such defendants from their own localities
and to drag them anywhere at all outside their own province,
in order that they may plead their case in the place where
they can be better prepared and can more easily find evidence.
Indeed, if those persons for whose fatigue We make provision
should suppose that they should petition Us, in accordance
with the wish of such defendants, We do not deny them the

right to come, and thus their adversaries shall be compelled by the governor of the province to appear in the presence of the Emperor.

3. Emperor Julian Augustus to Mamertinus.

We order that the governors shall be notified by Your Sublimity to issue the criminal, no less than the civil, records to those persons, of course, whose safety is called into jeopardy.

Given on the eleventh day before the kalends of December at Antioch in the year of the fourth consulship of Julian Augustus and the consulship of Sallustius.—November 21, 363; 362.

4. Emperors Gratian, Valentinian, and Theodosius Augustuses.

(Excerpt from the Records in the Consistory of Gratian Augustus)

Gratian Augustus said: "The judge shall make provision for the maintenance of his own official residence. But neither to a count nor to a governor of a province shall anything more be furnished than We grant in the subsistence allowances and cellar supplies."

Done in the Imperial Consistory in the year of the second consulship of the Most Noble Merobaudes and the consulship of the Most Noble Saturninus.—383.

INTERPRETATION: The judge must maintain his official residence from his own resources, and he must demand no more from the provincials than has been assigned to him by the Emperor in subsistence allowances and cellar supplies.

TITLE 27: THE JUDICIAL DECISIONS OF BISHOPS (DE EPISCOPALI DEFINITIONE)

1. Emperor Constantine Augustus.

Pursuant to his own authority, a judge must observe that if an action should be brought before an episcopal court, he shall maintain silence, and if any person should desire him to transfer his case to the jurisdiction of the Christian law and to observe that kind of court, he shall be heard, even though the action has been instituted before the judges, and whatever may be adjudged by them shall be held as sacred; provided, however, that there shall be no such usurpation of authority in that one of the litigants should proceed to the aforementioned tribunal and should report back his own unrestricted choice of a tribunal. For the judge must have the unimpaired right of jurisdiction of the case that is pending before him, in order that he may pronounce his decision, after full credit is given to all the facts as presented.

Given on the ninth day before the kalends of July at Constantinople in the year of the consulship of the Augustus and of Crispus Caesar.—June 23, 318(?)

2. Emperors Arcadius, Honorius, and Theodosius Augustuses to Theodorus, Praetorian Prefect.

The judgment of a bishop shall be valid for all persons who acquiesce in being heard by priests. For since private persons can hear those persons who have given their consent, even without the knowledge of the judge, We grant that this power shall be permitted to those persons whom We necessarily venerate, and We order that such reverence must be shown toward their adjudication as must be granted to your authority, from which it is not permitted to appeal. Also, in order that such cognizance may not be without effect, execution of judgment shall be granted through a public office staff.

Given on the ides of December in the year of the consulship of Bassus and Philippus.—December 13, 408.

TITLE 28: THE DEFENDERS OF THE SENATE (DE DEFENSORIBUS SENATUS)

1. Emperor Constantius Augustus to the Senate.

Your defense must be entrusted to those persons whose trustworthiness is esteemed to be commendable, so that in each and every province they may resist any demand which is made from Senators contrary to custom and justice or beyond the legal measure of payments, especially since those amounts only must be paid that are denoted by the hand of Our Clemency in the tax levy, or those which are demanded by the prefecture for the necessities of the State.

Given on the fifth day before the nones of May in the year of the consulship of Taurus and Florentius.—May 3, 361.

2. Emperors Valentinian and Valens Augustuses to Clearchus, Vicar of Asia.

Senators shall have the power to choose from their own body one or two persons for each and every province. Such persons shall protect the patrimonies of all by their devices and defenses, with alleviation also of payment of the capitation tax. For the imperial benefit granted by the sainted Julian, which is said to have been applied to decurions alone through the favoritism of the judges, We order to be extended by the common law not to decurions alone, but to the exhausted fortunes of all people.

Given on the day before the nones of May at Nicomedia in the year of the consulship of the sainted Jovian and of Varronianus.—May 6, 364.

3. Emperors Valens, Gratian, and Valentinian Augustuses to Vindaonius Magnus, Prefect of the City.

Whenever the regulations for fiscal obligations are being treated, neither the decurions nor the judges shall presume to make any arrangement in the absence of the defender of the Senate, lest they should scorn the method of justice in the boldness of lawless usurpation and should make some decree contrary to the interests of the Most August Assembly. We have also granted the following license to the defenders, namely, that if perchance to the contumely of the Senate, a divine imperial regulation should be disregarded, they shall hasten to refer the matter to Us.

Given on the fourth day before the kalends of June at Antioch in the year of the fifth consulship of Valens Augustus and the consulship of Valentinian Augustus.—May 29, 376.

4. Emperors Theodosius, Arcadius, and Honorius Augustuses to Aurelianus, Prefect of the City.

Defenders of those Senators who are settled throughout the provinces shall maintain freedom of action in the office which they have undertaken. Wherefore, whenever the privileges of this Most August Order are impaired by a judge ordinary and the power of resistance is denied to them, they shall not hesitate to refer the matter to Us, lest the injury of all should be increased by the diffidence of individuals.

Given on the third day before the kalends of March at Constantinople in the year of the third consulship of Theodosius Augustus and the consulship of the Most Noble Abundantius.—February 27, 393.

TITLE 29: THE DEFENDERS OF THE MUNICIPALITIES (DE DEFENSORIBUS CIVITATUM)

1. Emperors Valentinian and Valens Augustuses to Probus, Praetorian Prefect.

We have decreed quite beneficially that all the plebeians of Illyricum shall be defended by the offices of patrons against the ourages of the powerful. For each and every municipality of the aforesaid diocese Your Sincerity shall provide for the selection to this office of men of suitable character, whose past lives have been praiseworthy and who have either administered provinces or have performed terms of imperial service in the forum, or who have completed their service among the secret service or the palatines. You shall not entrust such duties to decurions; likewise, you shall not assign this service to those persons who at any time have served the office of Your Eminence or of any governors ordinary whatever. Certainly, the appointments made in each town shall be referred to Our Wisdom.

Given on the fifth day before the kalends of May in the year of the consulship of the sainted Jovian and of Varronianus.—April 27, 364; 368.

2. The same Augustuses to Seneca.

If any person should suppose that he ought to institute

an action before you about slight and unimportant matters, you shall conclude the proceedings in such minor cases, in such a way, of course, that if ever anyone should demand either a just debt or a slave who has escaped by flight or compensation for something he has paid beyond the tax levy or anything of the kind, you shall make restitution by your decision. But other cases which shall appear worthy of an important forum, you shall transfer with full information to the governor ordinary. (Etc.)

Given on the fifth day before the kalends of July at Tyr- in the year of the consulship of Valentinian and Valens Augustuses.—June 27, 365(?).

3. The same Augustuses to Probus, Praetorian Prefect.

Although We have carefully established many things in behalf of the plebeians, We believe that We have provided nothing for them unless We should give them suitable defenders. Therefore, appointments to this office shall be made not from the body of decurions, but from another, namely, from the administrators with the title of consular or of praeses in their administration, from the palatines, from the secret service, from those persons who have held the position of chief in the office staff of Your Eminence or that of the vicars, or from the advocates.

Given on the (third) day before the nones of November in the year of the consulship of Valentinian and Valens Augustuses.—November 3 (6), 368; 370; 373.

4. Emperors Valentinian, Valens, and Gratian Augustuses to Probus, Praetorian Prefect.

If any persons from the department of the secret service should serve the office of Your Eminence with the rank of chief of office staff, in a certain manner in Our name in accordance with Our order they shall be appointed among the other dignitaries as patrons of the plebeians of the various cities. Thus if Your Authority should suppose that any of the aforesaid persons should be chosen, they shall be entrusted with such a guardianship but you shall render them exempt from those duties.

Given on the eighth day before the ides of November at Trier in the year of the consulship of Valentinian Augustus and the second consulship of Valens Augustus.—November 6, 368(?).

5. The same Augustuses to the Senate.

In a useful manner wise provision has been made that innocent and peaceful rustics shall enjoy the benefit of a special protection. Thus they shall not be exhausted by the fraudulent practices of court trials and be harassed even when they demand satisfaction, while they either provide for a very avaricious advocate or win over the chief of the office staff with very large bribes, as he blocks the threshold, while the records of the case are purchased from the secretaries, and while in the name of a fee, the enforcement officer demands more from the winner of the suit than the loser will pay. The dignity of a Senator does not allow such practices, but with a speedy decision he settles the controversies that have arisen. For if anything has been wrongfully and violently taken away, he eliminates all dilatoriness and restores the property to its owner. 1. Without doubt, the authority of the governor shall be considered as the regular one, as it is maintained in the case of good men of higher status. For the governor endures the horror of human blood, while the Senatorial defender vindicates a harmless authority to himself.

Given on the fourth day before the ides of August at Hierapolis in the year of the fourth consulship of Valentinian and Valens Augustuses.—August 10, 370; 373.

6. Emperors Valentinian, Theodosius, and Arcadius Augustuses to Eusignius, Praetorian Prefect.

Those persons shall preferably be constituted defenders whom the municipalities shall choose by their decrees. But if any person should attain the position of defender by corrupt solicitation, Your Sincerity shall immediately reject him and compel him to pay five pounds of gold to the account of the fisc.

Given on the eighth day before the kalends of February in

*the year after the consulship of Emperor Designate Honorius
and the Most Noble Evodius.—January 25, 386; 387.*

INTERPRETATION: Those persons shall be instituted defenders of the municipalities who are known to have been chosen by the agreement of the citizens and the endorsement of all. But if any defender is proved to have attained to his post through his own cupidity without the interposition of a decree, he shall be compelled to pay five pounds of gold to the fisc for this presumption.

7. The same Augustuses to Potamius, Augustal Prefect.

Defenders shall vindicate nothing arrogantly for themselves, nothing which is not their due. They shall discharge only the duties indicated by their name; they shall impose no fines and conduct no judicial inquiries under torture; they shall only protect the plebeians and the decurions from all arrogance and lawlessness of wicked men, so that they shall not cease to be that alone which they are said to be.

*Given on the third day before the nones of March at Constantinople in the year of the second consulship of Arcadius
Augustus and the consulship of the Most Noble Rufinus.—
March (May) 5, 392.*

INTERPRETATION: Defenders, in accordance with their name, shall defend with all justice and equity the municipal councils and the plebeians committed to their care; they shall presume neither to condemn nor to flog any innocent person.

8. The same Augustuses to Tatianus, Praetorian Prefect.

Throughout all the regions in which the wild madness of brigands rages, a madness that is unaware of its own danger, all those defenders who are the most approved and the most severe shall assist in the discipline and supervise the everyday legal proceedings, and they shall not permit crime to grow strong with impunity. That protection shall be abolished which, by bestowing favors on the guilty ones and aid to criminals, has made crimes increase.

Given on the fifth day before the ides of April at Constantinople in the year of the second consulship of Arcadius

*Augustus and the consulship of the Most Noble Rufinus.—
April 9, 392.*

INTERPRETATION: Throughout all provinces such judges shall be appointed on account of their zeal for discipline that with all solicitude they shall abolish the protection of the powerful over criminals and brigands, and they shall not delay to exercise due strictness, lest through their negligence or venality crimes should flourish which ought to be punished.

TITLE 30: THE CURATORS OF THE MUNICIPALITIES (DE CURATORIBUS CIVITATUM)

TITLE 31: PETTY ADMINISTRATIVE OFFICES WITHIN THE CITY (DE ADMINISTRATIUNCULIS INTRA URBEM)

1. . . .

. . . shall be restored by those striving. For it is Our will that there shall be continued in this kind of administration, as in all others, that custom which the foresight and wisdom of ancient men has established, and that the activities of envious men shall not detract from anything which originates from the established functions and honorable customs of this administrative duty.

Given on the fourth day before the kalends of March in the year of the consulship of Valentinian and Valens Augustuses.—February 26 (27), 365; 368; 372.

2. The same Augustuses to Olybrius, Prefect of the City.

In accordance with ancient custom, the right to some petty profit had been assigned to the office staffs of administrations within the City; but henceforth, this custom of giving and receiving shall entirely cease, so that the fee which is called "formal" shall be completely eliminated from use. 1. Indeed, it shall be at the discretion of those who give, not within the power of those who receive, whether they wish to bestow anything upon each of these persons on account of his administrative services, in consideration of his expenses. But if it should appear that in such a case any person gave anything unwillingly and did not report this fact to the court, the severity of the public authority shall immediately be exerted against the giver no less vehemently than against the recipient.

Given on the day before the nones of April at Trier in the year of the consulship of Valentinian and Valens Augustuses.—April 4, 368; 370.

TITLE 32: PROCURATORS (DE PROCURATORIBUS)

1. Emperor Constantine Augustus to Felix.

Since through the procurators of the privy purse, of the dyeworks, and of the weaving establishments, Our private substance is being diminished and the materials manufactured in the weaving establishments are being ruined, and in the dyeworks the illegal mixture of the polluted dye produces stains, such procurators shall abstain from the patronage whereby they attain the aforesaid administrative positions, or if they should contravene this order, they shall be removed from the number of Roman citizens and struck down by the sword.

Given . . . kalends of November at Aquileia in the year of the consulship of Dalmatius and Zenophilus.—October 16-November 1, 333.

2. Emperors Valens, Gratian, and Valentinian Augustuses to Hesperius, Proconsul of Africa.

It is Our will that the risk of their property and life shall be set before the members of the office staffs, namely, that they shall not doubt that they themselves must compensate for the financial losses of Our household, unless they appoint administrators who have given sureties of such condition that their wealth shall be sufficient for Us to avoid loss by having recourse to it, if through fraud and avarice the administrators should commit anything to the detriment of Our privy purse.

Given on the eighth day before the ides of July at Trier in the year after the fifth consulship of Valens Augustus and the consulship of Valentinian Augustus.—July 8, 377(?).

3. The same Augustuses to Eucherius, Count of the Sacred Imperial Largesses.

When any person, acting as procurator in whatsoever name and service in Our largesses, has acquired an administration which obligates him to render an account, he shall first give most competent sureties, and then he shall undertake the service which he has sought. Then, within thirty days in the case of the treasures which belong to the lesser accounts, within fifty days, however, in the case of those of the larger accounts, he shall deliver the documents and all the records of the accounts. Of course, he shall deliver to the tax receivers a written statement showing what he received, what he issued, what remains deposited in the storehouses. 1. Furthermore, although he must deliver immediately what he has received, nevertheless, since in certain cases there is a valid regulation, he must count out the lesser money to his successor within thirty days from the time of his arrival, and all other things, which are supposed to be among the deposits, within four months. But if anything ever so little should be found to have been deferred by the procurator who has departed, he shall be forcibly deprived of the very appearance of honor, and stripped of all his former dignity, he shall incur the fitting punishment of flogging and torture in accordance with his character, and he shall suffer disgraceful and shameful punishments continuously until the whole undiminished amount of Our largesses is deposited among the stores. 2. This same condition shall apply to the procurators who are provosts of the weaving establishment, of the mints, and of the imposts.

Given on the fourth day before the kalends of April at Trier in the year of the fourth consulship of Gratian Augustus and the consulship of Merobaudes.—March 29, 377.

4. Emperors Gratian, Valentinian, and Theodosius Augustuses to Count Arborius.

Those palatine apparitors who serve in the office of Your Sincerity shall take care to be on guard, so that when any person obtains an administrative duty that requires a surety, he shall not be heard at all if he offers a decurion as a sponsor.

Given on the fifth day before the nones of May in the year of the consulship of Auxonius and Olybrius.—May 3, 379.

5. The same Augustuses to Eusignius, Praetorian Prefect.

Since the procurators of the mines within Macedonia, Midland Dacia, Moesia, and Dardania, who are customarily appointed from the decurions and who exact the usual tax collections, have removed themselves from this compulsory public service by pretending fear of the enemy, they shall be dragged back to the fulfillment of their duties. Henceforth no person shall be allowed the license to seek honors which are not due to him, before he completes by the faithful and skillful exaction of taxes the procuratorship which he must undertake.

Given on the fourth day before the kalends of August at Milan in the year of the consulship of Emperor Designate Honorius and of the Most Noble Evodius.—July 29, 386.

6. Emperors Valentinian, Theodosius, and Arcadius Augustuses to Cynegius, Praetorian Prefect.

Our procurators, who have been given the rank of Most Prefect, shall be protected from outrage, so that there shall be preserved for them also the full power to enter the private council chambers of the judges ordinary for the opportunity of making recommendations.

Given on the day before the kalends of January at Thessalonica in the year of the third consulship of Valentinian Augustus and the consulship of Eutropius.—December 31, 388; 387.

7. The same Augustuses to Cynegius, Praetorian Prefect.

We deem that it is in accordance neither with custom nor with any law that the procurators of Our household should be summoned to the task of restoration of public works.

Posted at Beirut in the year of the second consulship of

Theodosius Augustus and the consulship of the Most Noble Cynegius.—389; 388.

TITLE 33 (KR. 34): THE CHIEFS OF OFFICE STAFFS (DE PRIMICERIIS)

TITLE 34: ASSESSORS, CONFIDENTIAL ADVISERS, AND CHANCELLORS (DE ASSESSORIBUS, DOMESTICIS, ET CANCELLARIIS)

1. Emperors Arcadius and Honorius Augustuses to Caesarius, Praetorian Prefect.

If any judge should wish to take as his adviser either a citizen of the province which he governs, or at least a foreigner, he shall know that only four months have been assigned to him for retaining the person whom he took from the same province, until he has employed a person called from other districts to assist him in his acts, so that when four months have elapsed, it shall be considered a crime if anyone should suppose that he should retain an adviser beyond this time.

Given on the sixth day before the ides of December at Constantinople in the year of the consulship of Stilicho and Aurelianus.—December 8, 400; 396; 397.

2. Emperors Honorius and Theodosius Augustuses to Eustathius, Praetorian Prefect.

(After other matters.) When assessors who customarily assist administrators with their advice are subject to paternal power, they shall have the right, after the death of their father, to vindicate whatever they have been able to accumulate through permissible and honorable profits, as though it were a military peculium.

Given on the tenth day before the kalends of April at Constantinople in the year of the thirteenth consulship of Our Lord Honorius Augustus and the tenth consulship of Our Lord Theodosius Augustus.—March 23, 422.

INTERPRETATION: If any person should be attached to the

council of any judge while his father is living, he shall have the right to vindicate to himself whatever he has acquired by legal and proper means, just as does that son also who, while employed in the armed service, has acquired anything during the life of his father.

3. The same Augustuses to Asclepiodotus, Praetorian Prefect.

No judge shall dare to take with him to the province entrusted to him any person whom he designates as a confidential adviser or as a chancellor, nor shall he receive any person who has come to him from any other place whatsoever, lest he be punished by the brand of infamy together with the confiscation of his goods. For We order that, at the peril of the chiefs of their office staffs, chancellors shall be chosen under the trustworthiness of records, they shall be attached to the judges, and it shall be provided that they shall not leave the imperial service for an uninterrupted period of three years after they have surrendered their administrative position, and that they shall be present among the provincials, in order that those persons who wish may have the opportunity to accuse them. For if a suitable case should demand it, they shall be subjected to examination even under torture, for the purpose of revealing disgraceful acts of the judge. (Etc.)

Given on the day before the kalends of June at Constantinople in the year of the consulship of the Most Noble Asclepiodotus and Marinianus.—May 31, 423.

INTERPRETATION: Every judge shall clearly know that while he is in the province committed to him, he shall not attach to himself a chancellor or a confidential adviser, perhaps, from the same province from which he comes, or from any other region, unless such chancellor or adviser has been publicly assigned to him by the choice of the citizens; provided that if such governor should be removed later, the person who held the office of chancellor or confidential adviser shall not leave the province for a period of three years under another judge, so that, if there should perhaps

201

be an accuser, such chancellor or confidential adviser shall
render an account to the accusers. If, perchance, he should
wish to conceal in any way the deeds of the judge, he shall
be subjected to a public inquisition under torture.

THE JUSTINIAN CODE, 529-535*

One of the first acts of Flavius Ancius Justinianus, known to the world as Justinian, when he succeeded to the throne as Emperor of the Romans in Constantinople in 527 was to appoint a commission to collect and organize the Roman laws. This commission led by Tribonian collected the most comprehensive collection of Roman law or Corpus Juris Civilis. The Corpus intended to provide an orderly document from about 1,000 years of Roman legal development. The final work was more comprehensive and exhaustive than any previous work of that nature. The four parts of the Corpus or Code consist of the Codex, a collection of imperial constitutions since the time of Hadrian, first published by Gregorianus in 295, the Digest or Pandects, which contains selections from noted classical jurists such as Papinian, Paulus, Ulpian and Modestinus; the Institutes, published in 533, based largely upon the work of Gaius with numerous additions and changes; the Novellae, which were later additions to the Code. The great service of Justinian rests not only in the order he brought to the mass of Roman law but also in the preservation of knowledge about Roman and earlier laws which would no doubt have been lost had they not been published.

*From *Sources of Roman Civil Law,* by William Grapel, London, Macmillan and Company, 1857.

THE THREE PREFACES OF THE CODE OF JUSTINIAN

FIRST PREFACE
CONCERNING THE ESTABLISHMENT OF A NEW CODE

The Emperor Justinian to the Senate of the City of Constantinople. Those things which seem to many former Emperors to require correction, but which none of them ventured to carry into effect, We have decided to accomplish at the present time with the assistance of Almighty God; and to diminish litigation by the revision of the multitude of constitutions which are contained in the Three Codes; namely, the Gregorian, the Hermogenian, and the Theodosian, as well as in those other Codes promulgated after them by Theodosius of Divine Memory, and by other Emperors, who succeeded him, in addition to those which We Ourselves have promulgated, and to combine them in a single Code, under Our auspicious name, in which compilation should be included not only the constitutions of the three above-mentioned Codes, but also such new ones as subsequently have been promulgated.

(1) Therefore, having in view the accomplishment of this extensive work, as well as the maintenance of the public welfare, We have chosen, as being competent for a task involving such labor and care, John, a most eminent man, Ex-Quæstor of our Sacred Palace, and of consular, as well as patrician dignity; Leontius, a man of the highest standing, an officer in the army, an Ex-Prætorian Prefect, of consular and patrician dignity; Phocas, a most illustrious man, an officer of the army, also of consular and patrician dignity; Basilis, a most excellent man, Ex-Prætorian Prefect of the East, and of patrician rank; Thomas, a most glorious man, Quæstor of our Sacred Palace, and Ex-Consul; Tribonian, a distinguished man of great authority, and invested with

magisterial dignity; Constantine, an illustrious man, one of the Stewards of Our bounty, Master of Requests, and of Our Judicial Inquiries; Theophilus, a most eminent man, and one of the members of our Sacred Consistory, a Doctor of Laws in this Fair City; and Dioscorus and Praesentinus, most learned jurists of the Prætorian Tribunal.

(2) To these We have especially entrusted the suppression of superfluous preambles, so far as this can be done without affecting the efficacy of the laws, as well as of such enactments as are similar or contradictory, and in addition to this, the division of the laws; and it will be to the advantage to omit such as have fallen into desuetude, to give expression in concise terms to those which are included in the said three Codes, and in the New Constitutions, and to place them under suitable titles, adding and omitting portions of the same, and, indeed, changing their phraseology where convenience requires it, bringing under one head enactments which are scattered through various constitutions, and rendering their meaning clearer; so that the order of the said constitutions may appear not only from the days and the consulate when they were enacted, but also from their composition itself, by placing those primarily published in the first place, and those which follow in the second. And if any laws should be found in the three ancient codes without the date and the name of the consul, or if any new constitutions have been inserted among them, they should be so arranged that no doubt may arise with reference to their general application, in such a way that rescripts addressed to certain individuals, or originally issued by pragmatic sanction, may obtain the effect of general constitutions, where, for the public welfare, they have been included in a new code.

(3) Hence We have hastened to bring these matters to your notice, in order that you may be informed to what an extent Our daily care is occupied with matters having reference to the common welfare, by collecting such laws as are certain and clear, and incorporating them into a single code, so that, by means of this code, designated by Our auspicious name,

the citation of the various constitutions may cause decisions to be more readily rendered in all litigation.

Given at Constantinople, on the *Ides* of February, during the reign and second Consulship of the Emperor Justinian.

SECOND PREFACE
Concerning the Confirmation of the Code of Justinian

The maintenance of the integrity of the government depends upon two things, namely, the force of arms and the observance of the laws: and, for this reason, the fortunate race of the Romans obtained power and precedence over all other nations in former times, and will do so forever, if God should be propitious; since each of these has ever required the aid of the other, for, as military affairs are rendered secure by the laws, so also are the laws preserved by force of arms. Therefore, We have, with reason, directed Our attention, Our aims, and Our labors in the first place to the maintenance of the public welfare, and have corrected matters relating to the army in many ways, and thus provided for everything; as We have by means of old laws not only brought matters into a better condition, but We also have promulgated new laws, and by Our just administration, or with additional expense, We have preserved those already enacted, and afterwards by publishing new ones, have established them most firmly for the obedience of Our subjects.

(1) But as it was necessary to reduce the vast number of the constitutions contained in the three old codes, as well in the others compiled in former times, and to clear up their obscurity by means of proper definitions, We have applied Ourselves with willing mind to the accomplishment of this work for the common good; and, after having selected men conspicuous for their legal learning and ability, as well as for their experience in business, and tireless zeal for the interests of the State, We have committed this great task to them under certain limitations, and have directed them to collect

into a single code, to be designated by Our auspicious name, the constitutions of the three ancient codes, namely the Gregorian, Hermogenian, and Theodosian compilations, as well as all those subsequently promulgated by Theodosius of Divine Memory, and the other princes who have succeeded him; together with such constitutions as have been issued during Our reign; and to see that any preambles which are not confirmed by subsequent decrees, and any constitutions which are contradictory, or should be suppressed, as well as such as have been repealed by others of later date, or which are of the same character—except those which, by conferring upon them Our sanction to a certain extent, We have considered to be susceptible of division, and by such division of these ancient laws some new principle may appear to arise.

In addition to all this, many other matters relative to the composition of this Code have been placed by Our authority in the hands of these most wise men; and Almighty God has afforded this protection through Our zeal for the welfare of the State.

(2) The following persons have been chosen for this work, and the completion of a task of such importance, namely: that most excellent man, John, Ex-Quaestor of Our Palace, and of consular and patrician dignity; as well as that most eminent man, Leontius, Ex-Praetorian Prefect, of consular and patrician dignity; and also the most distinguished Phocas, officer of the army, also of consular and patrician dignity; and that most accomplished man of patrician dignity, Basilis, Ex-Praetorian Prefect of the East, now Praetorian Prefect of Illyria; also, the most illustrious Thomas, Quaestor of our Sacred Palace and Ex-Consul; and the eminent Tribonian, of exalted magisterial dignity; the distinguished Constantine, Steward of Our Imperial Largesses, Master of Requests, and of Judicial Inquiries; Theophilus, former magistrate and Doctor of Laws in this Fair City; as well as those most learned jurists, Dioscorus and Praesentinus, members of your bar; and all that We have directed them to do, they with God's assistance have, through assiduous and untiring industry,

brought to a successful conclusion, and offered to Us this new, systematically arranged Justinian Code, compiled in such a manner as to contribute to the common benefit, and meet the requirements of Our Empire.

(3) Therefore We have had in view the perpetual validity of this Code in your tribunal, in order that all litigants, as well as the most accomplished advocates, may know that it is lawful for them, under no circumstances, to cite constitutions from the three ancient codes, of which mention has just been made, or from those which at the present time are styled the New Constitutions, in any judicial inquiry or contest; but that they are required to use only the constitutions which are included in this Our Code, and that those who venture to act otherwise will be liable to the crime of forgery; as the citation of the said constitutions of Our Code, with the opinions of the ancient interpreters of the law, will be sufficient for the disposal of all cases.

No doubt as to their validity should arise where any of them appears without a date and without the name of the consul, or because they may have been addressed to certain private individuals; as there can be no question whatever that all have the force of general constitutions; and even if there should be some of them from which anything has been taken, or to which anything has been added, or which have been changed in certain respects (which We have specially permitted the most excellent men aforesaid to do), We grant to no one the right to cite the said constitutions, as they are stated in the books of the ancient authorities, but merely to mention the opinions of the latter, as being of legal effect when they are not opposed to the constitutions of this Our Code.

(4) Moreover, the pragmatic sanctions that are not included in Our Code, and which have been granted to cities, corporate bodies, bureaus, offices, or private individuals, shall remain in every respect valid, if they concede any privilege as a special favor; but where they have been promulgated for the settlement of some legal point We direct that they shall only hold when not opposed to the provisions

of Our Code. But in any matter which comes before your tribunal, or in any other civil or military proceeding, or in one which has reference to accounts forming part of the public expenses, or in such as have any relation to the public welfare, We decree that they shall remain valid as far as public convenience may require this to be done.

(5) Therefore let your illustrious and sublime authority, actuated by a desire for the common good, and with zeal for the execution of Our orders, cause information of this Code to be communicated to all peoples, by the promulgation of an edict in the customary way, and by sending into each province, subject to Our Empire, a copy bearing Our signature, so that in this manner the constitutions of this Our Code may be brought to the knowledge of all persons; and that during festival days, that is to say, from the sixteenth day of the *Kalends* of May of the seventh current indiction, and during the consulate of that most illustrious man Decius, citations of the constitutions shall be made from this Our Code.

Given at Constantinople, on the sixth of the *Ides* of April, during the Consulate of the illustrious Decius.

THIRD PREFACE

CONCERNING THE AMENDMENTS OF THE CODE OF OUR LORD JUSTINIAN, AND THE SECOND EDITION OF THE SAME

Our heart, Conscript Fathers, always induces Us to pay the strictest attention to matters concerning the public welfare, so that nothing which has been begun by Us may be left imperfect. Therefore, in the beginning of Our reign, we formed the design of collecting in a single body the Imperial Constitutions which were scattered through several volumes, and the most of which were either repetitions or conflicting, and free them from every defect. This work has now been perfected by certain most distinguished and learned men, and has been subsequently confirmed by Us, as is shown by Our two Constitutions prefixed hereto.

(1) But after We decreed that the ancient law should be observed, We rendered fifty decisions, and promulgated several constitutions relative to the advantages to be derived from the proposed work, by means of which the majority of the former enactments were amended and abridged; and We divested all the ancient law of superfluous prolixity, and then inserted the same in Our Institutes and Digest.

(2) But, as Our new decisions and constitutions, which were promulgated after the completion of Our Code, were distinct from the body of the same, and seemed to demand our care and attention, and as some of them, which were afterwards inserted, appeared to require alteration or correction, it seemed to Us necessary to have the said constitutions revised by that eminent man Tribonian, Ex-Quæstor and Ex-Consul, the authorized minister of our work; and also by the illustrious Dorotheus, Quæstor and Doctor of Laws of Berytus; and, in addition to these Menna, Constantine, and John, most eloquent men, and distinguished advocates of the bar of this City, who were ordered to divide said constitutions into separate chapters for the purpose of rendering them more available; to place them under proper titles; and to add them to those constitutions which had preceded them.

(3) We permitted the aforesaid distinguished and most learned jurists to do all these things, and when there was need of any correction, allowed them to make it without hesitation, relying upon Our authority; and where any of the constitutions were superfluous, or had been annulled by any of Our subsequent decrees; or where they were found to be similar or conflicting, to remove and separate them from the compilation of the Code itself; as well as to complete such as were imperfect, and to bring to light those that were shrouded in obscurity, so that not only the way of the Institutes and the Digest might appear clear and open, but also that the splendor of the Constitutions of Our Code

might be manifest to all, and no constitution which resembled another, or was contradictory or useless, should be retained, and no one should have any doubt that what was confirmed by the revision was both valid and sufficiently perspicuous. For, in the ancient Books, the authorities of former times not only called the first, but also the second editions, revisions; which can be readily ascertained from the works of that eminent jurist Ulpianus, on Sabinus, by those who desire to know.

(4) These things having been accomplished according to Our intention, and the Justinian Code having been purified and elucidated by the aforesaid most illustrious and learned men (all of this having been done in compliance with Our order, and the work offered to Us with its amplifications, and changes) , We ordered that it should be copied in accordance with the second edition, and not in accordance with the first, but as it was revised; and, by Our authority, We directed that it alone should be used in all tribunals, whenever the Divine Constitutions were applicable, from the fourth day of the *Kalends* of January of the most auspicious Consulate of Ourself and that illustrious man Paulinus; and that no constitution not contained in this Our Code should be cited, unless in the course of events some new question may arise which requires Our decision. For, if something better should be found hereafter, and it becomes necessary to revise a constitution, no one will doubt that We should do so, and incorporate into another compilation those laws which are designated by the name New Constitutions.

(5) Therefore, having repeated Our order that We shall permit none hereafter to quote anything from Our decisions, or from other constitutions, which We have previously promulgated, or from the first edition of the Justinian Code; but that only what may be found written in this Our present purified and amended Code shall be regarded as authority, and cited in all tribunals, We have ordered it to be transcribed without any ambiguity, as was done in the case of Our Institutes and Digest, so that everything which has been

compiled by Us shall be clear and intelligible, not only in the chirography, but also in the laws themselves, although on this account the matter contained in this Code has been considerably extended.

(6) Therefore, Most Reverend and Illustrious Fathers, in order that Our labors may become manifest to you and obtain authority through all time, We have presented this collection of laws to your most distinguished Order.

Given at Constantinople, on the seventeenth day of the *Kalends* of December, during the Consulate of Our Lord Justinian, for the fourth time Consul, and of Paulus.

Concerning the Most Exalted Trinity and the Catholic Faith, and Providing That No One Shall Dare to Publicly Oppose Them

1. *The Emperors Gratian, Valentinian, and Theodosius to the people of the City of Constantinople.*

We desire that all peoples subject to Our benign Empire shall live under the same religion that the Divine Peter, the Apostle, gave to the Romans, and which the said religion declares was introduced by himself, and which it is well known that the Pontiff Damasus, and Peter, Bishop of Alexandria, a man of apostolic sanctity, embraced; that is to say, in accordance with the rules of apostolic discipline and the evangelical doctrine, we should believe that the Father, Son, and Holy Spirit constitute a single Deity, endowed with equal majesty, and united in the Holy Trinity.

(1) We order all those who follow this law to assume the name of Catholic Christians, and considering others as demented as insane, We order that they shall bear the infamy of heresy; and when the Divine vengeance which they merit has been appeased, they shall afterwards be punished in accordance with Our resentment, which we have acquired from the judgment of Heaven.

Dated at Thessalonica, on the third of the *Kalends* of

March, during the Consulate of Gratian, Consul for the fifth time, and Theodosius.

2. *The Same Emperors to Eutropius, Prætorian Prefect.*

Let no place be afforded to heretics for the conduct of their ceremonies, and let no occasion be offered for them to display the insanity of their obstinate minds. Let all persons know that if any privilege has been fraudulently obtained by means of any rescript whatsoever, by persons of this kind, it will not be valid. Let all bodies of heretics be prevented from holding unlawful assemblies, and let the name of the only and the greatest God be celebrated everywhere, and let the observance of the Nicene Creed, recently transmitted by Our ancestors, and firmly established by the testimony and practice of Divine Religion, always remain secure.

(1) Moreover, he who is an adherent of the Nicene Faith, and a true believer in the Catholic religion, should be understood to be one who believes that Almighty God and Christ, the Son of God, are one person, God of God, Light of Light; and let no one, by rejection, dishonor the Holy Spirit, whom we expect, and have received from the Supreme Parent of all things, in whom the sentiment of a pure and undefiled faith flourishes, as well as the belief in the undivided substance of a Holy Trinity, which true believers indicate by the Greek word ὁμοούσιος. These things, indeed, do not require further proof, and should be respected.

(2) Let those who do not accept these doctrines cease to apply the name of true religion to their fraudulent belief; and let them be branded with their open crimes, and, having been removed from the threshold of all churches, be utterly excluded from them, as We forbid all heretics to hold unlawful assemblies within cities. If, however, any seditious outbreak should be attempted, We order them to be driven outside the walls of the City, with relentless violence, and We direct that all Catholic churches, throughout the entire

213

world, shall be placed under the control of the orthodox bishops who have embraced the Nicene Creed.

Given at Constantinople, on the fourth of the *Ides* of January, under the Consulate of Flavius Eucharius and Flavius Syagrius.

3. *The Emperor Martian to Palladius, Prætorian Prefect.*

No one, whether he belongs to the clergy, the army, or to any other condition of men, shall, with a view to causing a tumult and giving occasion to treachery, attempt to discuss the Christian religion publicly in the presence of an assembled and listening crowd; for he commits an injury against the most reverend Synod who publicly contradicts what has once been decided and properly established; as those matters relative to the Christian Faith have been settled by the priests who met at Chalcedony by Our order, and are known to be in conformity with the apostolic explanations and conclusions of the three hundred and eight Holy Fathers assembled in Nicea, and the hundred and fifty who met in this Imperial City; for the violators of this law shall not go unpunished, because they not only oppose the true faith, but they also profane its venerated mysteries by engaging in contests of this kind with Jews and Pagans. Therefore, if any person who has ventured to publicly discuss religious matters is a member of the clergy, he shall be removed from his order; if he is a member of the army, he shall be degraded; and any others who are guilty of this offence, who are freemen, shall be banished from this most Sacred City, and shall be subjected to the punishment prescribed by law according to the power of the court; and if they are slaves, they shall undergo the severest penalty.

Given at Constantinople, on the eighth of the *Ides* of February, under the consulship of Patricius.

4. *John, Bishop of the City of Rome, to his most Illustrious and Merciful Son Justinian.*

Among the conspicuous reasons for praising your wisdom

and gentleness, Most Christian of Emperors, and one which radiates light as a star, is the fact that through love of the Faith, and actuated by zeal for charity, you, learned in ecclesiastical discipline, have preserved reverence for the See of Rome, and have subjected all things to its authority, and have given it unity. The following precept was communicated to its founder, that is to say, the first of the Apostles, by the mouth of the Lord, namely: "Freed my lambs."

This See is indeed the head of all churches, as the rules of the Fathers and the decrees of Emperors assert, and the words of your most reverend piety testify. It is therefore claimed that what the Scriptures state, namely, "By Me Kings reign, and the Powers dispense justice;" will be accomplished in you. For there is nothing which shines with a more brilliant lustre than genuine faith when displayed by a prince, since there is nothing which prevents destruction as true religion does, for as both of them have reference to the Author of Life and Light, they disperse darkness and prevent apostasy. Wherefore, Most Glorious of Princes, the Divine Power is implored by the prayers of all to preserve your piety in this ardor for the Faith, in this devotion of your mind, and in this zeal for true religion, without failure, during your entire existence. For we believe that this is for the benefit of the Holy Churches, as it was written, "The king rules with his lips," and again, "The heart of the King is in the hand of God, and it will incline to whatever side God wishes"; that is to say, that He may confirm your empire, and maintain your kingdoms for the peace of the Church and the unity of religion; guard their authority, and preserve him in that sublime tranquillity which is so grateful to him; and no small change is granted by the Divine Power through whose agency a divided church is not afflicted by any griefs or subject to any reproaches. For it is written, "A just king, who is upon his throne, has no reason to apprehend any misfortune."

We have received with all due respect the evidences of

215

your serenity, through Hypatius and Demetrius, most holy men, my brothers and fellow-bishops, from whose statements we have learned that you have promulgated an Edict addressed to your faithful people, and dictated by your love of the Faith, for the purpose of overthrowing the designs of heretics, which is in accordance with the evangelical tenets, and which we have confirmed by our authority with the consent of our brethren and fellow bishops, for the reason that it is in conformity with the apostolic doctrine.

The following is the text of the letter of the Emperor Justinian, Victorious, Pious, Happy, Renowned, Triumphant, always Augustus, to John, Patriarch, and most Holy Archbishop of the fair City of Rome:

With honor to the Apostolic See, and to Your Holiness, which is, and always has been remembered in Our prayers, both now and formerly, and honoring your happiness, as is proper in the case of one who is considered as a father, We hasten to bring to the knowledge of Your Holiness everything relating to the condition of the Church, as We have always had the greatest desire to preserve the unity of your Apostolic See, and the condition of the Holy Churches of God, as they exist at the present time, that they may remain without disturbance or opposition. Therefore, We have exerted Ourselves to unite all the priests of the East and subject them to the See of Your Holiness, and hence the questions which have at present arisen, although they are manifest and free from doubt, and, according to the doctrine of your Apostolic See, are constantly firmly observed and preached by all priests, We have still considered it necessary that they should be brought to the attention of Your Holiness. For we do not suffer anything which has reference to the state of the Church, even though what causes the difficulty may be clear and free from doubt, to be discussed without being brought to the notice of Your Holiness, because you are the head of all the Holy Churches, for We shall exert Ourselves in every way (as has already been stated), to increase the honor and authority of your See.

(1) Therefore, We present to Your Holiness the fact that certain infidels and persons who do not belong to the Holy Catholic and Apostolic Church of God have, like Jews and apostates, dared to dispute matters which are properly accepted, glorified, and preached by all priests in accordance with your doctrines, denying that Our Lord Jesus Christ is the only begotten Son of God, and that Our Lord was born of the Holy Spirit and of the Holy, Glorious, and always Virgin Mary, the Mother of God, and became a man and was crucified, and that he is one of the persons of the Holy Trinity, who are all of one substance, and who should be adored and exalted along with the Father and the Holy Spirit, and that he is consubstantial with the Father according to divinity, and consubstantial with ourselves according to humanity, and susceptible of the sufferings of the flesh, but not susceptible of the same as a deity. For these persons refusing to acknowledge Our Lord Jesus Christ as the only begotten Son of God, and Our Lord as one of the Holy Trinity, and of the same substance with the other persons composing it, appear to follow the evil doctrine of Nestor, who asserts that there is one Son of God according to grace, whom he styles the Word of God, and another Son whom he calls Christ.

(2) All the priests of the Holy Catholic and Apostolic Church and the most Reverend Abbots of the Holy Monasteries, acknowledging Your Holiness, and solicitous for the prosperity and unity of the Holy Churches of God, which they receive from the Apostolic See of Your Holiness, making no changes in the ecclesiastical condition which has existed up to this time, and still exists; with one voice, confess, glorify, and preach that Our Lord Jesus Christ is the only begotten Son and the Word of God, and that Our Lord, born of His Father before all centuries and times, Who descended from Heaven in the last days, was born of the Holy Spirit and the Holy and Glorious Virgin Mary, the Mother of God; became a man and was crucified; is of the same substance as the Holy Trinity to be adored and glorified

with the Father and the Holy Spirit; for we do not acknowledge any other God, Word or Christ, but one alone, and the same of like substance with the Father, in accordance with divinity, and of like substance with us in accordance with humanity, Who could suffer in the flesh, but could not suffer as a deity; and Whom, Himself perfect in divinity as well as humanity, we receive and confess as being what the Greeks call ὁμοὐύσιος. And, as the only begotten Son and Word of God was born of His Father before centuries and times existed, and as He, in later times, descended from Heaven, was born of the Holy Spirit and the Holy ever Virgin Mary, the Mother of God, Our Lord Jesus Christ having become a man, is properly and truly God. Hence we say that the Holy and Glorious Virgin Mary is properly and truly the Mother of God, not for the reason that God obtained speech and origin from her, but because in the last days He descended from Heaven, and, incarnated through Her, became a man, and was born; whom we confess and believe (as has already been stated), to be of the same substance with the Father according to deity, and of the same substance with ouselves according to humanity, whose miracles and sufferings voluntarily sustained by Him while in the flesh we acknowledge.

(3) Moreover, we recognize four Sacred Councils, that is to say, the one composed of three hundred and eighteen Holy Fathers who assembled in the City of Nicea; and that of the hundred and fifty Holy Fathers who met in this Imperial City; and that of the Holy Fathers who first congregated at Ephesus; and that of the Holy Fathers who met at Chalcedony, as your Apostolic See teaches and proclaims. Hence, all priests who follow the doctrine of your Apostolic See believe, confess, and preach these things.

(4) Wherefore We have hastened to bring to the notice of Your Holiness, through the most blessed Bishops Hypatius and Demetrius (so it may not be concealed from Your Holiness), that these tenets are denied by some few wicked

and judaizing monks, who have adopted the perfidious doctrines of Nestor.

(5) Therefore We request your paternal affection, that you, by your letters, inform Us and the Most Holy Bishop of this Fair City, and your brother the Patriarch, who himself has written by the same messengers to Your Holiness, eager in all things to follow the Apostolic See of Your Blessedness, in order that you may make it clear to Us that Your Holiness acknowledges all the matters which have been set forth above, and condemns the perfidy of those who, in the manner of Jews, have dared to deny the true Faith. For in this way the love of all persons for you, and the authority of your See will increase, and the unity of the Holy Church will be preserved unimpaired, when all the most blessed bishops learn through you and from those who have been dispatched by you, the true doctrines of Your Holiness. Moreover, We beg Your Blessedness to pray for Us, and to obtain the beneficence of God in Our behalf.

The subscription was as follows: "May God preserve you for many years, Most Holy and Religious Father."

HERE FOLLOWS THE REMAINDER OF THE LETTER OF THE POPE.

It is then clear, Most Glorious Emperor (as the tenor of your message and the statements of your envoys disclose), that you have devoted Yourself to the study of apostolic learning as You are familiar with, have written, proposed and published to believers among the people, those matters having reference to the faith of the Catholic religion, which (as we have already stated), both the tenets of the Apostolic See and the venerated authority of the Holy Fathers have established, and which, in all respects, we have confirmed. Therefore, it is opportune to cry out with a prophetic voice, "Heaven will rejoice with You, and pour out its blessings upon You, and the mountains will rejoice, and the hills be glad with exceeding joy." Hence, you should write these things upon the tablets of Your heart, and preserve them as the apples of your eyes, for there is no one animated by the charity of Christ who will appear to impugn this confession of the just and true faith; as it is evident that You condemn the impiety of Nestor and Eutyches, and all other heretics, and that You firmly and inviolably, with devotion to God and reverent mind acknowledge the single, true, and Catholic Faith of Our Lord God, as revealed by the agency of Our Savior Jesus Christ; diffused everywhere by the preaching of the Prophets and Apostles; confirmed by the confessions of saints throughout the entire world, and united with the opinions of the Fathers and Doctors conformably to our doctrine.

Those alone who are opposed to your professions are they of whom the Holy Scriptures speak as follows: "They have based their hope on lying, and have expected to remain concealed through falsehood." And also those who, according to the prophet, say to the Lord, "Depart from us, we are unwilling to follow your ways"; on account of which Solomon said, "They have wandered through the paths of their own cultivation and gathered unfruitful things with their hands." This, then, is your true faith, this your true religion, which all the Fathers and heads of the Roman Church of happy memory (as we have already stated) and whom we follow in all things, have embraced; this is what the Apostolic See has preached up to this time, and has preserved inviolate, and if anyone should appear to oppose this confession, and this Faith, he must show himself to be outside of the communion and the Catholic Church. We have found Cyrus and his followers in the City of Rome, who came from the Cumitensian monastery, and whom we have attempted by our apostolic arguments to recall to the true faith, as sheep who are about to perish and are wandering, should be brought back to the fold of the owner. In order that, according to the prophet, stammering tongues may know how to speak matters which have reference to peace, the first of our apostles quotes the words of Isaiah, the prophet, through us to unbelievers, namely: "Continue in the light of the fire and the flame which you yourselves have kindled, but their heart is so hardened (as has been written), that they do not recognize the voice of the Shepherd, and the sheep which were not mine are unwilling to hear." With reference to such persons, we, observing what was established by the Pontiff on this point, do not receive them in our communion, and we order them to be excluded from every Catholic Church, unless, having renounced their errors, they adopt our doctrine, and announce their adherence to it, after having made a regular profession the same. For it is just that those who do not show obedience to the laws which we have established should be banished from the churches. But as the Church never closes her heart to those who return to her, I beseech Your Clemency, if they, having renounced their errors and abandoned their wicked designs, should wish to return to the bosom of the Church, to receive them in your communion, and abandon your feelings of indignation, and that through our intercession you pardon them, and grant them your indulgence.

Moreover, we pray God and Our Saviour Jesus Christ, that he may preserve you long in peace in this true religion and in the unity and veneration of the Apostolic See, and that your most Christian and pious Empire may, in all respects, long be maintained. Moreover, O most Serene of Princes, we praise Hypatius and Demetrius, your envoys, and our brothers and fellow-bishops, whose selection has shown that they are acceptable to Your Clemency; for the importance of such an embassy indicates that it could not be entrusted to anyone who is not perfect in Christ, and that You would not have deemed them worthy of a mission involving so much piety and reverence, unless they have been very dear to You.

The favor of Our Lord Jesus Christ, the love of God the Father, and the Communion of the Holy Spirit, remain forever with you, Most Pious son. Amen.

The subscription was as follows, "Most Glorious and Clement Son of the Emperor Augustus, may Almighty God guard your kingdom and your health with His eternal protection."

Given at Rome, on the eighth of the *Kalends* of April, during the Consulate of the Emperor Justinian, Consul for the fourth time, and of Paulinus, Consul for the fifth time.

CONCERNING THE MOST SACRED CHURCHES, THEIR PROPERTY AND THEIR PRIVILEGES.

1. *The Emperor Constantine to the People.*

Let everyone, at the time of his death, have the liberty to leave any portion of his property that he chooses to a most holy and venerable Catholic congregation, and let his dispositions not be set aside; for there is nothing to which men are more entitled than to have free power to exert their last will, as afterwards they cannot do so, and let them be unrestrained, for the right exercised then does not return.

Given at Rome, on the fifth of the *Nones* of July during the Consulate of Crispus and Constantine-Cæsar, each Consul for the second time, 321.

2. *The Emperors Gratian, Valentinian, and Theodosius to Pancratius, Urban Prefect.*

Let no one think that he has permission to bury human bodies in churches consecrated to the apostles or martyrs.

VI.

MEDIEVAL ACTS

POPE INNOCENT VIII
(1432-1492)

Pope Innocent VIII was a Genovese named Giovanni Battista
Cibo and was successor of Sixtus IV and predecessor of Alexander
VI. Like those before him Innocent wished to stop the Turkish
advance and succeeded by means other than the crusade he
originally planned for that purpose. He made peace with Charles
VIII of France and kept Djem, brother of Sultan Bajazet II,
captive in Rome. In 1490 Bajazet agreed to leave Europe in
peace if the Pope would continue to keep Djem captive.

BULL ON THE MARRIAGE OF HENRY VII
WITH ELIZABETH OF YORK

Our holy fadre, the Pope Innocent the viij. To the ppetuall
memory of this he (   ) to be hade, by his ppre mocion
without pcurement of our soverayn lord the Kyng or other
person for consernacyon of the vniuersal peas and eschewyng
of Sklaundres, and to engendre the contrary of the same.
Vnderstanding of the longe and greuous variaunce, contentions, and debates that hath ben in this Realme of Englond
betwene the house of the Duchre of Lancastre on the one
party, And the house of the Duchre of Yorke on that other
party. Wylling alle suche diuysions (   ) following to be
put apart By the Counsell and consent of his College of
Cardynalles approveth confirmyth and stablishyth the matri-
monye and coniuncion made betwene our soūayn lord King
Henre the seuenth of the house of Lancastre of that one party

And the noble Princesse Elyzabeth of the house of Yorke of that other (party) with all thaire Issue laufully borne betwene the same

And in lyke wise his holines cofermeth stablishith and approueth the right and title to the Crowne of England of the sayde oure souerayn lorde Henry the seuenthe, and the heires of his body laufully begoten to hym (　) pteynig aswel by reason of his nyghest and vndouted title of succession as by the right of his most noble (　) and by eleccyon of the lordes spyrituales and temporales, and other nobles of his Realme and by the (　) naunce and auctorite of parlyament made by the .iij. states of this lande

Also our saide holy Fadre the Pope of hys propur mocyon by hyegh and holy commaundement (　) requireth euy inhabitant of this lande and euery subgiect in the same of what degree, state or condicion (　) that non of theym by occasion of any successyon, or by any other coloure or cause within this Realme (by hym) selfe, or other mediate persones attempte, in worde, or dede ayenst the sayd oure sourayen lorde, or the (heires) of his body lawfully begoten, contrary to the peas of him and his Realme, vppon the payne of his grete curse (and Ana) theme, the whiche thay and euery of thaim that so attempteth, fallyth in forth right by that selfe dede done: the whiche curse and Anatheme noo man hath power to assoyle thaym: but our holy Fadre him selfe (or his speci) all depute to the same

Forthermore he approueth confirmeth and declareth. That yf hit please god that the sayde Elizabeth whiche God forbede shulde decesse withoute Issue bytwene oure souerayn lorde and hir of thair bodyes borne than suche Issue as bytwene hym and hir whome after that God shall ioyne him to shalbe hade and borne (　) heritours to the same croune and realme of Englande, Commaundyng that noo man attempte the (　) the payne of his grete curse, whiche thay and euery of thaym soo doynge fallyth in, in the selfe dede done and may not be assoyled but by hym or his speciall depute to the same.

Ouer this the same our holy Fadre yeueth his blyssing to alle princes nobles and other inhabitants of this Realme or outwarde that fauoureth aydeth and assisteth the sayde our souerayne lorde and his heires (   ) or thaire rebelles, Yeuing thayme that dye in his and thayr quarrall full and plenarye Pardon, and (remissi) on of all thaire synnes.

Fynally he commaundeth alle Metropolitanes and Bisshopes vpon the payne of interdiccion of (   ) the Chirche Abbotes Prioures Archydecones Pareshpriestes Priores and wardeyns of the frerys and (other) men of the chirche Exempte and not Exempte opon payn of his grete curse, whiche thay fallyth in (   ) it not to denuce and declare or cause to be denuced and declared alle suche contrary doers and rebelles (   ) suche time as thay to the same in the name of the sayd o souayn Lorde shalbe requyred with aggraua (tion of the) same curse yf the case shall so require So that if thay for drede shall not moue to publisshe the same (   ) them lefull to curse theire resistentis to the (   ) calle for theire assistence to the same in the sayde our holy fader's Name

And as touching the articles of this Bulle The Popys holines by this presente Bulle derog (   ) maketh voide all maner grauntes, Priueleges and Exempcions made by him or hys predecessors (   ) ny persone or place where as they shulde or myghte be preiudiciall to the execucion of this presetis (   ) alle suche as expressely reuoked by thys same as thaugh they were written worde by worde within the presentis Bulles as by hit ondre leyde here more largely doith apere

CONSULADO DEL MAR, 13TH CENTURY

The Consulado del Mar or Code of Barcelona, as it was also known, was first established in the thirteenth century and widely applied for about five centuries to the regulations involving trade at sea. Countless controversies arising from international maritime trade were resolved by the issue of the Consulado. The rules contained two hundred and fifty chapters and covered more detail than any previous maritime code. A printed edition appeared in 1494 and there were numerous translations into different languages.

The translation used here is taken from the Italian edition chiefly used by *Casa Regis,* and reprinted with his explications at Venice in 1737. He in turn derived his material from the French edition printed in 1577 at Marseille.

CHAPTER CCLXXIII

Of Merchant Vessels captured by an armed Ship

SECTION 1

If an armed ship, or cruizer, meet with a merchant vessel belonging to an enemy, and carrying a cargo the property of an enemy, common sense will sufficiently point out what is to be done; it is therefore unnecessary to lay down any rules for such a case.

2. If the captured vessel is neutral property, and the cargo the property of enemies, the captor may compel the merchant vessel to carry the enemy's cargo to a place of safety, where the prize may be secure from all danger of recapture, paying

to the vessel the whole freight, which she would have earned at her delivering port; and this freight shall be ascertained by the ship's papers, or in default of necessary documents, the oath of the master shall be received as to the amount of the freight.

3. Moreover, if the captor is in a place of safety, where he may be secure of his prize, yet is desirous to have the cargo carried to some other port, the neutral vessel is bound to carry it thither; but for this service, there ought to be a compensation agreed upon between them; or, in default of any special agreement, the merchant vessel shall receive for that service the ordinary freight that any other vessel would have earned for such a voyage, *or even more*; and this is to be understood of a ship that has arrived in the place where the captor may secure his prize; that is to say, in the port of a friend; and going on an ulterior voyage to that port, to which the captor wishes her to carry the cargo which he has taken.

4. If it shall happen that the master of the captured vessel, or any of the crew, shall claim any part of the cargo as their own, they ought not to be believed on their simple word; but the ship's papers or invoice shall be inspected; and in defect of such papers, the master and his mariners shall be put to their oaths; and if, on their oaths, they claim the property as their own, the captor shall restore it to them; regard being paid, at the same time, to the credit of those who swear, and make the claim.

5. If the master of the captured vessel shall refuse to carry the cargo, being enemy's property, to some such place of safety, at the command of the captor, the captor may sink the vessel, if he thinks fit, without control from any power or authority whatever, taking care to preserve the lives of those who are in her. This must be understood however, of a case where the whole cargo, or at least the greater part, is enemy's property.

6. If the ship should belong to the enemy, the cargo being either in the whole, or in part neutral property; some reasonable agreement should be entered into, on account of the

ship now become lawful prize, between the captor and the merchants owning the cargo.

7. If the merchants refuse to enter into such an agreement, the captor may send the vessel home to the country whose commission he bears; and in that case the merchants shall pay the freight, which they were to have paid at the delivering port; and if any damage is occasioned by this proceeding, the captor is not bound to make compensation; because the merchants had refused to treat respecting the ship; after it had become lawful prize; and for this farther reason also, that the ship is frequently of more value than the cargo she carries.

8. If, on the other hand, the merchants are willing to come to a reasonable agreement, and the captor, from arrogance, or other wrong motives, refuses to agree, and forcibly sends the cargo away, the merchants are not bound to pay the whole, nor any part of the freight; and besides, the captor shall make compensation for any damage he may occasion to them.

9. If the capture should be made in a place where the merchants have it not in their power to make good their agreement, but are nevertheless men of repute, and worthy to be trusted, the captor shall not send away the vessel without being liable to the damage; but if the merchants are not men of known credit, and cannot make good their stipulated payment, he may then act as it is above directed.

CHAPTER CCLXXXVII

Of Cases of Recapture

SECTION 1

If a ship is taken by the enemy, and afterwards another ship of a friend comes up, and effects a recapture; the vessel, and all that is in her, shall be restored to the former proprietors, on payment of a reasonable salvage for the expense, and trouble, and danger that have been incurred; but this is to be understood of recaptures effected within the seigniory, or territorial seas of the country, to which the captured vessel belongs, or before the enemy had secured the vessel to himself, in a place of safety.

2. If the recapture has been effected within the enemy's territory, or in a place where the enemy was in entire possession of his prize, that is, in a place of security, the proprietors shall not recover, nor shall the recaptors claim any salvage; for they are entitled to the whole benefit of the recapture, without opposition, from any rights of seigniory, or the claims of any person whatever.

3. If an enemy, having made a capture of a vessel, quits his prize on appearance of another vessel, either from fear, or from any doubt that he may entertain of her; and the vessel, on whose account the captured ship was abandoned, takes possession of the vessel that has been relinquished, and brings her into port; she shall be restored to the proprietor, or his heirs, without opposition, on payment of a reasonable salvage, to be fixed, by agreement between the parties, or if the parties cannot agree, by the arbitration of creditable persons.

4. If it should happen that any one abandons his vessel through fear of his enemy; and any friendly vessel falls in with the ship that has been deserted, and brings her into a place of security; that is to say, in a case where the finding vessel has not retaken the ship from the enemy, and where the enemy had not carried her into a place of security, and had not taken her from the owner; the finders shall have no claim to the vessel nor to the cargo on board; but, by the use and custom of the sea, they may demand a reasonable salvage, to be settled, either by agreement, or by reference to the arbitration of creditable persons; for it is not fit that any one should endeavour to take undue advantage of the misfortunes of another; since he cannot foresee what may happen to himself; and because, every one should be ready

to submit his disputes, especially in cases like the present, to the arbitration of two unexceptionable persons.

5. It is besides to be understood, in all that has been said, that every thing shall be done without fraud; for no man can tell what may be his own case; and it sometimes happens that the deceit and injury which a person attempts to practise on others, light upon himself; therefore, if any persons, knowing that a ship is going on a voyage, where she must be exposed to danger or alarm from the enemy, fit out a vessel with a view, and for the purpose of doing injury to that ship or any other, in making salvage at their expence; or with a design of getting possession of the ship and cargo; if it can be proved against them, that they went out with any such intention, such persons shall not be entitled to any salvage on the ship or cargo, although the owner may have abandoned her; nor even, although she may have been taken by the enemy.

6. If those, who fitted out the vessel, cannot establish, in proof, that they did not arm with any of the before-mentioned intentions, or if it should be proved against them, that they armed for the purpose of doing injury to any one, or generally to all, whom they might meet, in the form and manner of enemies, in such a case, whether they bring in a vessel, with or without a cargo—whether it shall be retaken from the enemy, or merely found by them, they shall take no benefit from it, but the whole shall be restored to the former proprietors; and moreover such persons, so arming, shall be delivered over to justice to be treated as robbers and pirates, if the fact can be established in proof.

7. If they are not convicted of such an intention, having either retaken or found a vessel in any of the situations abovementioned, they shall be entitled to their full right and benefit according to the preceding regulations. But if the matter shall remain in doubt, or if it shall rest with them to disprove the charge, neither they, nor any that were with them, nor any, that are interested in the event, shall be received to give evidence in their favour; nor shall any person of a

covetous disposition, nor any one, who may be suspected of being biased by money, be a witness for them.

8. If an enemy shall have made a capture of a vessel or cargo, and shall afterwards abandon it, voluntarily, and not from any fear or apprehension of any vessel coming upon him; and if any persons shall find the vessel or cargo that has been voluntarily abandoned, and bring it to a place of security, the property shall not be acquired to them, if any owner can be found; but they shall receive a reasonable salvage, to be fixed, at the discretion of reputable persons of the place, to which the ship or goods shall be carried.

9. If, after the expiration of a reasonable time, no owner comes forward, the finders shall receive for their salvage one half of the proceeds, and the other half shall be applied in the manner that has been expressed and declared in a preceding chapter.*

10. If the enemy, being in possession of any ship or cargo, shall not have deserted it voluntarily, but shall have been obliged to abandon it by storm or tempest, or on account of any ship or vessel by whom he may have been alarmed, the same rule shall be observed as if the enemy had quitted the same voluntarily, and of his own accord.

11. If the enemy, after a capture, comes to any place where he takes a ransom for his prize, if the proprietors wish to have their vessel or cargo again, he or they, who have ransomed her, are bound to deliver her up to the original owners, on payment of the debt and charges, and some further allowance besides, if they choose to accept it.

12. If an enemy, on capture of a ship or cargo, shall make a gift of it; such a donation or gift shall not be valid on

* In chapter 249, the same proportion of a moiety is given to the finder of goods found floating in port, &c. after the expiration of a year and a day, if no owner appears to claim. The other moiety was to be divided into two parts, of which the Lord of the Jurisdiction was to retain one; and to apply the other *to pious purposes,* for the soul of the proprietor.

any account; except that if a gift is made of the ship or cargo to those to whom it belonged, such donation shall be valid. But if the captor bargains with the master in these words, "We are willing to give you your ship for nothing, but must have a ransom for the cargo," such a donation shall not be good; because, in the case of which we are now speaking, the enemy had not carried it to a place of security, so as to say, that he might not lose it; notwithstanding that he might so far have obtained power over his prize, as to be able to burn or sink it.

VII.

CELTIC JUDGMENT

THE WRONG JUDGMENTS OF CARATNIA*

Composed in one of the oddest literary forms ever to stimulate legal thought, the Celtic Wrong Judgments of Caratnia are contained in one short book as a type of digest. Supposedly written by Caratnia the Scarred, an early judge, who is said to have lived in the second century A.D., the judgments or decisions are stated in abstract terms which are apparently unsound and paradoxical. The king questions these rulings and the judge explains the facts, applying an exception to the rule.

The oldest copy, found in an Irish law-text, goes back to the 1100's with the text dating as far back as 700.

Here follow the wrong judgments of Caratnia the Scarred. He was from the North, and was judge to King Conn of the Hundred Battles. He acquired great wealth. But his people maltreated him and deserted him; and he went to Conn's abode and was there healed. This Caratnia was deemed to blunder, when his judgments were heard by the many; but his judgments were correct, when examined by the few. Every case that was brought to Conn would be submitted by Conn to him. Then Conn would ask him, "What judgment seems meet to you?" [The judgments are now stated in dialogue between Caratnia and Conn.]

1. "I decided, A bargain, after a night has elapsed, cannot be revoked."—"You decided wrongly," said Conn.—"I did it wisely," said Caratnia, "for it was a silver thing, and its defect was concealed."

*From the German Translation of R. Thurneysen, Bonn University, *Aus dem Irischen Recht,* III.

2. "I decided, A contract for plowing with another man's oxen can be revoked."—"You decided wrongly," said Conn. —"I did it wisely, for the other man's oxen were taken away from him."

3. "I decided, The bard cannot claim pay for his hired eulogy."—"You decided wrongly," said Conn.—"I did it wisely; for it was sly praise, which amounted to a sneer."

4. "I decided, The tools of the smith descended to a relative not craft-skilled."—"You decided wrongly," said Conn.— "I did it wisely, for the relative was his son, who has first claim."

5. "I decided, A bondwoman wife must share the cost of her child's upbringing."—"You decided wrongly," said Conn. —"I did it wisely, for the child's father was himself a bondman."

6. "I decided, The surety for a son who contracts [without capacity] in his father's lifetime must pay."—"You decided wrongly," said Conn.—"I did it wisely, for the contract was for purchasing a wife and hiring land."

7. "I decided, An iron tool is acceptable as a pledge."— "You decided wrongly."—"I did it wisely, for this was a pledge to secure a liability for building a party-wall."

8. "I decided, The contract is binding, though the thing received was of less value."—"You decided wrongly."—"I did it wisely, for every adult man must suffer being overreached."

9. "I decided, The first choice of lands when an inheritance is divided lies with the eldest son-heir, without casting lots for it."—"You decided wrongly."—"I did it wisely, for in this case the younger yielded first choice to the elder without lots, even though it might be worse for him."

10. "I decided, The stealing of a morsel may go free of penalty."—"You decided wrongly."—"I did it wisely, for here it was a homeless outcast who eat it."

11. "I decided, For trespass by bees a pledge must be lodged with one's neighbor."—"You decided wrongly."—"I

did it wisely, for no one need supply feed to his neighbor gratis."

12. "I decided, The whole cost of the child's upbringing falls on the mother only."—"You decided wrongly."—"I did it wisely, for this was the child of a slut, which the father had not acknowledged before she sought to shuffle off liability."

13. "I decided, Excessive advantages in family shares may be retained."—"You decided wrongly."—"I did it wisely, for here the spouses, though not bringing equal marriage portions, were entitled to spend equally for family expenses."

14. "I decided, The gravid wife may be freed from a penalty."—"You decided wrongly."—"I did it wisely, it was a matter of saving life; the infant was not brought to birth."

15. "I decided, One of the animals put out to pasture on hired land may be kept by the land-owner."—"You decided wrongly."—"I did it wisely, for the animal, being kept as pay, was not of greater value than the rent."

16. "I decided, For breach of a clan-truce no fine need be paid."—"You decided wrongly."—"I did it wisely, for here the accused was wounding in defense of his life."

17. "I decided, An overpayment may be pleaded against a debtor."—"You decided wrongly."—"I did it wisely, for here it was a surety and a creditor, who pursued their claim until the debtor yielded."

18. "I decided, One oath makes good proof against two."—"You decided wrongly."—"I did it wisely, for the one oath was of a competent man who prosecuted two infamous men for a misdeed."

19. "I decided, Harm by an animal is payable like harm by a human [i.e. the full penalty-amount, not merely compensation]."—"You decided wrongly."—"I did it wisely, for here the animal had been kept by its owner after once doing harm and was notoriously vicious."

20. "I decided, Harm by a human is payable like harm by an animal."—"You decided wrongly."—"I did it wisely, for

harm by a minor or without intention calls only for compensation, not fine also."

21. "I decided, Harm done by a shepherd-dog carries no penalty."—"You decided wrongly."—"I did it wisely, for here it was attacked by animals that it had not hurt."

22. "I decided, The chief has not the power of judgment over his underlings."—"You decided wrongly."—"I did it wisely, for here the chief was disqualified as to his underlings."

23. "I decided, Children's contracts are binding on both sides."—"You decided wrongly."—"I did it wisely, for here it was an exchange of goods, made openly and without overreaching."

24. "I decided, A king's arrival [with ceremonies] does not excuse failure to fulfill one's attendance at court."—"You decided wrongly."—"I did it wisely, for here the king himself was to hold the court for this party."

25. "I decided, The exemption of a bard's cattle from attachment for debts of his followers is lost."—"You decided wrongly."—"I did it wisely, because the bard's followers exceeded the lawful number."

26. "I decided, The injured man, taken in with his followers by the injurer under his duty of treatment, need not be kept till the ninth day."—"You decided wrongly."—"I did it wisely, for a skilled physician pronounced that the man would be dead at the month's end, and the fine for death relieves the injurer from the usual duty to support for nine days."

27. "I decided, Liability for death accrues against him who is commissioned by his family-chief to fight in a regular duel." —"You decided wrongly."—"I did it wisely, for the man killed was feudal superior to the killer, and no necessity compelled the killing."

28. "I decided, The clan does not share liability for the the misdeed of one who by purchase became an adoptive member."—"You decided wrongly."—"I did it wisely, for

here the conditions of purchasing membership were not fulfilled."

29. "I decided, The son is free from the duty to support his father in old age."—"You decided wrongly."—"I did it wisely, for here the father had sold the son as a serf, and the duty to support had ceased."

30. "I decided, On division of property at divorce, the wife receives no share representing the fruits of her household toil, in spite of her service having been faithful."—"You decided wrongly."—"I did it wisely, for here the wife had waived her right when marrying a man of higher rank."

31. "I decided, A garment may be seized as a pledge."— "You decided wrongly."—"I did it wisely, for here the pledge was one required to be redeemed before nightfall."

32. "I decided, The chief's share of head-money for killing of a clansman need not be paid."—"You decided wrongly." —"I did it wisely, for here there was a counter-claim due from him."

33. "I decided, No fine is imposed for negligence on a bystander who by inaction causes the death of a helpless person."—"You decided wrongly."—"I did it wisely, for here the bystander himself scarcely escaped the same death."

34. "I decided, The oath of a woman against a cleric is void."—"You decided wrongly."—"I did it wisely, for here the suit was by one cleric against another."

35. "I decided, Of a treasure found no share goes to the rear man of those who chanced upon it."—"You decided wrongly."—"I did it wisely, for the rear man here was blind, who did not share the sight of it."

36. "I decided, He who takes possession of land in good faith as claimant obtains permanent possession."—"You decided wrongly."—"I did it wisely, for the one dispossessed had neither ownership nor consent of the owner."

37. "I decided, In a suit for injury to a chief, only one 'cumal' [= 3 cows] was awarded."—"You decided wrongly [for the head-money of a chief is 7 'cumal']."—"I did it wisely,

for here the insult was to the widow of a chief, and she was the mother of seven chiefs; therefore each claimant received only one 'cumal.' "

38. "I decided, To the woman who makes no outcry when forced, the fine is none the less payable."—"You decided wrongly."—"I did it wisely, for here she was forced in the wilderness."

39. "I decided, No fine is imposed for improper seizure of a man's wife in the guest-house."—"You decided wrongly."— "I did it wisely, for a wife among the house-serfs without the protection of her husband is deemed for the time not his wife."

40. "I decided, The deposit need not be restored."—"You decided wrongly."—"I did it wisely, for this deposit perished with the goods of the depositary."

41. "I decided a case on hearing one party only."—"You decided wrongly."—"I did it wisely, for the opponent in this case could not be found, and I decided after considering his side."

42. "I decided, The husband is freed from paying fine to the wife's family for causing her death."—"You decided wrongly."—"I did it wisely, for this wife was his by the family's consent and died in childbirth."

43. "I decided, The bride-price is to be paid back to the husband even after consummation of the marriage."—"You decided wrongly."—"I did it wisely, for here the marriage was for a term and the wife had deserted the husband before the term expired."

44. "I decided, The liability of a serf for a misdeed is shared by another serf."—"You decided wrongly."—"I did it wisely, for here the other serf had harbored the first."

45. "I decided, The man who brings complaint according to law is oathworthy."—"You decided wrongly."—"I did it wisely, for here his oath was fortified by one of the seven 'rocks' of proof."

46. "I decided, For a bard's song composed on the spot and therefore inadequate, the regular fee must be paid."—"You

decided wrongly."—"I did it wisely, for this was a song to invoke magic and must therefore be extemporized."

47. "I decided, The recaption of a pledge by the pledgor does not make him liable."—"You decided wrongly."—"I did it wisely, for this was a pledge unlawfully taken."

48. "I decided, The pound for keeping a pledge seized may be outside of clan-territory."—"You decided wrongly."—"I did it wisely, for the seizer here acted for a creditor in the other territory."

49. "I decided, A surety may repudiate the suretyship."—"You decided wrongly."—"I did it wisely, for this was a case where the man had been erroneously made surety against his will."

50. "I decided, The chief cannot claim that his honor was injured, in spite of the bard's insulting song."—"You decided wrongly."—"I did it wisely, for here the chief then demanded a eulogy, and it more than made up for the insult."

51. "I decided, No head-money is payable for a treacherous killing."—"You decided wrongly."—"I did it wisely, for here there was a set-off for seven deeds of violence on the other side."

VIII.

GOTHIC LAW

VISIGOTHIC LAWS

The original Visigothic laws, wholly based upon oral tradition, were first reduced to order and committed to writing by Euric, at Arles, in the latter half of the fifth century. At the beginning of the sixth century, Alaric II promulgated the *Breviarium Alaricianum,* a body of laws compiled mainly from the 3 Codes of Gregorianus, Hermogenianus and Theodosianus, which collection was the source of the subsequent Lombard and Bavarian Codes. From the two compilations of Euric and Alaric, under the reigns of Kings Chintasvintus and Recesvintus, 649-652, was formed the *Forum Judicum,* or Visigothic Code; the most remarkable monument of legislation which ever emanated from a semi-barbarian people, and the only substantial memorial of greatness or erudition bequeathed by the Goths to posterity. Like the Roman works on jurisprudence it is divided into twelve books, subdivided into titles and chapters. The language in which it is written is monkish Latin, a barbarous jargon, extremely difficult to translate, and vastly different from the polished idiom of Tacitus and Cicero. Its examination discloses many discrepancies, variations, ambiguities, and contradictions, unquestionably due to the ignorance of the various transcribers; a fact which is not surprising when the imperfect knowledge and defective education which prevailed in Spain during the seventh century are considered. There is no mention of the *Forum Judicum* during the Saracen domination, except that it is known to have been preserved by the Moors; and as Christians were permitted the use of their own laws, where they did not conflict with those of the conquerors, upon the regular payment of tribute, it may be presumed that it was the recognized legal authority of Christian magistrates during the period that Spain remained under the Moslem scepter. When Ferdinand III took

Cordova in the thirteenth century, he ordered the *Forum Judicum* to be adopted and observed by its citizens, and caused it to be rendered into Castilian.

THE LAWS OF THE JUDGES

BOOK I

CONCERNING LEGAL AGENCIES

TITLE: I. THE LAWMAKER

I. What the Method of Making Laws Should Be

We, whose duty it is to afford suitable assistance in the formation of the laws, should, in the execution of this undertaking, improve upon the methods of the ancients, disclosing as well the excellence of the law to be framed, as the skill of its artificer. The proof of this art will be the more plainly evident, if it seems to draw its conclusions not from inference and imitation but from truth. Nor should it stamp the force of argument with the subtlety of syllogism, but it should, with moderation, and by the use of pure and honorable precepts, determine the provisions of the law. And, indeed, reason plainly demands that the work be performed in this manner. For, when the master holds in his hand the finished product, in vain is sought the reason for its having been impressed with that particular form. On subjects that are obscure, reason eagerly seeks to be informed by examination; in matters, however, that are well known and established, action alone is required. Therefore, when the matter in question is not clear because its form is unfamiliar, investigation is desirable; but it is otherwise in affairs known to all men, where not speculation, but performance, becomes essential. As we are more concerned with morals than with eloquence, it is not our province to introduce the personality of the orator, but to define the rights of the governor.

II. How the Lawmaker Should Act

The maker of laws should not practise disputation, but should administer justice. Nor is it fitting that he should appear to have framed the law by contention, but in an orderly manner. For the transaction of public affairs does not demand, as a reward of his labors, the clamor of theatrical applause, but the law destined for the salvation of the people.

III. What Should be Required of the Lawmaker

First, it should be required that he make diligent inquiry as to the soundness of his opinions. Then it should be evident that he has acted not for private gain but for the benefit of the people; so that it may conclusively appear that the law has not been made for any private or personal advantage, but for the protection and profit of the whole body of citizens.

IV. What the Conduct of the Lawmaker Should Be in his Daily Life

The framer of laws and the dispenser of justice should prefer morals to eloquence, that his speech may be characterized rather by virtuous sentiments, than by elegance of expression. He should be more eminent for deeds than for words; and should discharge his duties rather with alacrity than with reluctance, and not, as it were, under compulsion.

V. How the Lawmaker Should Impart Advice

He should be mindful of his duty only to God and to himself; be liberal of counsel to persons of high and low degree, and easy of access to the citizens and common people; so that, as the guardian of the public safety, exercising the government by universal consent, he may not, for personal motives, abuse the privileges of his judicial office.

VI. What Manner of Speech the Lawmaker Should Use

He should be energetic and clear of speech; certain in opinion; ready in weighing evidence; so that whatever proceeds from the source of the law may at once impress all hearers that it is characterized by neither doubt nor perplexity.

VII. How the Lawmaker Should Act in Rendering Judgment.

The Judge should be quick of perception; firm of purpose; clear in judgment; lenient in the infliction of penalties; assiduous in the practice of mercy; expeditious in the vindication of the innocent; clement in his treatment of criminals; careful of the rights of the stranger; gentle toward his countrymen. He should be no respecter of persons, and should avoid all appearance of partiality.

VIII. How the Lawmaker Should Comport Himself in Private and Public Affairs

All public matters he should approach with patriotism and reverence; those concerning private individuals and domestic controversies he should determine according to his authority and power; so that the community may look up to him as a father, and the lower orders of the people may regard him as a master and a lord.

He should be assiduous in the performance of his duties so that he may be feared by the commonalty to such a degree that none shall hesitate to obey him; and be so just that all would willingly sacrifice their lives in his service, from their attachment to his person and to his office.

IX. What Instruction it is Fitting that the Lawmaker Should Give

Then, also, he should bear in mind that the glory and the majesty of the people consist in the proper interpretation of the laws, and in the manner of their administration. For, as the entire safety of the public depends upon the preservation of the law, he should attempt to amend the statutes of the country rather than the manners of the populace; and remember that there are some who, in controversies, apply the laws according to their will, and in pursuance of private advantage, to such an extent that what should be law to the public is to them private dishonor; so that, by perversion of the law, acts which are illegal are often perpetrated, which should obviously be abolished through the power of the law itself.

TITLE II. THE LAW

I. *What the Lawmaker Should Observe in Framing the Laws.*
II. *What the Law Is.*
III. *What the Law Does.*
IV. *What the Law Should Be.*
V. *Why the Law Is Made.*
VI. *How the Law Should Triumph over Enemies.*

I. What the Lawmaker Should Observe in Framing the Laws

In all legislation the law should be fully and explicitly set forth, that perfection, and not partiality, may be secured. For, in the formation of the laws, not the sophisms of argument, but the virtue of justice should ever prevail. And here is required not what may be prompted by controversy, but what energy and vigor demand; for the violation of morals is not to be coerced by the forms of speech, but restrained by the moderation of virtue.

II. What the Law Is

The law is the rival of divinity; the oracle of religion; the source of instruction; the artificer of right; the guardian and promoter of good morals; the rudder of the state; the messenger of justice; the mistress of life; the soul of the body politic.

III. What the Law Does

The law rules every order of the state, and every condition of man; it governs wives and husbands; youth and age; the learned and the ignorant; the polished and the rude. It aims to provide the highest degree of safety for both prince and people, and, in renown and excellence, it is as conspicuous as the noon-day sun.

IV. What the Law Should Be

The law should be plain, and not lead any citizen to commit error or fraud. It should be suitable to the place and the time, according to the character and custom of the state; prescribing justice and equity; consistent, honorable, worthy, useful, and necessary; and it should be carefully noted whether its provisions are framed rather for the convenience, than for the injury, of the public; so that it may be determined whether it sufficiently provides for the administration of justice; whether or not it appears to be contrary to religion, and whether it defends the right, and may be observed without detriment to any one.

V. Why the Law is Made

Laws are made for these reasons: that human wickedness may be restrained through fear of their execution; that the lives of innocent men may be safe among criminals; and that the temptation to commit wrong may be restrained by the fear of punishment.

VI. How the Law Should Triumph over Enemies

Domestic peace having been once established and the plague of contention having been entirely removed from prince, citizen, and the populace, expeditions then may be made safely against the enemy and he may be attacked confidently and vigorously, in the certain hope of victory; when nothing is to be anticipated or feared from dissensions at home. The entire body of the people being prosperous and secure, through the influence of peace and order, they can set forth boldly against the enemy and become invincible, where salutary arts are aided by just laws. For men are better armed with equity than with weapons; and the prince should rather employ justice against an enemy than the soldier his javelin; and the success of the prince will be more conspicuous when a reputation for justice accompanies him, and soldiers who are well governed at home will be all the more formidable to a foe. It is a matter of common experience, that justice, which has protected the citizen, overwhelms the enemy; and that those prevail in foreign contests who enjoy domestic peace; and while the moderation of the prince insures temperance in the enforcement of the law, so the united support of the citizens promotes victory over the enemy. For the administration of the law is regulated by the disposition and character of the king; from the administration of the law proceeds the institution of morals; from the institution of morals, the concord of the citizens; from the concord of the citizens, the triumph over the enemy. So a good prince ruling well his kingdom, and making foreign conquests, maintaining peace at home, and overwhelming his foreign adversaries, is famed both as the ruler of his state and a victor over his enemies, and shall have for the future eternal renown; after terrestrial wealth, a celestial kingdom; after the diadem and the purple, a crown of glory; nor shall he then cease to be king; for when he relinquished his earthly kingdom, and conquered a celestial one, he did not diminish, but rather increased his glory.

BOOK II
CONCERNING THE CONDUCT OF CAUSES

TITLE I. CONCERNING JUDGES AND MATTERS TO BE DECIDED IN COURT

I.   *When Amended Laws should come in Force.*
II. *The Royal Power, as well as the Entire Body of the People, should be Subject to the Majesty of Law.*
III. *It is Permitted to No One to be Ignorant of the Law.*

IV. *The Business of the King shall First be Considered, then that of the People.*

V. *How the Avarice of the King should be Restrained in the Beginning, and How Documents Issued in the Name of the King should be Drawn Up.*

VI. *Concerning Those who Abandon the King, or the People, or their Country, or who Conduct Themselves with Arrogance.*

VII. *Of Incriminating the King, or Speaking Ill of Him.*

VIII. *Of Annulling the Laws of Foreign Nations.*

IX. *No One shall presume to have in his Possession another Book of Laws except this which has just been Published.*

X. *Concerning Fast Days and Festivals, during which No Legal Business shall be Transacted.*

XI. *No Cause shall be Heard by the Judges which is not Sanctioned by the Law.*

XII. *When Causes have once been Determined, at no Time shall They be Revived; but They shall be Disposed of according to the Arrangement of this Book: the Addition of Other Laws being One of the Prerogatives of the King.*

XIII. *It shall be Lawful for No One to Hear and Determine Causes except Those Whom either the King, the Parties by Voluntary Consent, or the Judge, shall have Invested with Judicial Powers.*

XIV. *What Causes shall be Heard, and to what Persons Causes shall be Assigned for a Decision.*

XV. *Judges Shall Decide Criminal as well as Civil Causes.*

XVI. *Concerning the Punishment of Those who Presume to Act as Judges, who have not been Invested with Judicial Power.*

XVII. *Concerning Those who Ignore the Letters of the*

Judge, or His Seal, Calling Them to Court.

XVIII. Where a Judge Refuses to Hear a Litigant, or Decides Fraudulently or Ignorantly.

XIX. Where a Judge, either through Convenience to Himself, or through Want of Proper Knowledge, Decides a Cause Improperly.

XX. Where a Judge, either through Deceit or Cunning, imposes Needless Costs upon Either, or Both the Parties to a Suit.

XXI. What, First of All, a Judge should be Familiar With, in order that he may Understand a Case.

XXII. Where the Integrity of a Judge is said to be Suspected by Any One of Honorable Rank, or where a Judge presumes to render a Decision Contrary to Law.

XXIII. How a Judge should render Judgment.

XXIV. Concerning the Emoluments and the Punishment of the Judge, and of the Bailiff.

XXV. Everyone who is Invested with Judicial Power shall Legally bear the Title of Judge.

XXVI. Every Bond which is Exacted by a Judge, after an Unjust Decree, shall be held Invalid.

XXVII. An Unjust Decree or an Unjust Interpretation of the Law, Prompted by Fear of the Throne, or Made by Order of the King, shall be Invalid.

XXVIII. Concerning the Power, conferred upon Bishops, of Restraining Judges who Decide Wrongfully.

XXIX. The Judge, when Inquired of by a Party, should be able to give a Reason for His Decision.

XXX. Concerning the Punishment of Judges who Appropriate the Property of Others.

XXXI. Concerning those who Treat the Royal Order with Disdain.

XXXII. How the Judge should Inquire into Causes by the Ordeal of Hot Water.

I. When Amended Laws should come in Force

In assigning their place to laws which have been amended, we have considered it proper to give them the most important rank, for, as clearness in the laws is useful in preventing the misdeeds of the people, so obscurity in their provisions interferes with the course of justice. For many salutary edicts are drawn up in obscure and contradictory language, and are instrumental in promoting the controversies of litigants; and, while they should put an end to chicanery, they, in fact, give rise to new sophisms and abuses. For this reason, therefore, litigation increases; disputes between parties are encouraged; the judges become undecided, so that, in attempting to dispose of false claims and charges, they are unable to form definite conclusions, as all seems perplexed and uncertain. And because all questions which arise in suits at law, cannot be disposed of in a few words, except those which have been determined in our presence; we have decided that certain laws should be amended in this book; that doubtful matters should be made clear; that profit should be extracted from those things that are evil; clemency from those that are mortal; clearness from those that are obscure; and that perfection should be given to those that are incomplete; whereby the people of our kingdom, whom our peaceful government alone restrains, may be checked and controlled, hereafter, by the aid of said amended laws. And therefore, these laws as amended, and approved by us, and our new decrees, as set forth in this book and its titles, as well as such as may be subsequently added, shall be enforced from the second year of our reign, and the twelfth Kalends of November, and shall be binding thereafter upon all persons subject to our empire, irrespective of rank. Those laws, however, which we have promulgated against the offences of the Jews, we decree shall be valid from the date when they were confirmed by us.

THE GLORIOUS FLAVIUS RECESVINTUS, KING

II. The Royal Power, as well as the Entire Body of the

People, should be Subject to the Majesty of the Law.

The Omnipotent Lord of all, sole Founder and Provider of the means of human salvation, ordered the inhabitants of the earth to learn justice from the sacred precepts of the law. And, because the mandate of Divinity has been thus imposed upon the human race, it is fitting that all terrestrial creatures, of however exalted rank, should acknowledge the authority of Him whom even the celestial soldiery obey. Wherefore, if God should be obeyed, justice should be highly esteemed, which, if it were thus esteemed, would be constantly practised, as every one loves justice more truly and ardently when a feeling of equity unites him with his neighbor. Willingly, therefore, carrying out the Divine commands, let us give temperate laws to ourselves and to our subjects; laws such as we and our successors, and the whole body of the people, may readily obey; so that no person of whatever rank or dignity may refuse to submit to the power of the law, which the necessity and will of the King has deemed it proper and salutary to inculcate.

FLAVIUS RECESVINTUS, KING

III. It is Permitted to No One to be Ignorant of the Law

All true science declares that ignorance should be detested. For while it has been written, "he need not understand who desires to act with propriety," it is certain that he who does not wish to know, despises an upright life. Therefore, let no one think that he can do what is unlawful because he was ignorant of the provisions of the laws, and what is sanctioned by them; for ignorance does not render him innocent, whom guilt has subjected to the penalties of the criminal.

FLAVIUS RECESVINTUS, KING

IV. The Business of the King shall First be Considered, then that of the People

God, the Creator of all things, in his arrangement of the

257

human form, placed the head above the body, and caused all
the different members of the latter to originate from it, and
it is, therefore, called the head; there being formed the bright-
ness of the eyes, by which all things that produce injury can
be discerned; there being born also the power of intelligence,
through which the members connected with, and subject to,
the head, may be either controlled or protected. For this
reason it is the especial care of skillful physicians to provide
the remedies for the head before treating the other members
of the body; which, indeed, may not be thought unreasonable,
when properly explained; because, if the head should be
healthy, it is reasonable to suppose that the other members
can be readily cured. For if disease attacks the head, health
cannot be imparted by it to the members which are constantly
being wasted by weakness. The most important duties of the
prince are, therefore, the preservation of health and the defence of life; so that the proper method may be adopted in
the conduct of the affairs of the people; and while the health
of the king is cared for, the preservation of his subjects may
be the better maintained.

THE GLORIOUS FLAVIUS RECESVINTUS, KING

V. How the Avarice of the King should be Restrained in
the Beginning, and How Documents Issued in the Name of
the King should be Drawn Up.

Earthly greatness appears the more sublime when compassion for our neighbors is displayed; and, therefore, it
shoul be the duty of every monarch to pay more attention
to the safety of his subjects than to his own personal advantage. For the greater the number of his subjects, the greater
the benefit to be derived by him from them; as, however
much the king may desire to profit by his individual efforts
alone, there is little to be gained therefrom. Hence, the wellbeing of the people, whose bounds are not defined by the
will of one, but affect the prosperity of all, is directly concerned. Wherefore, that the favor of the prince may not

seem to be manifested rather in words than in deeds, he should be attentive to the unspoken wishes of his subjects; and thus unsolicited compassion may often effect what otherwise crowded assemblies would hardly be able to obtain.

For the reason that, in former times, the unbridled greed of princes despoiled the people of their possessions, and the wealth of the state was persistently wrung from the misery of its citizens; as we have already given laws to the subject, we deem it in accordance with the teachings of the Holy Spirit to place restraints upon the exactions of the prince. Hence, after sincere deliberation, as well for our own glory as for that of our successors; God being our mediator; we decree that no king shall, by any means, extort, or cause to be extorted, any documents whatever in acknowledgment of any debt, whereby any person can unjustly, and without his consent, be deprived of his property. And, if by the free will of any one the king should receive a gift, or should openly profit by any transaction, the character of the transaction or contribution should be clearly set forth in the document; by which means either the influence of the prince or the fraud of his accomplice may be readily detected. And, if it should appear that the document had been exacted from any one against his will, either the dishonesty of the prince shall be atoned for, and he shall cancel his corrupt contract, or, if he should be dead, the document shall be declared void as against him from whom it was extorted, or his heirs, and this shall be done without delay. But the ownership of property whose acquisition is free from all suspicion, shall vest absolutely in the prince, and be his own forever. And whatever disposition he wishes to make of any of these things, he can make according to his judgment. But as sincerity and truth confirm all matters of this kind, whenever any documents are made for the advantage of the prince, the witnesses who have attested those documents shall be carefully examined, and if no indication of corrupt or forcible influence by the prince is apparent, or should any fraud in the execution of the document be detected; according to these circumstances the instrument shall either stand as properly made, or, having been proved to be illegal, it shall be declared void.

Similar arrangements concerning lands, vineyards, and bodies of slaves shall be observed, even when such disposition has been made of them verbally and in the presence of witnesses. In regard to all property that has been acquired by princes since the time of King Chintilanus, or that hereafter shall be acquired by others; and whatever property a king has left, or shall leave undisposed of, when it is proved to have been acquired by the head of the government; we decree that it shall belong to his successor in the kingdom, and he shall have the power to dispose of it according to his pleasure. But property obtained from relatives, or inherited from parents, shall descend to his sons, or, if he have no sons, to his legitimate heirs, as their rights may appear, or as they are acknowledged by the laws of succession: but if it should happen that he has left undisposed of any property inherited from his parents or his relatives, or derived from any contribution, or obtained by any legal contract; it shall belong, not to the successor of the kingdom, but to the sons or heirs of him who has thus acquired it. For whatever the prince is known to have possessed before his accession to the throne, either as his own property, or gained through honorable transactions with others, he shall have absolute power to dispose of according to his will, and his sons shall have full right to its inheritance; but, if he should have no sons, such property as he did not dispose of, shall descend to his lawful heirs. This law shall apply solely to, and shall be observed in, the affairs of the prince, and shall be forever enforced, and no one shall ascend the royal throne before making oath that he will observe it in all its details.

Whoever, either through an insurrection of the people, or by secret machinations, shall attain to supreme power, shall, with all his adherents, be accursed, and shall be excommunicated from the society of all Christians; and every Christian who shall have any intercourse with him shall undergo the same condemnation and pay the same penalty. And if any one holding an office in the royal palace, shall, through malice, criticise this law, or evade it in any way, or murmur against it; or shall have been convicted of having openly condemned it; he shall be deprived of all his employments and privileges, shall be stripped of half of all his possessions, shall be forcibly restrained of his liberty, and be excluded from the society of the palace. Any one in holy orders who has shared his offense, shall undergo the same confiscation of his property.

FLAVIUS CHINTASVINTUS, KING

VI. Concerning Those who Abandon the King, or the People, or their Country, or who Conduct Themselves with Arrogance

The extent to which the country of the Goths has been afflicted by domestic strife, and by the injuries caused by deserters and their abominable pride, is not generally known; yet it is evident in the diminution of the population; and these disturbances are the source of more trouble to the country than enterprises against the enemy. Therefore, that such contemptible conduct may be abolished, and the manifest crimes of these transgressors may no longer go unpunished, we have decreed by this law, which shall prevail through all ages, that whoever, from the time of King Chintilanus of sacred memory, until the second year of our reign, has deserted, or shall desert to the enemy; or shall repair to any foreign country; or even has wished, or shall wish, at any time, to act with criminal intent against the Gothic people; or shall conspire against his country; or, perchance, has attempted at any time to conspire against it; and has been, or shall be captured or detected in the commission of any of these offences; and if, either from the first year of our reign has attempted, or, hereafter, any one within the limits of the country of the Goths shall attempt, to foment any disorder, or cause any scandal to the detriment of our government, or of the people; or, what is unworthy to be even mentioned,

261

may have seemed to have plotted our death or injury, or shall hereafter plot against subsequent kings; or has appeared, or shall appear, to manifest, in any way, the intentions of a traitor; whoever shall be found guilty of all of these crimes, or of any one of them, shall undergo sentence of death; nor shall any leniency be shown him, under any condition, except that his life alone may be spared through the considerate pity of the prince. But this shall not be done until his eyes have been put out, so that he may not see the wrong in which he wickedly took delight, and may henceforth drag out a miserable existence in constant grief and pain. The property of such atrocious criminals shall belong absolutely to the king, and whoever he bestows it upon shall possess it in security forever and no succeeding king, at any time, shall presume to review the cause, or shall interfere, in any way, with this sentence. But, as many are found who, having been implicated in these, and in similar wicked designs, and have fraudulently transferred their property to the Church, or to their wives, or to their sons and friends, or to other persons; or have secretly conveyed said property to foreign countries, in order that they may claim said property, and demand its possession thereafter; when, in fact, none of said property has been alienated, and the papers evidencing its transfer are fraudulent, making false representations under an appearance of truth; therefore, we have decided to abolish this most iniquitous fraud by the decree of this law; so that, wherever documents have been drawn up with a manifest intention to wrong or deceive, any property owned by a person who has been convicted of such criminal practices shall be confiscated for the use of the royal treasury; and it is hereby declared that all such property above mentioned shall be at the disposal of the king, and he shall hereafter do with it whatever his judgment dictates, but whatever other provisions relating to a fraud of this description are contained in other laws, are hereby confirmed in all their force.

All persons to whom pardon has been granted by preceding kings are expressly excepted from the penalties of this decree;

and if, through motives of humanity, the king should wish to bestow anything upon a criminal, it should not be taken from the property belonging to the malefactor, but must be obtained from such other source as it may please the king; and it shall be only lawful for him to give an amount equal to the twentieth part of the inheritance of the criminal.

THE GLORIOUS FLAVIUS RECESVINTUS, KING

VII. Of Incriminating the King, or Speaking Ill of Him

As we have forbidden all persons to either plot treason, or to institute violence against the king, so it shall also be unlawful to either accuse him of crime, or utter maledictions against him. For the authority of the Sacred Scriptures does not permit evil to be spoken of one's neighbor, and declares that he who curses the prince, is an offender against the people. Wherefore, whoever shall accuse the prince of crime or shall utter curses against him, and, instead of humbly and respectfully admonishing him as to his life, shall boldly insult him with pride and contumely; or, in order to degrade him, shall refer to him in ignominious, base, and injurious language; if the offender should belong to the nobility or to a family of high rank, no matter whether he is a member of the clergy or of the laity, as soon as he has been detected and convicted, he shall forfeit half of all his property, which the prince shall have the privilege of disposing of according to his pleasure. If, however, he should belong to the lower classes, or those without dignity and position, both his property and his person shall be at the absolute disposal of the king. And even should the king be dead, these same provisions shall apply to whoever dares to defame his memory. For the living vainly cast the darts of slander against the dead, who, having departed this life, cannot be affected by abuse, or influenced by criticism. But, for the reason that he is evidently insane who heaps detraction upon one who cannot comprehend it; the slanderer shall receive fifty lashes, and his presumption shall be silenced. But the privilege is given freely to all, while the prince is either living or dead, to discuss all matters pertaining to any cause he may have before the legal tribunals and to use such arguments as may be proper and right, and obtain such judgment as he may be entitled to; for, by this means, we endeavor to establish reverence for human dignity, as well as to maintain faithfully the justice of God.

FLAVIUS CHINTASVINTUS, KING

VIII. Of Annulling the Laws of Foreign Nations

We both permit and desire that the laws of foreign nations shall be studied for the sake of the useful knowledge that may be obtained from them, but we reject and prohibit their employment in the business of the courts. For although they may be couched in eloquent language, they abound in difficulties; and so long as the methods, principles and precepts contained in this body of laws suffice for the purposes of justice, we are unwilling that anything more be borrowed, either from the Roman laws, or from the institutions of foreigners.

THE GLORIOUS FLAVIUS RECESVINTUS, KING

IX. No One shall presume to have in his Possession another Book of Laws except this which has just been Published

No one of our subjects, whosoever, shall presume to offer to a judge as authority, in any legal proceeding, any book of laws excepting this one, or an authorized translation of the same; and any person who does this shall pay thirty pounds of gold to the treasury. And if any judge shall not at once destroy such a prohibited book when it is offered him, he shall undergo the above named penalty. But we decree that those shall be exempt from the operation of this law, who have cited former laws, not for the overthrow of ours, but in confirmation of causes which have previously been determined.

THE GLORIOUS FLAVIUS
CHINTASVINTUS, KING

X. Concerning Fast Days and Festivals, during which no Legal Business shall be Transacted

No litigation shall be commenced on Sunday, for religion should take precedence of all legal matters, and upon that day no one shall presume to subject another to annoyances either for the trial of a case, or for the payment of a debt; nor shall any person be permitted to bring a suit at Easter; that is, for fifteen days, the seven which precede the celebration of that festival, and the seven which follow it. The days of Christmas, of the Circumcision, of the Epiphany, of the Ascension, and of Pentecost shall be observed with the same reverence; and, in like manner, during the harvest festivals, from the fifteenth Kalends of August, to the fifteenth Kalends of September, the same pious conformity shall be required. But in the province of Carthage, by reason of the constant ravages of the locust, we decree that the harvest festival shall be celebrated from the fifteenth Kalends of July to the fifteenth Kalends of August; and, on account of the vintage, from the fifteenth Kalends of October to the fifteenth Kalends of November.

This provision we decree shall be obeyed by all; so that, during these festivals, no one may be summoned to court, or subjected to prosecution, unless the suit in which he is concerned has already been brought before the judge. For there can be no reason, if the action should still be undecided, that he who has been sued should be placed at any disadvantage on account of holidays. And if either of the parties is a person of credit and honor, he may depart the court, under his promise to return. But if he should be of doubtful faith. he shall provide securities for such time as is necessary; either until the cause has been decided, or until the judge shall appoint a time for it to be heard. An exception should be made, however, against those who have committed a crime punishable with death, who may be arrested upon any of the hereinbefore mentioned days, and kept in close custody, until Sunday or the above-named festivals shall have passed, when they shall be subjected to the vengeance of the presiding judge. The harvest or vintage festivals shall, in no way, interfere with the punishment of criminals and malefactors worthy of death. But the law shall not hold him excusable who, not yet having been brought into court, knows that he shall eventually be summoned there, and who, concealing himself for the rest of the time, appears in the presence of him to whom he is liable, only on the festival days aforesaid, thinking that, through no process of the law, he can be held until the cause is heard: such a person we decree shall be placed under restraint until the case of plaintiff shall have been disposed of. And if there should be any one concerning whose good faith there may be suspicions, and who cannot find security, he shall remain in custody, until, the holidays having expired, the cause in which he has been summoned shall be decided. And if any one shall presume to act contrary to the decree of this law, and shall come to the judge with a complaint upon the days which are prohibited, as aforesaid, he shall be scourged in public with fifty lashes.

XI. No cause shall be Heard by the Judges which is not Sanctioned by the Law

No one has a right to hear a cause which is not authorized by the laws; but the governor of the city or the judge, either in person, or by their messengers, may cause both parties to appear before the king, that the matter may be disposed of at his discretion; and after this promulgation, such decisions shall have all the force of law.

FLAVIUS RECESVINTUS, KING

XII. When Causes have once been Determined, at no Time shall They be Revived; but They shall be Disposed of according to the Arrangement of this Book: the Addition of Other Laws being One of the Prerogatives of the King

Whatever legal proceedings have heretofore been begun, but remain unfinished, we decree shall be disposed of according to these laws. But those causes which, before these laws have been amended by us, have been legally decided, that is, according to the tenor of the laws which prevailed previous to our reign, shall under no circumstances whatever be revived. But, if the judgment of the prince should approve it, and conditions require it, he shall have the right to add other laws, which shall have the same validity and force as those now in existence.

THE GLORIOUS FLAVIUS RECESVINTUS, KING

XIII. It shall be Lawful for No One to Hear and Determine Causes except Those Whom either the King, the Parties by Voluntary Consent, or the Judge, shall have Invested with Judicial Powers

It shall be lawful for no one to decide causes unless authorized either by the mandate of the prince, or by the consent of the parties evidenced by an agreement made in the presence of three witnesses, and attested by their seals or signatures. If those, however, who have received from the king authority to preside in court, or those who exercise judicial functions either through the appointment of magistrates or judges, should delegate their powers in writing to others who are properly qualified, the latter shall have the same power in determining or settling affairs pertaining to their offices, as the judges themselves, or the other officials from whom they received their commissions.

THE GLORIOUS FLAVIUS RECESVINTUS, KING

XIV. What Causes shall be Heard, and to what Persons Causes shall be Assigned for a Decision

While deputies are permitted to render judgment in certain criminal and civil cases, they must not presume to release criminals under the sentence of the law, but shall see that

267

said sentence is duly executed; and those who choose such deputies, should solemnly impress upon them that, during their absence, they should act with moderation and decide with justice.

THE GLORIOUS FLAVIUS RECESVINTUS, KING

XV. Judges Shall Decide Criminal as well as Civil Causes
The judges shall have all of the business of the court under their control, as they have full authority to dispose of all criminal and civil business. But Defenders of the Peace can not dispose of other causes than those which the royal power has permitted them to determine. The Defender of the Peace is he who has been appointed by the royal authority for the sole purpose of settling legal disputes between the parties.

FLAVIUS CHINTASVINTUS, KING

XVI. Concerning the Punishment of Those who Presume to Act as Judges, who have not been Invested with Judicial Power
No one shall presume, either by decree, or by means of a bailiff, to either imprison or oppress any person, in any way, in a district over which he has not been appointed, or where he has no judicial authority, unless by the order of the king, or by agreement of the parties, or under instructions of a governor or a judge, in accordance with what has been stated in a former law relating to the appointment of judges. And, where a non-appointed judge, as aforesaid, is guilty of usurpation, and unlawfully presumes to do things that are prohibited, as soon as this fact shall come to the knowledge of the governor of the province, whether he is acting in his own proper person, or by a deputy, he shall cause the illegal act to be punished; and the magistrate who has thus exceeded his authority shall pay a pound of gold to him whose rights have been affected, if insult or injury have alone been committed. But if said person who has illegally assumed judi-

cial functions, shall boldly deprive anyone of any property, or order it to be done, he shall not only make restitution, but shall be compelled to surrender an equal amount of his own property to the party injured. And if any judge shall appoint his own slave, or the slave of another, to transact any legal business, the judge who appointed him shall render full satisfaction to the law for whatever injustice said slave shall commit. Any bailiff who, acting under the orders of such an usurper of judicial authority, shall arrest or imprison any one, or remove any of his property, shall be scourged with a hundred lashes, and, in this way, shall pay the penalty of his insolence.

FLAVIUS CHINTASVINTUS, KING

XVII. Concerning Those who Ignore the Letters of the Judge, or His Seal, Calling Them to Court

When application has been made to the judge by a plaintiff, he may compel the other party to come into court, either by means of a letter or by his seal, in this manner, to wit: that the messenger of the judge shall offer the letter or seal to him who has been summoned, in the presence of respectable witnesses. And if, after having received said summons, he should either delay, or refuse to appear, he shall forfeit five golden *solidi* to the plaintiff, on account of his delay or refusal, and five more to the judge on account of contempt. But if he should not have the means to pay this fine, he shall, for each offence, receive fifty lashes in the presence of the judge, but they must be so inflicted as to place upon him no permanent mark of infamy. But if he should only be guilty of contempt, and should not have the means wherewith to render satisfaction, he shall receive thirty lashes, without further penalty. And if he who has been sued shall declare, before he receives punishment from the judge, that he has, in no way, been guilty of delay, or contempt, and shall be unable to prove this fact by witnesses, and shall make oath that, at no time, has he been guilty of contempt as aforesaid, he shall be exempt from the condemnation and punishment hereinbefore mentioned. But if any bishop, relying upon the privileges of the sacerdotal order, shall ignore the summons of the judge, and neglect to give security for his appearance, he shall, without delay, be compelled, either by the presiding judge, or by the governor or lord of the province, to pay a fine of fifty *solidi*: of which sum the judge shall receive twenty *solidi*, on account of contempt, and the plaintiff the remaining thirty. But if any priest, deacon, clerk, or monk, after receiving the letter or seal of the judge, should delay to answer either in his own person or by a representative, or should continue obstinately in contempt, he shall undergo the punishment hereinbefore mentioned, according to the provisions of the law relating to the laity; and if he should not have the means to pay his fine, the bishop may be notified, that he may have the privilege of paying the same for him, if he so desires. But if he should be unwilling to do so, the bishop must bind himself by oath, in the presence of the judge, that he will place the above-named person under such restraint that he shall be compelled to fast continuously for the space of thirty days, and shall only receive each day at sunset, a little bread and water; that, by this means, his contumacy may be punished in a proper manner. It shall always be in the discretion of the judge, that if it should be evident that, either through age or sickness, a severe sentence could not be endured; the judge shall not inflict the extreme penalty to any one belonging to any rank of the clergy, or upon a layman; but the illness or age of the offender being taken into consideration, he may impose such a penalty that the person in contempt may not thereby undergo either great weakness or exhaustion, or death. Any one who refuses to obey the mandate of the judge, and conceals himself, so that the judge cannot easily find him, and does not present himself in court within four days after the appointed time, but presents himself upon the fifth day, shall not be subject to the sentence of this law. In like manner, if any one, who, at the time, is distant more than a hundred miles, should appear upon the eleventh day after the appointed time, he shall not undergo the penalty of this law. And also, if he who is distant two hundred miles, should present himself in court on the twenty-first day after he has been summoned; he shall be free from punishment under this law. And a similar regulation shall prevail where the length of the journey is still longer. And, finally, if he to whom reasonable time has been given, should purposely delay, and does not appear, upon the last day prescribed by law, the judge shall at once grant the prayer of the plaintiff; and if, subsequently, the other party should appear in court, and the twenty-first day shall have passed, he shall be fined twenty *solidi* of gold. And if he that is distant more than a hundred miles, should exceed the term of eleven days, he shall be liable to a fine of ten *solidi*: of which the judge shall reserve for himself half, and the other half shall be given to the plaintiff. But if sickness should prevent one who is summoned from appearing; or if he should be hindered by an inundation; or his path across the mountains should be obstructed by snows; this must plainly appear; and the truth must be established either by credible witnesses, or by the oath of the party himself.

FLAVIUS CHINTASVINTUS, KING

XVIII. Where a Judge Refuses to Hear a Litigant, or Decides Fraudulently, or Ignorantly

If any one should file a complaint against another before a judge, and the latter should refuse to hear him, or deny him the use of his seal, or under different pretexts, should delay the trial of his cause, not permitting it to be heard, through favor to a client or a friend, and the plaintiff can prove this by witnesses, the judge shall give to him to whom he has refused a hearing, as compensation for his trouble, a sum equal to that which the plaintiff would have received from his adversary by due course of law; and he who brought the suit may have it continued until the time appointed by law;

and, when it comes before the court for trial, he shall receive the judgment to which he is entitled. But if the plaintiff should be unable to prove either the fraud or undue procrastination of the judge, the latter shall make oath that he, through no malice, nor through favor or friendship, has delayed the hearing, and, by reason of this oath, the judge shall in no manner be deemed guilty.

The judge shall be permitted, for two days in every week, or every day during the noon hour, to desist from holding court, and to repose in quiet at home. But, for the remaining time, he shall attend to the business of his office, and, without any unnecessary delay, determine such matters as may be brought before him.

XIX. Where a Judge, either through Convenience to Himself, or through Want of Proper Knowledge, Decides a Cause Improperly

If any judge should render judgment for the sake of gain, and direct that ony one should be treated with injustice, he who has been benefited by the decision of the said judge shall make restitution. And the judge himself, who has thus acted contrary to the precepts of equity, shall surrender to the losing party the same amount of his own property, as he has ordered him to be deprived of; that is to say, that in addition to the restitution that has been made, he shall, in satisfaction for his improper conduct, give to him whom he unjustly condemned, a sum equal to that which was disposed of by his decree. But if he should not have sufficient property wherewith to make amends, he shall be deprived of all that he is known to possess, and shall be delivered as a slave to him to whom he is indebted, or, after having been exposed in public, he shall receive fifty lashes. But if he shall have rendered an unjust judgment through ignorance, and can declare under oath that he has done this only through want of knowledge, and not through partiality or cupidity, or for the sake of profit, his judgment shall be invalid, and he himself shall not be considered guilty.

FLAVIUS CHINTASVINTUS, KING

XX. When a Judge, either through Deceit or Cunning, Imposes Needless Costs upon Either, or Both the Parties to a Suit

It is part of our duty quietly and carefully to admonish judges not to subject litigants to unnecessary delay, or impose heavy costs upon them. But, if it appears that, through craft or cunning, a judge has so delayed matters that one or both parties have suffered injury, he shall be compelled to refund to them all costs that have been incurred after eight days from the time the action was begun; the facts having been established under oath. But if either through illness or from considerations of public utility, the judge should be prevented from performing his duties, he shall not subject the litigants to delay, but shall dismiss them at once, and shall appoint a time for the hearing of the cause.

XXI. What, First of All, a Judge should be Familiar With, in order that he may Understand a Case

In order that he may be perfectly familiar with a case the judge should first interrogate the witnesses; then he should examine the documents, if any there be; and, that the truth may the more certainly be determined, the oaths of the parties should finally be taken with all due reverence. The true investigation of justice demands that written instruments should take precedence over everything else; and that necessity alone justifies the administration of oaths to the parties. But in those cases where there is no documentary evidence, or other proof, or where the judge shall not be able to decide without it, the parties to the suit shall be sworn.

FLAVIUS CHINTASVINTUS, KING

XXII. Where the Integrity of a Judge is said to be Suspected by Any One of Honorable Rank, or where a Judge presumes to render a Decision Contrary to Law

If any one should declare that he suspects the integrity of

273

either a judge, a governor, a vice-governor, or any other official, and demands access to his superior, or shall even allege that he has suspicion of that superior himself, he shall not be subject to delay on this account, especially if he should be poor. But those who decide the case shall do so with the bishop of the diocese, and their opinions and judgment shall be reduced to writing, and be signed by them; and he who has declared that he suspected the judge, should he desire to bring a suit against him, after judgment has been rendered in the case in question, shall have the right to summon that judge to appear before the king. And if a judge or an ecclesiastic should be convicted of having decided wrongfully in any cause, the property of which the complainant has been deprived shall be restored to him, and an equal quantity of property shall be given him by way of satisfaction, by those who are proved to have rendered an unrighteous judgment. And if anyone should lodge an unjust complaint against a judge, and it should appear that the cause in question has been properly decided, the accuser shall undergo the same penalty which the judge would have suffered. And if he should not have the property wherewith to make amends, after having been exposed in public he shall receive thirty lashes in the presence of the judge himself.

If anyone, however, should allege that he possesses information which relates to the interests of the Crown, access to our presence shall not be denied him.

FLAVIUS CHINTASVINTUS, KING

XXIII. How a Judge should render Judgment

If the lawsuit is important, or matters involving the ownership of valuable property are in question, the judge shall, in the presence of both parties, make two copies of the decree, which shall be exactly similar in text and signature, and each party shall be given one of them. But where affairs of minor importance are concerned, only such things as have been testified to in favor of him who prevailed, shall be reduced to writing by the judge. He who has been defeated shall be entitled to a transcript of the decree and of the testimony of the witnesses, should he desire it. But if the party who has been brought into court in any case, shall declare in the presence of the judge that it is not necessary for the plaintiff to introduce any evidence, the judge shall put the decree in writing, and confirm it with his signature, however insignificant the action may be, in order that the matter may not, under any circumstances, be brought up again in the future. But if, under an order of the court, one party should offer witnesses, and, at the time that their testimony is to be heard, the other party should be absent himself without the knowledge of the judge, the testimony of the witnesses shall be received, and what they have established by their evidence shall be given in writing, under seal, to him who produced them. It shall not be lawful for him who fraudulently left the court to afterwards offer any evidence in the case, but he shall have the privilege, before the death of any witness who has testified against him, to adduce any reasonable accusation against him, which shall be heard by the judge; and if the accused witness should have been manifestly guilty of perjury, his testimony shall be rejected. And if, after such examination, all the witnesses should be impeached but one, he who has offered the testimony, must produce other witnesses to prove his case, within the space of three months. But, if he is unable to find any, the property in question shall remain in the possession of him who formerly held it. The judge shall always keep copies of the judgment which he has rendered, to prevent a renewal of any controversies in the future.

FLAVIUS CHINTASVINTUS, KING

XXIV. Concerning the Emoluments and the Punishment of the Judge, and of the Bailiff

There are some judges who, on account of cupidity, and in violation of the provisions of the law, presume to reserve for themselves the third part of the property involved in the causes which are brought before them; wherefore, we now decree by the present law, in order to effectually abolish this practice, that no judge shall accept more for his trouble, after the case has been properly considered and decided, than has been fixed by a former law, to wit, twenty *solidi*. If any one should fraudulently attempt to extort more than this sum, he shall lose the entire compensation which he would have lawfully received; and also, because he has unjustly appropriated more than twenty *solidi*, contrary to the provisions of the law, he shall pay double that amount to him from whom he directed it should be taken. And likewise, because we are aware that certain bailiffs who busy themselves in the affairs of others, receive greater compensation for their labor than they deserve; we also decree by this law, that no bailiff who is employed in any lawsuit, shall have more than ten *solidi* for his fee. And if any one should presume to extort more than this established amount, he shall not only lose his legitimate fee, but also he shall restore to the person from whom he received it, double the amount which he has extorted. The fees of both judge and bailiff shall be paid by the party against whom judgment is rendered; and if a case should occur where a settlement cannot be made, the legal compensation of the judge and the bailiff shall be required of both parties. The same rule shall apply to a debtor who did not return upon the appointed day, the money which he has borrowed; as well as to one who unjustly retains the property of another; and also, in cases of partition, where both parties demand their rights from the judge, it shall be required of each of them, that he pay to the court his portion of the fees aforesaid. And, likewise, where no crime has been proved; or no contempt, unlawful possession, or indebtedness have been established; this provision shall be in force, and the fees of the judge and the bailiff shall be paid by both parties.

In cases of partition, where one of the parties causes unnecessary delay; as soon as the fact shall come to knowledge of the judge, he may exact his fee and that of the bailiff from him who has delayed to assert his claims within the specified time. If any corrupt bailiff should fail to execute an order of the judge, when the property involved is worth an ounce of gold, or less, the bailiff shall pay to him who is entitled to the judgment, a *solidus* of gold; and where the property is worth more, he shalll pay for every ounce, a *solidus,* on account of his delay. And if the property in question should be worth more than two ounces, and not more than a pound of gold, said bailiff shall receive ten lashes, and the number of lashes shall increase with the number of pounds of gold.

If the cause or the party is of minor importance, and the bailiff must travel to perform his duties, he shall be entitled to two common horses, from the plaintiff, in addition to his fees. But if the cause should be important, and the party of high rank, the bailiff shall not be entitled to demand more than six horses for the purpose of his journey.

FLAVIUS RECESVINTUS, KING

XXV. Every one who is Invested with Judicial Power shall legally bear the Title of Judge

As the remedies of the law are applied in many ways, it is decreed, that a duke, count, vicar, deputy, and any other official, who, either by the royal order, or by consent of the parties, has been, or shall be, selected to determine questions of law; or any person of whatever rank invested with the legal right to preside in court; as well as all to whom has been delegated the power to decide causes; shall be invested with the name of judge, and shall be entitled to the rights, and subject to the liabilities of that office, whether these relate to the emoluments or the penalties attaching to the same.

XXVI. Every Bond that is Exacted by a Judge, after an Unjust Decree, shall be held Invalid.

We occasionally find that justice is distorted, and deprived of its proper force, by unjust judges; and see injustice, confirmed by their decrees, prevail in its stead. And, indeed, certain judges after they have rendered unjust decrees, cause one or both the parties to bind themselves in writing, in order that the wrongful judgment that has been rendered may not at any time thereafter be remedied; but where such a transaction is not fair and honorable, but entered into with the manifest intention of oppressing any one whose cause is just, the matter may be reviewed; and all obligations relating thereto shall be declared invalid, and not, in any way, authorized by law.

FLAVIUS RECESVINTUS, KING

XXVII. An Unjust Decree, or an Unjust Interpretation of the Law, Prompted by Fear of the Throne, or Made by Order of the King, shall be Invalid

Sometimes the influence of power defeats the ends of justice, and although it often prevails, it is certain that it always inflicts injury; for, when the abuse of authority once causes oppression, it never permits the restoration of justice to its original integrity. Therefore, as judges through fear, or at the command of princes, sometimes decide questions contrary to law, for the sake of the peace of our kingdom we have determined, to cure two diseases with one remedy; declaring that when it should have been discovered that any document has been drawn up, or any judgment rendered, not according to justice or to the established laws, but by the command or through the dread of the king, then that which is evidently contrary to justice and to the laws shall be void; and those who have rendered the judgment or have caused it to be rendered, shall receive no mark of infamy, nor be subjected to any punishment whatever; and any judge shall be immune from the penalties of the law, if he will swear that he has decided wrongfully, not through his own depravity, but on account of royal compulsion.

FLAVIUS RECESVINTUS, KING

XXVIII. Concerning the Power, conferred upon Bishops, of Restraining Judges who Decide Wrongfully

We direct the ministers of God, to whom the Divine authority has been committed to remedy the misfortunes of oppression and poverty, that they admonish, with paternal piety, such judges as oppress the people with unjust decrees, by which means such wrongs may be remedied. But if any magistrate, invested with judicial functions, has either decided unjustly, or has imposed a wrongful sentence upon any one, then the bishop in whose diocese this has been done, shall summon the judge who is alleged to have acted unjustly, and shall render a just decision, sitting along with him, in the presence of ecclesiastics, or other persons of respectability. But if the judge, moved by perversity, refuses to correct the iniquitous judgment given by him, after the bishop has exhorted him to do so, then the bishop shall have the privilege of reviewing the case, and of rendering judgment alone; and the wrongful decision of the judge, subsequently set aside by him, as well as his own decision, shall be committed to writing, and be deposited among the records of the court. The bishop shall so act toward the party who has been oppressed, and liberated by him from that oppression, that truth may be established and confirmed by our authority. If the judge should prevent the party whom he has oppressed from appearing before the bishop, he shall forfeit two pounds of gold to the king.

FLAVIUS CHINTASVINTUS, KING

XXIX. The Judge, when Inquired of by a Party, should be able to give a Reason for His Decision

Every judge is hereby admonished that if a demand is made upon him by any one, he shall give the reasons in their proper order, for the decision he has made; and this he shall do, either in the presence of the governor of the city, or of those whom the governor has chosen to represent him. And if the matter has been brought before the king, those judges whom the king shall appoint for the purpose, shall decide the cause, without the presence of the bishop and the other judges. And if, after the action has been brought to an end, either before the bishop or before the governor, either of the parties should present himself, a second time, with the royal order, he who heard or decided the cause in the first place, must account for his conduct to those who have been specially appointed judges by the royal decree; so that in case he should be found to have rendered an improper decision, he may give satisfaction therefor to the plaintiff before the law. And if the plaintiff shall have filed an unjust complaint, he shall be condemned to suffer the legal penalty prescribed for the same.

FLAVIUS RECESVINTUS, KING

XXX. Concerning the Punishment of Judges who Appropriate the Property of Others

While it is evident that judges have been appointed for the purpose of remedying evils, some of them, on the other hand, with all the insolence of power, attempt to attack those very things which, according to the principles of equity, they ought to defend. For, once invested with authority, some judges do not hesitate to assume illegal control over the property of others; and do not fear, under almost any pretext, to subject them to unreasonable expense in the exercise of official tyranny. Henceforth, any judge who shall take any property belonging to another, contrary to an order of court, or in violation of law, or shall injure said property in any way, shall be condemned to suffer the same penalty which he, acting in his judicial capacity, would have imposed upon any one guilty of the same offence.

FLAVIUS RECESVINTUS, KING

XXXI. Concerning those who Treat the Royal Order with Disdain

Any freeman who shall have been convicted of having disobeyed the royal summons, or shall have been proved to have acted in such a manner that his duplicity is apparent, and shall say contrary to the truth, that he has neither seen nor received the summons; if he is a person of noble birth, he shall pay three pounds of gold to the treasury; but, if he should not have sufficient property to pay this fine, he shall receive a hundred lashes with the scourge, without any degradation of rank. But if he should have been prevented from travelling by sickness, tempest, inundation, or snow, or by unavoidable trouble of any kind, and this should be established by the testimony of reliable witnesses, he shall not be considered guilty of disobedience to the royal order; or be liable to any punishment, as it is evident that the delay was the result of manifest necessity.

XXXII. How the Judge should Inquire into Causes by the Ordeal of Hot Water

We are aware that many persons assert that they have received injuries at the hands of freeborn citizens; and it is our opinion that torture should be applied in such instances, where an amount exceeding three hundred *solidi* is involved; and we now declare this to be a salutary measure, and decree that whenever crime has been committed by anyone, where a small amount of property is concerned, the ordeal by hot water be instituted by the judge; and should the accused appear to be guilty, the judge shall not hesitate to put him to the torture, and after confession has been obtained, he shall inflict upon the criminal the sentence of the law provided in such cases. If, after the test, he should prove to be innocent, his accuser shall incur no reproach whatever. This test shall also be applied to suspicious persons who present themselves in court to give testimony against others.

IX.

PHILOSOPHIES OF CRIME AND MORALITY

GROTIUS (or DE GROTT)
(1583-1645)

The founder of the science of international law and a distinguished Dutch scholar. He was a theologian and brilliant jurist as well as an astute thinker. In Rotterdam he was Chief Magistrate but was banished as an opposer of the strict Calvinistic doctrine. Later he became the Swedish ambassador to France and wrote extensively. One of his most famous works—*"ON THE LAW OF WAR AND PEACE"*— is still used as a text on international law.

ON THE RIGHT OVER PRISONERS
OF WAR (1625)*

I. By the law of nature, in its primaeval state, apart from human institutions and customs, no men can be slaves: and it is in this sense that legal writers maintain the opinion that slavery is repugnant to nature. Yet in a former part of this treatise, it was shewn that there is nothing repugnant to natural justice, in deriving the origin of servitude from human actions, whether founded upon compact or crime.

But the law of nations now under consideration is of wider extent both in its authority over persons, and its effects. For, as to persons, not only those, who surrender their rights, or engage themselves to servitude, are considered in the light of slaves, but all, who are taken prisoners in public and solemn war, come under the same description from the time that they are carried into the places, of which the enemy is master.

Nor is the commission of crime requisite to reduce them to this condition, but the fate of all is alike, who are un-

* From *The Rights of War and Peace* translated from the original Latin by A. C. Campbell.

fortunately taken within the territories of an enemy, upon the breaking out of war.

II. and III. In ancient times, while slavery was permitted to exist, the offspring, born during captivity or servitude, continued in the same condition as the parents.—The consequences of such rules were of wide extent;—there was no cruelty, which masters might not inflict upon their slaves;—there was no service, the performance of which they might not compel;—the power even of life and death was in their hands. However the Roman laws at length set bounds to such wanton power, at least to the exercise of it within the Roman territories.

Every thing too, found upon the prisoner's person, became a lawful prize to the captor. For as Justinian observes, one who was entirely in the power of another could have no property of his own.

IV. and V. Incorporeal rights, gained by the enemy, along with the person so captured, cannot be considered in the light of primary and original acquisitions. And there are some rights so purely personal in their nature, that they cannot be lost even by captivity, nor the duties attached thereto ever be relinquished. Of such a nature was the paternal right among the Romans. For rights of this kind cannot exist but immediately with the person to whom they originally belonged.

All these rights to prizes, which were introduced by the law of nations, were intended as an inducement to captors to refrain from cruel rigour of putting prisoners to death; as they might hope to derive some advantage from sparing and saving them. From hence Pomponius deduces the origin of the word, SERVUS, or SLAVE, being one, who might have been put to death, but from motives of interest or humanity had been saved.

VI. (being the IX. of the original.) It has long been a maxim, universally received among the powers of Christendom, that prisoners of war cannot be made slaves, so as to be sold, or compelled to the hardships and labour attached to slavery. And they have with good reason embraced the latter principle. As it would be inconsistent with every precept of the law of charity, for men to refuse abandoning a cruel right, unless they might be allowed to substitute another, of great, though somewhat inferior rigour, in its place.

And this, as Gregoras informs us, became a traditionary principle among all who professed one common religion; nor was it confined to those, who lived under the authority of the Roman empire, but prevailed among the Thessalians, the Illyrians, the Triballians, and Bulgarians.— Though such an abolition of slavery, and mitigation of captivity may be considered as of trivial import, yet they were effects produced by the introduction of the Christian religion, especially upon recollection that Socrates tried, but without effect, to prevail upon the Greeks to forbear making slaves of each other.

In this respect the Mahometans act towards each other in the same manner as Christians do. Though it is still the practice among Christian powers to detain prisoners of war, till their ransom be paid, the amount of which depends upon the will of the Conqueror, unless it has been settled by express treaty. The right of detaining such prisoners has sometimes been allowed to the individuals, who took them, except where the prisoners were personages of extraordinary rank, who were always considered as prisoners of war to the state.

CESARE BECCARIA

Beccaria, an economist, jurist and criminologist, was born in Italy in 1738. A modest man, he nevertheless held several public offices in Italy and was effective in stimulating penal reform throughout Europe.

His most famous work was his *Essay on Crimes and Punishments,* an excerpt from which is presented here. Published in 1764, it was one of the first arguments against capital punishment and the inhumane treatment of prisoners. Over and above these practical points, however, the *Essay* is laced with a beautifully stated and high-minded utilitarian idealism that had considerable influence on such as Bentham and Voltaire.

AN ESSAY ON
CRIMES AND PUNISHMENTS

Consequences of the Right to Punish

The laws only can determine the punishment of crimes; and the authority of making penal laws can only reside with the legislator, who represents the whole society, united by the social compact. No magistrate then (as he is one of the society) can, with justice, inflict on any other member of the same society, punishment that is not ordained by the laws. But as a punishment, increased beyond the degree fixed by the law, is the just punishment, with the addition of another; it follows, that no magistrate, even under a pretense of zeal, or the public good, should increase the punishment already determined by the laws.

If every individual be bound to society, society is equally

bound to him, by a contract, which from its nature equally binds both parties. This obligation, which descends from the throne to the cottage, and equally binds the highest and lowest of mankind, signifies nothing more, than that it is the interest of all, that conventions, which are useful to the greatest number, should be punctually observed. The violation of this compact by any individual, is an introduction to anarchy.

The sovereign, who represents the society itself, can only make general laws, to bind the members; but it belongs not to him to judge whether any individual has violated the social compact, or incurred the punishment in consequence. For in this case there are two parties, one represented by the sovereign, who insists upon the violation of the contract, and the other is the person accused, who denies it. It is necessary then, that there should be a third person to decide this contest; that is to say, a judge, or magistrate, from whose determination there should be no appeal; and this determination should consist of a simple affirmation, or negation of fact.

If it can only be proved, that the severity of punishments, though not immediately contrary to the public good, or to the end for which they were intended, viz. to prevent crimes be useless: then such severity would be contrary to those beneficent virtues derived from that enlightened reason, which instructs the sovereign to wish rather to govern then in a state of freedom and happiness, than of slavery. It would also be contrary to justice, and the social compact.

Of the Interpretation of Laws

Judges, in criminal cases, have no right to interpret penal laws, because they are not legislators. They have not received the laws from our ancestors as a domestic tradition, or as a will which the survivors are bound only to obey; but they receive them from a society actually existing, or from the

289

sovereign, its representative. Even the authority of laws is not founded on any pretended obligation, or ancient convention; for such convention would be null, as it cannot bind those who did not exist at the time of its institution; and unjust, as it would reduce men, in the ages following, to a herd of brutes, without any power of judging or acting. The laws receive their force and authority from an oath of fidelity, either tacit or expressed, which living subjects have sworn to their sovereign, in order to restrain the intestine fermentation of the private interests of individuals. From hence springs their true and natural authority. Who then is their lawful interpreter? The sovereign, that is, the representative of society, and not the judge, whose office is only to examine, if a man have, or have not committed an action contrary to the laws.

In every criminal cause the judge should reason syllogistically. The *major* should be the general law; the *minor* the conformity of the action or its opposition to the laws, the *conclusion,* liberty, or punishment. If the judge be obliged by the imperfection of the laws, or to make any other, or more syllogisms than this, it will be an introduction to uncertainty.

There is nothing more dangerous than the common axiom: *the spirit of the laws is to be considered.* To adopt it is to give way to the torrent of opinions. This may seem a paradox to vulgar minds, which are more strongly affected by the smallest disorder before their eyes, than by the most pernicious, though remote, consequences produced by one false principle adopted by a nation.

Our knowledge is in proportion to the number of our ideas. The more complex these are, the greater is the variety of positions in which they may be considered. Every man hath his own particular point of view, and at different times sees the same objects in very different lights. The spirit of the laws will then be the result of the good or bad logic of the judge; and this will depend on his good or bad digestion;

on the violence of his passions; on the rank and condition of the accused, or on his connections with the judge, and on all those little circumstances which change the appearance of objects in the fluctuating mind of man. Hence we see the fate of a delinquent changed many times in passing through different courts of judicature, and his life and liberty victims to the false ideas or ill humor of the judge; who mistakes the vague result of his own confused reasoning for the just interpretation of the laws. We see the same crimes punished in a different manner at different times in the same tribunals; the consequence of not having consulted the constant and invariable voice of the laws, but the erring instability of arbitrary interpretation.

The disorders that may arise from a rigorous observance of the letter of penal laws, are not to be compared with those produced by the interpretation of them. The first are temporary inconveniences which will oblige the legislature to correct the letter of the law, the want of preciseness, and uncertainty of which has occasioned these disorders; and this will put a stop to the fatal liberty of explaining; the source of arbitrary and venal declamations. When the rule of right, which ought to direct the actions of the philosopher, as well as the ignorant, is a matter of controversy, not of fact, the people are slaves to the magistrates. The despotism of this multitude of tyrants is more insupportable, the less the distance is between the oppressor and the oppressed; more fatal than that of one, for the tyranny of many is not to be shaken off but by having recourse to that of one alone. It is more cruel, as it meets with more opposition, and the cruelty of a tyrant is not in proportion to his strength, but to the obstacles that oppose him.

These are the means by which security of person and property is best obtained; which is just, as it is the purpose of uniting in society; and it is useful as each person may calculate exactly the inconveniences attending every crime. By these means, subjects will acquire a spirit of independence and liberty; however it may appear to those who dare to call the weakness of submitting blindly to their capricious and interested opinions by the sacred name of virtue.

These principles will displease those who have made it a rule with themselves, to transmit to their inferiors the tyranny they suffer from their superiors. I should have every thing to fear, if tyrants were to read my book; but tyrants never read.

Of the Obscurity of Laws.

If the power of interpreting laws be an evil, obscurity in them must be another, as the former consequence of the latter. This evil will be still greater, if the laws be written in a language unknown to the people; who, being ignorant of the consequences of their own actions, become necessarily dependent on a few, the interpreters of laws, which, instead of being public and general, are thus rendered private and particular. What must we think of mankind, when we reflect, that such is the established custom of the greatest part of our polished and enlightened Europe? Crimes will be less frequent, in proportion as the code of laws is more universally read and understood; for there is no doubt that the eloquence of the passions is greatly assisted by the ignorance and uncertainty of punishments.

Hence it follows, that without written laws, no society will ever acquire a fixed form of government, in which the power is vested in the whole, and not in any part of the society; and in which the laws are not to be altered, but my the will of the whole, nor corrupted by the force of private interest. Experience and reason show us, that the probability of human traditions diminishes in proportion as they are distant from their sources. How then can laws resist the lasting monument of the social compact?

Hence we see the use of printing, which alone makes the public, and not a few individuals the guardians and defenders of the laws. It is this art, which, by diffusing literature, has gradually dissipated the gloomy spirit of cabal and intrigue.

To this art it is owing, that the atrocious crimes of our ancestors, who were alternately slaves and tyrants, are become less frequent. They who are acquainted with the history of the two or three last centuries, may observe, how from the lap of luxury and effeminacy, have sprung the most tender virtues, humanity, benevolence, and toleration of human errors. They may contemplate the effects of what was so improperly called ancient simplicity and good faith; humanity groaning under implacable superstition; the avarice and ambition of a few, staining with human blood the thrones and palaces of kings; secret treasons and public massacres; every noble a tyrant over the people: and the ministers of the gospel of Christ, bathing their hands in blood, in the name of the God of all mercy. We may talk as we please of the corruption and degeneracy of the present age, but happily we see no such examples of cruelty and oppression.

Of the Proportion between Crimes and Punishments

It is not only the common interest of mankind, that crimes should not be committed, but that crimes of every kind should be less frequent, in proportion to the evil they produce to society. Therefore the means made use of by the legislature to prevent crimes, should be more powerful, in proportion as they are destructive of the public safety and happiness, and as the inducements to commit them are stronger. Thence there ought to be a fixed proportion between crimes and punishments.

It is impossible to prevent entirely all the disorders which the passions of mankind cause in society. These disorders increase in proportion to the number of people, and the opposition of private interests, which cannot be directed with mathematical exactness to the public good, and instead of this exactness we must in political calculation substitute probability. If we consult history, we shall find disorders increasing, in every state, with the extent of dominion. That force, which continually impels us to our own private interest, like gravity, acts incessantly, unless it meets with an obstacle to oppose it. The effects of this force are the confused series of human actions. Punishments, which I would call political obstacles, prevent the fatal effects of private interest, without destroying the impelling cause, which is that sensibility inseparable from man. The legislator acts, in this case, like a skilful architect, who endeavors to counteract the force which may contribute to the strength of his edifice.

The necessity of uniting in society being granted, together with the conventions, which the opposite interests of individuals must necessarily require, a scale of crimes may be formed, of which the first degree should consist of those, which immediately tend to the dissolution of society, and the last, of the smallest possible injustice done to a private member of that society. Between these extremes will be comprehended, all actions contrary to the public good, which are called criminal, and which descend by insensible degrees, decreasing from the highest to the lowest. If mathematical calculation could be applied to the obscure and infinite combinations of human actions, there might be a corresponding scale of punishments, descending from the greatest to the least: but it will be sufficient that the wise legislator mark the principal divisions, without disturbing the order, lest to crimes of the *first* degree, be assigned punishments of the *last*. If there were an exact and universal scale of crimes and punishments, we should there have a common measure of the degree of liberty and slavery, humanity and cruelty of different nations.

Any action, which is not comprehended in the above mentioned scale, will not be called a crime, or punished as such, except by those who have an interest in the denomination. The uncertainty of the extreme points of this scale, hath produced a system of morality which contradicts the laws; a multitude of laws that contradict each other, and many, which expose the best men to the severest punishments, rendering the ideas of *vice* and *virtue* vague and fluctuating, and even their existence doubtful. Hence that fatal lethargy of political bodies, which terminates in their destruction.

Whoever reads, with a philosophic eye, the history of nations, and their laws, will generally find, that the ideas of virtue and vice, of a good or a bad citizen, change with the revolution of ages; not in proportion to the alteration of circumstances, and consequently conformable to the common good; but in proportion to the passions and errors by which the different law-givers were successively influenced. He will frequently observe, that the passions and vices of one age, are the foundation of the morality of the following; that violent passion, the offspring of fanaticism and enthusiasm, being weakened by time, which reduces all the phenomena of the natural and moral world to an equality, become, by degrees, the prudence of the age, and a useful instrument in the hands of the powerful, or artful politician. Hence the uncertainty of our notions of honour and virtue, an uncertainty which will ever remain, because they change with the revolutions of time, and names survive the things they originally signified; they change with the boundaries of states, which are often the same both in physical and moral geography.

Pleasure and pain are the only springs of action in beings endowed with sensibility. Even amongst the motives which incite men to acts of religion, the invisible legislator has ordained rewards and punishments. From a partial distribution of these, will arise that contradiction, so little observed, because so common; I mean, that of punishing by the laws, the crimes which the laws have occasioned. If an equal punishment be ordained for two crimes that injure society in different degrees, there is nothing to deter men from committing the greater, as often as it is attended with greater advantage.

JEREMY BENTHAM

Born in 1748, Bentham was educated at Oxford. Although he remains famous today as a philosopher and as the founder of *utilitarianism,* he was also an important jurist and political theorist of his time. Disillusionment with the practice of law occurred early in his career, and at length, abandoning all pretense at its practice, he turned his mind wholly to jurisprudence. Devoted to the possibilities of legislative reform, he spent his later years investigating the principles underlying legislation.

In THE PRINCIPLES OF MORALS AND LEGISLATION, his most renowned work, he derives from the ethics of utilitarianism a philosophy that concludes with a deterministic argument for bringing morals out of the remote mountains of abstract theory and into the field of practical legislation. He envisioned that, by so doing, the virtue and happiness of man could be secured through law.

THE LIMITS BETWEEN PRIVATE ETHICS

AND THE ART OF LEGISLATION

In the course of this enquiry—that part of it I mean which concerns the limits between the civil and the penal branch of law—it will be necessary to settle a number of points, of which the connection with the main question might not at first sight be suspected. To ascertain what sort of a thing *a* law is; what the *parts* are that are to be found in it; what it must contain in order to be *complete;* what the connection is between that part of a body of laws which belongs to the subject of *procedure* and the rest of the law at large:—all these, it will be seen, are so many problems which must be solved before any satisfactory answer can be given to the main question above mentioned.

Nor is this their only use: for it is evident enough that the notion of a complete law must first be fixed, before the legislator can in any case know what it is he has to do, or when his work is done.

Ethics at large may be defined, the art of directing men's actions to the production of the greatest possible quantity of happiness, on the part of those whose interest is in view.

What then are the actions which it can be in a man's power to direct? They must be either his own actions or those of other agents. Ethics, in as far as it is the art of directing a man's own actions, may be styled the *art of self-government,* or *private ethics.*

What other agents then are there which, at the same time they are under the influence of man's direction, are susceptible of happiness? They are of two sorts: (1) other human beings who are styled persons; (2) animals, which, on account of their interests having been neglected by the insensibility of the ancient jurists, stand degraded into the class of *things.* As to other human beings, the art of directing their actions to the above end is what we mean, or at least the only thing which upon the principle of utility we *ought* to mean, by the art of government: which, in as far as the measures it displays itself in are of a permanent nature, is generally distinguished by the name of *legislation;* as it is by that of *administration,* when they are of a temporary nature, determined by the occurrences of the day.

Now human creatures, considered with respect to the maturity of their faculties, are either in an *adult* or in a *non-adult* state. The art of government, in as far as it concerns the direction of the actions of persons in a non-adult state, may be termed the art of *education.* In as far as this business is entrusted with those who, in virtue of some private relationship, are in the main the best disposed to take upon them and the best able to discharge this office, it may be termed the art of *private education;* in as far as it is exercised by those whose province it is to superintend the conduct of the whole community, it may be termed the art of *public education.*

As to ethics in general, a man's happiness will depend, in the first place, upon such parts of his behavior as none but himself are interested in; in the next place, upon such parts of it as may affect the happiness of those about him. In as far as his happiness depends upon the first-mentioned part of his behavior, it is said to depend upon his *duty to himself.* Ethics then, in as far as it is the art of directing a man's actions in this respect, may be termed the art of discharging one's duty to oneself; and the quality which a man manifests by the discharge of this branch of duty (if duty it is to be called) is that of *prudence.* In as far as his happiness, and that of any other person or persons whose interests are considered, depends upon such parts of his behavior as may affect the interests of those about him, it may be said to depend upon his *duty to others;* or, to use a phrase now somewhat antiquated, his *duty to his neighbor.* Ethics then, in as far as it is the art of directing a man's actions in this respect, may be termed the art of discharging one's duty to one's neighbor. Now the happiness of one's neighbor may be consulted in two ways: (1) in a negative way, by forbearing to diminish it; (2) in a positive way, by studying to increase it. A man's duty to his neighbor is accordingly partly negative and partly positive: to discharge the negative branch of it, is *probity;* to discharge the positive branch, *beneficence.*

It may here be asked how it is that upon the principle of private ethics (legislation and religion out of the question) a man's happiness depends upon such parts of his conduct as affect, immediately at least, the happiness of no one but himself: this is as much as to ask, What motives (independent of such as legislation and religion may chance to furnish) can one man have to consult the happiness of another? By what motives, or, which comes to the same thing, by what obligations, can he be bound to obey the dictates of *probity* and *beneficence?* In answer to this, it cannot but be admitted that the only interests which a man at all times and upon all occasions is sure to find *adequate* motives for consulting, are his own. Notwithstanding this, there are no occasions in which a man has not some motives for consulting the happiness of other men. In the first place, he has, on all occasions, the purely social motive of sympathy or benevolence; in the next place, he has, on most occasions, the semi-social motives of love of amity and love of reputation. The motive of sympathy will act upon him with more or less effect according to the *bias* of his sensibility; the two other motives, according to a variety of circumstances, principally according to the strength of his intellectual powers, the firmness and steadiness of his mind, the quantum of his moral sensibility, and the characters of the people he has to deal with.

Now private ethics has happiness for its end; and legislation can have no other. Private ethics concerns every member, that is, the happiness and the actions of every member, of any community that can be proposed; and legislation can concern no more. Thus far, then, private ethics and the art of legislation go hand in hand. The end they have, or ought to have, in view, is of the same nature. The persons whose happiness they ought to have in view, as also the persons whose conduct they ought to be occupied in directing, are precisely the same. The very acts they ought to be conversant about, are even in a *great measure* the same. Where then lies the difference? In that the acts which they ought to be conversant about, though in a great measure, are not *perfectly and throughout* the same. There is no case in which a private man ought to direct his own conduct to the production of his own happiness and of that of his fellow-creatures; but there are cases in which the legislator ought not (in a direct way at least, and by means of punishment applied immediately to particular *individual* acts) to attempt to direct the conduct of the several other members of the community. Every act which promises to be beneficial upon the whole to the community (himself included) each individual ought to perform of himself; but it is not every such act that the legislator ought to compel him to perform. Every act which promises to be pernicious upon the whole to the community (himself included) each individual ought to abstain from of himself; but it is not every such act that the legislator ought to compel him to abstain from.

Where then is the line to be drawn? We shall not have far to seek for it. The business is to give an idea of the cases in which ethics ought, and in which legislation ought not (in a direct manner at least) to interfere. If legislation interferes in a direct manner, it must be by punishment. Now the cases in which punishment, meaning the punishment of the political sanction, ought not to be inflicted, have been already stated. If then there be any of these cases in which, although legislation ought not, private ethics does or ought to interfere, these cases will serve to point out the limits between the two arts or branches of science. These cases, it may be remembered, are of four sorts: (1) where punishment would be groundless, (2) where it would be inefficacious, (3) where it would be unprofitable, (4) where it would be needless. Let us look over all these cases, and see whether in any of them there is room for the interference of private ethics, at the same time that there is none for the direct interference of legislation.

(1) First then, as to the cases where punishment would be *groundless*. In these cases it is evident that the restrictive interference of ethics would be groundless too. It is because upon the whole there is no evil in the act, that legislation ought not to endeavor to prevent it. No more, for the same reason, ought private ethics.

(2) As to the cases in which punishment would be *inefficacious*. These, we may observe, may be divided into two sets or classes. The first do not depend at all upon the

nature of the act: they turn only upon a defect in the timing of the punishment. The punishment in question is no more than what, for anything that appears, ought to have been applied to the act in question. It ought, however, to have been applied at a different time: viz., not till after it had been properly denounced. These are the cases of an *ex post facto* law, of a judicial sentence beyond the law, and of a law not sufficiently promulgated. The acts here in question then might, for anything that appears, come properly under the department even of coercive legislation: of course do they under that of private ethics. As to the other set of cases in which punishment would be inefficacious, neither do these depend upon the nature of the act, that is, of the *sort* of act; they turn only upon some extraneous *circumstances,* with which an act of *any* sort may chance to be accompanied. These, however, are of such a nature as not only to exclude the application of legal punishment but in general to leave little room for the influence of private ethics. These are the cases where the will could not be deterred from any act even by the extraordinary force of artificial punishment—as in the cases of extreme infancy, insanity, and perfect intoxication: of course, therefore, it could not by such slender and precarious force as could be applied by private ethics. The case is in this respect the same under the circumstances of unintentionality with respect to the event of the action, unconsciousness with regard to the circumstances, and mis-supposal with regard to the existence of circumstances which have not existed, as also where the force, even of extraordinary punishment, is rendered inoperative by the superior force of a physical danger or threatened mischief. It is evident that in these cases, if the thunders of the law prove impotent, the whispers of simple morality can have but little influence.

(3) As to the cases where punishment would be *unprofitable*. These are the cases which constitute the great field for the exclusive interference of private ethics. When a punishment is unprofitable, or in other words too expensive, it is because the evil of the punishment exceeds that of the

offence. Now the evil of the punishment, we may remember, is distinguishable into four branches: (1) the evil of coercion, including constraint or restraint, according as the act commanded is of the positive kind or the negative, (2) the evil of apprehension, (3) the evil of sufferance, (4) the derivative evils resulting to persons in *connection* with those by whom the three above-mentioned original evils are sustained. Now with respect to those original evils, the persons who lie exposed to them may be two very different sets of persons: in the first place, persons who may have actually committed, or been prompted to commit, the acts really meant to be prohibited; in the next place, persons who may have performed, or been prompted to perform, such other acts as they fear may be in danger of being involved in the punishment designed only for the former. But of these two sets of acts, it is the former only that are pernicious: it is, therefore, the former only that it can be the business of private ethics to endeavor to prevent. The latter being by the supposition not mischievous, to prevent them is what it can no more be the business of ethics to endeavor at, than of legislation. It remains to show how it may happen that there should be acts really pernicious, which, although they may very properly come under the censure of private ethics, may yet be no fit objects for the legislator to control.

Punishment then, as applied to delinquency, may be unprofitable in both or either of two ways: (1) by the expense it would amount to, even supposing the application of it to be confined altogether to delinquency; (2) by the danger there may be of its involving the innocent in the fate designed only for the guilty. First then, with regard to the cases in which the expense of the punishment, as applied to the guilty, would outweigh the profit to be made by it. These cases, it is evident, depend upon a certain proportion between the evil of the punishment and the evil of the offence. Now were the offence of such a nature that a punishment which, in point of *magnitude,* should but just exceed the profit of it, would be sufficient to prevent it, it might be rather difficult perhaps to find an instance in which such punishment would clearly appear to be unprofitable. But the fact is, there are many cases in which a punishment, in order to have any chance of being efficacious, must, in point of magnitude, be raised a great deal above that level. Thus it is, wherever the danger of detection is, or, what comes to the same thing, is likely to appear to be, so small, as to make the punishment appear in a high degree uncertain. In this case it is necessary, as has been shown, if punishment be at all applied, to raise it in point of magnitude as much as it falls short in point of certainty. It is evident, however, that all this can be but guess-work; and that the effect of such a proportion will be rendered precarious by a variety of circumstances; by the want of sufficient promulgation on the part of the law; by the particular circumstances of the temptation; and by the circumstances influencing the sensibility of the several individuals who are exposed to it. Let the *seducing* motives be strong, the offence then will at any rate be frequently committed. Now and then indeed, owing to a coincidence of circumstances more or less extraordinary, it will be detected, and by the means punished. But for the purpose of example, which is the principal one, an act of punishment considered in itself is of no use: what use it can be of, depends altogether upon the expectation it raises of similar punishment, in future cases of similar delinquency. But this future punishment, it is evident, must always depend upon detection. If then the want of detection is such as must in general (especially to eyes fascinated by the force of the seducing motives) appear too improbable to be reckoned upon, the punishment, though it should be inflicted, may come to be of no use. Here then will be two opposite evils running on at the same time, yet neither of them reducing the quantum of the other: the evil of the disease and the evil of the painful and inefficacious remedy. It seems to be partly owing to some such considerations, that fornication, for example, or the illicit commerce between the sexes, has commonly either gone altogether unpunished, or been punished in a degree inferior to that in which, on other accounts, legislators might have been disposed to punish it.

Secondly, with regard to the cases in which political punishment as applied to delinquency may be unprofitable, in virtue of the danger there may be of its involving the innocent in the fate designed only for the guilty. Whence should this danger then arise? From the difficulty there may be of fixing the idea of the guilty action—that is, of subjecting it to such a definition as shall be clear and precise enough to guard effectually against misapplication. This difficulty may arise from either of two sources: the one permanent, to wit, the nature of the *actions* themselves; the other occasional, I mean the qualities of the *men* who may have to deal with those actions in the way of government. In as far as it arises from the latter of these sources, it may depend partly upon the use which the *legislator* may be *able* to make of language; partly upon the use which, according to the apprehension of the legislator, the *judge* may be *disposed* to make of it. As far as legislation is concerned, it will depend upon the degree of perfection to which the arts of language may have been carried, in the first place, in the nation in general; in the next place, by the *legislator* in particular. It is to a sense of this difficulty, as it should seem, that we may attribute the caution with which most legislators have abstained from subjecting to censure, on the part of the law, such actions as come under the notion of rudeness, for example, or treachery, or ingratitude. The attempt to bring acts of so vague and questionable a nature under the control of law, will argue either a very immature age, in which the difficulties which give birth to that danger are not desired, or a very enlightened age, in which they are overcome.

For the sake of obtaining the clearer idea of the limits between the art of legislation and private ethics, it may now be time to call to mind the distinctions above established with regard to ethics in general. The degree in which private ethics stands in need of the assistance of legislation, is different in the three branches of duty above distinguished. Of the rules of moral duty, those which seem to stand least in need of the assistance of legislation are the rules of *prudence*. It can only be through some defect in point of duty to himself. If he does wrong, there is nothing else that it can be owing to but either some *inadvertence* or some *mis-supposal* with regard to the circumstances on which his happiness depends. It is a standing topic of complaint that a man knows too little of himself. Be it so; but is it so certain that the legislator must know more? It is plain that of individuals the legislator can know nothing: concerning those points of conduct which depend upon the particular circumstances of each individual, it is plain, therefore, that he can determine nothing to advantage. It is only with respect to those broad lines of conduct in which all persons, or very large and permanent descriptions of persons, may be in a way to engage, that he can have any pretence for interfering; and even here the propriety of his interference will, in most instances, lie very open to dispute. At any rate, he must never expect to produce a perfect compliance by the mere force of the sanction of which he is himself the author. All he can hope to do is to increase the efficacy of private ethics by giving strength and direction to the influence of the moral sanction. With what chance of success, for example, would a legislator go about to extirpate drunkenness and fornication by dint of legal punishment? Not all the tortures which ingenuity could invent would compass it; and before he had made any progress worth regarding, such a mass of evil would be produced by the punishment, as would exceed a thousandfold the utmost possible mischief of the offence. The great difficulty would be in the procuring evidence: an object which could not be attempted, with any probability of success, without spreading dismay through every family, tearing the bonds of sympathy asunder, and rooting out the influence of all the social motives. All that he can do then, against offences of this nature, with any prospect of advantage, in the way of direct legislation, is to subject them, in cases of notoriety, to a slight censure, so as thereby to cover them with a slight shade of artificial disrepute.

It may be observed that with regard to this branch of duty, legislators have in general been disposed to carry their interference full as far as is expedient. The great difficulty here is to persuade them to confine themselves within bounds. A thousand little passions and prejudices have led them to narrow the liberty of the subject in this line, in cases in which the punishment is either attended with no profit at all, or with none that will make up for the expense.

The mischief of this sort of interference is more particularly conspicuous in the article of religion. The reasoning, in this case, is of the following stamp. There are certain errors, in matters of belief, to which all mankind are prone; and for these errors in judgment, it is the determination of a Being of infinite benevolence to punish them with an infinity of torments. But from these errors the legislator himself is necessarily free; for the men who happen to be at hand for him to consult with, being men perfectly enlightened, unfettered, and unbiassed, have such advantages over all the rest of the world, that when they sit down to enquire out the truth relative to points so plain and so familiar as those in question, they cannot fail to find it. This being the case, when the sovereign sees his people ready to plunge headlong into an abyss of fire, shall he not stretch out a hand to save them? Such, for example, seems to have been the train of reasoning, and such the motives, which led Louis the XIVth into those coercive measures which he took for the conversion of heretics and the confirmation of true believers. The groundwork, pure sympathy and loving-kindness; the superstructure, all the miseries which the most determined malevolence could have devised. But of this more fully in another place.

The rules of *probity* are those which in point of expediency stand most in need of assistance on the part of the legislator, and in which, in point of fact, his interference has been most extensive. There are few cases in which it *would* be expedient to punish a man for hurting *himself;* but there are few cases, if any, in which it would *not* be expedient to punish a man for injuring his neighbor. With regard to that branch of probity which is opposed to offenses against property, private ethics depends in a manner for its very existence upon legislation. Legislation must first determine what things are to be regarded as each man's property, before the general rules of ethics, on this head, can have any particular application. The case is the same with regard to offences against the state. Without legislation there would be no such thing as a *state*: no particular persons invested with powers to be exercised for the benefit of the rest. It is plain, therefore, that in this branch the interference of the legislator cannot anywhere be dispensed with. We must first know what are the dictates of legislation, before we can know what are the dictates of private ethics.

As to the rules of beneficence, these, as far as concerns matters of detail, must necessarily be abandoned in great measure to the jurisdiction of private ethics. In many cases the beneficial quality of the act depends essentially upon the disposition of the agent—that is, upon the motives by which he appears to have been prompted to perform it: upon their belonging to the head of sympathy, love of amity, or love of reputation, and not to any head of self-regarding motives, brought into play by the force of political constraint: in a word, upon their being such as denominate his conduct *free* and *voluntary,* according to one of the many senses given to those ambiguous expressions. The limits of the law on this head seem, however, to be capable of being extended a good deal farther than they seem ever to have been extended hitherto. In particular, in cases where the person is in danger, why should it not be made the duty of every man to save another from mischief, when it can be done without prejudicing himself, as well as to abstain from bringing it on him? This accordingly is the idea pursued in the body of the work.

To conclude this section, let us recapitulate and bring to a point the difference between private ethics considered as

an art or science, on the one hand, and that branch of jurisprudence which contains the art of science of legislation, on
the other. Private ethics teaches how each man may dispose
himself to pursue the course most conducive to his own happiness, by means of such motives as offer of themselves; the
art of legislation (which may be considered as one branch
of the science of jurisprudence) teaches how a multitude of
men, composing a community, may be disposed to pursue
that course which upon the whole is the most conducive to
the happiness of the whole community, by means of motives
to be applied by the legislator.

X.

LAWS OF LIBERATION

DECLARATION OF THE RIGHTS OF MAN, 1789 *

Drafted by Sieyès, and adopted by the French Constituent Assembly on August 26, 1789, the Declaration is a fundamental document in French constitutional history. It was embodied in the French Constitution of 1791 as a preamble.

The Declaration was based on the theories of J. J. Rousseau and the American Declaration of Independence and asserted the equality of men and the sovereignty of the people with whom the law should rest. It also provided for responsibility of officials to the people and financial control. Its effect in the nineteenth century was incalculable.

DECLARATION OF THE RIGHTS OF MAN AND OF THE CITIZEN OF 26 AUGUST 1789

(The preamble of the Constitution of 27 October 1946 expressly mentions this declaration.)

Art. 1. Men are born and remain free and equal in respect of rights. Social distinctions shall be based solely upon public utility.

Art. 2. The purpose of all civil associations is the preservation of the natural and imprescriptible rights of man. These rights are liberty, property, security, and resistance to oppression.

Art. 3. The nation is essentially the source of all sovereignty; nor shall any body of men or any individual exercise authority which is not expressly derived from it.

*English translation in *France-Amerique* 1776-1789-1917 Paris, R. Helieu, 1918.

Art. 4. Liberty consists in the power of doing whatever does not injure another. Accordingly, the exercise of the natural rights of every man has no other limits than those which are necessary to secure to every other man the free exercise of the same rights; and these limits are determinable only by the law.

Art. 5. The law ought to prohibit only actions hurtful to society. What is not prohibited by the law should not be hindered; nor should any one be compelled to do that which the law does not require.

Art. 6. The law is an expression of the common will. All citizens have a right to concur, either personally or by their representation, in its formation. It should be the same for all, whether it protects or punishes; and all, being equal in its sight, are equally eligible to all honours, places, and employments, according to their different abilities without any other distinction than that of their virtues and talents.

Art. 7. No one shall be accused, arrested, or imprisoned, save in the cases determined by law, and according to the forms which it has prescribed. All who solicit, promote, execute, or cause to be executed, arbitrary orders, ought to be punished and every citizen summoned or apprehended by virtue of the law, ought immediately to obey, and becomes culpable if he resists.

Art. 8. The law should impose only such penalties as are absolutely and evidently necessary; and no one ought to be punished but by virtue of a law promulgated before the offence, and legally applied.

Art. 9. Every man being counted innocent until he has been convicted, whenever his arrest becomes indispensable, all rigour more than is necessary to secure his person ought to be provided against by law.

Art. 10. No man is to be interfered with because of his opinions, not even because of religious opinions, provided his avowal of them does not disturb public order as established by law.

Art. 11. The unrestrained communication of thoughts or

opinions being one of the most precious rights of man, every citizen may speak, write, and publish freely, provided he be responsible for the abuse of this liberty, in the cases determined by law.

Art. 12. A public force being necessary to give security to the rights of men and of citizens, that force is instituted for the benefit of the community, and not for the particular benefit of the person to whom it is entrusted.

Art. 13. A common contribution being necessary for the support of the public force, and for defraying the other expenses of government, it should be divided equally among the members of the community, according to their abilities.

Art. 14. Every citizen has a right, either of himself or his representative, to a free voice in determining the necessity of public contributions, the appropriation of them, and their amount, mode of assessment, and duration.

Art. 15. The community has the right to demand of all its agents an account of their conduct.

Art. 16. Every community in which a security of rights and a separation of powers is not provided for needs a constitution.

Art. 17. The right to property being inviolable and sacred no one shall be deprived of it, except in cases of evident public necessity, legally ascertained, and on condition of a previous just indemnity.

THE CODE NAPOLEON*

As early as the sixteenth century Charles Dumoulin had pressed for a unification of French law, but nothing materialized until Jean Baptist Colbert (1619-1683), Comptroller-General to King Louis XIV, secured the establishment of a council to draft a set of standard national codes. Although described as "the greatest minister," Colbert died before the council completed the codes. They did, however create several sectional codes of considerable value, among them the *Commercial Code* and a *Criminal Code.*

The French legal codifiers who worked under the direction of Napoleon I were indebted to Robert Joseph Pothier (1699-1772), a Frenchman who virtually did the job for them in advance. It was his desire to combine the many customary law systems of France with early Roman law and what he considered the laws of nature into one central legal system. The final codification was started by a jurist named Jacques Régis Cambacérès (1753-1824) in 1796. Although interrupted by the French Revolution, the work was continued under Napoleon's direction and resulted in a *Civil Code,* to which the entire French bar contributed, in 1804, followed by the *Criminal Civil Procedure* and *Criminal Procedure.*

While Napoleon Bonaparte contributed little to the actual revision of the Codes, it is to his credit that he realized the need for a unified legal system, appointed a commission, encouraged their work and attended many of the commission's metings.

*From *The Code Napoleon, Being the French Civil Code,* by Robert Samuel Richards, New York, Wiley and Sons.

PRELIMINARY TITLE

Of the Publication, Effect, and Application of the Laws in General

Decreed 5th of March, 1803. Promulgated 15th of the same Month.

ARTICLE 1

The laws are executory throughout the whole French territory, by virtue of the promulgation thereof made by the first consul.

They shall be executed in every part of the republic, from the moment at which their promulgation can have been known.

The promulgation made by the first consul shall be taken to be known in the department which shall be the seat of government, one day after the promulgation; and in each of the other departments, after the expiration of the same interval augmented by one day for every ten myriameters (about twenty ancient leagues) between the town in which the promulgation shall have been made, and the chief place of each department.

2.

The law ordains for the future only; it has no retrospective operation.

3.

The laws of police and public security bind all the inhabitants of the territory.

Immoveable property, although in the possession of foreigners, is governed by the French law.

The laws relating to the condition and privileges of persons govern Frenchmen, although residing in a foreign country.

4.

The judge who shall refuse to determine under pretext of the silence, obscurity, or insufficiency of the law, shall be liable to be proceeded against as guilty of a refusal of justice.

5.

The judges are forbidden to pronounce, by way of general and legislative determination, on causes submitted to them.

6.

Private agreements must not contravene the laws which concern public order and good morals.

BOOK I
OF PERSONS

Decreed 8th of March, 1803. Promulgated 18th of the same Month.

TITLE I
Of the Enjoyment and Privation of Civil Rights

CHAPTER I
Of the Enjoyment of Civil Rights

7.

The exercise of civil rights is independent of the quality of citizen, which is only acquired and preserved conformably to the constitutional law.

8.

Every Frenchman shall enjoy civil rights.

9.

Every individual born in France of a foreigner, may, during the year which shall succeed the period of his majority, claim the quality of Frenchman; provided, that if he shall reside in France he declares his intention to fix his domicile in that country, and that in case he shall reside in a foreign country, he give security to become domiciled in France and establish himself there within a year, to be computed from the date of that undertaking.

10.

Every child born of a Frenchman in a foreign country is French. Every child born in a foreign country of a Frenchman who shall have lost the quality of Frenchman, may at any time recover this quality by complying with the formalities prescribed in the ninth article.

11.

A foreigner shall enjoy in France the same civil rights as are or shall be accorded to Frenchmen by the treaties of that nation to which such foreigner shall belong.

12.

The foreigner who shall have married a Frenchman, shall follow the condition of her husband.

13.

The foreigner who shall have been permitted by the government to establish his domicile in France, shall enjoy in that country all civil rights so long as he shall continue to reside there.

14.

A foreigner, although not resident in France, may be cited before the French courts, to enforce the execution of engagements contracted by him in France with a Frenchman; he may be summoned before the tribunals of France, on account of engagements entered into by him with Frenchmen in a foreign country.

15.

A Frenchman may be summoned before a French court, for engagements contracted by him in a foreign country, though with a foreigner.

16.

In all causes, except commercial ones, in which a foreigner shall be plaintiff, he shall be required to give security for the payment of the costs and damages incident to the suit, unless he possess in France immoveable property of value sufficient to guarantee such payment.

CHAPTER II
Of the Privation of Civil Rights

SECTION I
Of the Privation of Civil Rights by the Loss of the Quality of Frenchman

17.

The quality of Frenchman shall be lost, 1st, by naturalization in a foreign country; 2nd, by accepting, without the authority of government, public employments bestowed by a foreign power; 3dly, by adoption into any foreign corporation which shall require distinctions of birth; 4thly, in short, by any settlement made in a foreign country, without intention of return.

Commercial establishments shall never be considered as having been made without intention of return.

18.

A Frenchman, who shall have lost his quality of Frenchman, may at any time recover it by returning to France with the sanction of government, declaring at the same time his intention to settle there, and his renunciation of every distinction inconsistent with the law of France.

318

19.

A Frenchwoman, who shall espouse a foreigner, shall follow the condition of her husband.

If she become a widow, she shall recover the quality of Frenchwoman, provided she already reside in France, or that she return thither under the sanction of government, and declare at the same time her intention to fix there.

20.

The individuals who shall recover the quality of Frenchman or Frenchwoman in the cases provided for by Articles 10, 18, and 19, shall not be permitted to avail themselves of it until they have fulfilled the conditions imposed upon them by those articles, and only for the exercise of rights open to their advantage after that period.

21.

The Frenchman who, without the authority of the government, shall engage in military service with a foreign power, or shall enroll himself in any foreign military association, shall lose his quality of Frenchman.

He shall not be permitted to re-enter France without the permission of the government, nor to recover the quality of Frenchman except by complying with the conditions required for a foreigner in order to become a citizen; and this without affecting the punishments denounced by the criminal law against Frenchmen who have borne or shall bear arms against their country.

SECTION II

Of the Privation of Civil Rights in consequence of Judicial Proceedings

22.

Sentences to punishments, the effect of which is to deprive the party condemned of all participation in the civil rights hereafter mentioned, shall imply civil death.

23.

Sentence to natural death shall imply civil death.

24.

Other perpetual afflictive punishments shall not imply civil death, except so far as the law shall have attached that consequence to them.

25.

By civil death, the party condemned loses his property in all the goods which he possessed; and the succession is open for the benefit of his heirs, on whom his estate devolves, in the same manner as if he were naturally dead and intestate.

He no longer can inherit any estate, nor transmit, by this title, the property which he has acquired in consequence.

He is no longer capable of disposing of his property, in whole or in part, either by way of gift during his life, or by will, nor of receiving by similar title, except for the purpose of subsistence. He cannot be nominated guardian, nor concur in any act relative to guardianship.

He cannot be a witness in any solemn public act, nor be admitted to give evidence in any court. He cannot engage in any suit, whether as defendant or plaintiff, except in the name and by the intervention of a special curator appointed for him by the court in which the action is brought.

He is incapable of contracting a marriage attended by any civil consequences.

If he have previously contracted marriage, it is dissolved, as respects all civil effects. His wife and his heirs shall respectively exercise those rights and demands to which his natural death would have given rise.

26.

Peremptory sentences only import civil death, reckoning from the day of their execution, whether real or by representation.

27.

Condemnations for contumacy shall not import civil death until after five years from the execution of the sentence by representation, and during which the condemned party may make his appearance.

28.

Those condemned for contumacy shall, during five years, or until they shall make appearance or until their arrest during that period, be deprived of the exercise of civil rights. Their estate shall be administered and their rights exercised in the same manner as those of absent persons.

29.

When the party under sentence for contumacy shall appear voluntarily during the five years, to be reckoned from the day of the execution, or when he shall have been seized and made prisoner during that interval, the judgment shall be entirely reversed; the accused shall be restored to the possession of his property; he shall be tried afresh; and if by the new judgment he is condemned to the same punishment or a different punishment equally drawing after it civil death, it shall only take place from the date of the execution of the second judgment.

30.

When a party condemned for contumacy, who shall not have appeared or who shall not have been made prisoner until the expiration of the five years, shall be acquitted by this new judgment, or shall only be sentenced to a punishment that does not carry with it civil death, he shall be reinstated in the full enjoyment of his civil rights for the future, reckoning from the day on which he shall have reappeared in court; but the first judgment shall extend, as regards the past, to all consequences produced by civil death during the interval which elapsed between the period

321

of the expiration of the five years and the day of appearance in court.

31.

If the party under sentence for contumacy dies during the five years interval of grace without having appeared, or without having been seized or arrested, he shall be deemed dead as to the entirety of his rights; judgment of contumacy shall be reversed entirely, without prejudice nevertheless to the action of any civil plaintiff, which shall only be entered against the heirs of the party condemned according to the civil form.

32.

In no case shall efflux of time (prescription) after sentence restore a party condemned to his civil rights for the future.

33.

Property acquired by an outlawed person, after incurring civil death, and of which he shall be found possessed at the date of his natural death, shall belong to the nation by right of disherison. Nevertheless the government shall be allowed to make for the benefit of the widow, children, or relations of the party condemned, such disposition respecting it as humanity shall suggest.

TITLE II
Of Acts Before The Civil Authorities

CHAPTER I

General Ordinance

34.

The records of the civil power shall declare the year, the day, and hour, at which they shall be received; the Christian name, surname, age, profession, and domicile of all those who shall be therein mentioned.

35.

The officers of the civil courts shall insert nothing in the acts which they shall receive, either by way of note or of any explanation whatsoever, other than what is declared by the parties.

36.

In those cases in which parties interested are not bound to appear in person, it shall be allowed them to make appearance by means of a special and authentic warrant of attorney.

THE DECLARATION OF PARIS, 1856 *

The Declaration of Paris was directly and indirectly a result of the Crimean War, beginning in 1854 and ending in 1856. It was the first enactment of rules governing international law and covered much of the law of warfare at sea. It abolished privateering and established legislation regarding contraband and blockading.

In August, 1861, the Confederate States of America adopted the Declaration with some modification. In the Spanish-American War the United States followed the principles of the three last articles of the Declaration by official notification.

During World War I in the code of maritime warfare issued by the United States Navy Department, the second and third articles of the Declaration were literally included while the fourth article was in principle incorporated.

Considering that maritime law, in time of war, has long been the subject of deplorable disputes;

That the uncertainty of the law and of the duties in such a matter, gives rise to differences of opinion between neutrals and belligerents which may occasion serious difficulties, and even conflicts;

That it is consequently advantageous to establish a uniform doctrine on so important a point;

That the plenipotentiaries assembled in congress at Paris cannot better respond to the intentions by which their Governments are animated, than by seeking to introduce into international relations fixed principles in this respect;

*From *A Digest of International Law,* by John B. Moore, Washington, Government Printing Office, 1906.

The above-mentioned plenipotentiaries, being duly authorised, resolved to concert among themselves as to the means of attaining this object; and, having come to an agreement, have adopted the following solemn declaration:

1. Privateering is, and remains abolished.

2. The neutral flag covers enemy's goods, with the exception of contraband of war.

3. Neutral goods, with the exception of contraband of war, are not liable to capture under enemy's flag;

4. Blockades, in order to be binding, must be effective; that is to say, maintained by a force sufficient really to prevent access to the coast of the enemy.

The Governments of the undersigned plenipotentiaries engage to bring the present declaration to the knowledge of the states which have not taken part in the congress of Paris, and to invite them to accede to it.

Convinced that the maxims which they now proclaim cannot but be received with gratitude by the whole world, the undersigned plenipotentiaries doubt not that the efforts of their Governments to obtain the general adoption thereof, will be crowned with full success.

The present declaration is not and shall not be binding, except between those powers who have acceded, or shall accede, to it.

Done at Paris, the 16th of April, 1856.

Herlstet's Map of Europe by Treaty, II, 1282.

The foregoing declaration respecting maritime law was signed by the representatives of all the seven powers in the Congress of Paris, namely, Austria, France, Great Britain, Prussia, Russia, Sardinia, and Turkey.

ALEXANDER II
(1818-1881)

As Emperor and Tsar of Russia, Alexander was the son and successor of Nicholas I. Mainly through the teachings of the poet Zhukovsky and influenced by his liberal education and the outcome of the Crimean War Alexander II put into effect the great program of internal reforms of which the most important was the emancipation in 1861 of the serfs. This edict changed the entire social order of the empire despite the fact that many of its features—particularly the communal ownership of the land and the high cost to the peasants of their small plots—were factors in subsequent revolutionary movements.

Other major reforms initiated by Alexander were the Zemstvo system of local self government, a new judicial system and the interduction of compulsory military service.

Emancipation Ukase: The Emancipation of the Russian Serfs*

EDICT FOR THE LIBERATION OF THE SERFS

By the grace of God, we, Alexander II, Emperor and Autocrat of all the Russias, King of Poland, Grand Duke of Finland, etc., to all our faithful subjects make known:

Called by Divine Providence and by the sacred right of inheritance to the throne of our ancestors, we took a vow in our innermost heart so to respond to the mission which is intrusted to us as to surround with our affection and our Imperial solicitude all our faithful subjects of every rank and of every condition, from the warrior who nobly bears arms for the defence of the country to the humble artisan devoted to the works of industry, from the official in the

---

*The Annual Register, 1861, London; J. & F. H. A. Rivington, 1862.

career of the high offices of the State to the labourer whose plough furrows the soil.

In considering the various classes and conditions of which the State is composed we came to the conviction that the legislation of the empire having wisely provided for the organization of the upper and middle classes and having defined with precision their obligations, their rights, and their privileges, has not attained the same degree of efficiency as regards the peasants attached to the soil, thus designated because either from ancient laws or from custom they have been hereditarily subjected to the authority of the proprietors, on whom it was incumbent at the same time to provide for their welfare. The rights of the proprietors have been hitherto very extended and very imperfectly defined by the law, which has been supplied by tradition, custom, and the good pleasure of the proprietors. In the most favorable cases this state of things has established patriarchal relations founded upon a solicitude sincerely equitable and benevolent on the part of the proprietors, and on an affectionate submission on the part of the peasants; but in proportion as the simplicity of morals diminished, as the diversity of the mutual relations became complicated, as the paternal character of the relations between the proprietors and the peasants became weakened, and, moreover, as the seigneurial authority fell sometimes into hands exclusively occupied with their personal interests, those bonds of mutual good-will slackened, and a wide opening was made for an arbitrary sway, which weighed upon the peasants, was unfavourable to their welfare and made them indifferent to all progress under the conditions of their existence.

These facts had already attracted the notice of our predecessors of glorious memory, and they had taken measures for improving the conditions of the peasants, but among those measures some were not stringent enough, insomuch that they remained subordinate to the spontaneous initiative of such proprietors who showed themselves animated with liberal intentions; and others, called forth by peculiar circumstances, have been restricted to certain localities or simply adopted as an experiment. . . .

We thus came to the conviction that the work of a serious improvement of the condition of the peasants was a sacred inheritance bequeathed to us by our ancestors, a mission which, in the course of events, Divine Providence called upon us to fulfil.

We have commenced this work by an expression of our Imperial confidence towards the nobility of Russia, which has given us so many proofs of its devotion to the Throne, and of its constant readiness to make sacrifices for the welfare of the country. . . .

Having invoked the Divine assistance, we have resolved to carry this work into execution.

In virtue of the new dispositions [of the nobility], the peasants attached to the soil will be invested within a term, fixed by the law with all the rights of free cultivators.

The proprietors retaining their rights of property on all the land belonging to them grant to the peasants for a fixed regulated rental the full enjoyment of their close. . . . In this state, which must be a transitory one, the peasants shall be designated as "temporarily bound."

At the same time, they are granted the right of purchasing their close, and with the consent of the proprietors, they may acquire in full property the arable lands and other appurtenances which are allotted to them as a permanent holding. By the acquisition in full property of the quantity of land fixed, the peasants are free from their obligations towards the proprietors for land thus purchased, and they enter definitively into the condition of free peasants-landholders.

Although these dispositions, general as well as local, and the special supplementary rules for some particular localities, for the lands of small proprietors, and for the peasants who work in the manufactories and establishments of the proprietors, have been, as far as was possible, adapted to economical necessities and local customs, nevertheless, to preserve the existing state where it presents reciprocal advantages, we leave it to the proprietors to come to amicable terms with the peasants, and to conclude transactions relative to the extent of the territorial allotment, and to the amount of rental . . . observing, at the same time, the established rules to guarantee the inviolability of such agreements.

Aware of all the difficulties of the reform we have undertaken, we place above all things our confidence in the goodness of Divine Providence who watches over the destinies of Russia.

We also count upon the generous devotion of our faithful nobility, and we are happy to testify to that body the gratitude it has deserved from us, as well as from the country, for the disinterested support it has given to the accomplishment of our designs. Russia will not forget that the nobility, acting solely upon its respect for the dignity of man and its love for its neighbour, has spontaneously renounced rights given to it by serfdom actually abolished, and laid the foundation of a new future, which is thrown open to the peasants. We also entertain the firm hope that it will also nobly exert its ulterior efforts to carry out the new regulation by maintaining good order, in a spirit of peace and benevolence, and that each proprietor will complete, within the limits of his property, the great civic act accomplished by the whole body, by organizing the existence of the peasants domiciliated on his estates, and of his domestics, under mutual advantageous conditions, thereby giving to the country population the example of a faithful and conscientious execution of the regulations of the State. . . .

XI.

INTERNATIONAL CONVENTIONS

THE GENEVA CONVENTION, 1864

In 1862 a Swiss named Jean Henry Dunant wrote *Un Souvenir de Solférino* in which he described the suffering of the wounded on the battlefield of Solferino and urged the formation of neutral volunteer societies to offer aid during time of war. The Société genevoise d'Utilité, a Swiss welfare agency, endorsed Dunant's proposal and an international conference was held in 1864.

Of the sixteen countries represented at the conference twelve signed the original agreement for the "Amelioration of the Condition of the wounded and Sick of Armies in the Field." This document provided for the neutrality of personnel in the medical service attending the wounded, the humane treatment of wounded, the neutrality of civilians engaged in caring for the wounded and the establishment of an international emblem to mark personnel and supplies.

In honor of Dunant's nationality a red cross on a white background—the Swiss flag's colors reversed—was designated as the official emblem to mark supplies and medical installations.

Signatories to the original Geneva Convention and its subsequent revisions and allied treaties, such as the Hague Convention and the Prisoner of War Convention, include all civilized nations.

GENEVA CONVENTION

Whereas on the 22d day of August 1864, a convention was concluded at Geneva in Switzerland, between the Grand Duchy of Baden and the Swiss Confederation, the Kingdom of Belgium, the Kingdom of Denmark, the Kingdom of Spain, the French Empire, the Grand Duchy of Hesse, the Kingdom of Italy, the Kingdom of the Netherlands, the Kingdom of Portugal, the Kingdom of Prussia and the Kingdom of Würtemberg, for the amelioration of the wounded in armies in the field, the tenor of which convention is as follows:

The Swiss Confederation; His Royal Highness, the Grand-Duke of Baden; His Majesty the King of the Belgians; His Majesty the King of Denmark; Her Majesty the Queen of Spain; His Majesty the Emperor of the French; His Royal Highness the Grand-Duke of Hesse; His Majesty the King of Italy; His Majesty the King of the Netherlands; His Majesty the King of Portugal and of the Algarves; His Majesty the King of Prussia; His Majesty the King of Würtemberg, being equally animated with the desire to soften, as much as depends on them, the evils of warfare, to suppress its useless hardships and improve the fate of wounded soldiers on the field of battle, have resolved to conclude a Convention to that effect, and have named for their Plenipotentiaries, viz:

The Swiss Confederation:

Guillaume Henri Dufour, Grand Officer of the Imperial Order of the Legion of Honor, General in Chief of the federal army, Member of the Council of the States;

Gustave Moynier, President of the International Relief Committee for wounded soldiers and of the Geneva Society of Public Utility, and

Samuel Lehmann, federal Colonel, Doctor in Chief of the federal army, Member of the National Council;

His Royal Highness the Grand-Duke of Baden:

Robert Volz, Knight of the Order of the Lion of Zaehringen, M.D., Medical Councellor at the Direction of Medical Affairs, and

Adolphe Steiner, Knight of the Order of the Lion of Zaehringen, Chief of Staff Physician;

His Majesty the King of Denmark:

Auguste Visschers, Officer of the Order of Leopold, Councillor at the Council of Mines;

Charles Emile Fenger, Commander of the Order of Danebrog, decorated with the silver cross of the same Order; Grand Cross of the Order of Leopold of Belgium, etc., etc., His Councillor of State;

Her Majesty the Queen of Spain:

Don José Heriberto García de Quevedo, Gentleman of Her Chamber on active service, Knight of the Grand Cross of Isabella-the-Catholic, Numerary Commander of the Order of Charles III, Knight of the first class of the Royal and Military Order of St. Ferdinand, Officer of the Legion of Honor of France, Her Minister-Resident to the Swiss Confederation;

His Majesty the Emperor of the French:

Georges Charles Jagerschmidt, Officer of the Imperial Order of the Legion of Honor, Officer of the Order of Leopold of Belgium, Knight of the Order of the Red Eagle of Russia of the third class, etc., etc., Sub-Director at the Ministry of Foreign Affairs;

Henri Eugène Seguineau de Préval, Knight of the Imperial Order of the Legion of Honor, decorated with the Imperial Order of th Medjidié of fourth class, Knight of the Order of Saints Maurice and Lazarus of Italy, etc., etc., military Sub-Commissioner of first class, and

Martin François Boudier, Officer of the Imperial Order of the Legion of Honor, decorated with the Imperial Order of the Medjidié of the fourth class, decorated with the medal of Military Valor of Italy, etc., etc., doctor in chief of second class;

His Royal Highness the Grand-Duke of Hesse:

Charles Auguste Brodrück, Knight of the Order of Philip the Magnanimous, of the Order of St. Michael of Bavaria, Officer of the Royal Order of the Holy Savior, etc., etc., Chief of Battalion Staff Officer;

His Majesty the King of Italy:

Jean Capello, Knight of the Order of Saints Maurice and Lazarus, His Consul-General to Switzerland, and

Felix Baroffio, Knight of the Order of Saints Maurice and Lazarus, Doctor in Chief of medical division;

His Majesty the King of the Netherlands:

Bernard Ortuinus Theodore Henri Westenburg, Officer of His Order of the Crown of Oak, Knight of the Orders of of Nassau, L. D., His Secretary of Legation at Frankfort;

His Majesty the King of Portugal and of the Algarves:

José Antonio Marques, Knight of the Order of Christ, of Our Lady of the Conception of Villa Viciosa, of Saint Benedict of Aviz, of Leopold of Belgium, etc., M. D. Surgeon of Brigade, Sub-Chief to the Department of Health at the Ministry of War;

His Majesty the King of Prussia:

Charles Albert de Kamptz, Knight of the Order of the Red Eagle of second class, etc., etc., etc., His Envoy Extraordinary and Minister Plenipotentiary to the Swiss Confederation,
Private Councillor of Legation;

Godefroi Frederic François Loeffler, Knight of the Order of the Red Eagle of third class etc., etc., M. D. Physician in chief of the fourth Army Corps;

Gorges Hermann Jules Ritter, Knight of the Order of the Crown of third class, etc., etc., Private Councillor at the Ministry of War;

His Majesty the King of Würtemberg:

Christophe Ulric Hahn, Knight of the Order of Saints Maurice and Lazarus, etc., Doctor of Philosophy and Theology, Member of the Central Royal Direction for Charitable Institutions,

Who, after having exchanged their powers and found them in good and due form, agreed to the following articles:

Article I. Ambulances and Military hospitals shall be acknowledged to be neuter, and, as such, shall be protected and respected by belligerents so long as any sick or wounded may be therein.

Such neutrality shall cease if the ambulances or hospitals should be held by a military force.

Art. II. Persons employed in hospitals and ambulances comprising the staff for superintendence, medical service, administration, transport of wounded, as well as chaplains, shall participate in the benefit of neutrality whilst so employed, and so long as there remain any wounded to bring in or to succour.

Art. III. The persons designated in the preceding article may, even after occupation by the enemy, continue to fulfil their duties in the hospital or ambulance which they serve, or may withdraw in order to rejoin the corps to which they belong.

Under such circumstances, when these persons shall cease from their functions, they shall be delivered by the occupying army to the outposts of the enemy.

Art. IV. As the equipment of military hospitals remains subject to the laws of war, persons attached to such hospitals cannot, in withdrawing, carry away any articles but such as are their private property.

Under the same circumstances an ambulance shall, on the contrary, retain its equipment.

Art. V. Inhabitants of the country who may bring help to the wounded shall be respected, and shall remain free. The generals of the belligerent Powers shall make it their care to inform the inhabitants of the appeal addressed to their humanity, and of the neutrality which will be the consequence of it.

Any wounded man entertained and taken care of in a house shall be considered as a protection thereto. Any inhabitant who shall have entertained wounded men in his house shall be exempted from the quartering of troops, as well as from a part of the contributions of war which may be imposed.

Art. VI. Wounded or sick soldiers shall be entertained and taken care of, to whatever nation they may belong.

Commanders-in-Chief shall have the power to deliver immediately to the outposts of the enemy soldiers who have been wounded in an engagement, when circumstances permit this to be done, and with the consent of both parties.

Those who are recognized, after their wounds are healed, as incapable of serving, shall be sent back to their country.

The others may also be sent back, on condition of not again bearing arms during the continuance of the war.

Evacuations, together with the persons under whose directions they take place, shall be protected by an absolute neutrality.

Art. VII. A distinctive and uniform flag shall be adopted for hospitals, ambulances, and evacuations. It must on every occasion, be accompanied by the national flag. An arm-badge (brassard) shall also be allowed for individuals neutralized, but the delivery thereof shall be left to military authority.

The flag and the arm-badge shall bear a red cross on a white ground.

Art. VIII. The details of execution of the present convention shall be regulated by the commanders-in-chief of belligerent armies, according to the instructions of their respective Governments, and in conformity with the general principles laid down in this convention.

Art. IX. The high contracting Powers have agreed to communicate the present convention to those Governments which have not found it convenient to send plenipotentiaries to the International Conference of Geneva, with an invitation to accede thereto; the protocol is for that purpose left open.

Art. X. The present convention shall be ratified and the ratifications shall be exchanged at Berne in four months, or sooner, if possible.

In faith whereof the respective Plenipotentiaries have signed it and have affixed their seals thereto.

Done at Geneva, the twenty-second day of the month of August of the year one thousand eight hundred and sixty-four.

(L.S.) G'l G. H. Dufour.	(L.S.) Boudier.
(L.S.) G. Moynier.	(L.S.) Brodrück.
(L.S.) Dr. Lehmann.	(L.S.) Capello.
(LS) Dr. Robert Volz.	(L.S.) F. Baroffio.
(L.S.) Steiner.	(L.S.) Westenberg.
(L.S.) Visschers.	(L.S.) José Antonio Marques.
(L.S.) Fenger.	(L.S.) De Kamptz.
(L.S.) Y. Heriberto	(L.S.) Loeffler.
García de Quevedo.	
(L.S.) Ch. Jagerschmidt.	(L.S.) Ritter.
(L.S.) S. de Préval.	(L.S.) Dr. Hahn.

And whereas the several contracting parties to the said convention exchanged the ratifications thereof at Geneva on the 22d day of June 1865;

And whereas the several states hereinafter named have adhered to the said convention in virtue of Article IX thereof, to wit:

Sweden	December 13, 1864.
Greece	January 5-17, 1865.
Great Britain	February 18, 1865.
Mecklenburg-Schwerin	March 9, 1865.
Turkey	July 5, 1865.
Würtemberg	June 2, 1866.
Hesse	June 22, 1866.
Bavaria	June 30, 1866.
Austria	July 21, 1866.
Russia	May 10, 1867.
Persia	December 5, 1874.
Roumania	November 18|30, 1874.
Salvador	December 30 ,1874.
Montenegro	November 17-29, 1875.
Serbia	March 24, 1876.
Bolivia	October 16, 1879.
Chile	November 15, 1879.
Argentine Republic	November 25, 1879.
Peru	April 22, 1880.

And whereas the Swiss Confederation in virtue of the said Article IX of said convention has invited the United States of America to accede thereto.

And whereas on the 20th. October, 1868, the following additional articles were proposed and signed at Geneva on behalf of Great Britain, Austria, Baden, Bavaria, Belgium, Denmark, France, Italy, Netherlands, North Germany; Sweden and Norway, Switzerland, Turkey and Würtemberg.

The governments of North Germany, Austria, Baden, Bavaria, Belgium, Denmark, France, Great Britain, Italy; the Netherlands, Sweden and Norway, Switzerland, Turkey, and Würtemberg, desiring to extend to armies on the sea the advantages of the Convention concluded at Geneva the 22d of August, 1864, for the amelioration of the condition of wounded soldiers in armies in the field, and to further particularize some of the stipulations of the said Convention, have named for their commissioners . . .

(Names of commissioners follow.)

THE DECLARATION OF ST. PETERSBURG, 1868

The first attempt to regulate and establish rules of international law was the *Declaration of Paris* in 1856. This was the outgrowth of a small group of powers who joined in the establishment of fixed rules governing much of the warfare at sea, abolished privateering and set forth rules regarding blockading. It was signed by nine states and acceded to by most maritime powers.

In 1868 the Declaration of St. Petersburg was established which legislated the use of explosives and inflammable projectiles. The United States did not participate in the St. Petersburg conference, although an English translation of the Declaration was sent to the Department of State by the United States Minister to Russia in a dispatch on November 29, 1868.

Legation of the United States
St. Petersburg, Russia
Dec. 12th, 1868

Sir,

In the St. Petersburg Journal of today we have the official report of the Convention upon explosive projectiles, and final agreement signed by the Great Powers through their ministers.—The Convention or "Commission" was represented in part by experts in arms, and ministers here. They were from France, England, Prussia, Austria, Russia, Denmark; Norway, and Sweden, Switzerland, Italy, Turkey, Persia; Würtemberg, Bavaria, Brazil, Greece, (Pays Bas) Holland, and Belgium.

The following "Declaration," and signatures were made in the Foreign office; I translate from the French.

Declaration.

Upon the proposition of the Imperial Cabinet, of Russia, an international military commission being assembled in St. Petersburg, in order to examine the propriety of forbidding the use of certain projectiles in time of war between civilized nations, and that commission having determined by common consent the technical limits where the impetus of war ought to stop before the demands of Humanity, the undersigned are authorized by the owners of their governments to declare the following:

Whereas ("considerant,") the progress of civilization ought to have for its effect the ameliorating as much as possible the calamities of war: Considering that:

—Since the sole legitimate end the States ought to propose, during war, is the weakening the military strength ("forces") of the enemy:

—That for this result it is sufficient to put "hors du combat" the greatest possible number of men:

—That this end would be exceeded by the use of arms which would uselessly aggravate the sufferings of disabled men ("hors du combat") or render their deaths inevitable:

—That the employment of such arms would be, to that extent, contrary to the laws of humanity:

—The contracting parties mutually agree to renounce in case of war between them, the employment by their troops on land and sea, all projectiles under the weight of 400 "grammes," which may be explosive or charged with fulminating or inflamable materials.

They will invite all States which have not participated by sending delegates to the deliberation of the national military Commission Post at St. Petersburg, to join the present agreement.

That agreement is only obligatory upon the contracting parties or those joining, in case of war between two or more of them; it is not applicable to parties not contracting or who have not joined them.

It would cease also to be obligatory from the moment, where in a war between the contracting parties, and those joining them, a non contracting party or one who had not joined ("accede"), should aid one of the belligerents.

The contracting parties, or those joining, reserve to themselves to come to an understanding ultimately, every time that a definitive proposition should be formed, in view of the future perfection which science should make in the armament of troops, in order to maintain the principles which they have laid down and to reconcile the impetus of war with the laws of Humanity. Done at St. Petersburg, the 29 Nov.—11 Dec. 1868 (signed:)

Vitrua, Count Tauffkirchen, E. Uriad, Talleyrand, Andrew Buchanan, S. A. Metaxa, Bella Caracciolo, Baron Genaro, Mirza Assedullah Khan, H. von de Reuss, pour la Prussie et pour la conféderation de l'Allemande du Nord, Gontcharow, O, M. Bjoernstjerna, Ad. Glintz, Carathiodorf C. d'Abèle.

There, in the order in which they stand, are the chargé of Austria, the ministers of Bavaria, the ministers of Belgium, and of Denmark, the Ambassadors of France and Great Britain, the ministers of Greece, of Italy, of Holland, and of Persia, and of Portugal, and of the German Confederation—of Prussia, the new minister of Foreign Affairs, the ministers of Norway and Sweden, Switzerland, and the Chargé d'Affaires of Turkey, and Würtemberg. Spain had joined in the previous correspondence favorably to the project, but was not represented in the commission; and the Shah of Persia reserved the right of reviewing the proceedings. Brazil took no part.

I have nothing more to add to my former paper upon this subject. I am, Sir, your

C. W. Clay, Q. R.

Hon. Wm. H. Seward,
    Secretary of Note:
        Ve-Ve.
Obt. Wt. Q. L.

XII.

THE SOVIET CONSTITUTION

THE SOVIET CONSTITUTION *

The Soviet Constitution of 1922 retained the dictatorship of the proletariat and public ownership of the land and of the means of production such as had been proclaimed in 1917. There have been several revisions of the Soviet Constitution, but the underlying factors of the 1922 version were preserved in the Constitution of 1936 which continues to remain in effect. The country is ruled and administered by three separate hierarchies, with the legislative portion vested in counselors ranging from a local level to the supreme constitution of the USSR. The supreme constitution elects a permanent committee whose chairman acts as president of the republic. The executive portion is vested in a council of ministers appearing before this council.

The following excerpt tells of the organization of Soviet society, the right of work, the right of education, and equal rights of men and women as well as other "rights" given the Soviet citizen.

1. THE ORGANIZATION OF SOCIETY

1. *Chapter I of the Constitution of the USSR*

Art. 1. The Union of Soviet Socialist Republics is a socialist State of workers and peasants.

Art. 2. The Soviets of Working People's Deputies, which grew and attained strength as a result of the overthrow of the landlords and capitalists and the achievement of the dictatorship of the proletariat, constitute the political foundation of the USSR.

*State Publishing House of Political Literature, Moscow, 1938.

Art. 3. In the USSR all power belongs to the working people of town and country as represented by the Soviets of Working People's Deputies.

Art. 4. The socialist system of economy and the socialist ownership of the means and instruments of production firmly established as a result of the abolition of the capitalist system of economy, the abrogation of private ownership of the means and instruments of production and the abolition of the exploitation of man by man, constitute the economic foundation of the USSR.

Art. 5. Socialist property in the USSR exists either in the form of State property (the possession of the whole people), or in the form of cooperative and collective-farm property (property of a collective farm or property of a co-operative association).

Art. 6. The land, its natural deposits, waters, forests, mills, factories, mines, rail, water and air transport banks; post, telegraph and telephones, large State-organized agricultural enterprises (State farms, machine and tractor stations and the like), as well as municipal enterprises and the bulk of the dwelling-houses in the cities and industrial localities, are State property—that is, belong to the whole people.

Art. 7. Public enterprises in collective farms and co-operative organizations, with their livestock and implements, the products of the collective farms and co-operative organizations, as well as their common buildings, constitute the common, socialist property of the collective farms and co-operative organizations.

In addition to its basic income from the public collective-farm enterprise, every household in a collective farm has for its personal use a small plot of land attached to the dwelling and, as its personal property, a subsidiary establishment on the plot, a dwelling-house, livestock, poultry and minor agricultural implements in accordance with the statutes of the argricultural *artel.*

Art. 8. The land occupied by collective farms is secured

348

to them for their use free of charge and for an unlimited time—that is, in perpetuity.

Art. 9. Alongside the socialist system of economy, which is the predominant form of economy in the USSR, the law permits the small private economy of individual peasants and handicraftsmen based on their personal labour and precluding the exploitation of the labour of others.

Art. 10. The right of citizens to personal ownership of their incomes from work and of their savings, of their dwelling-houses and subsidiary household economy, their household furniture and utensils and articles of personal use and convenience, as well as the right of inheritance of personal property of citizens, is protected by law.

Art. 11. The economic life of the USSR is determined and directed by the State national economic plan with the aim of increasing the public wealth, of steadily improving the material conditions of the working people and raising their cultural level, of consolidating the independence of the USSR and strengthening its defensive capacity.

Art. 12. In the USSR work is a duty and a matter of honour for every able-bodied citizen, in accordance with the principle: "He who does not work, neither shall he eat."

The principle applied in the USSR is that of socialism: "From each according to his ability, to each according to his work."

2. *J. Stalin. From the report on the draft Constitution of the USSR*

The main basis of the draft of the new Constitution for the USSR consists of the principles of socialism, its basic supports, which have already been won and made effective: the socialist ownership of the land, forests, factories and other implements and means of production; the abolition of exploitation and of the exploiting classes; the abolition of poverty for the majority and luxury for the minority; the abolition of unemployment; work as an obligation and an honourable duty for every able-bodied citizen in accordance with the formula: "He who does not work, neither shall he eat." The right to work—that is to say, the right of each citizen to receive guaranteed employment—the right to rest and leisure, the right to education, and so forth—the draft of the new Constitution is founded on these and similar supports of socialism. It reflects them and consolidates them by legislation.

Such is the second distinctive feature of the draft of the new Constitution.

Furthermore, *bourgeois* constitutions are tacitly based on the supposition that society consists of antagonistic classes, of classes owning wealth and classes not owning wealth, that no matter what party comes into power, the guidance of society by the State (dictatorship) must be in the hands of the *bourgeoisie,* that the constitution is required in order to consolidate a social order acceptable and beneficial to the owner classes.

Unlike *bourgeois* constitutions, the draft of the new Constitution of the USSR is based on the fact that there are no longer any antagonistic classes in society; that society consists of two classes friendly to each other, of workers and peasants; that these same working classes are in power; that the guidance of society by the State (dictatorship) is in the hands of the working class, the most important class in society; and that the Constitution is required in order to consolidate a social order acceptable and beneficial to the workers.

Such is the third distinctive feature of the draft of the new Constitution.

Furthermore, *bourgeois* constitutions are tacitly based on the supposition that nations and races cannot have equal rights; that some nations have full rights and others do not have full rights; and that in addition there is yet a third category of nations or races—in the colonies, for example, which have even fewer rights than the nations without full rights. This means that all these constitutions are basically nationalistic; that is to say, they are constitutions of ruling nations.

Unlike these constitutions, the draft of the new Constitution of the USSR is, on the contrary, profoundly international. It is based on the fact that all nations and races have equal rights. It is based on the fact that neither difference of colour, language, cultural level or political development nor any other difference between nations and races can serve as grounds for justifying national inequality of rights. It is based on the fact that all nations and races, irrespective of their past or present position, irrespective of their strength or weakness, must enjoy equal rights in all fields of the economic, social, political and cultural life of the draft of the new Constitution.

The fifth distinctive feature of the draft of the new Constitution is its consistent democracy, carried to its logical conclusion. From the point of view of democracy, *bourgeois* constitutions may be divided into two groups: one group of constitutions either openly denies or in actual fact nullifies the equality of rights of citizens and democratic freedoms. The other group of constitutions willingly accepts and even advertises democratic principles, but at the same time introduces such reservations and limitations that democratic rights and freedoms are utterly distorted. They speak of equal electoral rights for all citizens, but at the same time limit them by residential, educational and even property qualifications. They speak of equal rights of citizens, but at the same time make reservations that this does not apply to women or only partially applies to them, and so forth.

A distinctive feature of the draft of the new Constitution of the USSR is that it is free from such reservations and limitations. It does not acknowledge the existence of active or passive citizens, for in so far as it is concerned all citizens are active. It acknowledges no difference between the rights of men and women "residents" and "non-residents", the "haves" and "have-nots", the educated and uneducated. All

351

citizens have equal rights in its eyes. It is not property status, national origin, sex, or official status, but personal ability and personal labour that determine the position of every citizen in society.

Finally, there is yet another distinctive feature of the draft of the new Constitution. *Bourgeois* constitutions usually confine themselves to establishing the formal rights of citizens, without concerning themselves with the conditions for exercising these rights, with the possibility of exercising them and with the means whereby they can be exercised. They speak of the equality of citizens, but forget that there can be no real equality between a master and a workman, between a landlord and a peasant if the former possess wealth and political influence in society, while the latter are deprived of both, if the former are exploiters and the latter the exploited. Again, they speak of the freedom of speech, assembly and the press, but forget that all these freedoms may become hollow words for the working class if the latter do not have at their disposal suitable premises for meetings, good printing presses, sufficient quantity of printing paper, and so forth.

A distinctive feature of the draft of the new Constitution is that is does not confine itself to establishing the formal rights of citizens, but shifts the centre of gravity to the question of the means whereby these rights may be exercised. It does not merely proclaim the equality of the rights of citizens, but also ensures it by legislative confirmation of the fact that the regime of exploitation had been abolished, of the fact that citizens have been freed from all exploitation. It does not merely proclaim the right to work, but ensures it by legislative confirmation of the fact that crises do not exist in Soviet society, of the fact that unemployment has been abolished. It does not merely proclaim democratic freedoms, but ensures them by legislation providing certain material means. It is obvious, therefore, that the democracy in the draft of the new Constitution is not "ordinary" and "universally accepted" democracy in general, but socialist democracy.

Such are the fundamental distinctive features of the draft of the new Constitution of the USSR.

3. *V. M. Molotov. From a speech delivered at the Extraordinary VIII Congress of the Soviets of the USSR*

The new Constitution will consolidate our profoundly democratic system still further. By the fact that, together with a clear indication of the definite duties of citizens of the USSR, it firmly guarantees such rights as the right to work, the right to rest and leisure, the right to material security in old age, the right to education, absolute equality of rights for men and women, absolute equality of rights for the nations and races of the USSR, and so forth, we loudly proclaim how socialist democracy should be interpreted.

4. *The electoral system, Constitution of the USSR, articles* 134-142

Art. 134. Members of all Soviets of Working People's Deputies—of the Supreme Soviet of the USSR, the Supreme Soviets of the Union Republics, the Soviets of Working People's Deputies of the territories and regions, the Supreme Soviets of the Autonomous Republics, the Soviets of Working People's Deputies of Autonomous Regions, area, district, city and rural (*stanitsa,* village, hamlet, *kishlak, aul*) Soviets of Working People's Deputies—are chosen by the electors on the basis of universal, direct and equal suffrage by secret ballot.

Art. 135. Elections of deputies are universal: all citizens of the USSR who have reached the age of eighteen, irrespective of race or nationality, religion, educational and residential qualifications, social origin, property status or past activities, have the right to vote in the election of deputies and to be elected, with the exception of insane persons and persons who have been convicted by a court of law and whose sentences include deprivation of electoral rights.

Art. 136. Elections of deputies are equal: each citizen has one vote; all citizens participate in elections on an equal footing.

Art. 137. Women have the right to elect and be elected on equal terms with men.

Art. 138. Citizens serving in the Red Army have the right to elect and be elected on equal terms with all other citizens.

Art. 139. Elections of deputies are direct: all Soviets of Working People's Deputies, from rural and city Soviets of Working People's Deputies to the Supreme Soviet of the USSR, inclusive, are elected by the citizens by direct vote.

Art. 140. Voting at elections of deputies is secret.

Art. 141. Candidates for election are nominated according to electoral areas.

The right to nominate candidates is secured to public organizations and societies of the working people: Communist Party organizations, trade unions, co-operatives, youth organizations and cultural societies.

Art. 142. It is the duty of every deputy to report to his electors on his work and on the work of the Soviet of Working People's Deputies, and he is liable to be recalled at any time in the manner established by law upon decision of a majority of the electors.

II. THE RIGHT TO WORK

5. *Constitution of the USSR, article* 118

Citizens of the USSR have the right to work, that is, are guaranteed the right to employment and payment for their work in accordance with its quantity and quality.

The right to work is ensured by the socialist organization of the national economy, the steady growth of the productive forces of Soviet society, the elimination of the possibility of economic crises, and the abolition of unemployment.

6. *From the Labour Code*
(*Sections* 109, 114, 115)

Sect. 109. Every employee shall be granted an uninterrupted weekly rest period of not less than forty-two hours. The weekly rest days shall be fixed by the local labour sections, in agreement with the trade union councils, and may be assigned on Sunday or on any other day of the week, according to the national and denominational composition of the body of wage-earning and salaried employees in each locality.

Sect. 114. Every person employed for remuneration who has worked uninterruptedly for not less than five and a half months shall be granted ordinary leave once a year for not less than twelve working days. The ordinary leave for persons who have not attained the age of eighteen years shall not be less than twenty-four working days.

Sect. 115. Persons employed in especially dangerous and noxious undertakings shall be granted an extra leave period of not less than twelve working days in addition to the leave specified in section 114.

III. THE RIGHT TO REST AND LEISURE

7. *Constitution of the USSR, article* 119
Citizens of the USSR have the right to rest and leisure.

The right to rest and leisure is ensured by the reduction of the working day to seven hours for the overwhelming majority of the workers, the institution of annual vacations with full pay for workers and employees and the provision of a wide network of sanatoria, rest homes and clubs for the accommodation of the working people.

IV. THE RIGHT TO MAINTENANCE IN OLD AGE, AND ALSO IN CASE OF SICKNESS OR LOSS OF CAPACITY TO WORK.

8. *Constitution of the USSR, article* 120
Citizens of the USSR have the right to maintenance in

old age and also in case of sickness or loss of capacity to work.

This right is ensured by the extensive development of social insurance of workers and employees at State expense, free medical service for the working people and the provision of a wide network of health resorts for the use of the working people.

9. *Government communication on social insurance*

The proletariat of Russia has set itself the aim of complete social insurance for hired workers and also for the poor in towns and villages. Neither the tsarist Government of landlords and capitalists nor the coalition reformist Government met the needs of the workers with regard to insurance. The Workers' and Peasants' Government, supported by the Soviets of Workers', Soldiers' and Peasants' Deputies declares to the working class of Russia and also to the poor in towns and villages that it intends forthwith to issue decrees on a complete system of social insurance, based on the following slogans of workers' insurance:

1. The extension of insurance to all hired workers without exception and also to the poor in towns and villages.

2. The extension of insurance to cover all forms of loss of capacity to work—namely, in cases of illness, disability, invalidism, old age, maternity, widowhood, orphanhood, and also unemployment.

3. The assumption of all expenditure on insurance by the employees.

4. Compensation of at least the full earnings in cases of unemployment and loss of capacity to work.

5. Complete freedom of action of insured persons in all insurance organizations.

10. *Leave for treatment at sanatoria and health resorts. Decree of the Council of People's Commissars of the USSR of 9 August 1937*

1. Able-bodied workers and employees shall be given

leave for treatment at sanatoria and health resorts with payment of an allowance from the Government social insurance fund, if the necessity for such treatment is confirmed by the Commission for Sanatoria and Health Resorts. Free travel shall be provided by the factory or local committee of the trade union concerned.

2. Leave for treatment in sanatoria and health resorts shall be granted to able-bodied workers and employees for the period necessary for such treatment and for the journey to and from the place of treatment, this period to include regular and any additional leave (during which time the wages shall continue at the place of work).

3. Workers and employees who are unable to work and are sent to sanatoria and health resorts in accordance with the findings of the Commission for Sanatoria and Health Resorts during the period when they already hold hospitalization certificates in respect of an illness requiring treatment at sanatoria or health resorts, shall be given leave for such treatment and for the journey to the place of treatment and back with payment of an allowance, irrespective of the source of the travel warrant and without the inclusion of their regular and additional leaves.

In cases where the total regular and additional leave of a worker or employee who is unable to work exceeds one month, the part of his leave period in excess of one month shall be included in the leave period for treatment at a sanatorium or health resort.

V. THE RIGHT TO EDUCATION

11. *Constitution of the USSR, article* 121

Citizens of the USSR have the right to education.

This right is ensured by universal, compulsory elementary education; by education, including higher education, being free of charge; by the system of State stipends for the

357

overwhelming majority of students in the universities and colleges; by instruction in schools being conducted in the native language, and by the organization in the factories, State farms, machine and tractor stations and collective farms of free vocational, technical and agronomic training for the working people.

VI. EQUAL RIGHTS OF MEN AND WOMEN

12. *Constitution of the USSR, article* 122

Women in the USSR are accorded equal rights with men in all spheres of economic, State, cultural, social and political life.

The possibility of exercising these rights is ensured to women by granting them an equal right with men to work, payment for work, rest and leisure, social insurance and education, and by State protection of the interests of mother and child, pre-maternity and maternity leave with full pay, and the provision of a wide network of maternity homes, nurseries and kindergartens.

13. *V. I. Lenin. "International Working Women's Day"*
(Volume XXV, pp. 63-64)

Not a single *bourgeois* State, not even the most progressive, republican, democratic State, has brought about complete equality of rights.

But the Soviet Republic of Russia promptly eliminated, without exception, all vestiges of inequality in the legal status of women and secured their complete equality in its laws.

It is said that the level of culture is best characterized by the legal status of women. There is a grain of profound truth in this saying. From this point of view, only the dictatorship of the proletariat, only the socialist State, could achieve and has achieved the highest level of culture.

A new, unparalleled, powerful impetus to the working women's movement is therefore inevitably linked with the establishment (and consolidation) of the first Soviet Republic.

14. *Decree of the Presidium of the Supreme Council of 8 July 1944 on increasing State aid to expectant mothers, mothers of large families and unmarried mothers, and protection of motherhood and childhood, the institution of the honorary title of Mother Heroine and the establishment of the Order of the Glory of Motherhood and the Motherhood Medal.*

The welfare of children and mothers and the consolidation of the family has always been one of the most important tasks of the Soviet State. In protecting the interests of mothers and children, the State extends substantial material assistance to expectant mothers and to mothers for the maintenance and upbringing of children. During and after the war, when many families are faced with more considerable material difficulties, measures for State aid must be further extended.

In order to increase material assistance to expectant mothers, mothers of large families and unmarried mothers, to encourage large families and to increase the protection of motherhood and childhood, the Presidium of the Supreme Council of the Union of Soviet Socialist Republics decrees:

I. *On increasing State aid to mothers of large families and unmarried mothers....*

1. That State allowances be granted to mothers of large families (whether the husband is living or not), on the birth of the third and each subsequent child, instead of the existing system of granting State allowances to mothers of large families who have six children, on the birth of the seventh and each subsequent child.

2. That the payment of State allowances to mothers of large families shall be effected in accordance with the following system and scale:

	Single grant	Monthly allow-ance roubles
To a mother of two children, on the birth of a third child	400	—
To a mother of three children, on the birth of a fourth child	1,300	80
To a mother of four children on the birth of a fifth child	1,700	120
To a mother of five children, on the birth of a sixth child	2,000	140
To a mother of six children, on the birth of a seventh child	2,500	200
To a mother of seven children, on the birth of an eighth child	2,500	200
To a mother of eight children, on the birth of a ninth child	3,500	250
To a mother of nine children, on the birth of a tenth child	3,500	250
To a mother of ten children, on the birth of each subsequent child	5,000	300

Monthly allowances to mothers of large families shall be paid from the second year after the child's birth and shall continue until the child reaches the age of five.

Mothers who have three, four, five or six children at the date of the issue of the present decree, shall receive allowances under the present article for each child born after the issue of the present decree.

Mothers who have seven or more children at the date of the issue of the present decree shall retain the right to receive large-family allowances in accordance with the system and scales established in the decree of the Central Executive Committee and the Council of the People's Commissars of the USSR of 27 June 1936; namely: for the seventh, eighth, ninth and tenth child, 2,000 roubles each annually for five years from the day of the child's birth; for the eleventh and each subsequent child, 5,000 roubles in a single grant and 3,000 roubles each annually for four years, from the second year after the child's birth. For every child born after the issue of the present decree, allowances shall be paid in accordance with the system and scales set forth in the present article of the decree.

Children killed or missing on the fronts of the Patriotic War shall be included in determining State allowances for large families.

3. That State allowances be granted to unmarried mothers, for the maintenance and upbringing of children born after the issue of the present decree, in accordance with the fol-

lowing scales: 100 roubles monthly for one child, 150 roubles for two children, and 200 roubles for three or more children.

State allowances to unmarried mothers shall be paid until the children reach the age of twelve.

Unmarried mothers with three or more children shall receive the State allowances provided for under the present article, in addition to the large-family allowances received in accordance with article 2 of the present decree.

Upon marriage, an unmarried mother shall retain the right to the allowances provided for under the present article.

Mothers of children born in 1944, before the issue of the present decree, shall not receive alimony for these children, but shall be entitled to receive the allowances provided for under the present article.

4. If an unmarried mother wishes to place her child in an institution for children, the said institution shall be obliged to accept the child, who will be maintained and brought up entirely at the expense of the State.

The mother shall have the right to reclaim the child from the children's institution and to bring it up herself.

While the child is in an institution for children the State allowance for it shall not be paid.

5. That single grants paid from social insurance funds and mutual aid funds of co-operative *artels* for new-born infants be increased from 45 roubles to 120 roubles. That facilities be extended for the sale to mothers of layettes for new-born infants for the amount indicated.

II. *On increasing facilities for expectant mothers and mothers and on measures for extending the network of institutions for the protection of mother and child*

6. Maternity leave for women factory workers and office employees from sixty-three calendar days shall be extended to seventy-seven calendar days, by establishing the length of leave at thirty-five calendar days before and forty-two calendar days after childbirth, with payment during this

period of a State allowance on the scales established heretofore. In the event of abnormal birth or the birth of twins, post-natal leave shall be extended to fifty-six calendar days.

Managers of works and institutions shall grant expectant mothers regular leave, which must be timed to fit in with maternity leave.

7. After four months of pregnancy, women shall not be given overtime work in works and institutions, and women with infants at the breast shall be exempted from night work throughout the period of nursing.

8. The additional food rations shall be doubled for expectant mothers from the sixth month of pregnancy, and for nursing mothers during four months of nursing.

9. Managers of enterprises and institutions shall render assistance to expectant and nursing mothers by supplying them with additional food from auxiliary organizations.

10. The fees shall be reduced by fifty per cent at kindergartens and nurseries for parents:

With three children, and with monthly earnings up to 400 roubles;

With four children, and with monthly earnings up to 600 roubles;

With five or more children, irrespective of earnings.

III. *On the institution of the Motherhood Medal and the Order of the Glory of Motherhood and on the establishment of the honorary title of Mother Heroine*

12. There shall be instituted the Motherhood Medal, first and second class, for award to mothers who have given birth to and reared: five children, second-class medal; six children, first-class medal.

13. There shall be instituted the Order of the Glory of Motherhood, first, second and third class, for award to mothers who have given birth to and reared: seven children, third-class order; eight children, second-class order; nine children, first-class order.

14. The title of Mother Heroine shall be conferred on

mothers who have given birth to and reared ten children, and such mother shall be presented with a scroll from the Presidium of the Supreme Council of the USSR.

15. The award of the Order of the Glory of Motherhood and the Motherhood Medal, as well as the title of Mother Heroine, shall take place when the last child born reaches the age of one year, if the other children of the same mother are living.

Children killed or missing at the fronts of the Patriotic War are to be included when these awards are made to mothers.

VII. EQUALITY OF RIGHTS OF CITIZENS OF THE USSR IRRESPECTIVE OF THEIR NATIONALITY OR RACE

15. *Constitution of the USSR, article* 123

Equality of rights of citizens of the USSR, irrespective of their nationality or race, in all spheres of economic, State, cultural, social and political life, is an indefeasible law.

Any direct or indirect restriction of the rights of or, conversely, any establishment of direct or indirect privileges for, citizens on account of their race or nationality, as well as any advocacy of racial or national exclusiveness or hatred and contempt, is punishable by law.

16. *From the decree of the Council of the People's Commissars of the USSR on the extirpation of the anti-semitic movement*

Any kind of baiting of any nation is inadmissible and shameful.

The Council of the People's Commissars declares that the anti-semitic movement and pogroms against Jews are fatal to the interests of the workers' and peasants' revolution, and calls upon the toiling people of Socialist Russia to combat this evil with all the means at their disposal.

17. *V. M. Molotov. From "The Constitution of Socialism"*

We should recall at this moment the withering words regarding anti-semites which Comrade Stalin used in his reply on 12 January 1931 to an inquiry made by the Jewish Telegraphic Agency of America.

In his reply, Comrade Stalin wrote:

"I reply to your inquiry. National and racial chauvinism is a survival of the misanthropic ethics characteristic of the period of cannibalism. Anti-semitism, as an extreme form of racial chauvinism, is the most dangerous survival of cannibalism. Anti-semitism benefits the exploiters, for it serves as a lightning-conductor to divert the blows of the workers from capitalism. Anti-semitism is dangerous to the workers, for it is a false track which diverts them from the right path and leads them into the jungle. Hence, Communists, as consistent internationalists, cannot but be irreconcilable and sworn foes to anti-semitism. In the USSR, anti-semitism is strictly prosecuted as a phenomenon profoundly hostile to the Soviet system. Under the laws of the USSR, active anti-semites are punished with death."

J. Stalin

18. *Declaration of Rights of the Peoples of Russia of 15 November* 1917

The October revolution of workers and peasants began under the banner of general emancipation.

The peasants are being emancipated from the power of the landlords, for there is no longer any ownership of land by landlords—it has been abolished. Soldiers and sailors are being emancipated from the authority of autocratic generals, for generals will henceforward be elected and removable. Workers are being emancipated from the capricious and arbitrary methods of capitalists, for henceforward the control of workers over factories and mills will be established. All that is alive and vital is being freed from hated chains.

There remain only the peoples of Russia, who have suffered and are still suffering oppression and arbitrary rule and whose emancipation must be accomplished decisively and irrevocably.

In the period of tsarism, the peoples of Russia were systematically incited against each other. The results of this policy are well known: slaughter and pogroms on the one hand, and slavery of the peoples on the other.

There must be no return to this shameful policy of incitement. Henceforward it must be replaced by a policy of voluntary and honest union of the peoples of Russia.

In the period of imperialism, after the February revolution, when the power passed into the hands of the "Cadet" *bourgeoisie*, the open policy of incitement gave way to a policy of cowardly distrust towards the peoples of Russia, a policy of persecution and provocation masked by verbal declarations of the "freedom" and "equality" of the peoples. The results of this policy are well known: increase in national hostility and the undermining of mutual confidence.

This unworthy policy of deceit and distrust, persecution and provocation must be brought to an end. Henceforward, it must give way to an open and honest policy, leading to absolute mutual confidence between the peoples of Russia.

An honest and lasting union of the peoples of Russia can only be achieved on the basis of such confidence.

Only on the basis of such a union can the workers and peasants of the peoples of Russia be welded into a single revolutionary force, capable of resisting all attacks from the imperialist and annexationist *bourgeoisie*.

The Congress of Soviets of June this year proclaimed the rights of the peoples of Russia to free self-determination.

The second Congress of Soviets in October this year confirmed this inalienable right of the peoples of Russia in a more decisive and definite form.

Carrying out the will of these Congresses, the Council of People's Commissars has resolved to base its activities with regard to the question of the nationalities of Russia on the following principles:

1. The equality and sovereignty of the peoples of Russia.

2. The right of the peoples of Russia to free self-determination, including separation and the formation of an independent State.

3. The abolition of all national and national-religious privileges and limitations.

4. The free development of national minorities and ethnic groups inhabiting the territory of Russia.

The concrete decrees arising out of these principles will be elaborated immediately after the establishment of a Commission on the Affairs of Nationalities.

In the name of the Russian Republic, *V. Ulianov (Lenin)*
Chairman of the Council of People's Commissars
Dzhugashvili (Stalin)
People's Commissar for the Affairs of Nationalities
15|2 November 1917

VIII. FREEDOM OF CONSCIENCE

19. *Constitution of the USSR, article* 124

In order to ensure to citizens freedom of conscience, the church in the USSR is separated from the State, and the school from the church. Freedom of religious worship and freedom of anti-religious propaganda is recognized for all citizens.

20. *V. I. Lenin. From "Socialism and Religion"*

The State must not concern itself with religion; religious societies must not be bound to the State. Everyone must be absolutely free to profess whatever religion he likes, or to profess no religion, that is to say, to be an atheist, as every socialist usually is. Discrimination in the rights of citizens on religious grounds is absolutely inadmissible.

IX. FREEDOM OF SPEECH, THE PRESS, ASSEMBLY, MASS MEETINGS, STREET PROCESSIONS AND DEMONSTRATIONS.

21. *Constitution of the USSR, article* 125

In conformity with the interests of the working people,

and in order to strengthen the socialist system, the citizens of the USSR are guaranteed by law:

(a) Freedom of speech;
(b) Freedom of the press;
(c) Freedom of assembly, including the holding of mass meetings;
(d) Freedom of street processions and demonstrations.

These civil rights are ensured by placing at the disposal of the working people and their organizations, printing presses, stocks of paper, public buildings, the streets, communications facilities and other material requisites for the exercise of these rights.

22. *J. Stalin. From an interview with Roy Howard*

It is difficult for me to imagine what "personal liberty" is enjoyed by an unemployed person, who goes about hungry, and cannot find employment. Real liberty can exist only where exploitation has been abolished, where there is no oppression of some by others, where there is no unemployment and poverty, where a man is not haunted by the fear of being tomorrow deprived of work, of home and of bread.

X. THE RIGHT OF CITIZENS TO UNITE IN PUB-LIC ORGANIZATONS

23. *Constitution of the USSR, article 126*

In conformity with the interests of the working people, and in order to develop the organizational initiative and political activity of the masses of the people, citizens of the USSR are ensured the right to unite in public organizations —trade unions, co-operative associations, youth organizations, sport and defence organizations, cultural, technical and scientific societies; and the most active and politically most conscious citizens in the ranks of the working class and other sections of the working people united in the Communist Party of the Soviet Union (Bolsheviks), which is the vanguard of the working people in their struggle to strengthen and develop the socialist system and is the leading core of all organizations of the working people, both public and State.

XI. THE INVIOLABILITY OF HOMES AND PRIVACY OF CORRESPONDENCE

24. *Constitution of the USSR, article* 128

The inviolability of the homes of citizens and privacy of correspondence are protected by law.

XII. THE DEFENCE OF HUMAN RIGHTS

25. *Constitution of the USSR, article* 129

The USSR affords the right of asylum to foreign citizens persecuted for defending the interests of the working people, or for their scientific activities, or for their struggle for national liberation.

26. *Constitution of the USSR, articles* 109-112

Art. 109. People's Courts are elected by the citizens of the district on the basis of universal, direct and equal suffrage by secret ballot for a term of three years.

Art. 110. Judicial proceedings are conducted in the language of the union republic, autonomous republic or autonomous region, persons not knowing this language being guaranteed every opportunity of fully acquainting themselves with the material of the case through an interpreter and likewise the right to use their own language in court.

Art. 111. In all courts of the USSR, cases are heard in public, unless otherwise provided for by law, and the accused is guaranteed the right to be defended by counsel.

Art. 112. Judges are independent and subject only to the law.

CONSTITUTION (FUNDAMENTAL LAW) OF THE UNION OF SOVIET SOCIALIST REPUBLICS

of 5 December 1936

Chapter X

FUNDAMENTAL RIGHTS AND DUTIES OF CITIZENS

Art. 118. Citizens of the USSR have the right to work, that is, are guaranteed the right to employment and payment for their work in accordance with its quantity and quality.

The right to work is ensured by the socialist organization of the national economy, the steady growth of the productive forces of Soviet society, the elimination of the possibility of economic crises, and the abolition of unemployment.

Art. 119. Citizens of the USSR have the right to rest and leisure.

The right to rest and leisure is ensured by the reduction of the working day to seven hours for the overwhelming majority of the workers, the institution of annual vacations with full pay for workers and employees and the provision of a wide network of sanatoria, rest homes and clubs for the accommodation of the working people.

Art. 120. Citizens of the USSR have the right to maintenance in old age and also in case of sickness or loss of capacity to work.

This right is ensured by the extensive development of social insurance of workers and employees at State expense, free medical service for the working people and the provision of a wide network of health resorts for the use of the working people.

Art. 121. Citizens of the USSR have the right to education.
This right is ensured by universal, compulsory elementary

education; by education, including higher education, being free of charge; by the system of State stipends for the overwhelming majority of students in the universities and colleges; by instruction in schools being conducted in the native language, and by the organization in the factories, state farms, machine and tractor stations and collective farms of free vocational, technical and agronomic training for the working people.

Art. 122. Women in the USSR are accorded equal rights with men in all spheres of economic, State, cultural, social and political life.

The possibility of exercising these rights is ensured to women by granting them an equal right with men to work, payment for work, rest and leisure, social insurance and education, and by State protection of the interests of mother and child, pre-maternity and maternity leave with full pay, and the provision of a wide network of maternity homes, nurseries and kindergartens.

Art. 123. Equality of rights of citizens of the USSR, irrespective of their nationality or race, in all spheres of economic, State, cultural, social and political life, is an indefeasible law.

Any direct or indirect restriction of the rights of, or, conversely, any establishment of direct or indirect privileges for, citizens on account of their race or nationality, as well as any advocacy of racial or national exclusiveness or hatred and contempt, is punishable by law.

Art. 124. In order to ensure to citizens freedom of conscience, the church in the USSR is separated from the State, and the school from the church. Freedom of religious worship and freedom of anti-religious propaganda is recognized for all citizens.

Art. 125. In conformity with the interests of the working people, and in order to strengthen the socialist system, the citizens of the USSR are guaranteed by law:

(a) Freedom of speech;

(b) Freedom of the press;

(c) Freedom of assembly, including the holding of mass meetings;

(d) Freedom of street processions and demonstrations.

These civil rights are ensured by placing at the disposal of the working people and their organizations printing presses, stocks of paper, public buildings, the streets, communications facilities and other material requisites for the exercise of these rights.

Art. 126. In conformity with the interests of the working people, and in order to develop the organizational initiative and political activity of the masses of the people, citizens of the USSR are ensured the right to unite in public organizations—trade unions, co-operative associations, youth organizations, sport and defence organizations, cultural, technical and scientific societies; and the most active and politically most conscious citizens in the ranks of the working class and other sections of the working people unite in the Communist Party of the Soviet Union (Bolsheviks) which is the vanguard of the working people in their struggle to strengthen and develop the socialist system and is the leading core of all organizations of the working people, both public and State.

Art. 127. Citizens of the USSR are guaranteed inviolability of the person. No person may be placed under arrest except by decision of a court or with the sanction of a procurator.

Art. 128. The inviolability of the homes of citizens and privacy of correspondence are protected by law.

Art. 129. The USSR affords the right of asylum to foreign citizens persecuted for defending the interests of the working people, or for their scientific activities, or for their struggle for national liberation.

Art. 130. It is the duty of every citizen of the USSR to abide by the Constitution of the Union of Soviet Socialist

Republics, to observe the laws, to maintain labour discipline, honestly to perform public duties, and to respect the rules of socialist intercourse.

Art. 131. It is the duty of every citizen of the USSR to safeguard and strengthen public, socialist property as the sacred and inviolable foundation of the Soviet system, as the source of the wealth and might of the country, as the prosperous and cultured life of all the working people.

Persons committing offences against public, socialist property are enemies of the people.

Art. 132. Universal military service is law.

Military service in the Workers' and Peasants' Red Army is an honourable duty of the citizens of the USSR.

Art. 133. To defend the fatherland is the sacred duty of every citizen of the USSR. Treason of the country—violation of the oath of allegiance, desertion to the enemy, impairing the military power of the State, espionage—is punishable with all the severity of the law as the most heinous of crimes.

XIII.

ENGLISH LEGAL DOCUMENTS

ANGLO-SAXON LAW

The law of the Anglo-Saxons, which like their architecture and their arts was influenced by the Romans, was mainly oral and traditional. The remains of the ancient poetry of the law of the Anglo-Saxons are few as compared with the ancient Britons.

The earliest of the Anglo-Saxon laws known to exist at the present time are the laws of King Aethelbirht, King of Kent, baptized by Augustine in A.D. 507; the laws of Hlothhaere and Eadrie in A.D. 673 to 686; and the laws of Wihtraed in A.D. 690 to 725 all kings of Kent.

The only ancient copy of these laws is in a manuscript, the *Textus Roffensis,* which was compiled under Ernulf, Bishop of Rochester, between 1115 and 1125.

In both warlike and political matters the best man rose to the top of his class. It was part of the Anglo-Saxon system to recognize principles.

JUDGMENTS

If a ceorl thrived, so that he had fully five hides of his own land, church and kitche, bell-house and burh-gate, seat special duty in the king's hall, then was he thenceforth of thane-right worthy.

So if a "thane" thrived, he became an "eorl." A merchant who fared thrice over the wide sea by his own means, was worthy of thane-right, and the "scholar" also found his suitable rank in the Church.

Every man might be entitled to justice, but the justice of the ealdorman was very different from that of the ceorl.

Let the word of a bishop and of the king be without an oath, incontrovertible. (King Wihtraed, 16.)

A mass-priest's oath and a secular thane's are in English law reckoned of equal value.

A twelf-hynde man's oath stands for six ceorls' oaths; because if a man should avenge a twelf-hynde man, he will be fully avenged on six ceorls, and his wer-gild will be six ceorls' wergilds. (Oaths, p. 78.)

The "wergild" due for the life of the earl was six-times the worth of the wergild due for the life of the ceorl. If an earl were slain, six ceorls might suffer as a recompense.

The king's "burh bryce," or breach of security, shall be cxx shillings.

An archbishop's, 90 shillings.

Any other bishop's and an ealdorman's, 60 shillings.

A twelfe-hynde man's, 30 shillings.

A six-hynde man's, 15 shillings.

A ceorl's edor-bryce, 5 shillings.

If aught of this happen when the "fyrd" (or land force) is out, or in Lent fast, let the "bot" (or amends) be two-fold. If any one in Lent put down holy law among the people without leave, let him make "bot" with cxx shillings. (King Alfred, 40.)

If a wite theow, and Englishman, steal himself away, let *him* be hanged and nothing paid to his lord. (King Ina, 24.)

(5.) if a man slay another in the king's "tun," let him make "bot" with 50 shillings. (13.) if in an eorl's tun, 12 shillings. (King Aethelred.)

If any one with a hloth slay an unoffending *twy-hynde* man, let him who acknowledged the death-blow pay wer and wite, and let every one who was of the party pay shillings as hloth-bot. If it be a *six-hynde* man, let every man pay lx shillings as hloth-bot, and the slayer wer and full wite. If it be a twelve-hynde man, let each of them pay 120 shillings, and the slayer wer and wite. If a hloth do this, and afterwards will deny it on oath, let them all be accused, and let them then all pay the wer in common, and all one wite, such as shall belong to the wer. (King Alfred, 29, 30, 31.)

The value of female chastity was determined by the "caste"

of the maiden. "If a man lie with the king's maiden (perhaps his Hebe or cup-bearer), let him pay a 'bot' of l shillings: if she be a grinding slave, let him pay a 'bot' of xxv shillings: the third class xii shillings. (14.) if a man lie with an eorl's berele or cup-bearer, let him make 'bot' with xii shillings. (16.) with a ceorl's berele, 6 shillings; with a slave of the second class, l scaetts (averaging from 15 to 19 grains of silver) ; and with one of the third, 30 scaetts." So ordained by King Aethelred.

One class committed a rape, and made compensation in money, another in his person. If a man commit a rape upon a ceorl's female slave, let him make bot to the ceorl with 5 shillings, and let the wite be lx shillings. If the male "theow" commit a rape upon a female "theow," let him make bot with his testicles. (King Alfred, 25.)

If a man lie with the wife of a twelve-hynde man, let him make "bot" to the husband with 120 shillings: to a six-hynde man, let him make "bot" with 100 shillings: to a "ceorlish" man, let him make "bot" with 40 shillings. (King Alfred, 10.)

If a man seize hold of the breast of a "ceorlish" woman, let him make "bot" to her with 5 shillings: if he throw her down, and do not lie with her, let him make "bot" with 10 shillings: if he lie with her, let him make "bot" with 60 shillings. If another man had before lain with her, then let the "bot" be half that. If she be charged therewith, let her clear herself with 60 hides, or forfeit half the "bot." *If this befal a woman more nobly born, let the "bot" increase according to the "wer."* (*King Alfred, II.*)

The author of the "Rise and Progress" points out that we still estimate the value of the crime by the station of the parties. "The inequality of the rights of the different classes may be stigmatized as an arbitrary violation of the equity of the law; and it may be said that justice was meted out in proportion to rank and property, and not in conformity to the nature of the crime. But before we prefer the accusation let us pause and substitute the word 'damages' for the word 'were,' and we shall find that we have not entirely abandoned the reasoning of the Anglo-Saxon law, although we have narrowed its application. If a father, for instance, is under the humiliating necessity of bringing an action against the seducer of his daughter, will not the advocate of the defendant loudly expatiate on the condition of the injured female? Should she be in humbler walks of life, will not the circumstance of her poverty be carefully proved, in order to effect a corresponding reduction in the price of her honour and her happiness?"

The graduated scale at which injuries were valued, and the recompense provided even for the most minute, are among the most prominent and curious features of the laws of the Anglo-Saxon kings. They constitute a large part of the "dooms" enacted by Aethelbert and Alfred.

"If a man be so severely wounded in the genitals that he cannot beget a child, let bot be made to him for that with 80s. shillings.

"If a man strike out another's eye, let him pay him lx shillings, and vi shillings and vi pennies, and a third part of a penny as bot. If it remain in the head, and he cannot see aught therewith, let one-third part of the bot be retained." (King Alfred, 47.)

"If a man's tongue be done out of his head by another man's deeds, that shall be like as eye-bot." (King Alfred, 52.)

"If a man's arm with the hand be entirely cut off before the elbow, let bot be made for it with shillings." (Alf. 66.)

"If the loin be maimed, there shall be lx shillings as bot; if he be pierced, let xv shillings be paid as bot; if he be pierced through, then shall there be xxx shillings as bot." (Alf. 68.)

"If a man be wounded in the shoulder, let bot be made with lxxx shillings if the man be alive." (Alf. 68.)

"If a man rupture the tendons on another's neck, and wound them so severely that he has no power of them, and nevertheless live so maltreated, let c shillings be given him as bot, unless the witan shall decree to him one juster and greater." (Alf. 77.)

"If a man strike out another's tooth in the front of his head, let him make 'bot' for it with viii shillings; if it be the canine tooth, let iv shillings be paid as 'bot.' A man's grinder is worth xv shillings." (King Alfred, 49.)

We have selected and classified the following, to bring in apposition the value of each injury—abridging the original language—and distinguishing the dooms respectively enacted by Aethelbert (AE.) and Alfred (Al) .

A nose struck off	60s	(Al. 48)
A shank struck off near the knee	80s	(Al.)
An eye struck out	50s	(AE. 43)
A shank broken	30s	(Al.)
A thigh pierced, 30s; broken	30s	(Al.)
Wounded in the belly, 30s; a thorough wound, each orifice	20s	(I.)
Sound on the shoulder so that the joint-oil flow out	30s	(Al.)
Arm-shanks broken	30s	(Al.)
Thumb struck off	30s	(Al.)
A shoulder lamed	30s	(AE. 38)
The great toe struck off	20s	(Al.)
Outward maim of the hand, if it can be healed	20s	(Al.)
If it fly off, then	40s	
A chin-bone broken	20s	(AE. 54)
A thumb struck off	20s	(AE. 50)
The gold or ring finger struck off	17s	(Al.)
The second toe struck off	15s	(Al.)
A broken cheek	15s	(Al.)
Arm broken above the elbow	15s	(Al.)
Shooting or fore-finger struck off	15s	(Al.)
A cloven chin-bone	12s	(Al.)
A pierced windpipe	12s	(Al.)
Middlemost finger be struck off	12s	(Al.)
Shank pierced beneath the knee	12s	(Al.)
An ear struck off	12s	(AE. 39)

Any injury on the mouth or eye	12s	(AE. 44)
A broken rib within the whole skin	10s	(Al.)
If the skin be broken, then	15s	
The little finger struck off	9s	(Al. lls.) (AE. 54)
The middlemost toe struck off	9s	(Al.)
A nose pierced	9s	(AE. 45)
An ear mutilated	6s	(AE. 42)
A nose mutilated	6s	(AE. 48)
A broken collar-bone	6s	(AE. 52)
The fourth toe struck off	6s	(Al.)
The little toe struck off	5s	(Al.)
A nail struck off	5s	(Al.)
An ear pierced	3s	(AE. 42)
For the smallest disfigurement of the face 3s; for the greater	6s	(AE. 56)
A bruise	1s	(AE. 58.)

"If any one fight in the king's house, let him be liable in all his property, and be it in the king's doom whether he shall or shall not have life. If any one fight in a minster, let him make 'bot' with one hundred and twenty shillings. If anyone fight in an ealdorman's house, or in any other distinguished 'witas,' let him make 'bot' with lx shillings, and pay a second lx shillings as 'wite.' But if he fight in a 'gofol-gelda's' house, or in a 'gebur's,' let him pay cxx shillings as 'wite,' and to the gebur vi shillings; and though it be fought on mid-field, let one hundred and twenty shillings be given as 'wite.' But if they have altercation at a feast, and one of them bear it with patience let the other give xxx shillings as 'wite.'" (King Ina, 6.)

"If a man come from afar, or a stranger go out of the highway and he then neither shout nor blow a horn, he is to be accounted a thief either to be slain or to be redeemed." (King Wihtraed, 28.)

"If a priest allow of illicit intercourse or neglect the baptism of a sick person, or be *drunk* to that degree that he cannot do it, let him abstain from his ministry until the doom of the bishop." (King Wihtraed, 6.)

Doom concerning Hot Iron and Water

"And concerning the ordeal we enjoin by command of God, and of the archbishop and of all bishops, that no man come within the church after the fire is borne in with which the ordeal shall be heated, except the mass-priest, and him who shall go thereto. And let there be measured nine feet from the stake to the mark by the man's feet who goes thereto. But if it be water, let it heat till it low to boiling. And be the kettle of iron or of brass, of lead or of clay; and if it be a single accusation let the hand dive after the stone up to the wrist; and if it be three-fold up to the elbow. And when the ordeal is ready, then let two men go in of either side, and be they agreed that it is so hot as we before have said. And let go in an equal number of men on either side, and stand on both sides of the ordeal along the church. And let these all be fasting and abstinent from their wives on that night. And let the mass-priest sprinkle holy water over them all, and let each of them taste of the holy water, and give them all the book and the image of Christ's rood to kiss, and let no man mend the fire any longer when the hallowing is begun, but let the iron lie upon the hot embers till the last collect; after that let it be laid upon the Stapela, and let there be no other speaking within except that they earnestly pray to Almighty God that he make manifest what is soothest. And let him go thereto, and let his hand be enveloped, and be it postponed till after the third day whether it be foul or clean within the envelope. And he who shall break this law be the ordeal with respect to him woid, and let him pay to the king cxx shillings as 'wite.'" (King Aethelstan, 7.)

Of Moneyers.

"That there be one money over all the king's dominions,

and that no man mint except within port. And if the moneyer be guilty, let the hand be struck off with which he wrought that offence, and be set up on the money smithy; but if it be an accusation and he is willing to clear himself, then let him go to the hot iron and clear the hand therewith with which he is charged that fraud to have wrought. And if at the ordeal he should be guilty, let the like be done as he is here before ordained.

"In Canterbury, VII moneyers: IV the king's and II the bishop's, I the abbot's.

"At Rochdale III; II the king's and I the bishops.

At London	VIII
At Winchester	VI
At Lewes	II
At Hastings	I
Another at Chichester	
At Hampton	II
At Wareham	II
At Exeter	II
At Shaftesbury	II
Else at the other burgs	I"

(King Aethelstan, 14.)

"That no shield-wright cover a shield with sheep's skin; and if he so do, let him pay xxx shillings." (King Aethelstan.)

"If a limb-maimed man who has been condemned to be forsaken and he after that live three days, after that any one who is willing to take care of sore and soul may help him with the bishop's leave." (Laws of Edward and Guthrum, 10.)

"If during her husband's life a woman lie with another man, and it become public, let her afterwards be for a worldly shame as regards herself, and let her lawful husband have all that she possessed, and let her then forfeit *both nose and ears,* and if it be a prosecution and the lad fail, let the bishop use his power and doom severely." (King Cnut, 54.)

THE DOMESDAY BOOK, 1086

In December of 1085, William the Conqueror, holding court at Gloucester, England, ordered that a special survey should be made of his kingdom. The main theme gathered by the royal agents in compiling the survey is financial in nature and provided the King with an exact record of the local contributions to the king's gold—or Danegeld—"the one great taxe levied over the whole of England."

Another reason for the survey was the threatened invasion from Scandinavia which the king learned of while in Normandy during the summer of 1085. In August of 1086, while the royal agents were carrying out their work on the survey, the King held the moot of Salisbury where he took a special oath of allegiance from many of his magnates. It may be assumed that the needs of defense made it advisable for the King to obtain more accurate information as to how the land of England had been allocated among his greater followers.

The royal agents, going through the shires of England, received sworn verdicts concerning each piece of land, its present and former holders, the method of holding and the population on it. The verdicts were recorded territorially, summarized and rearranged upon a feudal plan. Originally kept in the king's Treasury at Winchester, they are now preserved in the Public Record Office in London.

Because of the speed and thoroughness with which the survey was taken, the Domesday Book remains a masterpiece unsurpassed in medieval history and provides an invaluable historical source.

HUNTINGDONSHIRE

In the borough of Huntingdon there are 4 quarters.

In 2 quarters there were *T.R.E.*, and are now, 116 burgesses rendering all customs and the king's geld and under them there are 100 bordars who help them to pay the geld. Of these burgesses St. Benedict of Ramsey had 10 with sake and soke and every custom except that they paid geld *T.R.E.* Eustace took them away wrongfully from the abbey and they are, with the others, in the king's hand. Ulf Fenisc had 18 burgesses, now Gilbert of Ghent has them with sake and soke except for the king's geld.

The abbot of Ely has 1 toft with sake and soke except for the king's geld.

The bishop of Lincoln had in the site of the castle a messuage with sake and soke which has now disappeared.

Earl Siward had a messuage with a house with sake and soke, quit from all custom, which the Countess Judith has now.

In the site of the castle there were 20 messuages assessed to all customs, and rendering yearly 16 shillings and 8 pence to the king's 'farm.' These do not exist now.

In addition to these, there were and are 60 waste messuages within these quarters. These gave and give their customs. And in addition to these there are 8 waste messuages which *T.R.E.* were fully occupied. These gave all customs.

In the other 2 quarters there were and are 140 burgesses, less half a house, assessed to all customs and the king's geld, and these had 80 haws for which they gave and give all customs. Of these St. Benedict of Ramsey had 22 burgesses *T.R.E.* Two of these were quit of all customs, and 30 rendered 10 pence yearly each. All other customs belonged to the abbot, apart from the king's geld.

In these quarters Aluric the sheriff *T.R.E.* had 1 messuage which King William afterwards granted to his wife and sons. Eustace has it now, and the poor man, with his mother, is claiming it. In these 2 quarters there were and are 44 waste messuages which gave and give their customs. And in these 2 quarters Borred and Turchil *T.R.E.* had 1 church with 2 hides of land and 22 burgesses with houses belonging to the same church with sake and soke; Eustace has all this now. Wherefore these men claim the king's mercy; nevertheless these 22 burgesses give every custom to the king.

Geffrey the bishop has 1 church and 1 house from the aforesaid which Eustace took away from St. Benedict, and the same saint is still claiming them.

In this borough Gos and Hunef had 16 houses *T.R.E.* with sake and soke and toll and team. The Countess Judith has them now.

The borough of Huntingdon used to defend itself towards the king's geld for 50 hides as the fourth part of Hurstingstone hundred, but now it does not so pay geld in that hundred, after the king set a geld of money on the borough. From this whole borough 10 pounds came out *T.R.E.* by way of 'Landgable' of which the earl had the third part, and the king two-thirds. Of this rent 16 shillings and 8 pence, divided between the earl and the king, now remain upon 20 messuages where the castle is. In addition to these payments the king had 20 pounds and the earl 10 pounds from the 'farm' of the borough more or less according as each could make disposition of his part. One mill rendered 40 shillings to the king and 20 shillings to the earl. To this borough there belong 2 ploughlands and 40 acres of land and 10 acres of meadow, of which the king with two parts, and the earl with the third part, divide the rent. The burgesses cultivate this land and take it on lease through the servants of the king and the earl. Within the aforesaid rent there are 3 fishermen rendering 3 shillings. In this borough there were 3 moneyers paying 40 shillings between the king and the earl, but now they are not there. *T.R.E.* it rendered 30 pounds; now the same.

In Hurstingstone hundred demesne ploughlands are quit of the king's geld. Villeins and sokemen pay geld according to the hides written in the return, apart from Broughton where the abbot of Ramsey pays geld for 1 hide with the others.

Here are noted those holding lands in Huntingdonshire

1. King William
2. The bishop of Lincoln.
3. The bishop of Coutances.
4. The abbey of Ely.
5. The abbey of Crowland.
6. The abbey of Ramsey.
7. The abbey of Thorney.
8. The abbey of Peterborough.
9. Count Eustace.
10. The count of Eu.
11. Earl Hugh.
12. Walter Giffard.
13. William of Warenne.
14. Hugh of Bolbec.
15. Eudo, son of Hubert.
16. Sweyn of Essex.
17. Roger of Ivry.
18. Arnulf of Hesdins.
19. Eustace the sheriff.
20. The Countess Judith.
21. Gilbert of Ghent.
22. Aubrey 'de Vere.'
23. William, son of Ansculf.
24. Rannulf, the brother of Ilger.
25. Robert Fafiton.
26. William 'Ingania'.
27. Ralph, son of Osmund.
28. Rohais, the wife of Richard.
29. The king's thegns.

1. *The land of the king*

Hurstingstone hundred

A manor. In Hartford King Edward had 15 hides assessed to the geld. There is land for 17 ploughs. Rannulf the brother of Ilger keeps it now. There are 4 ploughs now on the demesne; and 30 villeins and 3 bordars have 8 ploughs. There is a priest; 2 churches; 2 mills rendering 4 pounds; and 40 acres of meadow. Woodland for pannage, 1 league in length and half a league in breadth. *T.R.E.* it was worth 24 pounds; now 15 pounds.

Normancross hundred

A manor. In Bottlebridge King Edward had 5 hides assessed to the geld. There is land for 8 ploughs. The king has 1 plough now on the demesne; and 15 villeins have 5 ploughs. There is a priest and a church; 60 acres of meadow and 12 acres of woodland for pannage in Northamptonshire. *T.R.E.* it was worth 100 shillings; now 8 pounds. Rannulf keeps it.

In this manor belonging to the king, and in other manors, the enclosure of the abbot of Thorney is doing harm to 300 acres of meadow.

In Stilton the king's sokemen of Normancross have 3 virgates of land assessed to the geld. There is land for 2 ploughs, and there are 5 ploughing oxen.

In Orton the king has soke over 3½ hides of land in the land of the abbot of Peterborough which was Godwine's.

Toseland hundred

A manor. In Gransden Earl Alfgar had 8 hides of land assessed to the geld. There is land for 15 ploughs. There are 7 ploughs now on the demesne; and 24 villeins and 8 bordars have 8 ploughs. There is a priest and a church; 50 acres of meadow; 12 acres of underwood. From the pasture come 5 shillings and 4 pence. *T.R.E.* it was worth 40 pounds; now 30 pounds. Rannulf keeps it.

Leightonstone hundred

A manor. In Alconbury, and in Gidding, which is an outlying estate, there were 10 hides assessed to the geld. There is land for 20 ploughs. There are now 5 ploughs belonging to the hall on 2 hides of this land; and 35 villeins have 13 ploughs there; 80 acres of meadow. *T.R.E.* it was worth 12 pounds; now the same. Rannulf, the brother of Ilger, keeps it.

A manor. In Keyston King Edward had 4 hides of land assessed to the geld. There is land for 12 ploughs. There are 2 ploughs now on the demesne; and 24 villeins and 8 bordars have 10 ploughs; 86 acres of meadow. Scattered woodland for pannage 5 furlongs in length and 1½ furlongs in breadth. *T.R.E.* it was worth 10 pounds; now the same. Rannulf, the brother of Ilger, keeps it.

A manor. In Brampton King Edward had 15 hides assessed to the geld. There is land for 15 ploughs. There are 3 ploughs now on the demesne; and 36 villeins and 2 bordars have 14 ploughs. There is a church and a priest; 100 acres of meadow. Woodland for pannage half a league in length and 2 furlongs in breadth. Two mills rendering 100 shillings. *T.R.E.* it was worth 20 pounds; now the same. Rannulf, the brother of Ilger, keeps it.

Soke.[1] In Graff there are 5 hides assessed to the geld. There is land for 8 ploughs. The soke is in Leightonstone hundred. There 7 sokemen and 17 villeins have 6 ploughs now and 6 acres of meadow. Woodland for pannage 1 league in length and 1 league in breadth. *T.R.E.* it was worth 5 pounds; now 10 shillings less.

A manor. In Godmanchester King Edward had 14 hides assessed to the geld. There is land for 57 ploughs. There are 2 ploughs now on the king's demesne on 2 hides of this land; and 80 villeins and 16 bordars have 24 ploughs. There is a priest and a church; 3 mills rendering 100 shillings; 160 acres of meadow; and 50 acres of woodland for pannage. From the pasture come 20 shillings. From the meadows come 70 shillings. *T.R.E.* it was worth 40 pounds; now it is worth the same 'by tale'.

---

[1] This term prefixed to estates in this survey indicates "a group of tenements—united to some manor by the ties of rent, the homage of the peasant landholders, and in most cases their suit of court to the manorial centre."

2. *The land of the bishop of Lincoln*

Toseland hundred

A manor. In 'Cotes' the bishop of Lincoln had 2 hides assessed to the geld. There is land for 3 ploughs. There are 2 ploughs now on the demesne; and 3 villeins have 2 oxen; 20 acres of meadow. *T.R.E.* it was worth 40 shillings; now the same. Thurstan holds it of the bishop.

A manor. In Staughton the bishop of Lincoln had 6 hides assessed to the geld. There is land for 15 ploughs. There are 2½ ploughs on the demesne; and 16 villeins and 4 bordars have 8 ploughs. There is a priest and a church; 24 acres of meadow; 100 acres of underwood. *T.R.E.* it was worth 10 pounds; now the same. Eustace holds it of the bishop. The abbot of Ramsey claims this manor against the bishop.

A manor. In Diddington the bishop of Lincoln had 2½ hides assessed to the geld. There is land for 2 ploughs. There are now 2 ploughs on the demesne and 5 villeins have 2 ploughs. A church, and 18 acres of meadow. Woodland for pannage half a league in length and half in breadth. *T.R.E.* it was worth 60 shillings; now 70 shillings. William holds it of the bishop.

A manor. In Buckden the bishop of Lincoln had 20 hides assessed to the geld. There is land for 20 ploughs. There are now 5 ploughs on the demesne; and 37 villeins and 20 bordars have 14 ploughs. There is a church and a priest; 1 mill worth 30 shillings; 84 acres of meadow. Woodland for pannage 1 league in length and 1 league in breadth. *T.R.E.* it was worth 20 pounds; now 16 pounds and 10 shillings.

Normancross hundred

A manor. In Denton Godric had 5 hides assessed to the geld. There is land for 2 ploughs. There is 1 plough on the demesne; and 10 villeins and 2 bordars have 5 ploughs. There is a church and a priest; 24 acres of meadow and 24 acres of underwood. *T.R.E.* it was worth 100 shillings; now 4 pounds. Thurstan holds it of the bishop.

A manor. In Orton Leuric had 3 hides and 1 virgate of land assessed to the geld. There is land for 2 ploughs and 1 ox. There is now 1 plough on the demesne; and 2 villeins and 9 acres of meadow. *T.R.E.* it was worth 20 shillings; now 10 shillings. John holds it of the bishop. The king claims the soke of this land.

A manor. In Stilton Tovi had 2 hides assessed to the geld. There is land for 2 ploughs and 7 oxen. There is now 1 plough on the demesne; and 6 villeins have 3 ploughs; 16 acres of meadow and 5 acres of underwood. *T.R.E.* it was worth 40 shillings; now the same. John holds it of the bishop. This land was given to Bishop Wulfwig *T.R.E.*

Leightonstone hundred
A manor. In Leighton Bromswold Turchil the Dane had 15 hides assessed to the geld. There is land for 17 ploughs. There are now 6 ploughs on the demesne; and 33 villeins and 3 bordars have 10 ploughs. One mill rendering 3 shillings; 3 knights hold 3 hides less 1 virgate of this land: they have 3 ploughs and 3 villeins with a half a plough. There are 30 acres of meadow and 10 acres of underwood. *T.R.E.* the bishop's demesne was worth 20 pounds and it is worth the same now. The land of knights is worth 60 shillings. Earl Waltheof gave this manor in alms to St. Mary of Lincoln.

In Pertenhall Alwin had 1 virgate of land assessed to the geld. There is land for half a plough. This land is situated in Bedfordshire but renders geld and service in Huntingdonshire. The king's servants claim this land for his use. *T.R.E.* it was worth 5 shillings; now the same. William holds it of Bishop Remigius and ploughs it with his own demesne.

3. *The land of the bishop of Coutances*
In Hargrave Semar had 1 virgate of land assessed to the geld. There is land for 2 oxen. The soke belongs to Leightonstone hundred. The same man himself holds it of the bishop of Coutances and ploughs there with 2 oxen and has 2 acres of meadow. *T.R.E.* it was worth 5 shillings; now the same.

4. *The land of the abbey of Ely*

Hurstingstone hundred

A manor. In Colne the abbey of Ely had 6 hides assessed to the geld. There is land for 6 ploughs and in demesne the abbey has land for 2 ploughs apart from the 6 hides. There are now 2 ploughs on the demesne, and 13 villeins and 5 bordars have 5 ploughs; 10 acres of meadow. Woodland for pannage 1 league in length and half a league in breadth; marsh of the same extent. *T.R.E.* it was worth 6 pounds; now 100 shillings.

A manor. In Bluntisham the abbey of Ely had 6½ hides assessed to the geld. There is land for 8 ploughs, and, apart from these hides, the abbey has land for 2 ploughs in demesne. There are now 2 ploughs on the demesne; and 10 villeins and 3 bordars have 3 ploughs. There is a priest and a church; 20 acres of meadow. Woodland for pannage 1 league in length and 4 furlongs in breadth. *T.R.E.* it was worth 100 shillings; now the same.

A manor. In Somersham the abbey of Ely had 8 hides assessed to the geld. There is land for 12 ploughs, and, apart from these hides, the abbey has land for 2 ploughs in demesne. There are now 2 ploughs on the demesne; and 32 villeins and 9 bordars have 9 ploughs. There are 3 fisheries rendering 8 shillings, and 20 acres of meadow. Woodland for pannage 1 league in length and 7 furlongs in breadth. *T.R.E.* it was worth 7 pounds; now 8 pounds.

A manor. In Spaldwick the abbey of Ely had 15 hides assessed to the geld. There is land for 15 ploughs. There are now 4 ploughs on the demesne on 5 hides of this land; and 50 villeins and 10 bordars have 25 ploughs. There is 1 mill rendering 2 shillings; and 160 acres of meadow; and 60 acres of woodland for pannage. *T.R.E.* it was worth 16 pounds; now 22 pounds.

A manor. In Little Catworth, outlying estate of Spaldwick, there are 4 hides assessed to the geld. Land for 4 ploughs; 7 villeins have 2 ploughs there now.

5. *The land of the abbey of Crowland*

A manor. In Morborne the abbey of Crowland has 5 hides assessed to the geld. There is land for 9 ploughs. There are now 2 ploughs on the demesne on 1 hide of this land; and 16 villeins and 3 bordars have 7 ploughs. There is a church and a priest; 40 acres of meadow; 1 acre of underwood. *T.R.E.* it was worth 100 shillings; now the same.

In Thurning there are 1½ hides assessed to the geld. There is land for 1½ ploughs. The soke belongs to the king's manor of Alconbury. Eustace holds it now from the abbot of Crowland, and had 1 plough there and 1 villein with half a plough and 6 acres of meadow. *T.R.E.* it was worth 20 shillings; now the same.

6. *The land of St. Benedict of Ramsey*

[This is similarly described as lying in Stukeley; Abbot's Ripton; Broughton; Wistow; Upwood; Holywell; St. Ives; Houghton; Wyton; Warboys; Sawtry; Elton; Lutton; Yelling; Hemingford Abbots; Offord; Dillington; Gidding; Bythorn; Bringtin; Old Weston; Ellington.]

7. *The land of St. Mary of Thorney*

[This is similarly described as lying in Yaxley; Stranground; Woodstone; Haddon; Water Newton; Sibson; Stibbington.]

8. *The land of St. Peter of Peterborough*

[This is similarly described as lying at Fletton; Alwalton; Orton Waterville.]

9. *The land of Count Eustace*

[This is similarly described as lying at Glatton; Chesterton; Sibson.]

10. *The land of the count Eu*

[This is similarly described as lying at Buckworth.]

11. *The land of Earl Hugh*

[This is similarly described as lying in Upton; Coppingford.]

12. *The land of Walter Giffard*
[This is similarly described as lying at Folksworth.]

13. *The land of William of Warenne*
[This is similarly described as lying at Kimbolton; Keysoe; Catworth.]

14. *The land of Hugh of Bolbec*
[This is similarly described as lying at Wood Walton.]

15. *The land of Eudo, son of Hubert*
[This is similarly described as lying at Hamerton.]

16. *The land of Sweyn of Essex*
[This is similarly described as lying at Waresley.]

17. *The land of Roger of Ivry*
[This is similarly described as lying at Covington.]

18. *The land of Arnulf of Hesdins*
[This is similarly described as lying in Offord Cluny.]

19. *The land of Eustace the sheriff*
[This is similarly described as lying in Sawtry; Caldecot; Washingley; Orton Longueville; Stilton; Chesterton; Bottlebridge; Swineshead; Catworth; Hargrave; Gidding; Winwick Thurning; Luddington; Weston; Wooley; Hemingford; Offord; Warsley; Hail Weston; Southoe; Perry; Catworth.]

20. *The land of the Countess Judith*
[This is similarly described as lying in Conington; Sawtry; Stukeley; Molesworth; 'Cotes'; Eynesbury; Offord; Diddington; Paxton.]

21. *The land of Gilbert of Ghent*
[This is similarly described as lying in Fen Stanton.]

22. *The land of Aubrey 'de Vere'*
[This is similarly described as lying in Yelling; Hemingford.]

23. *The land of William, son of Ansculf*
[This is similarly described as lying in Waresley.]

24. *The land of Rannulf, brother of Ilger*
[This is similarly described as lying in Everton.]

25. *The land of Robert Fafiton*
[This is similarly described as lying in Hail Weston; South-hoe.]

26. *The land of William 'Ingania'*
[This is similarly described as lying in Gidding.]

27. *The land of Ralph, son of Osmund*
[This is similarly described as lying in Hemingford.]

28. *The land of Rohais, wife of Richard fitz Gilbert*

Toseland hundred
A manor. In Eynesbury Robert, son of Wimarc, had 15 hides assessed to the geld. There is land for 27 ploughs. Rohais, the wife of Richard, has 7 ploughs on the demesne there now. In the same place St. Neot has from her 3 ploughs on the demesne, and in the same village 19 villeins and 5 bordars have 7 ploughs. There is 1 mill worth 23 shillings, and 1 fishery which is valued with the manor; 65½ acres of meadow. *T.R.E.* it was worth 24 pounds; now it is worth 21 pounds apart from that which is assigned to the food of the monks, which is valued at 4 pounds. William 'Brito' holds 2 hides and 1 virgate of this land from Rohais and has half a plough on the demesne; and 3 villeins and 4 bordars have 1 plough. It is worth 30 shillings.

29. *The land of the king's thegns*

A manor. In Washingley, Chetelebert had 2½ hides assessed to the geld. There is land for 4 ploughs. He himself holds from the king and has 1 plough there; and 10 villeins have 4 ploughs. There is a church and a priest; 12 acres of meadow. Woodland for pannage 7 furlongs in length and 10½ furlongs in breadth. *T.R.E.* it was worth 10 shillings; now the same.

Leightonstone hundred

In Keysoe Alwine had 1 virgate of land assessed to the geld with sake and soke. There is land for 2 oxen. It belongs to Bedfordshire, but gives geld in Huntingdonshire. He himself holds now of the king and has 1 villein there with 2 oxen in a plough. *T.R.E.* it was worth 16 pence; now the same.

A manor. In Catworth Avic had 3 hides assessed to the geld. There is land for 4 ploughs. Eric holds it now of the king. And the same man has under the king 1 hide assessed to the geld. There is land for 1 plough. He has 2 villeins there, and 6 acres of meadow. *T.R.E.* it was worth 40 shillings; now 20 shillings.

In Brampton Elric has 1 hide and 1 virgate of land assessed to the geld. There is land for 10 oxen. There are 3 bordars and 1 plough. It is worth 30 shillings.

A manor. In Wooley Golde and Uluric, his son, had 3 hides assessed to the geld. There is land for 6 ploughs. They themselves now have it from the king. There is 1 plough on the demesne; and 14 villeins have 5 ploughs; 20 acres of meadow. *T.R.E.* it was worth 60 shillings; now the same.

In Sawtry Alwine had half a carucate assessed to the geld. There is land for 6 oxen. His wife holds it now of the king, and has 1 plough there and 2 acres. *T.R.E.* it was worth 10 shillings; now the same.

[Claims]

The jurors of Huntingdon say that the church of St. Mary of the borough and the land which is annexed to it belonged

395

to the church of Thorney, but the abbot gave it in pledge to the burgesses. Moreover, King Edward gave it to Vitalis and Bernard, his priests, and they sold it to Hugh, chamberlain to King Edward. Moreover, Hugh sold it to two priests of Huntingdon, and in respect of this they have the seal of King Edward. Eustace has it now without livery, without writ, and without seisin.

Eustace took away wrongfully the house of Leveve and gave it to Oger of London.

They bear witness that the land of Hunef and Gos was under the hand of King Edward on the day when he was alive and dead and that they held of him and not of the earl. But the jurors say that they heard that King William was said to have given it to Waltheof.

Touching the 5 hides of Broughton the jurors say that it was the land of sokemen *T.R.E.*, but that the same king gave the land and the soke over the men to St. Benedict of Ramsey in return for a service which Abbot Alwin did for him in Saxony, and ever afterwards the Saint had it.

The shire bears witness that the land of Bricmer 'Belehorne' was 'reeveland' *T.R.E.* and belonged to the king's 'farm'.

They bear witness that the land of Alwin the priest was to the abbot. . . .

They bear witness that Aluric's land of Yelling and Hemingford belonged to St. Benedict and that it was granted to Aluric for the term of his life on the condition that after his death it ought to return to the church, and 'Bocstede' with it. But this same Aluric was killed in the battle of Hastings, and the abbot took back his lands and held them until Aubrey 'de Vere' deprived him of possession.

Touching 2 hides which Ralph, son of Osmund, holds in Hemingford, they say that one of them belonged to the demesne of the church of Ramsey in King Edward's day, and that Ralph holds it against the abbot's will. Touching the other hide, they say that Godric held it from the abbot, but when the abbot was in Denmark, Osmund, Ralph's father, seized it from Sawin the fowler, to whom the abbot had given it for love of the king.

Touching Summerlede they say that he held his land from Turulf who gave it to him, and afterwards from the sons of Turulf, and they had sake and soke over him.

The jurors say that the land of Wulwine Chit of Weston was a manor by itself, and did not belong to Kimbolton, but that nevertheless he was a man of Earl Harold.

Touching a hide and a half of land which was Ælget's the jurors say that this Ælget held them from Earl Tosti with sake and soke and afterwards of Waltheof.

Godric the priest likewise held 1 hide of land from Earl Waltheof *T.R.E.*, and Eustace holds it now.

They say that the land of Godwine of Weston in no way belonged to Saxi, Fafiton's predecessor.

The men of the shire bear witness that King Edward gave Swineshead to Earl Siward with sake and soke, and so Earl Harold had it, except that the men paid geld in the hundred, and performed military service with them.

Touching the land of Fursa, the soke was the king's. King Edward had soke over 1 virgate of land of Alwin Deule in Pertenhall.

The jurors say that the hide of land which Wulwine Chit had in Catworth was in the king's soke and that Earl Harold did not have it.

In Little Catworth the same Wulwine had 1 hide over which King Edward always had sake and soke. But Wulwine could give and sell the land to whom he wished. But the men of the countess say that the king gave the land to Earl Waltheof.

The shire bears witness that the third part of half a hide which lies in Easton and pays geld in Bedfordshire belongs to the abbot of Ely's manor of Spaldwick. The abbot of Ely thus held it *T.R.E.*, and for five years after the coming of King William, Eustace seized this land wrongfully from the church, and kept it.

The jurors say that Keystone was and is of the 'farm' of King Edward, and although Aluric the sheriff resided in that village, he nevertheless always paid the king's 'farm' therefrom, and his sons after him, until Eustace took the sheriffdom. They have never seen or heard of a seal of King Edward that he put it outside his 'farm'.

Alwold and his brother claim that Eustace took away their land from them, and the men of the shire deny that they have ever seen a seal, or seen anyone who gave Eustace seisin of it.

On the day when King Edward was alive and dead, Gidding was an outlying estate of Alconbury in the king's 'farm'.

The men of the shire bear witness that Buckworth was an outlying estate of Paxton *T.R.E.*

They say that 36 hides of land in Brampton which Richard 'Ingania' claims to belong to the forest were of the king's demesne 'farm', and did not belong to the forest.

They say that Graffham was and is the king's sokeland, and that they have not seen the writ, or anyone who gave legal possession of this to Eustace.

Touching 6 hides in Conington they said they had heard that these formerly belonged to the church of Thorney, and that they were granted to Turchill on condition that after [his] death they ought to return to the church with the other 3 hides in the same village. The jurors said that they had heard this, but they had not seen evidence of it, nor were they present when the arrangement was made.

Touching the land of Tosti of Sawtry, they say that Eric, his brother, bequeathed it to the church of Ramsey after his death and after the death of his brother and sister.

Touching Fletton the jurors say that *T.R.E.* the whole belonged to the church of Peterborough, and so it should.

Touching Leuric's land the jurors say that it was in the king's soke, but Bishop Remigius shows the writ of King Edward by which he gave Leuric with all his land to the bishopric of Lincoln with sake and soke.

206. Domesday Book, vol. I, fols. 4 and 4b: The Knights of Lanfranc

Domesday Book normally alludes to the holdings of knights only incidentally as they occur on the estates of the king's tenants-in-chief. In the description of Kent, however, a separate section is exceptionally allotted to the estates of the knights of the archbishop of Canterbury in that country. It should be compared with the description of the barony of the archbishop given below in No. 222. This is printed in the edition (1783) of the Record Commission. A translation is in the *Victoria County History: Kent,* vol. III (1932), p. 213.

LAND OF THE ARCHBISHOP OF CANTERBURY

Land of his knights

In Axton hundred

Ansgot holds Farningham from the archbishop. It is assessed at 1 suling. There is land for   .[1] In the desmene there are 2 ploughs, and 13 villeins with 5 bordars have 3½ ploughs. There are 6 acres of meadow, and woodland for 20 pigs, and of this same woodland Richard of Tonbridge holds as much again in his lowy. *T.R.E.* this manor was worth 7 pounds; now 11 pounds. Of this the monks of Canterbury have 4 pounds to provide for their clothing.

Ralph, son of Unspac, holds Eynsford from the archbishop. It is assessed at 6 suling. There is land for   .[1] In the demesne there are 5 ploughs, and 29 villeins with 9 bordars have 15 ploughs. There are 2 churches and 9 slaves, and 2 mills worth 43 shillings and 29 acres of meadow. Woodland for 20 pigs. *T.R.E.* it was worth 16 pounds; now 20. Of this manor Richard of Tonbridge holds as much woodland as can sustain 20 pigs, and 1 mill worth 5 shillings and 1 fishpond in his lowy.

Mauger holds from the archbishop 3 yokes in Orpington, and it was assessed for as much apart from Orpington. Now it is assessed for 2 yokes within Orpington, and for a third

[1] A space is left for the number of ploughs.

yoke apart from Orpington. There is land for   .[1] In the demesne there is 1 plough; and 4 villeins with 1 bordar and 4 slaves have half a plough; 3 acres of meadow, and woodland for 11 pigs. *T.R.E.* it was worth 40 shillings; when received, 20 shillings; now 50 shillings.

Haimo the sheriff holds Brasted from the archbishop. It is assessed at 1½ sulings. There is land for 10 ploughs. In the demesne there are 2 ploughs; and 34 villeins with 16 bordars have 12 ploughs. There is a church; 15 slaves; and 2 mills worth 24 shillings; woodland for 80 pigs; and 9 shillings and 6 pence from herbage. *T.R.E.* it was worth 10 pounds; when received the same; now 17 pounds. Alnod the abbot held this manor from the archbishop.

The count of Eu holds Ulcombe from the archbishop. It is assessed at 2½ sulings *T.R.E.*, and is now assessed at 2 sulings. There is land for 9 ploughs. In the demesne are 2 ploughs; and 23 villeins with 7 bordars have 7 ploughs. There is a church; a mill worth 4 shillings; 8 acres of meadow; woodland for 80 pigs. In all it was worth *T.R.E.* 10 pounds; when received 8 pounds; now 11 pounds. Alfer held this manor from the archbishop.

In Eyhorne hundred

Ralph, the son of Turold, holds Boughton from the archbishop. It is assessed at half a suling and it is included in the 6 sulings of Hollingbourne. There is land for 1½ ploughs. In the demesne is 1 plough; and 3 villeins with 2 bordars have 1 plough. There is a church; 2 acres of meadow; and woodland for 16 pigs. In all it is worth, and always was worth, 40 shillings.

In Faversham hundred

Richard, a man of the archbishop, holds Leaveland from him. It is assessed for 1 suling. There is land for   .[1] In the demesne is 1 plough, and 2 villeins with 1 bordar have 1

[1] A space is left for the number of ploughs.

plough. Woodland for 5 pigs. *T.R.E.* and afterwards it was worth 30 shillings. Now 20 shillings.

In Boughton-under-Blean hundred

The same Richard holds Graveney from the archbishop. It is assessed at 1 suling. There is land for   .[1] In the demesne is 1 plough; and 8 villeins with 10 bordars have 2 ploughs. There are 5 slaves; 10 acres of meadow; and 4 salt-pans worth 4 shillings. *T.R.E.* and afterwards it was worth 100 shillings; now 6 pounds. Out of this the monks of Canterbury have 20 shillings.

In Calehill hundred

Godfrey the steward holds Lenham from the archbishop. It is assessed for 2 sulings. There is land for   .[1] In the demesne are 2 ploughs, and 15 villeins with 2 bordars have 4 ploughs. There are 4 slaves; 6 acres of meadow; 1 mill worth 7 shillings; and woodland for 10 pigs. In all it was worth 8 pounds, but it renders 12 pounds and 10 shillings.

In Teynham hundred

The same Godfrey holds from the archbishop, in Sheppey, half a suling. There is land for   .[1] In the demesne is 1 plough with 2 bordars and 4 slaves. *T.R.E.* and afterwards it was worth 30 shillings; now 4 pounds, but it renders 100 shillings.

In Eastry hundred

Osbern, the son of Letard, holds 1 yoke from the archbishop in Buckland, and there he has in demesne 1 plough; and it is worth 10 shillings.

William Folet holds Tilmanstone from the archbishop. It was assessed at 1 suling. In the demesne there are 2 ploughs and 5 bordars. Once it was worth 20 shillings. Now 30 shillings.

[1] A space is left for the number of ploughs.

William Folet holds Finglesham from the archbishop. It is assessed at half a suling. There he has 6 villeins with 1½ ploughs. The same William holds Statenborough from the archbishop. It was assessed at half a suling. There he has 12 villeins with 1½ ploughs. These lands *T.R.E.* were worth *40 shillings. When the archbishop received them, 10 shillings.* Now 30 shillings.

In Heane hundred

Hugh of Montfort-sur-Risle holds Saltwood from the archbishop. It was assessed at 7 sulings, *T.R.E.*, and now it is assessed at 3 sulings. There is land for 15 ploughs. In the demesne there are 2 ploughs; and 33 villeins with 12 bordars have 9½ ploughs. There is a church; 2 slaves; 9 mills worth 20 shillings; 33 acres of meadow; woodland for 80 pigs. To this manor belong 225 burgesses in Hythe. The borough and the manor together were *T.R.E.* worth 16 pounds; when received 8 pounds. Now it is altogether worth 29 pounds, 6 shillings, and 4 pence.

In Street hundred

William of Adisham holds Berwick from the archbishop, for a manor. It is assessed at half a suling. There is land for 3 ploughs. In demesne there are 2 ploughs, and 9 villeins with 9 bordars have 1½ ploughs. There are 18 acres of meadow, and woodland for 20 pigs. *T.R.E.* it was worth 60 shillings, and afterwards 20 shillings. Now it is worth 7 pounds, but it renders 11 pounds.

In Langport hundred

Robert of Romney holds Langport from the archbishop. It is assessed for 1½ sulings. There is land for 6 ploughs. In demesne are 2 ploughs, and 29 villeins with 9 bordars have 9 ploughs. There are 7 salt-pans worth 8 shillings and 9 pence. To this manor belong 21 burgesses who are in Romney. From these the archbishop has the three forfeitures: theft, breach of the peace, and public violence. The king, however, has all their service, and they themselves have all customs and the other forfeitures in return for their sea-service. They are in the hand of the king. *T.R.E.* and afterwards it was worth 10 pounds; now 16 pounds.

207. Domesday Book, vol. I, fol. 56: The Customs of Berkshire

Printed in the Record Commission's edition of Domesday Book (1783) and in W. Stubbs, *Select Charters.* Translated in *Victoria County History: Berkshire,* vol. I, p. 326.

When in the time of King Edward a general geld was given, each hide throughout the whole of Berkshire used to give 3 pence and 1 halfpenny before Christmas and as much again at Pentecost.

If the king was sending out an army anywhere, only one soldier went out from each 5 hides, and for his provision or pay 4 shillings for 2 months was given him from each hide. The money, however, was not sent to the king but given to the soldiers. If anyone summoned to serve in an expedition failed to do so, he forfeited all his land to the king. If anyone secured a substitute and that substitute failed to serve, the lord of the substitute was fined 50 shillings.

When a thegn, or a demesne warrior of the king was dying he sent all his weapons to the king as a 'relief', and 1 horse saddled and 1 horse unsaddled. If he possessed hounds or falcons, these were offered to the king for his acceptance if he wished to have them.

If anyone slew a man who was under the protection of the king's peace, his person and his possessions were forfeit to the king. If anyone broke into a town by night, he paid 100 shillings to the king and not to the sheriff. If anyone summoned to drive deer for the king's hunting failed to do so, he paid 50 shillings to the king.

THE MAGNA CHARTA, 1215

The Great Charter, or the "Charter of Liberties of the English People" as it was called, was a careful revision and reproduction of the old Anglo-Saxon principles and tenets of governments which had been suppressed by the Norman conquerors and their immediate successors, and may be considered the most important instrument of English constitutional history.

King John by his continual extortions of money and violation of feudal customs had aroused the anger of not only the nobility but the knights and townspeople to the point of rebellion. The lower classes, such as serfs and artisans, were not actively rebellious, but, though the uprising of 1213-15 was dominated by the barons, it was in a sense a national reaction. King John, compelled by superior force, was forced to enter into parleys with the barons at Runnymede. On June 15, 1215, after numerous attempts at evasion, King John placed his seal upon the preliminary draft of demands presented to him by the barons.

The resulting document was put forth in the form of a charter granted by the King. The original charter, in Latin, is a relatively brief document of some 70 clauses, many of which were of only transient significance.

The charter contains provisions guaranteeing the freedom of the church and the customs of the town. It implies that there are laws protecting the rights of the King's subjects which the King is required to observe or else be compelled to do so by force. Most important were the guarantees of trial by jury and habeas corpus, the latter two being later interpretations of original charter grants.

MAGNA CHARTA;

or,

The Great Charter of Liberties,

GRANTED BY

KING JOHN to the PEOPLE of England, on the 15th of June, 1215.*

————

JOHN, by the grace of God, King of England, Lord of Ireland, Duke of Normandy and Aquitaine, and Earl of Anjou; to the Archbishops, bishops, abbots, earls, barons, judiciaries of the forests, sheriffs, governors, officers, and to all bailiffs, and other his faithful subjects, greeting. Know ye that We, in the presence of God, and the health of our soul, and the souls of our ancestors, and to the honour of God, and the exaltation of his holy Church, and amendment of our kingdom, by advice of our venerable fathers, Stephen, Archbishop of Canterbury, Primate of all England, and Cardinal of the Holy Roman Church; Henry, Archbishop of Dublin; William, Bishop of London; Peter, of Winchester; Jocelin, of Bath and Glastonbury; Hugh, of Lincoln; Walter of Worcester; William, of Coventry, Benedict, of Rochester, Bishops; and Master Pandulph, the Pope's sub-deacon and ancient servant; Brother Aymerick, Master of the Temple in England, and the noble persons, William Marescall, Earl of Pembroke; William, Earl of Salisbury; William, Earl of Warren; William, Earl of Arundel; Alan de Gallaway, Constable of Scotland; Warin Fitz-Gerald, Peter Fitz-Herebert, and Hubert de Burgh, Seneschal of Poicton; Hugh de Neville, Matthew Fitz-Herebert, Thomas Basset, Allan Basset, Philipp de Albiney, Robert de Ropele, John Marescall, John Fitz-Hugh, and others our liegemen; have in the first place granted to God, and by this our present Charter, confirmed for us and our heirs for ever.

1. That the Church of England shall be free, and enjoy

* We are indebted to the Cottonian Library, at Oxford, for this authentic copy of the original *Magna Charta.*

her whole rights and liberties inviolable. And we will have them so to be observed, which appears from hence, that the freedom of elections, which was reckoned most necessary for the Church of England, of our own free will and pleasure, we have granted and confirmed by our Charter, and obtained the confirmation of, from Pope Innocent the Third, before the discord between us and our barons, which Charter we shall observe, and do will it to be faithfully observed by our heirs for ever.

2. We have also granted to all the freemen of our kingdom, for us and our heirs for ever, all the under-written liberties, to have and to hold them and their heirs, of us and our heirs.

3. If any of our Earls, or Barons, or others, who hold of us in chief by military service, shall die, and at the time of his death his heirs shall be of full age, and owe a relief, he shall have his inheritance by the ancient relief; that is to say, the heir or heirs of an Earl, for a whole Earl's barony, by a hundred pounds; the heir or heirs of a Baron, for a whole barony, by a hundred pounds; the heir or heirs of a knight, for a whole knight's fee, by a hundred shillings at most; and he that oweth less shall give less, according to the ancient custom of fees.

4. But if the heir of any such shall be under age, and shall be in ward, when he comes of age, he shall have his inheritance without relief or without fine.

5. The warden of the land of such heir who shall be under age, shall take of the land of such heir, only reasonable issues, reasonable customs, and reasonable services; and that without destruction and waste of the men or things. And if we shall commit the guardianship of these lands to the Sheriff, or any other who is answerable to us for the issues of the land; and if he shall make destruction and waste upon the ward-lands, we will compel him to give satisfaction, and the land shall be committed to two lawful and discreet tenants of that fee, who shall be answerable for the issues to us, or to him whom we shall assign. And if we shall give

or sell the wardship of such lands to any one, and he makes destruction or waste upon them, he shall lose his wardship, which shall be committed to two lawful and discreet tenants of that fee, who shall in like manner be answerable to us, as hath been said.

6. But the warden, so long as he shall have the wardship of the land, shall keep up and maintain the houses, parks, warrens, ponds, mills, and other things pertaining to the land, out of the issues of the same land; and shall restore to the heir, when he comes of full age, his whole land stocked with plows and carriages, according as the time of wainage shall require, and the issues of the land can reasonably bear.

7. Heirs shall be married without disparagement, [so as that before matrimony shall be contracted, those who are nearest to the heir in blood shall be made acquainted with it.]

8. A widow, after the death of her husband, shall forthwith, and without any difficulty, have her marriage, and her inheritance, nor shall she give any thing for her dower, or marriage, or her inheritance, which her husband and she held at the day of his death. And she may remain in the capital messuage or mansion-house of her husband 40 days after his death; within which term her dower shall be assigned.

9. No widow shall be destrained to marry herself so long as she has a mind to live without a husband. But yet she shall give security that she will not marry without our assent, if she holds of us; or without the consent of the lord of whom she holds, if she holds of another.

10. Neither we nor our bailiffs shall seize any land or rent for any debt, so long as there shall be chattels of the debtor's upon the premises, sufficient to pay his debt. Nor shall the sureties of the debtor be destrained, so long as the principal debtor is sufficient for the payment of the debt.

11. And if the principal debtor fail in the payment of the debt, not having wherewithal to discharge it, then the sure-

ties shall answer the debt, and if they will they shall have the lands and rents of the debtor, until they shall be satisfied for the debt which they paid for him; unless the principal debtor can show himself acquitted thereof, against the said sureties.

12. [If any one have borrowed any thing of the Jews, more or less, and dies before the debt be satisfied, there shall be no interest paid for that debt, so long as the heir is under age, of whomsoever, he may hold; and if the debt falls into our hands, we will take only the chattels mentioned in the Charter of instrument.]

13. [And if any one shall die indebted to the Jews, his wife shall have her dower, and pay nothing of that debt; and if the deceased left children under age, they shall have necessaries provided for them according to the tenement (or real estate) of the deceased, and out of the residue the debt shall be paid; saving however the service of the lords. In like manner let it be with the debts due to other persons than the Jews.]

14. No *Scuttage* or aid shall be imposed in our kingdom, unless by the common council of our kingdom, except to redeem our person, and to make our eldest son a knight, and once to marry our eldest daughter; and for this there shall only be paid a reasonable aid.

15. [In like manner it shall be concerning the aids of the city of London; and] the city of London shall have all its ancient liberties and free customs, as well by land as by water.

16. Furthermore, we will and grant that all other cities and boroughs, and towns and ports, shall have all their liberties and free customs; and shall have the common council of the kingdom concerning the assessments of their aids, except in the three cases aforesaid.

17. [And for the assessing of scuttages, we shall cause to be summoned the archbishops, bishops, abbots, earls, and great barons of the realm singly by our letters.]

18. [And furthermore we shall cause to be summoned in

general by our sheriffs and bailiffs, all others who hold of us in chief, at a certain day, that is to say, forty days, (before their meeting) at least to a certain place; and in all letters of such summons, we will declare the cause of the summons.]

19. [And summons being thus made, the business shall proceed on the day appointed, according to the advice of such as shall be present, although all that were summoned come not.]

20. We will not for the future grant to any one, that he may take aid of his own free tenants, unless to redeem his body, and to make his eldest son a knight, and once to marry his eldest daughter; and for this there shall only be paid a reasonable aid.

21. No man shall be destrained to perform more service for a knight's fee or other free tenement, than is due from thence.

22. Common Pleas shall not follow our court, but shall be holden in the same certain place; trials upon the writs of *Novel Desseisin* and of *Mort d'Ancestor,* and of *Darreine Presentment,* shall be taken but in their proper counties, and after this manner: We, or (if we shall be out of the realm) our chief judiciary, shall send two judiciaries through every county, four times a year; who, with the four knights chosen out of every shire by the people, shall hold the said assizes in the county, on the day, and at the place appointed.

23. And if any matters cannot be determined on the day appointed to hold the assizes in each county, so many of the knights and freeholders as have been at the assizes aforesaid, shall be appointed to decide them as is necessary, according as there is more or less business.

24. A free man shall not be amerced for a small fault, but according to the degree of the fault, and for a great crime, in proportion to the heinousness of it, saving to him his contenement, and after the same manner a merchant, saving to him his merchandise.

25. And a villain shall be amerced after the same manner,

saving to him his wainage, if he falls under our mercy: and none of the aforesaid amerciaments shall be assessed, but by the oath of honest men of the neighbourhood.

26. Earls and barons shall not be amerced but by their peers, and according to the quality of the offence.

27. No ecclesiastical person shall be amerced, but according to the proportion aforesaid, and not according to the value of ecclesiastical benefice.

28. Neither a town, nor any person, shall be destrained to make bridges over rivers, unless that anciently, and of right they are bound to do it.

29. No sheriff, constables, coroners, or other our bailiffs, shall hold pleas of the crown.

30. [All counties, hundreds, wapentakes, and trethings, shall stand at the old ferm, without any encrease except in our demesne lands.]

31. If any one that holds of us a lay fee, dies, and the sheriff or our bailiff show our letters-patent of summons concerning the debt, due to us from the deceased; it shall be lawful for the sheriff and our bailiff to attach and register the chattels of the deceased found upon his lay-fee, to the value of the debt, by the view of lawful men, so as nothing be removed until our whole debt be paid; and the rest shall be left to the executors to fulfill the will of the deceased; and if there be nothing due from him to us, all the chattels shall remain to the deceased, save to his wife and children their reasonable shares.

32. [If any freeman dies intestate, his chattels shall be distributed by the hands of his nearest relations and friends, by view of the church, saving to every one his debts, which the deceased owed.]

33. No constable or bailiff of ours shall take corn or other chattels of any man, unless he presently gives him money for it, or hath respite of payment from the seller.

34. No constable shall distrain any knight to give money for castle-guard, if he himself shall do it in his own person, or by another able man, in case he shall be hindered by any

reasonable cause.

35. And if we shall lead him, or if we shall send him into the army, he shall be free from castle-guard, from the time he shall be in the army, by our command.

36. No sheriff or bailiff of ours, or any other, shall take horses or carts of any for carriage.

37. Neither shall we or our officers or others, take any man's timber for our castles, or other uses, unless by the consent of the owner of the timber.

38. We will retain the lands of those that are convicted of felony but for one year and a day, and then they shall be delivered to the lord of the fee.

39. All wares for the time to come shall be demolished in the river Thames and Medway, and throughout all England, except upon the sea-coast.

40. The writ which is called *Praecipe* for the future, shall not be granted to any one of any tenement, whereby a freeman may lose his cause.

41. There shall be one measure of wine, and one of ale, through our whole realm; and one measure of corn, that is to say, the London quarter; and one breadth of dyed cloth and russets and haberjects, that is to say, two ells within the list; and the weights shall be as the measures.

42. From henceforward nothing shall be give nor taken for a writ of inquisition from him that desires an inquisition of life or limbs, but shall be granted *gratis* and not denied.

43. If any one holds of us by fee-farm or socage, or burgage and holds land of another by military service, We will not have the wardship of the heir or land, which belongs to another man's fee, by reason of what he holds of Us, by fee-farm, socage or burgage; nor will we have the wardship of the fee-farm, socage, or burgage, unless the fee-farm is bound to perform military service.

44. We will not have the wardship of an heir, nor of any land, which he holds of another by military service, by reason of any *petit serjeanty* he holds of us, as by the service of giving us daggers, arrows, or the like.

411

45. No bailiff for the future shall put any man to his law, upon his single accusation, without credible witnesses produced to prove it.

46. No freeman shall be taken or imprisoned, or disseised, or outlawed, or banished, or anyways destroyed; nor will we pass upon him, or commit him to prison, unless by the legal judgment of his peers, or by the law of the land.

47. We will sell to no man, we will deny no man, nor defer right or justice.

48. All merchants shall have safe and secure conduct to go out of, and come into England; and to stay there, and to pass, as well by land as by water; to buy and sell by the ancient and allowed customs, without any evil tolls, except in time of war, or when they shall be of any nation in the war with us.

49. And if there shall be found any such in our land in the beginning of the war, they shall be attached, without damage to their bodies or goods, until it may be known unto us, or our chief justiciary, how our merchants be treated in the nation at war with us; and if ours be safe there, they shall be safe in our land.

50. [It shall be lawful, for the time to come, for any one to go out of our kingdom, and return safely and securely by land or by water, saving his allegiance to us; unless in time of war by some short space from the common benefit of the kingdom, except prisoners and outlaws (according to the law of the land) and people in war with Us, and merchants who shall be in such condition as is above mentioned.]

51. If any man holds of any escheat, as of the honour of Wallingford, Nottingham, Bologne, Lancaster, or of other escheats, which are in our hands, and are baronies; and dies his heirs shall not give any other relief, or perform any other service to Us than he would to the baron, if the barony were in possession of the baron. We will hold it after the same manner the baron held it.

52. [Those men who dwell without the forest, from henceforth shall not come before our justiciaries of the forest upon summons, but such as are impeached, or are pledges for any

that were attached for something concerning the forest.]

53. We will not make any justiciaries, constables, sheriffs, or bailiffs, but what are knowing in the law of the realm, and are disposed duly to observe it.

54. All barons, who are founders of abbeys, and have charters of the kings of England for the advowson, or are entitled to it by ancient tenure, may have the custom of them, when void, as they ought to have.

55. All woods that have been taken into the forest in our own time, shall forthwith be laid out again; and the like shall be done with the rivers that have been taken or fenced in by us, during our reign.

56. All evil customs, concerning forests, warrens, and foresters, warreners, sheriffs, and their officers, rivers, and their keepers, shall forthwith be enquired into in each county, by twelve knights of the same shire, chosen by the most creditable persons in the same county, and upon oath; and, within forty days after the said inquest, be utterly abolished, so as never to be restored.

57. We will immediately give up all hostages and engagements, delivered unto us by our English subjects, as securities for their keeping the peace, and yielding us faithful service.

58. We will entirely remove from our bailiwicks the relations of Gerard de Athyes, so as for the future they shall have no bailiwick in England. We will also remove Enegelard de Cygony, Andrew, Peter, and Gyon de Cygony, Geoffrey de Martyn and his brothers; Philip Mark and his brothers, and his nephew Geoffrey and their whole retinue.

59. And as soon as peace is restored, we will send out of the kingdom all foreign soldiers, cross bowmen, and stipendiaries, who are come with horses and arms to the injury of our people.

60. If any one hath been dispossessed, or deprived by us, without the legal judgment of his peers, of his lands, castles, liberties, or right, we will forthwith restore them to him; and if any dispute arise upon this head, let the matter be decided by the five and twenty barons hereafter mentioned,

for the preservation of the peace.

61. As for those things, of which any person has, without the legal judgment of his peers, been dispossessed, or deprived either by King Henry our father, or our brother King Richard, and which we have in our hands, or are possessed by others, and we are bound to warrant and make good, we shall have respite till the term usually allowed the croises; excepting those things about which there is a suit depending, or whereof an inquest hath been made by our order, before we undertook the crusade. But when we return from our pilgrimage, or if we do not perform it, we will immediately cause full justice to be administered therein.

62. The same respite we shall have for disafforesting the forests, which Henry our father, or our brother Richard have afforested; and for the wardship of the lands which are in another's fee, in the same manner as we have hitherto enjoyed those wardships, by reason of a fee, held of us by knight's service; and for the abbeys founded in any other fee than our own, in which the Lord of the fee claims a right. And when we return from our pilgrimage, or if we should not perform it, we will immediately do full justice to all the complainants in this behalf.

63. No man shall be taken or imprisoned, upon the appeal of a woman, for the death of any other man than her husband.

64. All unjust and illegal fines, and all amerciaments, imposed unjustly, and contrary to the law of the land, shall be entirely forgiven, or else be left to the decision of the five and twenty barons hereafter mentioned for the preservation of the peace, or of the major part of them, together with the aforesaid Stephen, Archbishop of Canterbury, if he can be present, and others whom he shall think fit to take along with him. And if he cannot be present, the business shall, notwithstanding, go on with him. But so that, if one or more of the twenty five barons be plaintiffs in the same cause, they shall be set aside, as to what concerns this particular affair; and others be chosen in their room, out of the said five and twenty, and sworn by the rest to decide the matter.

65. If we have disseised or dispossessed the Welch of any lands, liberties, or other things, without the legal judgment of their peers, they shall be immediately restored to them. And if any dispute arises upon this head, the matter shall be determined in the Marches, by the judgment of their peers. For tenements of England according to the law of England. For tenements in Wales according to the law of Wales. The same shall the Welch do to Us and our subjects.

66. As for all those things, of which any Welshman hath without the legal judgment of his peers, being deseised or deprived, by King Henry our Father, or our Brother King Richard, and which we either have in our hands, or others are possessed of, and we are obliged to warrant it: we shall have a respite till the time generally allowed the croises; excepting those things about which a suit is depending, or whereof an inquest has been made by our order, before we undertook the crusade. But when we return, or if we stay at home, and not perform our pilgrimage, we will immediately do them full justice according to the laws of the Welch, and the parts afore-mentioned.

67. We will without delay dismiss the son of Lewelin, and all the Welch hostages, and release them from the engagements they entered into with Us, for the preservation of the peace.

68. We shall treat with Alexander, King of Scots, concerning the restoring of his sister and hostages, and his right and liberties, in the same form and manner as we shall do to the rest of our barons of England; unless by the engagements which his father William, late King of Scots, hath entered into with Us, it ought to be otherwise; and this shall be left to the determination of his peers in our court.

69. All the aforesaid customs and liberties, which we have granted to be holden in our kingdom, as much as it belong to us towards our people: all our subjects, as well clergy as laity, shall observe as far as they are concerned towards their dependents.

70. And whereas, for the honour of God, and the amend-

ment of our kingdom, and for quieting the discord that has arisen between Us and our barons, we have granted all the things aforesaid; willing to render them firm and lasting, we do give and grant our subjects the following security: namely, that the barons may choose five and twenty barons of the kingdom, whom they think convenient, who shall take care, with all their might, to hold and observe, and cause to be observed, the peace and liberty we have granted them, and by this our present charter confirmed. So as that if we, our justiciary, our bailiffs, or any of our officers, shall in any case fail in the performance of them, towards any person; or shall break through any of these articles of peace and security, and the offence is notified to four barons, chosen out of the five-and-twenty aforementioned, the said four barons shall repair to Us, or our justiciary, if we are out of the realm, and laying open the grievance, shall petition to have it redressed without delay; and if it is not redressed by Us, or, if we should chance to be out of the realm, if it is not redressed by our justiciary within forty days, reckoning from the time it has been notified to Us, or to our justiciary if we should be out of the realm; the four barons shall lay the cause before the rest of the twenty-five barons, and the said twenty-five barons, together with the community of the whole kingdom, shall distrain and distress us all the ways possible, namely, by seizing our castles, lands, possessions, and in any other manner they can, till the grievance is redressed according to their pleasure, saving harmless our own person, and the person of our queen and children; and when it is redressed, they shall obey Us as before.

71. And any person whatsoever in the kingdom may swear that he will obey the orders of the five and twenty barons aforesaid, in the execution of the premises, and that he will distress us, jointly with them, to the utmost of his power; and we give public and free liberty to any one that will swear to them, and never shall hinder any person from taking the same oath.

72. As for all those of our subjects, who will not, of their

own accord, swear to join the five and twenty barons in distraining and distressing us, we will issue our order to make them take the same oath, as aforesaid.

73. And if any one of the five and twenty barons dies, or goes out of the kingdom, or is hindered any other way, from putting the things aforesaid in execution, the rest of the said five and twenty barons may choose another in his room, at their discretion who shall be sworn in like manner, as the rest.

74. In all things that are committed to the charge of these five and twenty barons, if, when they are all assembled together, they should happen to disagree about any matter, or some of them, when summoned, will not, or cannot come, whatever is agreed upon or enjoined by the major part of those who are present, shall be reputed as firm and valid, as if all the five and twenty had given their consent, and the aforesaid five and twenty shall swear that all the premises they shall faithfully observe, and cause with all their power to be observed.

75. And we will not, by ourselves, or others, procure any thing, whereby any of these concessions and liberties be revoked or lessened; and if any such thing be obtained, let it be null and void:—neither shall we ever make use of it, either by ourselves or any other.

76. And all the ill-will, anger, and malice, that hath arisen between us and our subjects, of the clergy and laity from the first breaking out of the dissension between us, we do fully remit and forgive. Moreover, all trespasses occasioned by the said dissension, from Easter in the sixteenth year of our reign, till the restoration of peace and tranquillity, we hereby entirely remit, to all clergy, as well as laity, and far as in Us lies, do fully forgive.

77. We have moreover granted them our letters patent testimonial of Stephen Lord Archbishop of Canterbury, Henry Lord Archbishop of Dublin, and the Bishops aforesaid, as also of Master Pandulph, for security of concessions aforesaid.

417

78. Wherefore we will, and firmly enjoin, that the church of England be free, and that all men in our kingdom have and hold, all the aforesaid liberties, rights, and concessions, truly and peaceably, freely and quietly, fully and wholly to themselves and their heirs of Us and our heirs in all things and places for ever, as aforesaid.

79. It is also sworn, as well on our part, as on the part of the barons, that all the things aforesaid shall faithfully and sincerely be observed.

Given under our hand in the presence of the witnesses above-named, and many others, in the Meadow called Running-mede *between* Windlesore *and* Stanes, *the 15th day of June, in the 17th year of our reign.*

o——So as we are first acquainted therewith, or our justiciary, if we should not be in England.

——o And in the same manner, about administering justice, deafforesting the forests, letting them continue.

Either in England or Wales—

For ever—

The above are the articles contained in the two copies of the original, which are of undoubted antiquity, and as old as King John. Another is in the British Museum. They all begin with "SO," and end with "FOR EVER," a sure mark of their intended immortal duration.

THE STATUTE OF MERCHANTS

EDWARD I (1239-1307)

As the son of Henry III and King of England from 1272-1307, Edward gained new claims in France and strengthened the English rights to Gascony by his marriage to Eleanor of Castile. His reign was characterized by constant warfare and in 1284 Edward extended the English administration into Wales. From 1286 to 1289 he attempted to improve the administration of Gascony. He was an astute general and planner and was outstanding in his efforts to extend the English rule to all of Britain. Most important, however, were those developments in law and constitution that he inaugurated during his reign, causing him to be praised as the English Justinian. His *quo warranto* writs were aimed at strengthening the central government by reducing and restricting private feudal courts. In 1285 his law of *Circumspecte Agatis* forced church courts to confine themselves to ecclesiastical cases. The three statutes of Westminster formulated the advancements of a century of common law. His statute of mortmain in 1279 prohibited grants of land to the church without the king's permission.

In 1295 Edward's Model Parliament marked a tremendous forward step in the development of a powerful governmental body representative of all three estates. In 1297 Edward was forced to issue the confirmation of the Charters, including the Magna Charta and those signed by Henry III. Although Edward later revoked part of the confirmation, this doctrine survived to become the basis of "no taxation without representation."

The Statute of MERCHANTS, made at *Westminster Anno*
13 Edw. I. Stat. 3. and *Anno Dom. 1285.*

CAP I.

The Form of knowledging a Statute Merchant. The Creditor's Remedy if his Debt be not paid. The King's Seals shall be sent to Keepers of Fairs. Taking of Recognisance.

Forasmuch as Merchants, which heretofore have lent their Goods to divers Persons, be fallen in Poverty, because there is no speedy Remedy provided, whereby they may shortly recover their Debt at the Day of Payment; (2) *and for this Cause many merchants do refrain to come into the Realm with their Merchandise, to the Damage of such Merchants and of all the Realm;* (3) the King and his Council at his Parliament holden at *Aeton burnel,* after the *Feast of St. Michael,* the eleventh Year of his Reign, hath ordained these Establishments thereupon for the Remedy of such Merchants; which Ordinances and Establishments, the King commandeth that they shall be firmly kept and observed throughout this Realm, whereby Merchants may have Remedy, and less Trouble and Business to recover their Debt, than they have had heretofore. (4) *But forasmuch as Merchants after complained unto the King, that Sheriffs misinterpreted his Statutes, and sometimes by Malice and false Interpretation delayed the Execution of the Statute, to the great Damage of Merchants;* (5) The King at his Parliament holden at *Westminster* after *Easter,* the thirteenth Year of his Reign, caused the said Statute made at *Aeton Burnel* to be rehearsed; (6) and for the Declaration of certain Articles in the Statute aforesaid hath ordained and established, That a Merchant who will be sure of his Debt, shall cause his Debtor to come before the Mayor of *London,* or before some chief Warden of a City, or of another good Town, where the King shall appoint, (7) and before the Mayor and chief Warden, or other sufficient Men chosen and sworn thereto, when the Mayor or chief Warden cannot attend, (8) and before one of the Clerks that the King shall thereto assign, when both cannot attend, he shall knowledge the Debt and the Day of payment; (9) and the Recognisance shall be inrolled by one of the Clerks Hands being known, and the Roll shall be double, whereof one Part shall remain with the Mayor or chief Warden, and the other with the Clerks that thereto shall be first named; (10) and further, one of the said Clerks with his own Hand shall write an Obligation, to which Writing the Seal of the Debtor shall be put with the King's Seal provided for the same Intent; which Seal shall be of two Pieces, whereof the greater Piece shall remain in the Custody of the Mayor, or the Chief Warden, and the other Piece in the keeping of the foresaid Clerk. (11) And if the Debtor do not pay at the Day limited unto him, then shall the Merchant come to the Mayor and Clerk with his Obligation; (12) and if it be found by the Roll or Writing that the Debt was knowledged, and the Day of Payment expired, the Mayor or chief Warden shall cause the Body of the Debtor to be taken (if he be Lay) whensoever he happeneth to come in their Power; and shall commit him to the Prison of the Town, if there be any, and he shall remain there at his own Costs, until he hath agreed for the Debt. (13) And it is commanded that the Keeper of the Town Prison shall retain him upon the Delivery of the Mayor or Warden; and if the Keeper shall not receive him, he shall be answerable for the Debt, if he have whereof; and if he have not whereof, he that committed the Prison to his keeping shall answer. (14) And if the Debtor cannot be found in the Power of the Mayor, or chief Warden, then shall the Mayor or chief Warden send into the Chancery, under the King's Seal, the Recognisance of the Debt; and the Chancellor shall direct a Writ unto the Sheriff, in whose Shire the Debtor shall be found, for to take his Body (if he be Lay) and safely to keep him in Prison until he hath agreed for the Debt; (15) and within a Quarter of a Year after that he is taken, his Chattels shall be delivered him, so that by his own he may levy and pay the Debt; (16) and it shall be lawful unto him, during

421

the same Quarter, to sell his Lands and Tenements for the Discharge of his Debts, and his Sale shall be good and effectual. (17) And if he do not agree within the Quarter, next after the Quarter expired all the Lands and Goods of the Debtor shall be delivered unto the Merchant by a reasonable Extent, to hold them until such Time as the Debt is wholly levied; and nevertheless the Body shall remain in Prison as before is said; (18) and the Merchant shall find him Bread and Water, (19) and the Merchant shall have such Seisin in the Lands and Tenements delivered unto him or his Assignee, that he may maintain a Writ of *Novel disseisin,* if he be put out, and Redisseisin also, as of Freehold, to hold to him and and his Assigns until the Debt be paid; (20) and as soon as the Debt is levied, the Body of the Debtor shall be delivered with his Lands. (21) And in such Writs as the Chancellor doth award, Mention shall be made, that the Sheriff shall certify the Justices of the one Bench or of the other, how he hath performed the King's Commandment, at a certain Day, at which Day the Merchant shall sue before the Justices, if Agreement be not made: (22) and if the Sheriffs do not return the Writ, or do return that the Writ came too late, or that he hath directed it to the Bailiffs of some Franchise, the Justices shall do as it is contained in the latter Statute of *Westminster.* (23) And if in case the Sheriff return, that the Debtor cannot be found, or that he is a Clerk, the Merchant shall have Writs to all the Sheriffs where he shall have Land, and that they shall deliver unto him all the Goods and Lands of the Debtor by a reasonable Extent, to hold unto him and his Assigns in the Form aforesaid; and at the last he shall have a Writ to what Sheriff he will, to take his Body (if he be Lay) and to retain it in Manner aforesaid. (24) And let the Keeper of the Prison take Heed, that he must answer for the Body, or for the Debt. (25) And after the Debtor's Lands be delivered to the Merchant, the Debtor may lawfully sell his Land, so that the Merchant have no Damage of the Approvements; (26) and the Merchants shall always be allowed for their Damages, and all Costs, Labours,

Suits, Delays, and Expences reasonable. (27) And if the Debtor find Sureties which do acknowledge themselves to be principal Debtors, after the Day passed the Sureties shall be ordered in all Things as is said of the principal Debtor, as to the Arrest of Body, Delivery of Lands, and other Things. (28) And when the Lands of the Debtors be delivered unto the Merchant, he shall have Seisin of all the Lands that were in the Hand of the Debtor, the Day of the Recognisance made, in whose Hands soever that they come after, either by Feoffment, or otherwise. (29) And after the Debt paid, the Debtor's Lands, and the Issues of Lands of Debtors by Feoffment shall return again, as well to the Feoffee, as the other Lands unto the Debtors. (30) And if the Debtor or his Sureties die, the Merchant shall have no Authority to take the Body of his Heir, but he shall have his Lands, as before is said, if he be of Age, or when he shall be of full Age until he hath levied of the Lands the Amountance and Value of the Debt. (31) And a Seal shall be provided, that shall serve for Fairs, and the same shall be sent unto every Fair under the King's Seal by a Clerk sworn, or by the Keeper of the Fair. (32) And of the Commonalty of the Merchants of the City of *London* two Merchants shall be chosen, that shall swear, and the Seal shall be opened before them, and the one Piece shall be delivered unto the foresaid Merchants, and the other shall remain with the Clerk; and before them, or one of the Merchants (if both cannot attend) the Recognisances shall be taken, as before is said. (33) And before that any Recognisance be inrolled, the Pain of the Statute shall be openly read before the Debtor, so that after he cannot say that any did put another Penalty than that whereto he bound himself. (34) And to maintain the Costs of the said Clerk, the King shall take of every Pound a Penny, in every Town where the Seal is, except Fairs, where he shall take one Penny Halfpenny of the Pound. (35) This Ordinance and Act the King willeth to be observed from henceforth throughout his Realm of *England* and *Ireland,* amongst the which People they that will may make such Recognisances

423

(except *Jews,* to whom this Ordinance shall not extend.) (36) And by this Statute a Writ of Debt shall not be abated; (37) and the Chancellor, Justices of the one Bench and the other, the Barons of the Exchequer, and Justices Errants, shall not be estopped to take Recognisances of Debts before them knowledged and made: (38) But the Execution of Recognisances made before them shall not be done in the Form aforesaid but by the Law and Manner before used, and otherwise provided in other Statutes.

THE STATUTES OF WESTMINSTER

EDWARD 1

Under the reign of Edward I some of the greatest changes in
English Constitutional Law were enacted, intended to strengthen
the power of the crown by judicial and clear definition of its
privileges. The movement in this direction started with *"The
First Statute of Westminster"* enacted in 1275 which was directed
primarily to the improvement of administrative details, and
which was accompanied by a grant to the king of permanent
customs revenue on imports and exports. This source of income
for the crown soon became more valuable than the old feudal
taxes on land.

These be the acts of King Edward, son of King Henry,
made at Westminster at his first Parliament general after
his coronation, on the Monday of Easter Utas, the third year
of his reign, by his council and by the assent of archbishops,
bishops, abbots, priors, earls, barons, and [all] the commonalty of the realm, being thither summoned: Because our
lord the King had great zeal and desire to redress the state
of the realm in such things as required amendment for the
common profit of holy church, and of the realm: And because the state of the holy church had been evil kept, and
the prelates and religious persons of the land grieved many
ways, and the people otherwise intreated than they ought
to be, and the peace less kept, and the laws less used, and
the offenders less punished, than they ought to be, by reason
whereof the people [of the land] feared the less to offend;
the King hath ordained and established these acts under-

written, which he intendeth to be necessary and profitable unto the whole realm.

V. *Freedom of election*

And because elections ought to be free, the King commandeth upon great forfeiture, that [no man] by force of arms, nor by malice, or menacing, shall disturb any to make free election.

VI. *Amerciaments shall be reasonable*

And that no city, borough, nor town, nor any man be amerced, without reasonable cause, and according to the quantity of his trespass; that is to say, every freeman saving his (freehold) a merchant saving his merchandise, a villain saving his waynage, and that by his or their peers.

IX. *Pursuit of felons*

And forasmuch as the peace of this realm hath been (evil observed) heretofore for lack of quick and fresh suit making after felons in due manner, and namely, because of franchises, where felons are received; it is provided, that all generally be ready and apparelled, at the commandment and summons of sheriffs, and at the cry of the country, to (sue) and arrest felons, when any need is, as well within franchise as without; and they that will not so do, and thereof be attainted, shall make a grievous fine to the King: And if default be found in the lord of the franchise, the King (shall take the same franchise to himself) and if default be in the bailiff, he shall have one year's imprisonment, and after shall make a grievous fine; and if he have not whereof, he shall have imprisonment of two years. And if the sheriff, coroner, or any other bailiff, within such franchise or without for reward, or for prayer, (or for fear) or for any manner of affinity conceal, consent, or procure to conceal, the felonies done in their liberties, or otherwise (will not attach nor) arrest such felons there as they may, or otherwise (will not do) their office for favour borne to such mis-doers, and be attainted thereof ;they shall have one year's imprisonment, and after make a grievous fine (at the King's pleasure, if they have wherewith;) and if they have not whereof, they shall have imprisonment of (three) years.

X. *Who shall be chosen coroners. Their duty*

And forasmuch as mean persons, and undiscreet, now of late are commonly chosen to the office of coroners, where it is requisite that persons honest, lawful, and wise, should occupy such offices: It is provided, that through all shires sufficient men shall be chosen to be coroners, of the most wise and discreet knights, which know, will, and may best attend upon such offices and which lawfully shall attach and present pleas of the crown; and that sheriffs shall have counter rolls with the coroners, as well of appeals, as of enquests, of attachments, or of other things which to that office belong; and that no coroner demand nor take any thing of any man to do his office, upon pain of great forfeiture to the King.

XV. *Prisoners and bail*

And forasmuch as sheriffs, and other, which have taken and kept in prison persons, (detected) of felony, and (incontinent) have let out by replevin such as were not replevisable, and have kept in prison such as were replevisable, because they would gain of the one party, and grieve the other: And forasmuch as before this time, it was not determined which persons were replevisable, and which not, but only those that were taken for the death of man, or by commandment of the King, or of his justices, or for the forest; it is provided and by the King commanded, that such prisoners as before were outlawed, and they which have abjured the realm, provors and such as be taken with the manour and those which have broken the King's prison, thieves openly defamed and known, and such as be appealed by provors, so long as the provors be living, if they be not of good name, and such as

427

be taken for house-burning feloniously done, or for false money, or for counterfeiting the King's seal, or persons excommunicate, taken at the request of the bishop, or for manifest offences, or for treason touching the King himself shall be in no wise replevisable by the common writ, nor without writ: But such as be indicted of larceny, by enquests taken before sheriffs or bailiffs by their office, or of light suspicion, or for petty larceny that amounteth not (above the value) of twelve-pence, if they were not (guilty) of some other larceny aforetime, or (guilty) of receipt of felons, or of commandment, or force, or of aid in felony done; or (guilty of) some other trespass for which one ought not to lose life nor member, and a man appealed by a provor after the death of the provor, if he be no common thief, nor defamed, shall from henceforth be let out by sufficient surety whereof the sheriff will be answerable, and that without giving aught to their goods. (So much of this statute as provides what prisoners shall not be replevisable and what shall be so, rep., 7 Geo. 4. c. 64. s. 32.) And if the sheriff, or any other, let any go at large by surety, that is not replevisable if he be sheriff or constable or any other bailiff of fee which hath keeping of prisons, and thereof be attainted, he shall lose his fee and office for ever: and if the under sheriff, constable, or bailiff of such as have fee for keeping of prisons, (do it) contrary to the will of his lord, or any other bailiff being not of fee, they shall have three years imprisonment, and make fine at the King's pleasure. And if any withhold prisoners replevisable, after that they have offered sufficient surety, he shall pay a grievous amerciament to the King; and if he take any reward for the deliverance of such, he shall pay double the prisoner, and also shall (be in the great mercy of) the King.

XVI. *None shall drive a distress out of the county; See Stat. Marlb. ch. 4, 15.) nor distrain out of his own fee*

In right thereof, that some persons take, and cause to be taken, the beasts of other, chasing them out of the shire where the beasts were taken; it is provided also that none (from henceforth) do so; and if any do, he shall make a grievous fine, as is contained in the Statute of Marlebridge, made in the time of King Henry, father to the King that now is. And likewise it shall be done to them which take beasts (wrongfully,) and distrain out of their fee; and shall be more grievously punished, if the manner of the trespass do so require.

XIX. *Sheriffs, &c. receiving the King's debts shall acquit the debtor*

In right of the sheriffs, or other, which answer by their own hands unto the Exchequer, and which have received the King's father's debts, or the King's own debts before this time, and have not acquitted the debtors in the Exchequer; it is provided, that the King shall send good and lawful men through every shire, to hear all such as will complain thereof, and to determine the matters (there) that all such as can prove that they have paid, shall be thereof acquitted for ever, whether the sheriffs or other be living or dead, in a certain form that shall be delivered them; and such as have not so done, if they be living, shall be grievously punished; and if they be dead, their heirs shall answer, and be charged with the debt. And the King hath commanded, that sheriffs and other aforesaid shall from henceforth lawfully acquit the debtors at the next accompt after they have received such debts; and then the debt shall be allowed in the Exchequer, so that it shall no more come in the summons; and if the sheriff otherwise do, and there of be attainted, he shall pay to the plaintiff thrice as much as he hath received, and shall make fine at the King's pleasure. And let every (sheriff) take heed, that he have such a receiver, for whom he will answer; for the King will be recompensed of all, of the sheriffs and their heirs. And if any other, that is answerable to the Exchequer by his own hands so do, he shall render thrice so much to the plaintiff, and make fine in like manner. And that the sheriffs shall make tallies to all such as have paid their debt to the King; and that the summons of the Exchequer be showed to all debtors that demand a sight thereof, without denying to any, and that (without taking any reward, and without giving any thing;) and he that doth contrary, the King shall punish him grievously.

XXI. *Lands in ward shall be duly kept*

In right of lands of heirs being within age, which be in ward of their lords; it is provided, that the guardians shall keep and sustain the land, without making destruction of any thing; and that of such manner of wards shall be done in all points, as is contained in the Great Charter of Liberties made in the time of King Henry, father to the King that now is, and that it be so used from henceforth; and in the same manner shall archbishopricks, bishopricks, abbacies, churches and all spiritual dignities be kept in time of vacation.

XXIV. *Unlawful disseisin by escheators, &c.*

It is provided also, that no escheator, sheriff, nor other bailiff of the King, by colour of his office, without special warrant or commandment or authority certain pertaining to his office, disseise any man of his freehold, nor of any thing belonging to his freehold; and if any do, it shall be at the election of the disseisee, whether that the King by office shall cause it to be amended at his complaint, or that he will sue at the common law by a writ of novel disseisin; And he that is attainted thereof shall pay double damages to the plaintiff, and shall be grievously amerced unto the King.

XXV. *Champerty by the King's officers*

No officer of the King by themselves, nor by other, shall maintain pleas, suits, or matters hanging in the King's courts, for lands, tenements or other things for to have part or profit thereof by covenant made between them; and he that doth, shall be punished at the King's pleasure.

XXVI. *Extortion by the King's officers*

And that no sheriff, nor other the King's officer, take any reward to do his office, but shall be paid of that which they take of the King: and he that so doth, shall yield twice as much, and shall be punished at the King's pleasure.

XXVIII. *Maintenance by officers of courts*

And that none of the King's clerks, nor of any justicer, from henceforth shall receive the presentment of any church, for the which any plea or debate is in the King's court, without special license of the King; and that the King forbiddeth, upon pain to lose (the church, and) his service. And that no clerk of any justicer, or sheriff (take part) in any quarrels (of) matters depending in the King's court, nor shall work any fraud, whereby common right may be delayed or disturbed; and if any so do, he shall be punished by the pain aforesaid, or more grievously, if the trespass do so require.

XXIX. *Deceits by pleaders*

It is provided also, that if any serjeant, pleader, or other do any manner of deceit or collusion in the King's court or consent (unto it,) in deceit of the court, (or) to beguile the court, or the party, and thereof be attainted, he shall be imprisoned for a year and a day, and from thenceforth shall not be heard to plead in (that) court for any man; and if he be no pleader, he shall be imprisoned in like manner by the space of a year and a day at least; and if the trespass require greater punishment, it shall be at the King's pleasure.

XXXI. *Excessive toll in market town*

Touching them that take outragious toll, contrary to the common custom of the realm, in market towns; it is provided, that if any do so in the King's town, which is let in fee farm the King shall seize into his own hand the franchise of the market; and if it be another's town, and the same be done by the lord of the town, the King shall do in like manner; and if it be done by a bailiff, (or any mean officer,) without the commandment of his lord, he shall restore to the plaintiff as much more for the outragious taking, as he (had) of him, if he had carried away his toll, and shall have forty days imprisonment.

Touching citizens and burgesses, to whom the King or his father hath granted murage to inclose their towns, which take such murage otherwise than it was granted unto them, and thereof be attainted; it is provided, that they shall lose their grant for ever, and shall be grievously amerced unto the King.

XXXIV. *Of slanderous reports*

Forasmuch as there have been oftentimes found in the country (devisors) of tales, whereby discord (or occasion) of discord, hath many times arisen between the King and his people, or great men of this realm; for the damage that hath and may thereof ensue; it is commanded, that from henceforth none be so hardy to tell or publish any false news or tale, whereby discord, (or occasion) of discord or slander may grow between the King and his people, or the great men of the realm; and he that doth so, shall be taken and kept in prison, until he hath brought him into court, (which was the first author of the tale.)

XXXV. *Excess of jurisdiction in franchises*

Of great men and their bailiffs, and other, the King's officers only excepted unto whom especial authority is given, which at the complaint of some, or by their own authority, attach other passing through their jurisdiction with their goods, (compelling them) to answer afore them upon contracts, covenants, and trespasses, done out of their power and their jurisdiction, where indeed they hold nothing of them nor within the franchise, where their power is, in prejudice of the King and his crown, and to the damage of the people; it is provided, that none from henceforth so do; and if any do, he shall pay to him, that by this occasion shall be attached, his damages double, and shall be grievously amerced to the King.

L. *Saving for the crown*

And forasmuch as the King hath ordained these things

unto the honour of God and holy church and for the commonwealth, and for the remedy of such as be grieved, he would not that at any other time it should turn in prejudice of himself, of his crown; but that such right, as appertains to him, should be saved in all points.

THE STATUTE OF WINCHESTER

EDWARD I

The Statute of Winchester may be considered the second great
Legislative Act of 1285. Passed under the reign of Edward I it
was mainly concerned with the keeping of the peace in the realm.
It revised the organization and armament of the militia and provided a useful police force for the repression of disorder and
robbery. Basically this Statute may be considered as one more
device passed during Edward's thirty-five year reign aimed at
strengthening the power of the crown.

I. Forasmuch as from day to day, robberies, murders,
burnings and thefts be more often used than they have
been heretofore, and felons cannot be attainted by the oath
of jurors which had rather suffer felonies done to strangers
to pass without pain, than to indite the offenders of whom
great part be people of the same country, or at least if the
offenders be of another country the receivers be of places
near; and they do the same because an oath is not put unto
jurors, nor upon the country where such felonies were done
as to the restitution of damages, hitherto no pain hath been
limited for their concealment and laches; our lord the king
for to abate the power of felons, hath established a pain
in this case, so that from henceforth, for fear of the pain
more than from fear of any oath, they shall not spare any
nor conceal any felonies; and doth command that cries shall
be solemnly made in all counties, hundreds, markets, fairs,
and all other places where great resort of people is, so
that none shall excuse himself by ignorance that from

henceforth every country be so well kept that immediately upon such robberies and felonies committed fresh suits shall be made from town to town and from country to country.

II. Likewise when need requires, inquests shall be made in towns by him that is lord of the town, and after in the hundred and in the franchise and in the county, and sometimes in two, three, or four counties, in case when felonies shall be committed in the marches of shires, so that the offenders may be attainted. And if the country will not answer for the bodies of such manner of offenders, the pain shall be such, that every country, that is to wit, the people dwelling in the country, shall be answerable for the robberies done and also the damages; so that the whole hundred where the robbery shall be done, with the franchises being within the precinct of the same hundred, shall be answerable for the robberies done. And if the robbery be done in the division of two hundreds, both the hundreds and the franchises within them shall be answerable; and after that the felony or robbery is done, the country shall have no longer space than forty days, within which forty days it shall behove them to agree for the robbery or offence, or else that they will answer for the bodies of the offenders.

III. And forasmuch as the king will not that his people should be suddenly impoverished by reason of this penalty, that seemeth very hard to many, the king granteth that it shall not be incurred immediately, but it shall be respited until Easter next following, within which time the king may see how the country will order themselves, and whether such felonies and robberies do cease. After which term let them all be assured that the foresaid penalty shall run generally; that is to say, every country, that is to wit, the people in the country, shall be answerable for felonies and robberies done among them.

IV. And for the more surety of the country, the king hath commanded that in great towns being walled, the gates shall be closed from the sun-setting until the sun-rising; and that no man do lodge in suburbs, nor in any place out of the town, from nine of the clock until day, without his host will answer for him; and the bailiffs of towns every week, or at the least every fifteenth day, shall make inquiry of all persons being lodged in the suburbs or in foreign places of the towns; and if they do find any that have lodge or received any strangers or suspicious person against the peace, the bailiffs shall do right therein. And the king commandeth, that from henceforth all watches be made as it hath been used in times past, that is to wit, from the day of the Ascension until the day of S. Michael, in every city by six men at every gate; in every borough, twelve men; every town, six or four, according to the number of the inhabitants of the town, and they shall watch the town continually all night from the sun-setting unto the sun-rising. And if any stranger do pass by them he shall be arrested until morning; and if no suspicion be found he shall go quit; and if they find cause of suspicion, they shall forthwith deliver him to the sheriff, and the sheriff may receive him without damage, and shall keep him safely, until he be acquitted in due manner. And if they will not obey the arrest, they shall levy hue and cry upon them, and such as keep the watch shall follow with hue and cry with all the town and the towns near, and so hue and cry shall be made from town to town, until that they be taken and delivered to the sheriff as before is said; and for the arrestments of such strangers none shall be punished.

V. And further, it is commanded that highways leading from one market town to another shall be enlarged, whereas bushes, woods, or dykes be, so that there be neither dykes, tree, nor bush whereby a man may lurk to do hurt within two hundred foot of the one side and two hundred foot on the other side of the way; so that this statute shall not extend unto oaks, nor unto great trees, so as it shall be clear underneath. And if by default of the lord that will not abate the dyke, underwood, or bushes, in the manner aforesaid, any robberies be done therein, the lord shall be answerable for the felony; and if murder be done the lord shall make a fine at the king's pleasure. And if the lord be not able to fell the underwoods the country shall aid him therein. And the king willeth that in his demesne lands and woods, within his forest and without, the ways shall be enlarged, as before is said. And if per case a park be near to the highway, it is requisite that the lord shall minish his park the space of two hundred foot from the highways, as before is said, or that he make such a wall, dyke, or hedge that offenders may not pass, nor return to do evil.

VI. And further it is commanded that every man have in his house harness for to keep the peace after the ancient assize; that is to say, every man between fifteen years of age and sixty years, shall be assessed and sworn to armour according to the quantity of their lands and goods; that is to wit, from fifteen pounds lands, and goods forty marks an hauberke an helme of iron, a sword, a knife, and a horse; and from ten pounds of lands and twenty marks goods, an hauberke, an helme of iron, a sword, and a knife; and from five pound lands an doublet, an helme of iron, a sword, and a knife; and from forty shillings of land, a sword, a bow and arrows, and a knife; and he that hath less than forty shillings yearly shall be sworn to keep gisarmes, knives, and other less weapons; and he that hath less than twenty marks in goods, shall have swords, knives, and other less weapons; and all other that may shall have bows and arrows out of the forest, and in the forest bows and boults. And that view of armour be made every year two times. And in every hundred and franchise two constables shall be chosen to make the view of armour; and the constables aforesaid shall present before justices assigned such defaults as they do see in the country about armour, and of the suits, and of watches, and of highways; and also shall present all such as do lodge strangers in uplandish towns, for whom they will not answer. And the justices assigned shall present at every parliament unto the king such defaults as they shall find, and the king shall provide remedy therein. And from henceforth let sheriffs take good heed, and bailiffs within their franchises and without, be they higher or lower, that have any bailiwick or forestry in fee or otherwise, that they shall follow the cry with the country, and after, as they are bounden, to keep horses and armour, so to do; and if there be any that do not, the defaults shall be presented by the constables to the justices assigned, and after by them to the king; and the king will provide remedy as afore is said. And the king commandeth and forbiddeth that from henceforth neither fairs nor markets be kept in churchyards, for the honor of the church. Given at Winchester, the eighth of October, in the thirteenth year of the reign of the king. (*Statutes of the Realm*, i. 96-98.)

THE PETITION OF RIGHT, 1628

Drafted in 1628 by Edward Coke, one of the greatest proponents of the English legal system, the petition was sent by the English Parliament to Charles I. The refusal by Parliament to finance the king's foreign policy had caused his government to impose illegal taxes and the quartering of troops in citizens' houses as an economy measure. Arbitrary arrest and confinement to those opposing these policies had created in Parliament a violent anger directed toward Charles and the Duke of Buckingham.

The Petition of Right is based upon earlier charters and statutes securing recognition of four basic principles: taxes may not be levied without the consent of Parliament; no person could be imprisoned for refusing to make payments which had not been legally established by Parliament; no person could be imprisoned for any offense without cause and without an opportunity to answer the charge; soldiers and mariners could not be housed in the homes of the citizenry and martial law may not be used in time of peace.

In return for his acceptance of the Petition of Right in June of 1628, King Charles I was granted certain subsidies. The Petition of Right remains as one of the landmarks of British freedom.

THE PETITION OF RIGHT

Presented to His Majesty, Charles the First,

By the Lords Spiritual and Temporal, and Commons, in Parliament assembled, concerning divers Rights and Liberties of the subjects.

To the King's Most Excellent Majesty.

Humbly shew unto our Sovereign Lord the King, the

Lords Spiritual and Temporal, and Commons, in Parliament assembled, That, whereas it is declared and enacted by statute made in the time of the reign of King Edward I. commonly called *Statutum de tallago non concedendo,* that no tallage or age shall be laid or levied by the King or his heirs in this realm, without the good will and assent of the Archbishops, Earls, Barons, Knights, Burgesses, and other the freemen of the commonality of this realm: And by the authority of Parliament holden in the five and twentieth year of the reign of King Edw. III. it is declared and enacted, That, from thenceforth, no person shall be compelled to make any loans, to the King against his will, because such loans were against reason, and the franchise of the land; And, by other laws of this realm, it is provided, that none should be changed by any charge or imposition called benevolence, or by such like charge: By which the statutes before mentioned and other the good laws and statutes of this realm, your subjects have inherited this freedom, that they should not be compelled to contribute to any tax, tallage, aid, or other like charge, nor set by common consent in Parliament.

II. Yet nevertheless, of late, divers commissions directed to sundry commissions in several counties, with instructions, have issued; by means whereof your people have been in divers places assembled, and required to lend certain sums of money unto your Majesty, and many of them, upon their refusal so to do, have had an oath administered unto them not warrantable by the laws or statutes of this realm, and have been constrained to become bound to make appearance and give attendance before your Privy Council and in other places; and others of them have been therefore imprisoned, confined, and sundry other ways molested and disquieted. And divers other charges have been laid and levied upon your people in several counties, by Lord Lieutenants, Deputy Lieutenants, Commissioners for Musters, Justices of Peace, and others, by command or direction from your Majesty, or your Privy Council, against the laws and free customs of this realm.

III. And whereas also, by the statute called, *The Great Charter of the Liberties of England,* it is declared and enacted, That no freeman may be taken or imprisoned, or be disseised of his freehold or liberties, or of his customs, or be outlawed or exiled, or in any manner destroyed, but by the lawful judgment of his peers, or by the law of the land.

IV. And in the eighth and twentieth year of the reign of King Edward III. it was declared and enacted, by authority of Parliament, That no man, of what estate or condition that he be, should be put out of his land or tenements, nor taken, nor imprisoned, nor disherited, nor put to death, without being brought to answer by the due process of law.

V. Nevertheless, against the tenour of the said statutes, and other the good laws and statutes of your realm to that end provided, divers of your subjects have of late been imprisoned without any cause showed; and when for their deliverance, they were brought before justices, by your Majesty's writs of *Habeas Corpus,* there to undergo and receive as the Court should order, and their keepers commanded to certify the cause of their detainer, no cause was certified, but that they were detained by your Majesty's special command, signified by the Lords of your Privy Counsel, and yet were returned back to several prisons, without being charged with any thing to which they might make answer according to the law.

VI. And whereas of late, great companies of soldiers and mariners have been dispersed into divers countries of the realm, and the inhabitants against their wills have been compelled to receive them into their houses, and there to suffer them to sojourn against the laws and customs of this realm, and to the great grievance and vexation of the people.

VII. And whereas also, by authority of Parliament, in the five and twentieth year of the reign of King Edward III. it is declared and enacted, That no man shall be forejudged of life, or limb against the form of the *Great Charter,* and the law of the land; and, by the said *Great Charter,* and other the laws and statutes of this your realm, no man ought to be judged to death but by the laws established in this your realm, either by the customs of the realm, or by Acts of Parliament: And whereas no offender, of what kind soever, is exempted from the proceedings to be used, and punishments to be inflicted by the laws and statutes of this your realm: Nevertheless, of late divers commissions, under your Majesty's great seal, have issued forth, by which certain persons have been assigned and appointed commissioners, with power and authority to proceed within the land, according to the justice of martial law against such soldiers and mariners, or other dissolute persons joining with them, as should commit any murder, robbery, felony, mutiny, or other outrage or misdemeanour whatsoever, and by summary course and order as is agreeable to martial law, and as is used by armies in time of war, to proceed to the trial and condemnation of such offenders, and them to cause to be executed and put to death according to the law martial.

VIII. By pretext whereof some of your Majesty's subjects have been, by some of the said commissioners, put to death, when and where, if by the laws and statutes of the land, they had deserved death, by the same laws and statutes also they might, and by no other, ought to have been judged and executed.

IX. And also sundry grievous offenders, by colour thereof claiming an exemption, have escaped the punishments due to them by the laws and statutes of this your realm, by reason that divers of your officers and ministers of justice have unjustly refused or forborn to proceed against such offenders, according to the same laws and statutes, upon pretence that the said offenders were punishable only by martial law, and by authority of such commissioners as aforesaid: Which commissioners, and all other of like nature, are wholly and directly contrary to the said laws and statutes of this your realm.

X. They do therefore humbly pray your most excellent Majesty; That no man hereafter be compelled to make or yield any gift, loan, benevolence, tax, or such like charge, without common consent, by Act of Parliament: And that none be called to make answer, or take such oath, or to give attendance, or be confined or otherwise molested or disquieted, concerning the same or for refusal thereof: And that no freemen, in any such manner as is before mentioned, be imprisoned or detained: And that your Majesty would be pleased to remove the said soldiers and mariners, and that your people may not be so burdened in time to come: and that the aforesaid commissioners, for proceeding by martial law, may be revoked and annulled: And that hereafter no commissions of like nature may issue forth to any person or person whatsoever, to be executed as aforesaid, lest by colour of them, any of your Majesty's subjects be destroyed, or put to death, contrary to the laws and franchise of the land.

XI. All which they most humbly pray of your most excellent Majesty as their rights and liberties, according to the laws and statutes of this realm: And that your Majesty would also vouch to declare, That the awards, doings, and proceedings to the prejudice of your people, in any of the premises, shall not be drawn hereafter into consequence or example: And that your Majesty would be also graciously pleased, for the further comfort and safety of your people, to declare your royal will and pleasure, that in the things aforesaid, all your officers and ministers shall serve you according to the laws and statutes of this realm, as they tender the honour of your Majesty, and the prosperity of this kingdom.

His Majesty's Answer
TO THE
PETITION OF RIGHT.

The Petition being read, the King's answer was delivered unto it, as follows:

"The King willeth that right be done, according to the laws and customs of the realm, and that the statutes be put in due execution, that his subjects may have no cause to complain of any wrong, or oppressions, contrary to their just rights and liberties. To the preservation whereof, he holds himself in conscience as well obliged, as of his prerogative."

But this answer not giving satisfaction, the King was again petitioned unto, that he would give a full and satisfactory answer to their Petition, in full Parliament; whereupon the King in person, upon the seventh of June, 1628, made this second answer:

"My Lords and Gentlemen,

"The answer I have already given you, was made with so good a deliberation, and approved by the judgment of so many wise men, that I could not have imagined but that it should have given you satisfaction; but to avoid all ambiguous interpretations, and shew you that there is no doubleness in my meaning, I am willing to please you in words as well as in substance; read your Petition, and you shall have an answer that I am sure will please you."

And then causing the Petition to be read distinctly by the Clerk of the Crown; the Clerk of the Parliament read the King's answer thereunto in those words: *"Soit droit fait comme est désiré,"* which is,

LET RIGHT BE DONE AS IS DESIRED.

THE ACT OF SETTLEMENT, 1701

Interest in the Act of Settlement passed by the English Parliament in 1701 rests in its similarity to the American Bill of Rights. The Act provided that if William III and Princess Anne, later Queen Anne, should die without heirs, the throne of England should pass to Sophia, granddaughter of James I. There were also requirements that the king must join in communion with the Church of England and that he might not leave the country without Parliamentary consent. Foreign-born kings were not to use English armies in defense of foreign soil without the Parliament's consent. It further provided that no pensioner or appointee of the king should sit in the House of Commons.

AN ACT FOR THE FURTHER LIMITATION OF THE CROWN, AND BETTER SECURING THE RIGHTS AND LIBERTIES OF THE SUBJECT

Whereas in the first year of the reign of your Majesty, and of our late most gracious sovereign lady Queen Mary (of blessed memory) an act of parliament was made, intituled, An act for declaring the rights and liberties of the subject, and for settling the succession of the crown, wherein it was (amongst other things) enacted, established, and declared, That the crown and regal government of the kingdoms of England, France, and Ireland, and the dominions thereunto belonging, should be and continue to your Majesty and the said late Queen, during the joint lives of your Majesty and the said Queen, and to the survivor: and that after the decease of your Majesty and of the said Queen, the said crown and regal government should be and remain to the heirs of the body of the said late Queen; and for default of such issue, to her royal highness the princess Anne

445

of Denmark, and the heirs of her body: and for default of
such issue, to the heirs of the body of your Majesty. And it
was thereby further enacted, That all and every person and
persons that then were, or afterwards should be reconciled to,
or should hold communion with the see or church of Rome,
or should profess the popish religion, or marry a papist,
should be excluded, and are by that act made for ever un-
capable to inherit, possess, or enjoy the crown and government of this realm, and Ireland, and the dominions thereunto
belonging, or any part of the same, or to have, use, or exercise any regal power, authority, or jurisdiction within the
same: and in all and every such case and cases the people of
these realms shall be and are thereby absolved of their
allegiance: and that the said crown and government shall
from time to time descend to and be enjoyed by such person
or persons, being protestants, as should have inherited and
enjoyed the same, in case the said person or persons, so reconciled, holding communion, professing or marrying, as
aforesaid, were naturally dead. After the making of which
statute, and the settlement therein contained, your Majesty's
good subjects, who were restored to the full and free possession and enjoyment of their religion, rights and liberties,
by the providence of God giving success to your Majesty's just
undertakings and unwearied endeavours for that purpose,
had no greater temporal felicity to hope or wish for, than
to see a royal progeny descending from your Majesty, to
whom (under God) they owe their tranquility, and whose
ancestors have for many years been principal assertors of
the reformed religion and the liberties of Europe, and from
our said most gracious sovereign Lady, whose memory will
always be precious to the subjects of these realms: and it
having since pleased Almighty God to take away your said
sovereign Lady, and also the most hopeful prince William
duke of Gloucester (the only surviving issue of her royal
highness the princess Anne of Denmark) to the unspeakable
grief and sorrow of your Majesty and your said good subjects,

446

who under such losses being sensibly put in mind, that it standeth wholly in the pleasure of Almighty God to prolong the lives of your Majesty and of her royal Highness, and to grant your Majesty, or to her royal Highness such issue as may be inheritable to the crown and regal government aforesaid, by the respective limitations in the said recited act contained, do constantly implore the divine mercy for these blessings: and your Majesty's said having daily experience of your royal care and concern for the present and future welfare of these kingdoms, and particularly recommending from your throne a further provision to be made for the succession of the crown in the protestant line, for the happiness of the nation, and the security of our religion; and it being absolutely necessary for the safety, peace, and quiet of this realm, to obviate all doubts and contentions in the same, by reason of any pretended title to the crown, and to maintain a certainty in the succession thereof, to which your subjects may safely have recourse for their protection, in case the limitations in the said recited act should determine: therefore for a further provision of the succession of the crown in the protestant line, we your Majesty's most dutiful and loyal subjects, the lords spiritual and temporal, and commons, in this present parliament assembled, do beseech your Majesty that it may be enacted and declared, and be it enacted and declared by the King's most excellent majesty, by and with the advice and consent of the lords spiritual and temporal, and commons, in this present parliament assembled, and by the authority of the same, That the most excellent princess Sophia, electress and dutchess dowager of Hanover, daughter of the most excellent princess Elizabeth, late Queen of Bohemia, daughter of our late sovereign lord King James the First, of happy memory, be and is hereby declared to be the next in succession, in the protestant line, to the imperial crown and dignity of the said realms of England, France, and Ireland, with the dominions and territories thereunto belonging, after his Majesty, and the princess Anne of Denmark, and in default of issue of the said princess Anne, and of his Majesty respectively: and that from and after the decease of his said Majesty, our now sovereign lord, and of her royal highness the princess Anne of Denmark, and for default of issue of the said princess Anne, and of his Majesty respectively, the crown and regal government of the said kingdoms of England, France, and Ireland, and of the dominions thereunto belonging, with the royal state and dignity of the said realms, and all honours, stiles, regalities, prerogatives, powers, jurisdictions and authorities, to the fame belonging and appertaining, shall be, remain, and continue to the said most excellent princess Sophia, and the heirs of her body, being protestants: and thereunto the said lords spiritual and temporal, and commons, shall and will, in the name of all the people of this realm, most humbly and faithfully submit themselves, their heirs and posterities; and do faithfully promise, That after the decease of his Majesty, and her royal highness, and the failure of the heirs of their respective bodies, to stand to, maintain, and defend the said princess Sophia, and the heirs of her body, being protestants, according to the limitation and succession of the crown in this act specified and contained, to the utmost of their powers, with their lives and estates, against all persons whatsoever that shall attempt any thing to the contrary.

II. Provided always, and it is hereby enacted, That all and every person and persons, who shall or may take or inherit the said crown, by virtue of the limitation of this present act, and is, are or shall be reconciled to, or shall hold communion with, the fee or church of Rome, or shall profess the popish religion, or shall marry a papist, shall be subject to such incapacities, as in such case or cases are by the said recited act provided, enacted, and established; and that every King and Queen of this realm, who shall come to and succeed in the imperial crown of this kingdom, by virtue of this act, shall have the coronation oath administered to him, her or them, at their respective coronations, according to the act of parliament made in the first year of the reign of his

Majesty, and the said late Queen Mary intituled, An act for establishing the coronation oath, and shall make, subscribe, and repeat the declaration in the act first above recited mentioned or referred to, in the manner and form thereby prescribed.

III. And whereas it is requisite and necessary that some further provision be made for securing our religion, laws and liberties, from and after the death of his Majesty and the princess Anne of Denmark, and the default of issue of the body of the said princess, and of his Majesty respectively; be it enacted by the King's most excellent majesty, by and with the advice and consent of the lords spiritual and temporal, and commons, in parliament assembled, and by the authority of the same,

That whoever shall hereafter come to the possession of this crown, shall join in communion with the church of England, as by law established.

That in case the crown and imperial dignity of this realm shall hereafter come to any person, not being a native of this kingdom of England, this nation be not obliged to engage in any war for the defense of any dominions or territories which do not belong to the crown of England, without the consent of parliament.

That no person who shall hereafter come to the possession of this crown, shall go out of the dominions of England, Scotland, or Ireland, without consent of parliament.

That from and after the time that the further limitation by this act shall take effect, all matters and things relating to the well governing of this kingdom, which are properly cognizable in the privy council by the laws and customs of this realm, shall be transacted there, and all resolutions taken thereupon shall be signed by such of the privy counsel as shall advise and consent to the same.

That after the said limitation shall take effect as aforesaid, no person born out of the kingdoms of England, Scotland, or Ireland, or the dominions thereunto belonging (although he be naturalized or made a denizen, except such as are born of English parents) shall be capable to be of the privy council, or a member of either house of parliament, or to enjoy any office or place of trust, either civil or military, or to have any grant of lands, tenements or hereditaments from the crown, to himself or to any other or others in trust for him.

That no person who has an office or place of profit under the King, or receives a pension from the crown, shall be capable of serving as a member of the house of commons.

That after the said limitation shall take effect as aforesaid, judges commissions be made quamdiu se bene gesserint and their salaries ascertained and established; but upon the address of both houses of parliament it may be lawful to remove them.

That no pardon under the great seal of England be pleadable to an impeachment by the commons in parliament.

IV. And whereas the laws of England are the birth-right of the people thereof, and all the Kings and Queens, who shall ascend the throne of this realm, ought to administer the government of the same according to the said laws, and all their officers and ministers ought to serve them respectively according to the same: the said lords spiritual and temporal, and commons, do therefore further humbly pray, That all the laws and statutes of this realm for securing the established religion, and the rights and liberties of the people thereof, and all other laws and statutes of the same now in force, may be ratified and confirmed, and the same are by his Majesty, by and with the advice and consent of the said lords spiritual and temporal, and commons, and by authority of the same, ratified and confirmed accordingly.

THE DECLARATION OF LONDON

The *Declaration of London,* established on February 26, 1909, provided rules governing blockade, contraband and other conditions regulating naval warfare. Although a well-thought-out and carefully worded document, the House of Lords evidently seemed to think it was too favorable to neutrals, and England failed to ratify the Declaration.

Considering that the general principles of international law are often in their practical application the subject of divergent procedure;

Animated by the desire to insure henceforward a greater uniformity in this respect;

Hoping that a work so important to the common welfare will meet with general approval;

Have appointed as their Plenipotentiaries, that is to say:

(Names of Plenipotentiaries)

Who, after having communicated their full powers, found in good and due form, have agreed to make the present Declaration:—

Preliminary Provision

The Signatory Powers are agreed in declaring that the rules contained in the following Chapters correspond in substance with the generally recognized principles of international law.

451

Chapter I.—*Blockade in time of War*

Article 1

A blockade must be limited to the ports and coasts belonging to or occupied by the enemy.

Article 2

In accordance with the Declaration of Paris of 1856 a blockade, in order to be binding, must be effective—that is to say, it must be maintained by a force sufficient really to prevent access to the enemy coast.

Article 3

The question whether a blockade is effective is a question of fact.

Article 4

A blockade is not regarded as raised if the blockading forces are temporarily driven off by bad weather.

Article 5

A blockade must be applied impartially to the ships of all nations.

Article 6

The commander of a blockading force may grant to a war ship permission to enter, and subsequently to leave, a blockaded port.

Article 7

In circumstances of distress, acknowledged by an authority of the blockading forces, a neutral vessel may enter a place under blockade and subsequently leave it, provided that she has neither discharged nor shipped any cargo there.

Article 8

A blockade, in order to be binding, must be declared in accordance with Article 9, and notified in accordance with Articles 11 and 16.

Article 9

A declaration of blockade is made either by the blockading Power or by the naval authorities acting in its name.

It specifies—

(1.) The date when the blockade begins;

(2.) The geographical limits of the coast blockaded;

(3.) The delay to be allowed to neutral vessels for departure.

Article 10

If the blockading Power, or the naval authorities acting in its name, do not establish the blockade in conformity with the provisions, which, in accordance with Article 9 (1) and (2), must be inserted in the declaration of blockade, the declaration is void, and a new declaration is necessary in order to make the blockade operative.

Article 11

A declaration of blockade is notified—

(1) To the neutral Powers, by the blockading Power by means of a communication addressed to the Governments themselves, or to their representatives accredited to it;

(2) To the local authorities, by the officer commanding the blockading force. These authorities will, on their part, inform, as soon as possible, the foreign consuls who exercise

their functions in the port or on the coast blockaded.

Article 12

The rules relative to the declaration and to the notification of blockade are applicable in the case in which the blockade may have been extended, or may have been re-established after having been raised.

Article 13

The voluntary raising of a blockade, as also any limitation which may be introduced, must be notified in the manner prescribed by Article 11.

Article 14

The liability of a neutral vessel to capture for breach of blockade is contingent on her knowledge, actual or presumptive, of the blockade.

Article 15

Failing proof to the contrary, knowledge of the blockade is presumed if the vessel left a neutral port subsequently to the notification of the blockade made in sufficient time to the Power to which such port belongs.

Article 16

If a vessel which approaches a blockaded port does not know or cannot be presumed to know of the blockade, the notification must be made to the vessel itself by an officer of one of the ships of the blockading force. This notification must be entered in the vessel's logbook, with entry of the day and hour, as also of the geographical position of the vessel at the time.

A neutral vessel which leaves a blockaded port must be allowed to pass free if, through the negligence of the officer commanding the blockading force, no declaration of blockade has been notified to the local authorities, or, if, in the declaration, as notified no delay has been indicated.

Article 17

The seizure of neutral vessels for violation of blockade may be made only within the radius of action of the ships of war assigned to maintain an effective blockade.

Article 18

The blockading forces must not bar access to the ports or to the coasts of neutrals.

Article 19

Whatever may be the ulterior destination of the vessel or of her cargo, the evidence of violation of blockade is not sufficiently conclusive to authorize the seizure of the vessel if she is at the time bound toward an unblockaded port.

Article 20

A vessel which in violation of blockade has left a blockaded port or has attempted to enter the port is liable to capture so long as she is pursued by a ship of the blockading force. If the pursuit is abandoned, or if the blockade is raised, her capture can no longer be effected.

Article 21

A vessel found guilty of violation of blockade is liable to condemnation. The cargo is also liable to condemnation, unless it is proved that at the time the goods were shipped the

455

shipper neither knew nor could have known of the intention to violate the blockade.

Chapter II.—Contraband of War

Article 22

The following articles and materials are, without notice, regarded as contraband, under the name of absolute contraband:

1. Arms of all kinds, including arms for sporting purposes, and their unassembled distinctive parts.

2. Projectiles, charges, and cartridges of all kinds, and their unassembled distinctive parts.

3. Powder and explosives specially adapted for use in war.

4. Gun carriages, caissons, limbers, military wagons, field forges, and their unassembled distinctive parts.

5. Clothing and equipment of a distinctively military character.

6. All kinds of harness of a distinctively military character.

7. Saddle, draught, and pack animals suitable for use in war.

8. Articles of camp equipment and their unassembled distinctive parts.

9. Armor plates.

10. Warships and boats and their unassembled parts specially distinctive as suitable for use only in a vessel of war.

11. Implements and apparatus made exclusively for the manufacture of munitions of war, for the manufacture or repair of arms or of military material, for use on land or sea.

Article 23

Articles and materials which are exclusively used for war may be added to the list of absolute contraband by means of a notified declaration.

The notification is addressed to the Governments of other Powers, or to their representatives accredited to the Power which makes the declaration. A notification made after the opening of hostilities is addressed only to neutral Powers.

Article 24

The following articles and materials susceptible of use in war as well as for the purposes of peace, are without notice, regarded as contraband of war, under the name of conditional contraband:—

(1) Food.

(2) Forage and grain suitable for feeding animals.

(3) Clothing and fabrics for clothing, boots and shoes, suitable for military use.

(4) Gold and silver in coin or bullion; paper money.

(5) Vehicles of all kinds available for use in war, and their unassembled parts.

(6) Vessels, craft, and boats of all kinds, floating docks, parts of docks, as also their unassembled parts.

(7) Fixed railway material and rolling stock, and material for telegraphs, radio telegraphs, and telephones.

(8) Balloons and flying machines and their unassembled distinctive parts as also their accessories, articles and materials distinctive as intended for use in connection with balloons or flying machines.

(9) Fuel; lubricants.

(10) Powder and explosives which are not specially adapted for use in war.

(11) Barbed wire as also the implements for placing and cutting the same.

(12) Horseshoes and horseshoeing materials.

(13) Harness and saddlery material.

(14) Binocular glasses, telescopes, chronometers, and all kinds of nautical instruments.

Article 25

Articles and materials susceptible of use in war as well as for purposes of peace, and other than those enumerated in Articles 22 and 24, may be added to the list of conditional contraband by means of a declaration, which must be notified in the manner provided for in the second paragraph of Article 23.

Article 26

If a Power waives, so far as it is concerned, the right to regard as contraband of war articles and materials which are comprised in any of the classes enumerated in Articles 22 and 24, it shall make known its intention by a declaration notified in the manner provided for in the second paragraph of Article 23.

Article 27

Articles and materials which are not susceptible of use in war are not to be declared contraband of war.

Article 28

The following are not to be declared contraband of war:

(1.) Raw cotton, wool, silk, jute, flax; hemp; and other raw materials of the textile industries and also yarns of the same.

(2.) Nuts and oil seeds; copra.

(3.) Rubber resins, gums and lacs; hops.

(4.) Raw hides, horns, bones, and ivory.

(5.) Natural and artificial manures, including nitrates and phosphates for agricultural purposes.

(6.) Metallic ores.

(7.) Earths, clays, lime, chalk, stone, including marble; bricks, slates, and tiles.

(8.) Chinaware and glass.

(9.) Paper and materials prepared for its manufacture.

(10.) Soap, paint and colours, including articles exclusively used in their manufacture, and varnishes.

(11.) Bleaching powder, soda ash, caustic soda, salt cake, ammonia, sulphate of ammonia, and sulphate of copper.

(12.) Agricultural, mining, textile, and printing machinery.

(13.) Precious stones, semi-precious stones, pearls, mother-of-pearl, and coral.

(14.) Clocks and watches, other than chronometers.

(15.) Fashion and fancy goods.

(16.) Feathers of all kinds, hairs, and bristles.

(17.) Articles of household furniture and decoration; office furniture and accessories.

Article 29

Neither are the following to be regarded as contraband of war:

(1.) Articles and materials serving exclusively for the care of the sick and wounded. They may, nevertheless, in case of urgent military necessity and subject to the payment of compensation, be requisitioned, if their destination is that specified in Article 30.

(2.) Articles and materials intended for the use of the vessel in which they are found, as well as those for the use of her crew and passengers during the voyage.

Article 30

Absolute contraband is liable to capture if it is shown to be destined to territory belonging to or occupied by the enemy, or to the armed forces of the enemy. It is immaterial whether the carriage of the goods is direct or entails either transshipment or transport over land.

Article 31

Proof of the destination specified in Article 30 is complete in the following cases:

1. When the goods are documented to be discharged in a port of the enemy, or to be delivered to his armed forces.

2. When the vessel is to call at enemy ports only, or when she is to touch at a port of the enemy or to join his armed forces, before arriving at the neutral port for which the goods are documented.

Article 32

The ship's papers are complete proof of the voyage of a vessel transporting absolute contraband, unless the vessel is encountered having manifestly deviated from the route which she ought to follow according to the ship's papers and being unable to justify by sufficient reason such deviation.

Article 33

Conditional contraband is liable to capture if it is shown that it is destined for the use of the armed forces or of a government department of the enemy State, unless in this latter case the circumstances show that the articles cannot in fact be used for the purposes of the war in progress. This latter exception does not apply to a consignment coming under Article 24 (4).

Article 34

There is presumption of the destination referred to in Article 33 if the consignment is addressed to enemy authorities, or to a merchant, established in the enemy country, and when it is well known that this merchant supplies articles and material of this kind to the enemy. The presumption is the same if the consignment is destined to a fortified place of the enemy, or to another place serving as a base for the armed forces of the enemy; this presumption, however, does not apply to the merchant vessel herself bound for one of these places and of which vessel it is sought to show the contraband character.

Failing the above presumptions, the destination is presumed innocent.

The presumptions laid down in this Article admit proof to the contrary.

Article 35

Conditional contraband is not liable to capture, except when on board a vessel bound for territory belonging to or occupied by the enemy, or for the armed forces of the enemy, and when it is not to be discharged at an intervening neutral port.

The ship's papers are conclusive proof of the voyage of the goods, unless the vessel is encountered having manifestly deviated from the route which she ought to follow according to the ship's papers and being unable to justify by sufficient reason such deviation.

Article 36

Notwithstanding the provisions of Article 35, if the territory of the enemy has no seaboard, conditional contraband is liable to capture if it is shown that it has the destination referred to in Article 33.

Article 37

A vessel carrying articles liable to capture as absolute or conditional contraband may be captured on the high seas or in the territorial waters of the belligerents throughout the whole course of her voyage, even if she has the intention to touch at a port of call before reaching the hostile destination.

Article 38

A capture is not to be made on the ground of a carriage of contraband previously accomplished and at the time completed.

Article 39

Contraband is liable to condemnation.

Article 40

The confiscation of the vessel carrying contraband is allowed if the contraband forms, either by value, by weight, by volume, or by freight, more than half the cargo.

Article 41

If a vessel carrying contraband is released the expenses incurred by the captor in the trial before the national prize court as also for the preservation and custody of the ship and cargo during the proceedings are chargeable against the ship.

Article 42

Goods which belong to the owner of the contraband and which are on board the same vessel are liable to condemnation.

Article 43

If a vessel is encountered at sea making a voyage in ignorance of the hostilities or of the declaration of contraband affecting her cargo, the contraband is not to be condemned except with indemnity; the vessel herself and the remainder of the cargo are exempt from condemnation and from the expenses referred to in Article 41. The case is the same if the master after becoming aware of the opening of hostilities or of the declaration of contraband, has not yet been able to discharge the contraband.

A vessel is deemed to be aware of the state of war, or of the declaration of contraband, if she left a neutral port after there had been made in sufficient time the notification of the opening of hostilities, or of the declaration of contraband, to the power to which such port belongs. A vessel is also deemed to be aware of a state of war if she left an enemy port after the opening of hostilities.

Article 44

A vessel stopped because carrying contraband, and not liable to condemnation on account of the proportion of contraband, may, according to circumstances, be allowed to continue her voyage if the master is ready to deliver the contraband to the belligerent ship.

The delivery of the contraband is to be entered by the captor on the logbook of the vessel stopped, and the master of the vessel must furnish the captor duly certified copies of all relevant papers.

The captor is at liberty to destroy the contraband which is thus delivered to him.

Chapter III.—Unneutral service

Article 45

A neutral vessel is liable to be condemned and, in a general way, is liable to the same treatment which a neutral vessel would undergo when liable to condemnation on account of contraband of war:

(1) If she is making a voyage especially with a view to the transport of individual passengers who are embodied in the armed force of the enemy, or with a view to the transmission

of information in the interest of the enemy.

(2) If, with the knowledge of the owner, of the one who charters the vessel entire, or of the master, she is transporting a military detachment of the enemy, or one or more persons who, during the voyage, lend direct assistance to the operations of the enemy.

In the cases specified in the preceding paragraphs, (1) and (2), goods belonging to the owner of the vessel are likewise liable to condemnation.

The provisions of the present Article do not apply if when the vessel is encountered at sea she is unaware of the opening of hostilities, or if the master, after becoming aware of the opening of hostilities, has not been able to disembark the passengers. The vessel is deemed to know of the state of war if she left an enemy port after the opening of hostilities, or a neutral port after there had been made in sufficient time a notification of the opening of hostilities to the Power to which such port belongs.

Article 46

A neutral vessel is liable to be condemned and, in a general way, is liable to the same treatment which she would undergo if she were a merchant vessel of the enemy:

(1) If she takes a direct part in the hostilities.

(2) If she is under the orders or under the control of an agent placed on board by the enemy Government.

(3) If she is chartered entire by the enemy Government.

(4) If she is at the time and exclusively either devoted to the transport of enemy troops or to the transmission of information in the interest of the enemy.

In the cases specified in the present Article, the goods belonging to the owner of the vessel are likewise liable to condemnation.

Article 47

Any individual embodied in the armed force of the enemy,

and who is found on board a neutral merchant vessel, may be made a prisoner of war, even though there be no ground for the capture of the vessel.

Chapter IV.— *Destruction of Neutral Prizes*

Article 48

A captured neutral vessel is not to be destroyed by the captor, but must be taken into such port as is proper in order to determine there the rights as regards the validity of the capture.

Article 49

As an exception, a neutral vessel captured by a belligerent ship, and which would be liable to condemnation, may be destroyed if the observance of Article 48 would involve danger to the ship of war or to the success of the operations in which she is at the time engaged.

Article 50

Before the destruction, the persons on board must be placed in safety, and all the ship's papers and other documents which those interested consider relevant for the decision as to the validity of the capture must be taken on board the ship of war.

Article 51

A captor who has destroyed a neutral vessel must, as a condition precedent to any decision upon the validity of the capture, establish in fact that he only acted in the face of an exceptional necessity such as is contemplated in Article 49. Failing to do this, he must compensate the parties interested without examination as to whether or not the capture was valid.

Article 52

If the capture of a neutral vessel, of which the destruction has been justified, is subsequently held to be invalid, the captor must compensate those interested, in place of the restitution to which they would have been entitled.

Article 53

If neutral goods which were not liable to condemnation have been destroyed with the vessel, the owner of such goods is entitled to compensation.

Article 54

The captor has the right to require the giving up of, or to proceed to destroy, goods liable to condemnation found on board a vessel which herself is not liable to condemnation, provided that the circumstances are such as, according to Article 49, justify the destruction of a vessel liable to condemnation. The captor enters the goods delivered or destroyed in the logbook of the vessel stopped, and must procure from the master duly certified copies of all relevant papers. When the giving up or destruction has been completed, and the formalities have been fulfilled, the master must be allowed to continue his voyage.

The provisions of Articles 51 and 52 respecting the obligations of a captor who has destroyed a neutral vessel are applicable.

Chapter V.—Transfer of Flag

Article 55

The transfer of an enemy vessel to a neutral flag, effected

466

before the opening of hostilities, is valid, unless it is proved that such transfer was made in order to evade the consequences which the enemy character of the vessel would involve. There is, however, a presumption that the transfer is void if the bill of sale is not on board in case the vessel has lost her belligerent nationality less than sixty days before the opening of hostilities. Proof to the contrary is admitted.

There is absolute presumption of the validity of a transfer effected more than thirty days before the opening of hostilities if it is absolute, complete, conforms to the laws of the countries concerned, and if its effect is such that the control of the vessel and the profits of her employment do not remain in the same hands as before the transfer. If, however, the vessel lost her belligerent nationality less than sixty days before the opening of hostilities, and if the bill of sale is not on board, the capture of the vessel would not give a right to compensation.

Article 56

The transfer of an enemy vessel to a neutral flag, effected after the opening of hostilities, is void unless it is proved that such transfer was not made in order to evade the consequences which the enemy character of the vessel would involve.

There is, however, absolute presumption that a transfer is void:

(1) If the transfer has been made during a voyage or in a blockaded port.

(2) If there is a right of redemption or of revision.

(3) If the requirements upon which the right to fly the flag depends according to the laws of the country of the flag hoisted have not been observed.

Chapter VI.—*Enemy Character*

Article 57

Subject to the provisions respecting the transfer of flag, the neutral or enemy character of a vessel is determined by the flag which she has the right to fly.

The case in which a neutral vessel is engaged in a trade which is reserved in time of peace, remains outside the scope of, and is in no wise affected by, this rule.

Article 58

The neutral or enemy character of goods found on board an enemy vessel is determined by the neutral or enemy character of the owner.

Article 59

If the neutral character of goods found on board an enemy vessel is not proven, they are presumed to be enemy goods.

Article 60

The enemy character of goods on board an enemy vessel continues until they reach their destination, notwithstanding an intervening transfer after the opening of hostilities while the goods are being forwarded.

If, however, prior to the capture, a former neutral owner exercises, on the bankruptcy of a present enemy owner, a legal right to recover the goods they regain their neutral character.

Chapter VII.—*Convoy*

Article 61

Neutral vessels under convoy of their national flag are

exempt from search. The commander of a convoy gives, in writing, at the request of the commander of a belligerent ship of war, all information as to the character of the vessels and their cargoes, which could be obtained by visit and search.

Article 62

If the commander of the belligerent ship of war has reason to suspect that the confidence of the commander of the convoy has been abused, he communicates his suspicions to him. In such a case it is for the commander of the convoy alone to conduct an investigation. He must state the result of such investigation in a report, of which a copy is furnished to the officer of the ship of war. If, in the opinion of the commander of the convoy, the facts thus stated justify the capture of one or more vessels, the protection of the convoy must be withdrawn from such vessels.

Chapter VIII.—*Resistance to search*

Article 63

Forcible resistance to the legitimate exercise of the right of stoppage, visit and search, and capture, involves in all cases the condemnation of the vessel. The cargo is liable to the same treatment which the cargo of an enemy vessel would undergo. Goods belonging to the master or owner of the vessel are regarded as enemy goods.

Chapter IX.—Compensation

Article 64

If the capture of a vessel or of goods is not upheld by the

prize court, or if without being brought to judgment the captured vessel is released, those interested have the right to compensation, unless there were sufficient reasons for capturing the vessel or goods.

Final Provisions

Article 65

The provisions of the present Declaration form an indivisible whole.

Article 66

The Signatory Powers undertake to secure the reciprocal observance of the rules contained in this Declaration in case of a war in which the belligerents are all parties to this Declaration. They will therefore issue the necessary instructions to their authorities and to their armed forces, and will take the measures which are proper in order to guarantee the application of the Declaration by their Courts and more particularly by their prize courts.

Article 67

The present Declaration shall be ratified as soon as possible.

The ratifications shall be deposited in London.

The first deposit of ratifications shall be recorded in a Protocol signed by the Representatives of the Powers taking part therein, and by His Britannic Majesty's Principal Secretary of State for Foreign Affairs.

The subsequent deposits of ratifications shall be made by means of a written notification addressed to the British Government, and accompanied by the instrument of ratification.

A duly certified copy of the Protocol relating to the first

deposit of ratification, and of the notifications mentioned in the preceding paragraph as well as of the instruments of ratification which accompany them, shall be immediately sent by the British Government, through the diplomatic channel, to the Signatory Powers. The said Government shall, in the cases contemplated in the preceding paragraph, inform them at the same time of the date on which it received the notification.

Article 68

The present Declaration shall take effect, in the case of the Powers which were parties to the first deposit of ratifications, sixty days after the date of the Protocol recording such deposit, and, in the case of the Powers which shall ratify subsequently, sixty days after the notification of their ratification shall have been received by the British Government.

Article 69

In the event of one of the Signatory Powers wishing to denounce the present Declaration, such denunciation can only be made to take effect at the end of a period of twelve years beginning sixty days after the first deposit of ratifications, and, after that time, at the end of successive periods of six years, of which the first will begin at the end of the period of twelve years.

Such denunciation must be notified in writing, at least one year in advance, to the British Government, which shall inform all the other Powers.

It will only operate in respect of the Power which shall have made the notification.

Article 70

The Powers represented at the London Naval Conference attach particular value to the general recognition of the rules which they have adopted, and express the hope that the Powers which were not represented there will adhere to the present Declaration. They request the British Government to invite them to do so.

A Power which desires to adhere notifies its intention in writing to the British Government, in transmitting the act of adhesion, which will be deposited in the archives of the said Government.

The said Government shall forthwith transmit to all the other Powers a duly certified copy of the notification, as also of the act of adhesion, stating the date on which such notification was received. The adhesion takes effect sixty days after such date.

The position of the adhering Powers shall be in all matters concerning the Declaration similar to the position of the Signatory Powers.

Article 71

The present Declaration, which shall bear the date of the 26th February, 1909, may be signed in London until the 30th June, 1909, by the Plenipotentiaries of the Powers represented at the Naval Conference.

In faith whereof the Plenipotentiaries have signed the present Declaration and have thereto affixed their seal.

Done at London, the twenty-sixth day of February, one thousand nine hundred and nine, in a single original, which shall remain deposited in the archives of the British Government, and of which duly certified copies shall be sent through the diplomatic channel to the Powers represented at the Naval Conference.

XIV.

LEGAL DOCUMENTS OF AMERICA

THE LEYDEN AGREEMENT, 1618

A group of London Separatists had settled in Amsterdam, Holland, as early as 1593. In 1607-8 Separatists from the Scrooby Congregation joined the congregation in Amsterdam, but shortly moved to Leyden. In 1617 the Scrooby-Leyden group determined to move to America and applied to the Virginia Company (*see* Mayflower Compact) for a patent to land in Virginia. To further this application, the congregation drew up these Seven Articles as assurance to the King of loyalty and orthodoxy. The King, however, promised only that "he would connive at them and not molest them provided they carried themselves peaceably."

Seven Artikes which ye Church of Leyden sent to ye Counsell of England to bee considered of in respeckt of their judgements occationed about theer going to Virginia Anno 1618.

1. To ye confession of fayth published in ye name of ye Church of England & to every artikell theerof wee do wth ye reformed churches wheer wee live & also els where assent wholy.
2. As wee do acknolidg ye docktryne of fayth theer tawght so do wee ye fruites and effeckts of ye same docktryne to ye begetting of saving fayth in thousands in ye land (conformistes and reformistes as ye are called) wth whom also as wth our brethren wee do desyer to keepe sperituall communion in peace and will pracktis in our parts all lawfull thinges.
3. The Kings Majesty wee acknoledge for Supreame Governer in his Dominion in all causes and over all parsons,

and ye none maye decklyne or apeale from his authority or judgement in any cause whatsoever, byt y in all thinges obedience is dewe unto him, ether active, if ye thing commanded by not agaynst God's woord, or passive yf itt bee, except pardon can bee obtayned.

4. Wee judg itt lawfull for his Majesty to apoynt bishops; civill overseers, or officers in awthority under hime, in ye severall provinces, dioses, congregations or parrishes to oversee ye Churches and governe them civilly according to ye Lawes of ye Land, untto who ye ar in all thinges to give an account & by them to bee ordered according to Godlyness.

5. The authority of ye present bishops in ye Land wee do acknowlidg so far forth as ye same is indeed derived from his Majesty untto them and as ye proseed in his name, whom we will also theerein honor in all things and hime in them.

6. Wee beleeve yt no sinod, classes, convocation or assembly of Ecclesiasticall officers hath any power or awthority att all but as ye same by ye Majestraet geven unto them.

7. And lastly, wee desyer to geve untto all Superiors dew honnor to preserve ye untiy of ye speritt wth all ye feare God, to have peace wth all men what in us lyeth & wheerin wee err to bee instructed by any.

> Subscribed by
> John Robinson
> and
> Willyam Bruster

THE MAYFLOWER COMPACT

November 11, 1620

The Separatists living in Leyden, Holland, desired for various reasons to transplant their colony to America. In 1619 they secured from the Virginia Company a patent for a private plantation. The Pilgrims, reinforced by some seventy persons from London, sailed from Plymouth in September, 1620, and arrived off Cape Cod in November. Some of the London recruits were an "undesirable lot" and, Bradford tells us, boasted that they were not under the jurisdiction of the Virginia Company and "would use their owne libertie." In order to establish some form of government, therefore, the Pilgrim leaders drew up the famous Mayflower Compact. The Compact was not intended as a constitution, but was an extension of the customary church covenant to civil circumstances. Inasmuch as the Plymouth settlers were never able to secure a charter, the Mayflower compact remained the only form of constitution for the colony.

In The Name of God, Amen. We, whose names are underwritten, the Loyal Subjects of our dread Sovereign Lord King *James,* by the Grace of God, of *Great Britain, France,* and *Ireland,* King, *Defender of the Faith,* &c. Having undertaken for the Glory of God and Advancement of the Christian Faith, and the Honor of our King and Country, a Voyage to plant the first colony in the northern Parts of Virginia; Do by these Presents, solemnly and mutually in the Presence of God and one another covenant and combine ourselves together into a civil Body Politic, for our better Ordering and Preservation, and Furtherance of the Ends aforesaid; And by Virtue hereof do enact, constitute, and frame, such just and equal Laws, Ordinances, Acts, Constitutions, and Offices, from time to time, as shall be thought most meet and convenient for the general Good of the Colony; unto which we promise all due Submission and Obedience. In Witness whereof we have hereunto subscribed our names at *Cape Cod* the eleventh of *November,* in the Reign of our Sovereign Lord King *James* of *England, France,* and *Ireland,* the eighteenth and of *Scotland,* the fifty-fourth. *Anno Domini.* 1620.

Mr. John Carver	Digery Priest
Mr. William Bradford	Thomas Williams
Mr. Edward Winslow	Gilbert Winslow
Mr. William Brewster	Edmund Margesson
Isaac Allerton	Peter Brown
Miles Standish	Richard Bitteridge
John Alden	George Soule
John Turner	Edward Tilly
Francis Eaton	John Tilly
James Chilton	Francis Cooke
John Craxton	Thomas Rogers
John Billington	Thomas Tinker
Joses Fletcher	John Ridgate
John Goodman	Edward Fuller
Mr. Samuel Fuller	Richard Clark
Mr. Christopher Martin	Richard Gardiner
Mr. William Mullins	Mr. John Allerton
Mr. William White	Thomas English
Mr. Richard Warren	Edward Doten
John Howland	Edward Liester.
Mr. Stephen Hopkins	

BENJAMIN FRANKLIN

The Articles of Confederation have been so discredited by the weakness of the country while they were in force, and have been so overshadowed by the late Federal Constitution, that their constitutional history has been neglected. Yet those Articles were as great an advance over the old state of things as the Constitution was over the Confederation. They defined, by a bold experiment, a federal government in many respects better than any of the European federal systems which had preceded it, and a considerable part of the Articles was incorporated by the Convention of 1787 into the new instrument of government.

The first appearance of a systematic plan of a federal government is Franklin's draft of 1775. Franklin had already shown in the Albany Plan of 1754 (text in American History Leaflet No. 17) his readiness to sketch out a Colonial federal government. As soon as it became evident that the Second Continental Congress would stand by the Massachusetts people in their armed resistance, Franklin foresaw the necessity of a formal Union; and drew up the plan printed below, which was presented to Congress July 21, 1775. In the manuscript journals there is no reference to the submission of the plan, but the manuscript is preserved in the State Department in Franklin's firm and unmistakable hand, with the date of its reception endorsed upon it. From the impossible terms of adjustment which he suggests in the last paragraph, it is clear that he wished to create a permanent and independent Union. The manuscript has several interlineations, one of which—"upon the continent of North America"—is manifestly contradictory to some of the words which follow.

A year later, after the ignoring of the petition of Congress and the steady drifting into a general war, Congress came to see the necessity of both independence and union. On June 11, 1776, a committee was created to draw up a Declaration of Independence; and another committee was provided for to frame the form of a Confederation: the two plans were meant to stand together. The first committee reported on July 1, and its report was adopted July 4. The other reported ten days later in a draft in the handwriting of John Dickinson of Delaware, chairman of the committee. This draft was printed for the benefit of the members and then underwent searching and repeated debate. Notwithstanding the need of a settled government, it was not adopted by Congress till November 15, 1777, when the Secretary of Congress made up a new draft, including all amendments; and it was therefore submitted to the States for ratification July 9, 1778, the members then in Congress from States which had already ratified, signed an engrossed roll of the Articles; and, as other states ratified, their members also signed; last of all the delegates from Maryland, March 1, 1781.

THE ARTICLES OF CONFEDERATION

Article I
The name of this Confederacy shall henceforth be *The United Colonies of North America.—*

Article II
The said United Colonies hereby severally enter a firm League of Friendship with each other, binding on themselves and their Posterity for their common Defense against their Enemies, for the Security of their Liberties & Property, the Safety of their Persons and Families, and their mutual and general Welfare. [1]

Article III
That each Colony shall enjoy and retain as much as it may think fit of its own present Laws, Customs, Rights, Privileges and peculiar Jurisdictions within its own Limits; and may amend its own constitution as shall seem best to its own Assembly or Convention.

Article IV

That for the more convenient Management of general Interests, Delegates shall be annually elected in each Colony to meet in General Congress at such Time and Place as shall be agreed on in the next preceding Congress. Only where particular Circumstances do not make a Deviation necessary, it is understood to be a Rule, that each succeeding Congress be held in a different Colony till the whole Number be gone through, and so in perpetual Rotation; and that accordingly the next Congress after the present shall be held at Annapolis in Maryland.

Article V

That the Power and Duty of the Congress shall extend to Gen. Officers as Treasurer Secy. the Determining on War and Peace, the sending and receiving ambassadors, and entering into Alliances, (the Reconciliation with Great Britain;) the settling of all Disputes & Differences between Colony about Limits or any other cause if such should arise; and the Planting of new Colonies; when proper. The Congress shall also make general Ordinances as tho' necessary to the General Welfare, particular Assemblies cannot be competent to; viz. those that may relate to our general Commerce; or general Currency; to the Establishment of Posts: & the Regulation of our Common Forces. The Congress shall also have the Appointment of all General Officers civil and military, appertaining to the general Confederacy, such as General Treasurer, Secretary, etc.

Article VI

All Charges of Wars, and all other general Expenses to be incurr'd for the common Welfare, shall be defray'd out of a common Treasury, which is to be supply'd by each Colony in proportion to its Number of Male Polls between 16 & 60 Years of Age; the Taxes for paying that proportion are to be laid and levied by the Laws of each Colony.

481

Article VII

The Number of Delegates to be elected and sent to the Congress by each Colony, shall be regulated from time to time by the Number of such Polls return'd so as that one Delegate be allow'd for every (5000) Polls. And the Delegates are to bring with them to every Congress an authenticated Return of the number of Polls in their respective Provinces, which is to be triennially taken, for the Purposes above mentioned.

Article VIII

At every Meeting of the Congress One half of the Members returning exclusive of Proxies be necessary to make a Quorum, and Each Delegate at the Congress, shall have a Vote in all Cases; and if necessarily absent, shall be allowed to appoint any other Delegate from the same Colony to be his Proxy, who may vote for him.

Article IX

An executive Council shall be appointed by the Congress out of their own Body, consisting of (12) Persons; of whom in the first Appointment one third, viz. (4), shall be one Year, (4) for two Years, and (4) for three Years; and as the said Terms expire, the Vacancies shall be filled by Appointments for three Years, whereby One Third of the Members will be changed annually. And each Person who has served the said Term of three Years as Counsellor, shall have a Respite of three years, before he can be elected again. This Council (of whom two thirds shall be a Quorum) in the Recess of the Congress is to execute what shall have been enjoin'd thereby; to manage the general continental Business and Interests; to receive Applications from foreign Countries; to prepare Matters for the Consideration of the Congress; to fill up (Pro tempore) continental Offices that fall vacant; and to draw on the General Treasurer for such Monies as may be necessary for general Services, appropriated by the Congress to such Services.

Article X

No Colony shall engage in an offensive War with any Nation of Indians without the Consent of the Congress, or grand Council abovementioned, who are first to consider the Justice and Necessity of such War.

Article XI

A perpetual Alliance offensive and defensive, is to be entered into as soon as may be with the Six Nations; their Limits ascertain'd & to be secur'd to them; their Land not to be encroach'd on, nor any private or Colony Purchases made of them hereafter to be held good; nor any Contract for Lands to be made but between the Great Council of the Indians at Onondaga & the General Congress. The Boundaries and Limits of all the other Indians shall also (be) ascertain'd & secured to them in the same manner; and Persons appointed to reside among them in proper Districts, who shall take care to prevent Injustice in the Trade with them and be enabled at our general Expense by occasional small Supplies, to relieve their personal Wants and Distresses. And all Purchases from them shall be by the Congress for the General Advantage & Benefit of the United Colonies.

Article XII

As all new Institutions may have Imperfections which only Time and Experience can discover, it is agreed, that the General Congress from time to time shall propose such Amendments of this Constitution as may be found necessary; which being approv'd by a Majority of the Colony Assemblies shall be equally binding with the rest of the Articles of this Confederation.

Article XIII

Any and every Colony from Great Britain upon the Continent of North America not at present engag'd in our Association, upon Application and joining the said Association, be receiv'd into this Confederation, viz. (Ireland) the

West India Islands, Quebec, St. Johns, Nova Scotia, Bermuda, & the East & West Floridas: and shall thereupon be entitled to all the Advantages of our Union, mutual Assistance and Commerce.

`These Articles shall be propos'd to the several Provincial Conventions or Assemblies, to be by them consider'd, and if approv'd they are advis'd to impower their Delegates to agree to and ratify the same in the ensuing Congress. After which the Union establish'd shall continue firm till the Terms of Reconciliation proposed in the Petition of the last Congress to the King are agreed to; till the Acts since made restraining the American Commerce & Fisheries are repeal'd; till Reparation is made for the injury done to Boston by shutting up its Port; for the Burning of Charlestown; & for the expense of this unjust War; and till all the British Troops are withdrawn from America. On the Arrival of these Events, the Colonies shall return to their former Connection and Friendship with Britain: But on Failure thereof this Confederation is to be perpetual.

(Endorsement. [2])
Sketch of Articles of Confederation
July 75.
Read before Congress
July 21, 1775

Manuscript in Papers of the Continental Congress, No. 47, Vol. 1. June 11, 1776—APPOINTMENT OF A COMMITTEE

Resolved that the committee to prepare the Declaration consist of five members.

The members chosen Mr. Jefferson, Mr. J. Adams, Mr. Franklin, Mr. Sherman and Mr. R. R. Livingston.

Resolved That a committee be appointed to prepare and digest the form of a confederation to be entered into between these colonies.—*Manuscript Journal of Congress*, Vol. 3.

July 12, 1776—REPORT OF THE COMMITTEE

The Committee appointed to prepare articles of confederation brought in a draft which was read.—*Manuscript Journal of Congress*, Vol. 3. July 12, 1776—DICKINSON'S DRAFT.

Articles of Confederation and perpetual Union between the Colonies of New Hampshire or at Philadelphia the day of 1776.

Art. 1st The Name of this Confederacy shall be "The United States of America."

Art. 2nd The said Colonies unite themselves so as never to be divided by any Act whatever, and hereby severally enter into a firm League of Friendship with each other, for their common Defence, the Security of their Liberties, and their mutual and general Welfare, binding the (said) Colonies to assist one another against all Force offered to or Attacks made upon them or any of them, on Account of Religion, Sovereignty, Trade, or any other Pretence whatever.

Art. 3rd Each Colony shall retain and enjoy as much of its present Law, Rights (and Customs,) as it may think (fit, and) reserves to itself the sole and exclusive Regulation and Government of its internal Police, in all Matters that shall not interfere with the Articles of this Confederation.

Art. 4th No Colony or Colonies, without the Consent of the United States assembled shall send any Embassy to or receive any Embassy from, or enter into any Treaty, Convention or Conference with the King or Kingdom of Great Britain, or any foreign Prince or State, nor shall any Colony or Colonies, nor any Servant or Servants of the United States, or of any Colony or Colonies, accept of any Present Emolument, Office, or title of any kind whatever, from the King or Kingdom of Great-Britain, or any foreign Prince or state; nor shall the United States assembled, or any Colony grant any Title of Nobility.

Art. 5th No two or more Colonies shall enter into any Treaty, Confederation or Alliance whatever between them, without the previous and free Consent and Allowance of the United States assembled, specifying accurately the purposes for which the same is to be entered into, and how long it shall continue.

Art. 6th The Inhabitants of each Colony shall hence-forth always have the same Rights, Liberties, Privileges, Immunities and Advantages, in the other Colonies, which the said Inhabitants, now have, in all Cases whatever, except in those provided for by the next following article.

Art. 7th The Inhabitants of each Colony shall enjoy all the Rights, Privileges, Immunities, and Advantages, in Trade Navigation and Commerce, in any other Colony, and in going to and from the same from and to any Part of the World, which the Natives of such Colony, (or any Commercial Society established by its Authority, shall) enjoy.

Art. 8th Each Colony may assess or lay such Imposts or Duties as it thinks proper, on Importation or Exportations, provided such Imposts or Duties do not interfere with any Stipulations in Treaties hereafter entered into by the United States assembled, with the King or Kingdom of Great-Britain, or any foreign Prince or State.

Art. 9th No standing Army or Body of Forces shall be kept up by any Colony or Colonies in Time of Peace, except such a Number only as may be requisite to garrison the Forts necessary for the Defence of such Colony or Colonies: But every Colony shall always keep up a well regulated and disciplined Militia, sufficiently armed and accoutred; and shall provide and constantly have ready for Use in public Stores, a due Number of Field Pieces and Tents, and a proper Quantity of Ammunition and Camp Equipage.

Art. 10th When Troops are raised in any of the Colonies for the Common Defence, the Commission Officers, proper for the Troops raised in each Colony, except the General Officers, shall be appointed by the Legislature of each Colony respectively, or in such Manner as shall by them be directed.

Art. 11th All Charges of Wars and all Expences that shall be incurred for the Common Defence, or general Welfare, and allowed by the United States Assembled, shall be defrayed out of a Common Treasury, which shall be supplied by the several Colonies in Proportion to the Number of Inhabitants of every Age, Sex and Quality, except Indians not paying Taxes in each Colony, a true Account of which, distinguishing the white Inhabitants, shall be triennially taken and transmitted to the Assembly of the United States. The Taxes for paying that Proportion shall be laid and levied by the Authority and Direction of the Legislatures of the several Colonies, within the Time agreed upon by the United States assembled.

Art. 12th Every Colony shall abide by the Determinations of the United States assembled, concerning the Services performed and Losses or Expences incurred by every Colony for the Common Defence or General Welfare, and no Colony or Colonies shall in any Case whatever endeavor by Force to procure Redress of any Injury or Injustice supposed to be done by the United States to such Colony or Colonies in not granting such Satisfaction, Indemnifications, Compensation, Retributions, Exemptions or Benefits of any Kind, as such Colony or Colonies may think just or reasonable.

Art. 13th No Colony or Colonies shall engage in any War without the previous Consent of the United States assembled, unless such Colony or Colonies be actually invaded by Enemies, or shall have received certain Advice of a Resolution being formed by some Nation of Indians to invade such Colony or Colonies, and that Danger is so imminent as not to admit of a Delay, till the other Colonies can be consulted: Nor shall any Colony or Colonies grant Commissions to any Ships or Vessels of War, nor Letters of Marque or Reprisal, except it be after a Declaration of War by the United States assembled, and then only against the Kingdom or State and the Subjects thereof, against which War has been so declared, and under such Regulations as shall be established by the United States assembled.

Art. 14th No Purchases of Lands hereafter to be made of the Indians by Colonies or private Persons before the Limits of the Colonies are ascertained, to be valid; all purchases of Lands not included within these Limits, when ascertained, to be made by Contracts between the United States assembled, or by Persons for that Purpose authorized by them, and the great Councils of the Indians, for the general Benefit of all the united Colonies.

Art. 15th When the Boundaries of any Colony shall be ascertained by Agreement, or in the Manner hereinafter directed, all the other Colonies shall guarantee to such Colony the full and peaceable Possession of and the free and entire Jurisdiction in and over the Territory included within such Boundaries.

Art. 16th For the more convenient Management of the general Interests of the United States, Delegates shall be annually appointed in such Manner as the Legislature of each Colony shall direct, to meet at the City of Philadelphia, in the Colony of Pennsylvania, until otherwise ordered by the United States assembled, which Meeting shall be on the first Monday of November in every Year, with a Power reserved to those who appointed the said Delegates respectively to recall them or any of them at any time within the Year, and to send new Delegates in their stead for the Remainder of the Year. Each Colony shall support its own Delegates in a Meeting of the States, and while they act as Members of the Council of State, hereinafter mentioned.

Art. 17th In determining Questions each Colony shall have one Vote.

Art. 18th The United States assembled, shall have the sole and exclusive Right and Power of determining on Peace and War, except in the Cases mentioned in the thirteenth Article—of establishing Rules for deciding in all Cases, what Capture on Land or Water shall be legal—in what Manner Prizes taken by Land or naval Forces in the Service of the United States shall be divided or appropriated—granting Letters of Marque and Reprisal in Time of Peace—appointing Courts for the Trial of all Crimes Frauds and Piracies committed on the High Seas, or on any navigable River, not within the Body of the County or Parish—establishing Courts for receiving and determining finally Appeals in all Cases of Capture—sending and receiving Ambassadors under any Character—Entering into Treaties and Alliances—settling all Disputes and Differences now subsisting or that hereafter may arise between two or more Colonies concerning Boundaries, Jurisdictions, or any other Cause whatever—coining Money and regulating the Value thereof—regulating the Trade, and managing all Affairs with the Indians—limiting the Bounds of those Colonies, which by Charter or Proclamation, or under any Pretence, are said to extend to the South Sea, and ascertaining these Bounds of any other Colony, that appear to be indeterminate—assigning Territories for new Colonies, either in Lands to be thus separated from Colonies and heretofore purchased or obtained by the Crown of Great Britain from the Indians, or hereafter to be purchased or obtained from them—disposing of all such Lands for the general Benefit of all the United Colonies—ascertaining Boundaries to such new Colonies, within which Forms of Government are to be established on the Principles of Liberty—establishing and regulating Post Offices throughout all the United Colonies, on the Lines of Communication from one Colony to another—appointing General officers of the Land Forces in the Service of the United States—commissioning such other officers of the said Forces as shall be appointed by Virtue of the tenth Article—appointing all the officers of the naval Forces in the Service of the United States—Making Rules for the Government and Regulation of the said Land and Naval Forces—appointing a Council of State, and such Committees and civil officers as may be necessary for managing the general affairs of the United States, under their Direction while assembled, and in their Recess, of the Council of State—Appointing one of their number to preside, and a suitable person for a secretary—and adjourning to any Time within the Year.

The United States assembled shall have Authority for the Defence and Welfare of the United Colonies and every one of them, to agree upon and fix the necessary Sums and Expences—to emit Bills or to borrow Money on the Credit of the united Colonies—to raise naval Forces—to agree upon the Number of Land Forces to be raised, and to make Requisitions from the Legislatures of each Colony, or the person therein authorized by the Legislature to execute such Requisitions, for the Quota of each Colony, which is to be in Proportion to the Number of white Inhabitants in that Colony, which Requisitions shall be binding, and thereupon the Legislature of each Colony or the persons authorized as aforesaid, shall appoint the Regimental Officers, raise the Men and arm and equip them in a soldierlike Manner, and the Officers and Men so armed and equiped shall march to the Place appointed and within the Time agreed on by the United States assembled—

But if the United States assembled shall on Consideration of Circumstances judge proper, that any Colony or Colonies should not raise Men or should raise a smaller Number than the Quota or Quotas of such Colony or Colonies, and that any other Colony or Colonies should raise a greater number of men than the Quota or Quotas thereof, such extra numbers shall be raised officered, armed and equiped in the same Manner as the Quota or Quotas of such Colony or Colonies, unless the legislature of such Colony or Colonies respectively, shall judge that such extra-Numbers cannot be safely spared out of the same, in which Case they shall raise officer arm and equip as many of such extra-Numbers as they judge can be safely spared; and the Officers and Men so armed and equiped shall march to the Place appointed, and within the Time agreed on by the United States assembled.

To establish the same Weights and Measures throughout the United Colonies.

But the United States assembled shall never impose or levy any Taxes or Duties, except in managing the Post Offices, nor interfere in the internal Police of any Colony, any farther than such Police may be affected by the Articles of this Confederation. The United States assembled shall never engage the United Colonies in a War, nor grant Letters of Marque and Reprisal in Time of Peace, nor enter into any Treaties or Alliances, nor coin Money nor regulate the Value thereof, nor agree upon nor fix the Sums and Expenses necessary for the Defence and Welfare of the United Colonies or any of them, nor emit Bills, nor borrow Money on the Credit of the United Colonies, nor raise naval Forces, nor agree upon the Number of Land Forces to be raised, unless the Delegates of nine Colonies freely assent to the same: nor shall a Question on any other Point, except for adjourning, be determined, unless the Delegates of seven Colonies vote in the Affirmative.

No person shall be capable of being a Delegate for more than Three Years in any Term of six Years.

No person holding any Office under the United States, for which he, or another for his Benefit, receives any Salary Fees or Emolument of any kind, shall be capable of being a Delegate.

The Assembly of the United States to publish the Journal of their proceedings monthly, except such Parts thereof relating to Treaties Alliances, or military Operations, as in their Judgment require Secrecy—the Yeas and Nays of the Delegates of each Colony on any Question to be entered on the Journal, when it is desired by any Delegate; and the Delegates of a Colony or any of them, at his or their Request to be furnished with a Transcript of the said Journal, except such Parts as are above excepted, to lay before the Legislatures of the several Colonies.

Art. 19th The Council of State shall consist of one Delegate from each Colony, to be named annually by the Delegates of each Colony, and where they cannot agree, by the United States assembled.

This Council shall have power,

To receive and open all Letters directed to the United States, and to return proper answers, but not to make any Engagements that shall be binding on the United States—to correspond with the Legislature of every Colony, and all

Persons acting under the Authority of the United States, or of the said Legislature—to apply to such Legislatures, or to the Officers in the several Colonies, who are entrusted with the executive powers of Government, for occasional Aid whenever and wherever necessary—to give Counsel to the Commanding Officers, and to direct military Operations by Sea and Land, not changing any Objects or Expeditions determined on by the United States assembled, unless an Alteration of Circumstances which shall come to the Knowledge of the Council after the Recess of the States, shall make such Change absolutely necessary—to attend to the Defence and Preservation of Forts and strong Posts, and to prevent the Enemy from acquiring new Holds—to procure Intelligence of the Condition and Designs of the Enemy—to expedite the Execution of such Measures as may be resolved on by the United States assembled, in pursuance of the Powers hereby given to them—to draw upon the Treasurers for such Sums as may be appropriated by the United States assembled, and for the Payment of such Contracts as the said Council may make in Pursuance of the Powers hereby given to them—to superintend and control or suspend all officers civil and military acting under the Authority of the United States—in case of the Death or Removal of any Officer within the Appointment of the United States assembled, to employ a person to fulfill the Duties of such Office until the Assembly of the States Meet to publish and summon an Assembly of the States at an earlier Day than that appointed for their next meeting, if any great and unexpected Emergency should render it necessary for the Safety or Welfare of the United Colonies or any of them— to prepare Matters for the Consideration of the United States, and to lay before them at their next Meeting all Letters and Advices received by the Council, with a Report of their proceedings to appoint a proper Person for their Clerk; who shall take an Oath of Secrecy and Fidelity before he enters on the Exercise of his Office—Seven Members shall have power to act—in case of the Death of any member, the

Council shall immediately apply to his surviving Colleagues to appoint some one of themselves to be a Member thereof till the Meeting of the States, and if only one survives, they shall give him immediate Notice, that he may take his Seat as a Councillor till such Meeting.

Art. 20: Canada according to this Confederation, and entirely joining in the Measures of the United Colonies, shall be admitted into and entitled to all the Advantages of this Union: But no other Colony shall be admitted into the same, unless such Admission be agreed to by the Delegates of nine Colonies.

These Articles shall be proposed to the Legislatures of all the United Colonies, to be by them considered, and if approved by them, they are advised to authorize their Delegates to ratify the same in the Assembly of the United States, which being done, the Articles of this Confederation shall inviolably be observed by every Colony, and the Union is to be perpetual: Nor shall any Alteration be at any Time hereafter made in these Articles or any of them, unless such Alteration be agreed to in an Assembly of the United States, and be afterward confirmed by the Legislatures of every Colony.

(Endorsement on the Manuscript)
Report of Articles of Confederation
Nov. 15, 1777—ARTICLES AGREED TO
BY CONGRESS

A copy of the Confederation being made out and sundry amendments made in the diction without altering the sense the same was agreed to and is as follows:

July 9, 1778—ARTICLES OF CONFEDERATION
(OFFICIAL ENGROSSED TEXT)
TO ALL TO WHOM

these presents shall come, we the undersigned Delegates of the States affixed to our Names send greeting. Whereas the Delegates of the United States of America in Congress assembled did on the fifteenth day of November in the Year of Our Lord One thousand seven Hundred and Seventy seven, and in the second Year of the Independence of America agree to certain articles of Confederation and perpetual Union between the States of Newhampshire, Massachusetts-bay, Rhodeisland and Providence Plantations, Connecticut, New York, New Jersey, Pennsylvania, Delaware, Maryland, Virginia, North-Carolina, South-Carolina, and Georgia in the Words following, viz. ARTICLES OF CONFEDERATION and perpetual Union between the States of Newhampshire, Massachusetts-bay, Rhodeisland and Providence Plantations, Connecticut, New-York, New-Jersey, Pennsylvania, Delaware, Maryland, Virginia, North-Carolina, South-Carolina and Georgia.

Notes:

1. Franklin appears to have written this passage at first: "for Defence and Offence, the Security of their Liberties and Property, the Safety of their persons and Families, and their Common and general Welfare."

2. The first three lines of the endorsement are in the same handwriting as the body of the instrument. The last two lines appear to be in the handwriting of Thompson, Secretary of Congress. A later endorsement is: "This Sketch in handwriting of Doct Franklin."

THE DECLARATION OF INDEPENDENCE, 1776

On June 7, 1776, Richard Henry Lee of Virginia introduced three resolutions to the Continental Congress, one of which states that the "Colonies are, and of right ought to be free and independent states." This resolution grew out of increasing discontent and anger directed toward England and the King in particular. The King had refused to hear a petition sent to him by the Continental Congress, had called the colonists rebels, had sent his ships to blockade and burn their towns and had hired mercenary troops to put down "the rebellion." At this time Thomas Paine published *Common Sense,* a pamphlet which presented many reasons why America should separate from England. Virginia took a leading part in the movement toward independence by instructing her delegates in Congress to vote for independence.

On the 10th of June, 1776, a committee was appointed to prepare a declaration of independence; the committee consisted of Jefferson, John Adams, Franklin, Sherman and R. R. Livingston. This committee brought in its draft on the 28th of June and on the 2nd of July a resolution declaring independence was adopted. On July 4th the Declaration of Independence was agreed to, signed by Hancock and sent to the legislatures of the states.

The unanimous Declaration of the thirteen united States of America,
In Congress, July 4, 1776

When in the course of human events, it becomes necessary

for one people to dissolve the political bands which have connected them with another, and to assume among the Powers of the earth, the separate and equal station to which the Laws of Nature and of Nature's God entitle them, a decent respect to the opinions of mankind requires that they should declare the causes which impel them to the separation.

We hold these truths to be self-evident, that all men are created equal, that they are endowed by their Creator with certain unalienable Rights, that among these are Life, Liberty and the pursuit of Happiness. That to secure these rights, Governments are instituted among Men, deriving their just powers from the consent of the governed, That whenever any Form of Government becomes destructive of these ends, it is the Right of the People to alter or to abolish it and to institute new Government, laying its foundation on such principles and organizing its powers in such form, as to them shall seem most likely to effect their Safety and Happiness. Prudence, indeed, will dictate that Governments long established should not be changed for light and transient causes; and accordingly all experience hath shown, that mankind are more disposed to suffer, while evils are sufferable, than to right themselves by abolishing the forms to which they are accustomed. But when a long train of abuses and usurpations, pursuing invariably the same Object evinces a design to reduce them under absolute Despotism, it is their right, it is their duty, to throw off such Government, and to provide new Guards for their future security.— Such has been the patient sufferance of the Colonies; and such is now the necessity which constrains them to alter their former Systems of Government. *The history of the present King of Great Britain is a history of repeated injuries and usurpations, all having in direct object the establishment of an absolute Tyranny over these States. To prove this, let Facts be submitted to a candid world.*

He has refused his Assent to Laws, the most wholesome and necessary for the public good.

He has forbidden his Governors to pass Laws of immediate

and pressing importance unless suspended in their operation till his Assent should be obtained; and when so suspended, he has utterly neglected to attend to them.

He has refused to pass other Laws for the accommodation of large districts of people, unless those people would relinquish the right of Representation in the Legislature, a right inestimable to them and formidable to tyrants only.

He has called together legislative bodies at places unusual, uncomfortable, and distant from the depository of their Public Records, for the sole purpose of fatiguing them into compliance with his measures.

He has dissolved Representative Houses repeatedly, for opposing with manly firmness his invasions on the rights of the people.

He has refused for a long time, after such dissolutions, to cause others to be elected; whereby the Legislative Powers, incapable of Annihilation, have returned to the People at large for their exercise; the State remaining in the mean time exposed to all the dangers of invasion from without, and convulsions within.

He has endeavoured to prevent the population of these States; for that purpose obstructing the Laws of Naturalization of Foreigners; refusing to pass others to encourage their migration hither, and raising the conditions of new Appropriations of Lands.

He has obstructed the Administration of Justice, by refusing his Assent to Laws for establishing Judiciary Powers.

He has made Judges dependent on his Will alone, for the tenure of their offices, and the amount and payment of their salaries.

He has erected a multitude of New Offices, and sent hither swarms of Officers to harass our People, and eat out their substance.

He has kept among us, in times of peace, Standing Armies without the Consent of our legislature.

He has affected to render the Military independent of and superior to the Civil Power.

He has combined with others to subject us to a jurisdiction foreign to our constitution, and unacknowledged by our laws; giving his Assent to their acts of pretended legislation:

For quartering large bodies of armed troops among us:

For protecting them, by a mock Trial, from Punishment for any Murders which they should commit on the Inhabitants of these States:

For cutting off our Trade with all parts of the world:

For imposing taxes on us without our Consent:

For depriving us in many cases, of the benefits of Trial by Jury:

For transporting us beyond Seas to be tried for pretended offences:

For abolishing the free System of English Laws in a neighbouring Province, establishing therein an Arbitrary government and enlarging its Boundaries so as to render it at once an example and fit instrument for introducing the same absolute rule into these Colonies:

For taking away our charters, abolishing our most valuable Laws, and altering fundamentally the Forms of our Governments:

For suspending our own Legislature, and declaring themselves invested with Power to legislate for us in all cases whatsoever.

He has abdicated Government here, by declaring us out of his Protection and waging War against us.

He has plundered our seas, ravaged our Coasts, burnt our towns, and destroyed the lives of our people.

He is at this time transporting large armies of foreign mercenaries to compleat the works of death, desolation and tyranny, already begun with circumstances of Cruelty & perfidy scarcely paralleled in the most barbarous ages, and totally unworthy the Head of a civilized nation.

He has constrained our fellow Citizens taken Captive on the high Seas to bear Arms against their Country, to become the executioners of their friends and Brethren, or to fall themselves by their Hands.

He has excited domestic insurrections amongst us, and has endeavored to bring on the inhabitants of our frontiers, the merciless Indian Savages, whose known rule of warfare. is an undistinguished destruction *of all ages,* sexes and conditions.

In every stage of the Oppressions We have Petitioned for Redress in the most humble terms: Our repeated Petitions have been answered only by repeated injury. A Prince whose character is thus marked by every act which may define a Tyrant, is unfit to be the ruler of a free People.

Nor have We been wanting in attention to our British brethren. We have warned them from time to time of attempts by their legislature to extend an unwarrantable jurisdiction over us. We have reminded them of the circumstances of our emigration and settlement here. We have appealed to their native justice and magnanimity, and we have conjured them by the ties of our common kindred to disavow these usurpations, which would inevitably interrupt our connections and correspondence. They too have been deaf to the voice of justice and of consanguinity. We must, therefore, acquiesce in the necessity, which denounces our Separation, and hold them, as we hold the rest of mankind, Enemies in War, in Peace Friends.

We, therefore, the Representatives of the united States of America, in General Congress, Assembled, appealing to the Supreme Judge of the world for the rectitude of our intentions, do, in the Name and by the Authority of the good People of these Colonies, solemnly publish and declare, That these United Colonies are, and of Right ought to be Free and Independent States; that they are Absolved from all Allegiance to the British Crown, and that all political connection between them and the State of Great Britain, is and ought to be totally dissolved; and that as Free and Independent States, they have full Power to levy War, conclude Peace. contract Alliances, establish Commerce, and so do all other Acts and Things which Independent States may of right do. And for the support of this Declaration, with a firm reliance on the Protection of Divine Providence, we mutually pledge to each other our Lives, our Fortunes and our sacred Honor.

JOHN HANCOCK

New Hampshire
Josiah Bartlett,
Wm. Whipple,
Matthew Thornton.

Massachusetts-Bay
Saml. Adams,
John Adams,
Robt. Treat Paine,
Elbridge Gerry.

Rhode Island
Step. Hopkins,
William Ellery.

Connecticut.
Roger Sherman,
Sam'el Huntington,
Wm. Williams,
Oliver Wolcott.

Georgia
Button Gwinnett,
Lyman Hall,
Geo. Walton.

Maryland
Samuel Chase,
Wm. Paca,
Thos. Stone,
Charles Carroll of Carrollton.

Virginia
George Wythe,
Richard Henry Lee,
Th. Jefferson,
Benja. Harrison,
Ths. Nelson, Jr.,
Francis Lightfoot Lee,
Carter Braxton.

New York
Wm. Floyd,
Phil. Livingston,
Frans. Lewis,
Lewis Morris.

Pennsylvania
Robt. Morris,
Benjamin Rush,
Benja. Franklin,
John Morton,
Geo. Clymer,
Jas. Smith,
Geo. Taylor,
James Wilson,
Geo. Ross.

Delaware
Caesar Rodney,
Geo. Read,
Tho. M'Kean.

North Carolina
Wm. Hooper,
Joseph Hewes,
John Penn.

South Carolina
Edward Rutledge,
Thos. Heyward, Junr.,
Thomas Lynch, Junr.,
Arthur Middleton.

New Jersey
Richd. Stockton,
Jno. Witherspoon,
Fras. Hopkinson,
John Hart,
Abra. Clark.

THE OHIO VALLEY TRUST, 1787

With the achievement of independence, the young United States was confirmed in its possession of the trans-Allegheny West. The boundaries of the new republic stretched westward to the Mississippi, from the Great Lakes on the north to Spain's Gulf Coast holdings on the south. The Ohio River, cutting through this vast territory from east to west, dictated the course of the westward advance for the ensuing forty years. By 1820, eleven states had been added to the original thirteen, and more than two million people—close to a third of the total population of the United States—were residing west of the mountains. Pressed by prospective purchasers—speculators, veterans, and farm-seeking settlers, the government of the new nation worked out a plan for administering its transmontane domain. This was the justly famous Ordinance of 1787 for the government of the Northwest Territory, which set the pattern by which the United States was to evolve from a nation of thirteen states to one of fifty. Of major importance was the provision that after a period of territorial status, during which the Federal Government would exert the chief control, eligible portions of the West could achieve statehood on the basis of equality with the existing states. Its assurance of eventual statehood, together with its guarantees on the subject of religion, education, equality in property descent, and freedom from human bondage, make the Ordinance of 1787 the most significant single piece of legislation dealing with the development of the American West.

AN ORDINANCE FOR THE GOVERNMENT OF THE TERRITORY OF THE UNITED STATES, NORTHWEST OF THE RIVER OHIO

Sec. 3. *Be it ordained* . . . That there shall be appointed . . . , by Congress, a governor, whose commission shall comtinue in force for the term of three years . . . ; he shall reside in the district, and have a freehold estate therein in one thousand acres of land, while in the exercise of his office.

Sec. 4. There shall be appointed . . . , by Congress, a secretary, whose commission shall continue in force for four years . . . ; he shall reside in the district, and have a freehold estate therein, in five hundred acres of land, while in the exercise of his office. . . . There shall also be appointed a court, to consist of three judges, any two of whom to form a court, who shall have a common-law jurisdiction and reside in the district, and have each therein a freehold estate, in five hundred acres of land, while in the exercise of their offices. . . .

Sec. 5. The governor and judges, or a majority of them, shall adopt and publish in the district such laws of the original States, criminal and civil, as may be necessary, and best suited to the circumstances of the district. . . . which laws shall be in force . . . until the organization of the general assembly therein, unless disapproved of by Congress; but afterwards the legislature shall have authority to alter them as they shall think fit. . . .

Sec. 9. So soon as there shall be five thousand free male inhabitants, of full age, in the district, . . . they shall receive authority . . . to elect representatives from their counties or townships, to represent them in the general assembly: . . . *Provided,* That no person be eligible or qualified to act as a representative, unless he shall have been a citizen of one of the United States three years, and be a resident in the district, or unless he shall have resided in the district three years; and, in either case, shall likewise hold in his own right, in fee-simple, two hundred acres of land within the same: *Provided, also,* That a freehold in fifty acres of land in the district, having been a citizen of one of the States, and being resident in the district, shall be necessary to qualify a man as an elector of a representative. . . .

Sec. 11. The general assembly, or legislature, shall consist of the governor, legislative council, and a house of representatives. The legislative council shall consist of five members, to continue in office five years; . . . and the members of the council shall be . . . appointed in the following manner, to wit: As soon as representatives shall be elected . . . they shall nominate ten persons, residents in the district, and each possessed of a freehold in five hundred acres of land, . . . five of whom Congress shall . . . commission to serve as aforesaid. . . . And the governor, legislative council, and house of representatives shall have authority to make laws in all cases. . . . And all bills, having passed by a majority in the house, and by a majority in the council, shall be referred to the governor for his assent; but no bill . . . shall be of any force without his assent. . . .

Sec. 12. . . . As soon as a legislature shall be formed in the district, the council and house assembled, in one room, shall have authority, by joint ballot, to elect a delegate to Congress who shall have a seat in Congress, with a right of debating, but not of voting, during this temporary government. . . .

Sec. 14. It is hereby ordained . . . that the following articles shall be considered as articles of compact, between the original States and the people and States in the said territory, and forever remain unalterable, unless by common consent, to wit:

Article I.

No person, demeaning himself in a peaceable and orderly manner, shall ever be molested on account of his mode of worship.

Article II.

The inhabitants . . . shall always be entitled to the benefits of the writ of *habeas corpus,* and of the trial by jury; of a proportionate representation of the people in the legislature, and of judicial proceedings according to the course of common law. . . .

Article III.

Religion, morality, and knowledge being necessary to good government and the happiness of mankind, schools and the means of education shall forever be encouraged. The utmost good faith shall always be observed towards the Indians. . . .

504

Article IV.

The said territory, and the States which may be formed therein, shall forever remain a part of . . . the United States of America. . . .

Article V.

. . . whenever any of the said States shall have sixty thousand free inhabitants therein, such States shall be admitted, by its delegates, into the Congress of the United States, on an equal footing with the original States, in all respects whatever; and shall be at liberty to form a permanent constitution and State government: *Provided,* The constitution and government, so to be formed, shall be republican. . . .

Article VI.

There shall be neither slavery nor involuntary servitude in the said territory. . . .

THE CONSTITUTION OF THE
UNITED STATES, 1788

On the same day the Continental Congress appointed a committee to draft the Declaration of Independence a committee headed by John Dickinson was appointed to draft articles of union. Submitted to the Second Continental Congress on July 12, 1777, the first draft of the Articles of Confederation caused much debate which lasted for 16 months. It was finally adopted by Congress in 1777, but not ratified by the states until 1781.

The constitution, signed on September 17, 1787, and ratified by nine states by June 21, 1788, superseded the original charter of the United States in force since 1781 and established a system of Federal government which began functioning in 1789.

Although the original Articles of Confederation had a preamble and 13 articles, the new Constitution contained 7 articles, a preamble and eventually 22 amendments.

While Benjamin Franklin may be considered the father of the Articles of Confederation, his modified version of his Albany plan submitted to the Continental Congress in 1775 received little notice. While Dickinson's committee did not use Franklin's plan, much of the wording in the final Articles can be traced to Franklin.

PREAMBLE

WE THE PEOPLE of the United States, in Order to form a more perfect Union, establish Justice, insure domestic Tranquility, provide for the common defence, promote the general Welfare, and secure the Blessings of Liberty to ourselves and our

Posterity, do ordain and establish this Constitution for the United States of America.

Art. I

Sec. 1. All legislative Powers herein granted shall be vested in a Congress of the United States, which shall consist of a Senate and House of Representatives.

Sec. 2. The House of Representatives shall be composed of Members chosen every second Year by the People of the several States, and the Electors in each State shall have the Qualifications requisite for Electors of the most numerous Branch of the State Legislature.

No Person shall be a Representative who shall not have attained to the Age of twenty five Years, and been seven Years a Citizen of the United States, and who shall not, when elected, be an Inhabitant of that State in which he shall be chosen.

Representatives and direct Taxes shall be apportioned among the several States which may be included within this Union, according to their respective Numbers, which shall be determined by adding to the whole Number of free Persons, including those bound to Service for a Term of Years, and excluding Indians not taxed, three fifths of all other Persons. The actual Enumeration shall be made within three Years after the first Meeting of the Congress of the United States, and within every subsequent Term of ten Years, in such Manner as they shall by Law direct. The Number of Representatives shall not exceed one for every thirty Thousand, but each State shall have at Least one Representative; and until such enumeration shall be made, the State of New Hampshire shall be entitled to chuse three, Massachusetts eight, Rhode-Island and Providence Plantations one, Connecticut five, New-York six, New Jersey four, Pennsylvania eight, Delaware one, Maryland six, Virginia ten, North Carolina five, South Carolina five and Georgia three.

When vacancies happen in the Representation from any State, the Executive Authority thereof shall issue Writs of Election to fill such Vacancies.

The House of Representatives shall chuse their Speaker and other Officers; and shall have the sole Power of Impeachment.

Sec. 3. The Senate of the United States shall be composed of two Senators from each State, chosen by the Legislature thereof, for six Years; and each Senator shall have one Vote.

Immediately after they shall be assembled in Consequence of the first Election, they shall be divided as equally as may be into three Classes. The Seats of the Senators of the first Class shall be vacated at the Expiration of the second Year, of the second Class at the Expiration of the fourth Year, and of the third Class at the Expiration of the sixth Year, so that one third may be chosen every second Year; and if Vacancies happen by Resignation, or otherwise, during the Recess of the Legislature of any State, the Executive thereof may make temporary Appointments until the next Meeting of the Legislature, which shall then fill such Vacancies.

No Person shall be a Senator who shall not have attained the Age of thirty Years, and been nine Years a Citizen of the United States, and who shall not, when elected, be an Inhabitant of that State for which he shall be chosen.

The Vice President of the United States shall be President of the Senate, but shall have no Vote, unless they be equally divided.

The Senate shall chuse their other Officers, and also a President pro tempore, in the Absence of the Vice President or when he shall exercise the Office of President of the United States.

The Senate shall have the sole Power to try all Impeachments. When sitting for that Purpose, they shall be on Oath or Affirmation. When the President of the United States is tried, the Chief Justice shall preside: And no Person shall be convicted without the Concurrence of two thirds of the Members present.

Judgment in Cases of Impeachment shall not extend further than to removal from office, and disqualification to hold and enjoy any Office of honor, Trust or Profit under the United States: but the Party convicted shall nevertheless be liable and subject to Indictment, Trial, Judgement and Punishment, according to Law.

Sec. 4. The Times, Places and Manner of holding Elections for Senators and Representatives shall be prescribed in each State by the Legislature thereof; but the Congress may at any time by Law make or alter such Regulations, except as to the Places of chusing Senators.

The Congress shall assemble at least once in every Year, and such Meeting shall be on the first Monday in December, unless they shall by Law appoint a different Day.

Sec. 5. Each House shall be the Judge of the Elections, Returns and Qualifications of its own Members, and a Majority of each shall constitute a Quorum to do Business; but a smaller Number may adjourn from day to day, and may be authorized to compel the Attendance of absent Members, in such Manner, and under such Penalties as each House may provide.

Each House may determine the Rules of its Proceedings, punish its Members for disorderly Behaviour, and, with the Concurrence of two thirds, expel a Member.

Each House shall keep a Journal of its Proceedings, and from time to time publish the same, excepting such Parts as may in their Judgment require Secrecy; and the Yeas and Nays of the Members of either House on any question shall, at the Desire of one fifth of those Present, be entered on the Journal.

Neither House, during the Session of Congress, shall, without the Consent of the other, adjourn for more than three days, nor to any other Place than that in which the two Houses shall be sitting.

Sec. 6. The Senators and Representatives shall receive a Compensation for their services, to be ascertained by Law, and paid out of the Treasury of the United States. They shall in all Cases, except Treason, Felony and Breach of the Peace, be privileged from Arrest during their Attendance at the Session of their respective Houses, and in going to and returning from the same; and for any Speech or Debate in either House, they shall not be questioned in any other Place.

No Senator or Representative shall, during the Time for which he was elected, be appointed to any civil Office under the Authority of the United States which shall have been created, or the Emoluments whereof shall have been encreased during such time; and no Person holding any Office under the United States, shall be a Member of either House during his Continuance in Office.

Sec. 7. All Bills for raising Revenue shall originate in the House of Representatives; but the Senate may propose or concur with Amendments as on other Bills.

Every Bill which shall have passed the House of Representatives and the Senate, shall, before it become a Law, be presented to the President of the United States; If he approve he shall sign it, but if not he shall return it, with his Objections to that House in which it shall have originated, who shall enter the Objections at large on their Journal, and proceed to reconsider it. If after such Reconsideration two thirds of that House shall agree to pass the Bill, it shall be sent, together with the Objections, to the other House, by which it shall likewise be reconsidered, and if approved by two thirds of that House, it shall become a Law. But in all such Cases the Votes of both Houses shall be determined by yeas and Nays, and the Names of the Persons voting for and against the Bill shall be entered on the Journal of each House respectively. If any Bill shall not be returned by the President within ten Days (Sundays excepted) after it shall have been presented to him, the Same shall be a Law, in like Manner as if he had signed it, unless the Congress by their

Adjournment prevent its Return, in which Case it shall not be a Law.

Every Order, Resolution, or Vote to which the Concurrence of the Senate and House of Representatives may be necessary (except on a question of Adjournment) shall be presented to the President of the United States; and before the Same shall take Effect, shall be approved by him, or being disapproved by him, shall be repassed by two thirds of the Senate and House of Representatives, according to the Rules and Limitations prescribed in the Case of a Bill.

Sec. 8. The Congress shall have Power To lay and collect Taxes, Duties, Imposts and Excises, to pay the Debts and provide for the common Defence and general Welfare of the United States; but all Duties, Imposts and Excises shall be uniform throughout the United States;

To borrow Money on the credit of the United States;

To regulate Commerce with foreign Nations, and among the several States, and with the Indian Tribes;

To establish an uniform Rule of Naturalization, and uniform Laws on the subject of Bankruptcies, throughout the United States;

To coin Money, regulate the Value thereof, and of foreign Coin, and fix the Standard of Weights and Measures;

To provide for the Punishment of counterfeiting the Securities and current Coin of the United States;

To establish Post Offices and post Roads;

To promote the Progress of Science and useful Arts, by securing for limited Times to Authors and Inventors the exclusive Right to their respective Writings and Discoveries;

To constitute Tribunals inferior to the supreme Court;

To define and punish Piracies and Felonies committed on the high Seas, and Offences against the Law of Nations;

To declare War, grant Letters of Marque and Reprisal, and make Rules concerning Captures on Land and Water;

To raise and support Armies, but no Appropriation of Money to that Use shall be for a longer Term than two Years;

To provide and maintain a Navy;

To make Rules for the Government and Regulation of the land and naval Forces;

To provide for calling forth the Militia to execute the Laws of the Union, suppress Insurrections and repel Invasions;

To provide for organizing, arming, and disciplining, the Militia, and for governing such Part of them as may be employed in the Service of the United States, reserving to the States respectively, the Appointment of the Officers, and the Authority of training the Militia according to the discipline prescribed by Congress;

To exercise exclusive Legislation in all Cases whatsoever, over such District (not exceeding ten Miles square) as may, by Cession of particular States, and the Acceptance of Congress, become the Seat of the Government of the United States, and to exercise like Authority over all Places purchased by the Consent of the Legislature of the State in which the Same shall be, for the Erection of Forts, Magazines, Arsenals, dock-Yards, and other needful Buildings;—And

To make all Laws which shall be necessary and proper for carrying into Execution the foregoing Powers and all other Powers vested by this Constitution in the Government of the United States, or in any Department or Officer thereof.

Sec. 9. The Migration or Importation of such Persons as any of the States now existing shall think proper to admit, shall not be prohibited by the Congress prior to the Year one thousand eight hundred and eight, but a Tax or duty may be imposed on such Importation, not exceeding ten dollars for each Person.

No Money shall be drawn from the Treasury but in Consequence of Appropriations made by Law; and a regular Statement and Account of the Receipts and Expenditures of all public Money shall be published from time to time.

The Privilege of the Writ of Habeas Corpus shall not be suspended, unless when in Cases of Rebellion or Invasion the public Safety may require it.

No Bill of Attainder or ex post facto Law shall be passed.

No Capitation, or other direct, Tax shall be laid, unless in Proportion to the Census or Enumeration herein before directed to be taken.

No Tax or Duty shall be laid on Articles exported from any States.

No Title of Nobility shall be granted by the United States: And no Person holding any Office of Profit or Trust under them, shall, without the Consent of the Congress, accept of any present, Emolument, Office or Title of any kind whatever, from any King, Prince or foreign State.

Sec. 10. No State shall enter into any Treaty, Alliance, or Confederation; grant Letters of Marque and Reprisal; coin Money; emit Bills of Credit; make any Thing but gold and silver Coin a Tender in Payment of Debts; pass any Bill of Attainder, ex post facto Law, or Law impairing the Obligation of Contracts, or grant any Title of Nobility.

No State shall, without the Consent of the Congress, lay any Imposts or Duties on Imports or Exports, except what may be absolutely necessary for executing it's inspection Laws: and the net Produce of all Duties and Imposts, laid by any State on Imports or Exports, shall be for the Use of the Treasury of the United States; and all such Laws shall be subject to the Revision and Controul of the Congress.

No State shall, without the Consent of Congress, lay any Duty of Tonnage, keep Troops, or Ships of War in time of Peace, enter into any Agreement or Compact with another State, or with a foreign Power, or engage in War, unless actually invaded, or in such imminent Danger as will not admit of delay.

Art. II

Sec. 1. The executive Power shall be vested in a President of the United States of America. He shall hold his Office during the Term of four Years and, together with the Vice President, chosen for the same Term, be elected, as follows

Each State shall appoint, in such Manner as the Legislature

thereof may direct, a Number of Electors, equal to the whole Number of Senators and Representatives to which the State may be entitled in the Congress: but no Senator or Representative, or Person holding an Office of Trust or Profit under the United States, shall be appointed an Elector.

The Electors shall meet in their respective States, and vote by Ballot for two Persons, of whom one at least shall not be an Inhabitant of the same State with themselves. And they shall make a List of all the Persons voted for, and of the Number of Votes for each; which List they shall sign and certify, and transmit sealed to the Seat of the Government of the United States, directed to the President of the Senate. The President of the Senate shall, in the Presence of the Senate and House of Representatives, open all the Certificates, and the Votes shall then be counted. The Person having the greatest Number of Votes shall be the President, if such Number be a Majority of the whole Number of Electors appointed; and if there be more than one who have such Majority, and have an equal Number of Votes, then the House of Representatives shall immediately chuse by Ballot one of them for President; and if no person have a Majority, then from the five highest on the List the said House shall in like Manner chuse the President. But in chusing the President, the Votes shall be taken by States, the Representation from each State having one Vote; A quorum for this Purpose shall consist of a Member or Members from two thirds of the States, and a Majority of all the States shall be necessary to a Choice. In every Case, after the Choice of the President, the Person having the greatest Number of Votes of the Electors shall be the Vice President. But if there should remain two or more who have equal Votes, the Senate shall chuse from them by Ballot the Vice President.

No Preference shall be given by any Regulation of Commerce or Revenue to the Ports of one State over those of another: nor shall Vessels bound to, or from, one State, be obliged to enter, clear, or pay Duties in another.

The Congress may determine the Time of chusing the

Electors, and the Day on which they shall give their Votes; which Day shall be the same throughout the United States.

No Person except a natural born Citizen, or a Citizen of the United States, at the time of the Adoption of this Constitution, shall be eligible to the Office of President; neither shall any Person be eligible to that Office who shall not have attained to the Age of thirty five Years, and been fourteen Years a Resident within the United States.

In Case of the Removal of the President from Office, or of his Death, Resignation, or Inability to discharge the Powers and Duties of the said Office, the Same shall devolve on the Vice President, and the Congress may by Law provide for the Case of Removal, Death, Resignation or Inability, both of the President and Vice President, declaring what Officer shall then act as President, and such Officer shall act accordingly, until the Disability be removed, or a President shall be elected.

The President shall, at stated Times, receive for his Services, a Compensation which shall neither be encreased nor diminished during the Period for which he shall have been elected, and he shall not receive within that Period any other Emolument from the United States, or any of them.

Before he enter on the Execution of his Office, he shall take the following Oath or Affirmation:—"I do solemnly swear (or affirm) that I will faithfully execute the Office of President of the United States, and will to the best of my Ability, preserve, protect and defend the Constitution of the United States."

Sec. 2. The President shall be Commander in Chief of the Army and Navy of the United States, and of the Militia of the several States, when called into the actual Service of the United States; he may require the Opinion, in writing, of the principal Officer in each of the executive Departments, upon any Subject relating to the Duties of their respective Offices, and he shall have Power to grant Reprieves and Pardons for Offences against the United States, except in Cases of Impeachment.

515

He shall have Power, by and with the Advice and Consent of the Senate, to make Treaties, provided two thirds of the Senators present concur; and he shall nominate, and by and with the Advice and Consent of the Senate, shall appoint Ambassadors, other public Ministers and Consuls, Judges of the supreme Court, and all other Officers of the United States, whose Appointments are not herein otherwise provided for, and which shall be established by Law: but the Congress may by Law vest the Appointment of such inferior Officers, as they think proper, in the President alone, in the Courts of Law, or in the Heads of Departments.

The President shall have Power to fill up all Vacancies that may happen during the Recess of the Senate, by granting Commissions which shall expire at the End of their next Session.

Sec. 3. He shall from time to time give to the Congress Information of the State of the Union, and recommend to their Consideration such Measures as he shall judge necessary and expedient; he may, on extraordinary Occasions, convene both Houses, or either of them, and in Case of Disagreement between them, with Respect to the Time of Adjournment, he may adjourn them to such Time as he shall think proper; he shall receive Ambassadors and other public Ministers; he shall take Care that the Laws be faithfully executed, and shall Commission all the Officers of the United States.

Sec. 4. The President, Vice President and all civil Officers of the United States, shall be removed from Office on Impeachment for, and Conviction of, Treason, Bribery, or other high Crimes and Misdemeanors.

Art. III

Sec. 1. The judicial Power of the United States shall be vested in one supreme Court, and in such inferior Courts as the Congress may from time to time ordain and establish. The Judges, both of the supreme and inferior Courts, shall hold their Offices during good Behaviour, and shall, at stated

Times, receive for their Services, a Compensation which shall not be diminished during their Continuance in Office.

Sec. 2. The judicial Power shall extend to all Cases, in Law and Equity, arising under this Constitution, the Laws of the United States, and Treaties made, or which shall be made, under their Authority;—to all Cases affecting Ambassadors, other public Ministers and Consuls; to all Cases of admiralty and maritime Jurisdiction;—to Controversies to which the United States shall be a Party;—to Controversies between two or more States;—between a State and Citizens of another State;—between Citizens of different States—between Citizens of the same State claiming Lands under Grants of different States, and between a State, or the Citizens thereof, and foreign States, Citizens or Subjects.

In all Cases affecting Ambassadors, other public Ministers and Consuls, and those in which a State shall be Party, the supreme Court shall have original Jurisdiction. In all the other Cases before mentioned, the Supreme Court shall have appellate Jurisdiction, both as to Law and Fact, with such Exceptions, and under such Regulations as the Congress shall make.

The Trial of all Crimes, except in Cases of Impeachment, shall be by Jury; and such Trial shall be held in the State where the said Crimes shall have been committed; but when not committed within any State, the Trial shall be at such Place or Places as the Congress may by Law have directed.

Sec. 3. Treason against the United States, shall consist only in levying War against them, or in adhering to their Enemies, giving them Aid and Comfort. No Person shall be convicted of Treason unless on the Testimony of two Witnesses to the same overt Act, or on Confession in open Court.

The Congress shall have Power to declare the Punishment of Treason, but no Attainder of Treason shall work Corruption of Blood, or Forfeiture except during the Life of the Person attainted.

Art. IV

Sec. 1. Full Faith and Credit shall be given in each State to the Public Acts, Records, and judicial Proceedings of every other State. And the Congress may by general Laws prescribe the Manner in which such Acts, Records and Proceedings shall be proved, and the Effect thereof.

Sec. 2. The Citizens of each State shall be entitled to all Privileges and Immunities of Citizens in the several States.

A Person charged in any State with Treason, Felony, or other Crime, who shall flee from Justice, and be found in another State, shall on Demand of the executive Authority of the State from which he fled, be delivered up, to be removed to the State having Jurisdiction of the Crime.

No Person held to Service or Labour in one State, under the Laws thereof, escaping into another, shall, in Consequence of any Law or Regulation therein, be discharged from such Service or Labour, but shall be delivered up on Claim of the Party to whom such Service or Labour may be due.

Sec. 3. New States may be admitted by the Congress into this Union; but no new States shall be formed or erected within the Jurisdiction of any other State; nor any State be formed by the Junction of two or more States, or Parts of States, without the Consent of the Legislatures of the States concerned as well as of the Congress.

The Congress shall have Power to dispose of and make all needful Rules and Regulations respecting the Territory or other Property belonging to the United States; and nothing in this Constitution shall be so construed as to Prejudice any Claims of the United States, or of any particular State.

Sec. 4. The United States shall guarantee to every State in this Union a Republican Form of Government, and shall protect each of them against Invasion; and on Application of the Legislature, or of the Executive (when the Legislature cannot be convened) against domestic Violence.

Art. V

The Congress, whenever two thirds of both Houses shall deem it necessary, shall propose Amendments to this Constitution, or, on the Application of the Legislatures of two thirds of the several States, shall call a Convention for proposing Amendments, which, in either Case shall be valid to all Intents and Purposes, as Part of this Constitution, when ratified by the Legislatures of three fourths of the several States, or by Conventions in three fourths thereof, as the one or the other Mode of Ratification may be proposed by the Congress; Provided that no Amendment which may be made prior to the Year One thousand eight hundred and eight shall in any Manner affect the first and fourth Clauses in the Ninth Section of the first Article; and that no State, without its Consent, shall be deprived of it's equal Suffrage in the Senate.

Art. VI

All Debts contracted and Engagements entered into, before the Adoption of this Constitution, shall be as valid against the United States under this Constitution, as under the Confederation.

This Constitution, and the Laws of the United States which shall be made in Pursuance thereof; and all Treaties made, or which shall be made, under the Authority of the United States, shall be the supreme Law of the Land; and the Judges in every State shall be bound thereby, any Thing in the Constitution or Laws of any State to the Contrary notwithstanding.

The Senators and Representatives before mentioned, and the Members of the several State Legislatures, and all executive and judicial Officers, both of the United States and of the several States, shall be bound by Oath or Affirmation, to support this Constitution; but no religious Test shall ever be required as a Qualification to any Office or public Trust under the United States.

Art. VII

The Ratification of the Conventions of nine States, shall be sufficient for the Establishment of this Constitution between the States so ratifying the Same.

Done in Convention by the Unanimous Consent of the States present the Seventeenth Day of September in the Year of our Lord one thousand seven hundred and Eighty seven and of the Independence of the United States of America the Twelfth. In witness whereof We have hereunto subscribed our Names,

G° WASHINGTON—Presid^t
and deputy from Virginia

New Hampshire
John Langdon
Nicholas Gilman

Massachusetts
Nathaniel Gorham
Rufus King

Connecticut
Wm Saml Johnson
Roger Sherman

New York
Alexander Hamilton

New Jersey
Wil: Livingston
David Brearley
Wm Paterson
Jona: Dayton

Pennsylvania
B Franklin
Thomas Mifflin

Robt Morris
Geo. Clymer
Thos FitzSimons
Jared Ingersoll
James Wilson
Gouv Morris

Delaware
Geo: Read
Gunning Bedford
John Dickinson
Richard Bassett
Jaco: Broom

Maryland
James McHenry
Dan of St Thos Jenifer
Danl Carroll

Virginia
John Blair—
James Madison Jr.

North Carolina	Charles Cotesworth Pinckney
Wm Blount	Charles Pinckney
Richd Dobbs Spaight	Pierce Butler
Hu Williamson	
	Georgia
South Carolina	William Few
J. Rutledge	Abr Baldwin

Articles in addition to, and Amendments of the Constitution of the United States of America, proposed by Congress, and ratified by the Legislatures of the several States, pursuant to the fifth Article of the original Constitution.

(The first ten amendments went into effect November 3, 1791.)

Art. I

Congress shall make no law respecting an establishment of religion, or prohibiting the free exercise thereof; or abridging the freedom of speech, or of the press; or the right of the people peaceably to assemble, and to petition the government for a redress of grievances.

Art. II

A well regulated Militia, being necessary to the security of a free State, the right of the people to keep and bear Arms, shall not be infringed.

Art. III

No Soldier shall, in time of peace be quartered in any house, without the consent of the Owner, nor in time of war, but in a manner to be prescribed by law.

Art. IV

The right of the people to be secure in their persons,

521

houses, papers, and effects, against unreasonable searches and seizures, shall not be violated, and no Warrants shall issue but upon probable causes supported by Oath or affirmation, and particularly describing the place to be searched, and the persons or things to be seized.

Art. V

No person shall be held to answer for a capital, or otherwise infamous crime, unless on a presentment or indictment of a Grand Jury, except in cases arising in the land or naval forces, or in the Militia, when in actual service in time of War or public danger; nor shall any person be subject for the same offence to be twice put in jeopardy of life or limb; nor shall be compelled in any criminal case to be a witness against himself, nor be deprived of life, liberty, or property, without due process of law; nor shall private property be taken for public use, without just compensation.

Art. VI

In all criminal prosecutions, the accused shall enjoy the right to a speedy and public trial, by an impartial jury of the State and district wherein the crime shall have been committed, which district shall have been previously ascertained by law, and to be informed of the nature and cause of the accusation; to be confronted with the witnesses against him; to have compulsory process for obtaining witnesses in his favor, and to have the Assistance of Counsel for his defence.

Art. VII

In Suits at common law, where the value in controversy shall exceed twenty dollars, the right of trial by jury shall be preserved, and no fact tried by a jury, shall be otherwise re-examined in any Court of the United States, than according to the rules of the common law.

522

Art. VIII

Excessive bail shall not be required, nor excessive fines imposed, nor cruel and unusual punishments inflicted.

Art. IX

The enumeration in the Constitution, of certain rights, shall not be construed to deny or disparage others retained by the people.

Art. X

The powers not delegated to the United States by the Constitution, nor prohibited by it to the States, are reserved to the States respectively, or to the people.

Art. XI
Jan. 8, 1798

The Judicial power of the United States shall not be construed to extend to any suit in law or equity, commenced or prosecuted against one of the United States by Citizens of another State, or by Citizens or Subjects of any Foreign State.

Art. XII
Sept. 25, 1804

The Electors shall meet in their respective states, and vote by ballot for President and Vice-President, one of whom, at least, shall not be an inhabitant of the same state with themselves; they shall name in their ballots the person voted for as. President, and in distinct ballots the person voted for as Vice-President, and they shall make distinct lists of all persons voted for as President, and of all persons voted for as Vice-President, and of the number of votes for each, which lists they shall sign and certify, and transmit sealed

to the seat of the government of the United States, directed
to the President of the Senate;—The President of the Senate
shall, in the presence of the Senate and House of Representatives, open all the certificates and the votes shall then be
counted;—The person having the greatest number of votes
for President shall be the President, if such number be a
majority of the whole number of Electors appointed; and
if no person have such majority, then from the persons
having the highest numbers not exceeding three on the list
of those voted for as President, the House of Representatives
shall choose immediately, by ballot, the President. But in
choosing the President, the votes shall be taken by states, the
representation from each state having one vote; a quorum
for this purpose shall consist of a member or members from
two-thirds of the states, and a majority of all the states shall
be necessary to a choice. And if the House of Representatives
shall not choose a President whenever the right of choice
shall devolve upon them, before the fourth day of March
next following, then the Vice-President shall act as President, as in the case of the death or other constitutional disability of the President.—The person having the greatest
number of votes as Vice-President, shall be the Vice-
President, if such number be a majority of the whole
number of Electors appointed, and if no person have a
majority, then from the two highest numbers on the list,
the Senate shall choose the Vice-President; a quorum for
the purpose shall consist of two-thirds of the whole number
of Senators, and a majority of the whole number shall be
necessary to a choice. But no person constitutionally ineli-
gible to the office of President shall be eligible to that of
Vice-President of the United States.

Art. XIII
Dec. 18, 1865

Sec. 1. Neither slavery nor involuntary servitude, except
as a punishment for crime whereof the party shall have been

duly convicted, shall exist within the United States, or any place subject to their jurisdiction.

Sec. 2. Congress shall have power to enforce this article by appropriate legislation.

Art. XIV
July 28, 1868

Sec. 1. All persons born or naturalized in the United States, and subject to the jurisdiction thereof, are citizens of the United States and of the State wherein they reside. No State shall make or enforce any law which shall abridge the privileges or immunities of citizens of the United States; nor shall any State deprive any person of life, liberty, or property, without due process of law; nor deny to any person within its jurisdiction the equal protection of the laws.

Sec. 2. Representatives shall be apportioned among the several States according to their respective numbers, counting the whole number of persons in each State, excluding Indians not taxed. But when the right to vote at any election for the choice of electors for President and Vice President of the United States, Representatives in Congress, the Executive and Judicial officers of a State, or the members of the Legislature thereof, is denied to any of the male inhabitants of such State, being twenty-one years of age, and citizens of the United States, or in any way abridged, except for participation in rebellion, or other crime, the basis of representation therein shall be reduced in the proportion which the number of such male citizens shall bear to the whole number of male citizens twenty-one years of age in such State.

Sec. 3. No person shall be a Senator or Representative in Congress, or elector of President and Vice President, or hold any office, civil or military, under the United States, or under any State who, having previously taken an oath, as a member of Congress, or as an officer of the United

States, or as a member of any State legislature, or as an executive or judicial officer of any State, to support the Constitution of the United States, shall have engaged in insurrection or rebellion against the same, or given aid or comfort to the enemies thereof. But Congress may by a vote of two-thirds of each House, remove such disability.

Sec. 4. The validity of the public debt of the United States, authorized by law, including debts incurred for payment of pensions and bounties for services in suppressing insurrection or rebellion, shall not be questioned. But neither the United States nor any State shall assume or pay any debt or obligation incurred in aid of insurrection or rebellion against the United States, or any claim for the loss or emancipation of any slave; but all such debts, obligations and claims shall be held illegal and void.

Sec. 5. The Congress shall have power to enforce, by appropriate legislation, the provisions of this article.

Art. XV
March 30, 1870

Sec. 1. The right of citizens of the United States to vote shall not be denied or abridged by the United States or by any State on account of race, color, or previous condition of servitude—

Sec. 2. The Congress shall have power to enforce this article by appropriate legislation—

Art. XVI
February 25, 1913

The Congress shall have power to lay and collect taxes on incomes, from whatever source derived, without apportionment among the several States and without regard to any census or enumeration.

Art. XVII
May 31, 1913

The Senate of the United States shall be composed of two senators from each State, elected by the people thereof, for six years; and each Senator shall have one vote. The electors in each State shall have the qualifications requisite for electors of the most numerous branch of the State legislature.

When vacancies happen in the representation of any State in the Senate, the executive authority of such State shall issue writs of election to fill such vacancies: *Provided,* That the legislature of any State may empower the executive thereof to make temporary appointments until the people fill the vacancies by election as the legislature may direct.

This amendment shall not be so construed as to affect the election or term of any senator chosen before it becomes valid as part of the Constitution.

Art. XVIII
January 29, 1919

After one year from the ratification of this article, the manufacture, sale, or transportation of intoxicating liquors within, the importation thereof into, or the exportation thereof from the United States and all territory subject to the jurisdiction thereof for beverage purposes is hereby prohibited.

The Congress and the several States shall have concurrent power to enforce this article by appropriate legislation.

This article shall be inoperative unless it shall have been ratified as an amendment to the Constitution by the legislatures of the several States, as provided in the Constitution, within seven years from the date of the submission hereof to the States by Congress.

527

Art. XIX
August 26, 1920

The right of citizens of the United States to vote shall not be denied or abridged by the United States or by any States on account of sex.

The Congress shall have power by appropriate legislation to enforce the provisions of this article.

Art. XX
February 6, 1933

Sec. 1. The terms of the President and Vice-President shall end at noon on the twentieth day of January, and the terms of Senators and Representatives at noon on the third day of January, of the years in which such terms would have ended if this article had not been ratified; and the terms of their successors shall then begin.

Sec. 2. The Congress shall assemble at least once in every year, and such meeting shall begin at noon on the third day of January, unless they shall by law appoint a different day.

Sec. 3. If, at the time fixed for the beginning of the term of the President, the President-elect shall have died, the Vice-President-elect shall become President. If a President shall not have been chosen before the time fixed for the beginning of his term, or if the President-elect shall have failed to qualify, then the Vice-President-elect shall act as President until a President shall have qualified; and the Congress may by law provide for the case wherein neither a President-elect nor a Vice-President-elect shall have qualified, declaring who shall then act as President, or the manner in which one who is to act shall be selected, and such person shall act accordingly until a President or Vice-President shall have qualified.

Sec. 4. The Congress may by law provide for the case of the death of any of the persons from whom the House of Representatives may choose a President whenever the right of choice shall have devolved upon them, and for the case of the death of any of the persons from whom the Senate may choose a Vice-President whenever the right of choice shall have devolved upon them.

Sec. 5. Sections 1 and 2 shall take effect on the 15th day of October following the ratification of this article.

Sec. 6. This article shall be inoperative unless it shall have been ratified as an amendment to the Constitution by the legislatures of three-fourths of the several States within seven years from the date of its submission.

Art. XXI
December 5, 1933

Sec. 1. The eighteenth article of amendment to the Constitution of the United States is hereby repealed. . . .

Art. XXII
February 26, 1951

Sec. 1. No person shall be elected to the office of the President more than twice, and no person who has held the office of President, or acted as President for more than two years of a term to which some other person was elected President shall be elected to the office of the President more than once. But this Article shall not apply to any person holding the office of President when this Article was proposed by the Congress, and shall not prevent any person who may be holding the office of President, or acting as President, during the term within which this Article becomes operative from holding the office of President or acting as President during the remainder of such term.

THE JUDICIARY ACT OF 1789

(September 24, 1789)

The Federal Constitution provided only for a Supreme Court and "such inferior Courts as the Congress may from time to time establish," thus leaving the whole question of the nature and the organization of the judiciary to the discretion of Congress. Consequently one of the first things Congress did when it convened under the new Constitution was to appoint a committee to bring in a bill to organize the federal judiciary. The chairman of this committee, Oliver Ellsworth, was assisted by seven other committee members, five of which had been members of the Constitutional Convention.

The Act created a Supreme Court of five associate justices and one Chief Justice, fifteen District Courts with two Circuit Courts standing between the District Courts and the Supreme Court as intervening courts of appeal.

The Supreme Court had jurisdiction over cases involving a state, minister, consul, or ambassador and was also an appellate court. The judges' appointments were made by the President with the approval of the Senate and were to hold office for life with impeachment being the only method of removal.

AN ACT TO ESTABLISH THE JUDICIAL COURTS OF THE UNITED STATES

Sec. 1. *Be it enacted,* That the supreme court of the United States shall consist of a chief justice and five associate justices, any four of whom shall be a quorum, and shall hold anually at the seat of government two sessions, the one commencing the first Monday of February, and the other the first Monday of August. That the associate justices shall have precedence according to the date of their commissions, or when the commissions of two or more of them bear date on the same day, according to their respective ages.

Sec. 2. That the United States shall be, and they hereby are, divided into thirteen districts, to be limited and called as follows, . . .

Sec. 3. That there be a court called a District Court in each of the aforementioned districts, to consist of one judge, who shall reside in the district for which he is appointed, and shall be called a District Judge, and shall hold annually four sessions, . . .

Sec. 4. That the beforementioned districts, except those of Maine and Kentucky, shall be divided into three circuits, and be called the eastern, the middle, and the southern circuit. That the eastern circuit shall consist of the districts of New Hampshire, Massachusetts, Connecticut, and New York; that the middle circuit shall consist of the districts of New Jersey, Pennsylvania, Delaware, Maryland, and Virginia; and that the southern circuit shall consist of the districts of South Carolina and Georgia; and that there shall be held annually in each district of said circuits two courts which shall be called Circuit Courts, and shall consist of any two justices of the Supreme Court and the district judge of such districts, any two of whom shall constitute a quorum. *Provided,* That no district judge shall give a vote in any case of appeal or error from his own decision; but may assign the reasons of such his decision. . . .

Sec. 9. That the district courts shall have, exclusively of the courts of the several States, cognizance of all crimes and offences that shall be cognizable under the authority of the United States, committed within their respective districts, or upon the high seas; where no other punishment than whipping, not exceeding thirty stripes, a fine not exceeding one hundred dollars, or a term of imprisonment not exceeding six months, is to be inflicted; and shall also have exclusive original cognizance of all civil cases of admiralty and maritime jurisdiction, including all seizures under laws of impost, navigation, or trade of the United States. . . . And shall also have cognizance, concurrent with the courts of the several States, or the circuit courts, as the case may be, of all causes where an alien sue for a tort only in violation of the law of nations or a treaty of the United States. And shall also have cognizance, concurrent as last mentioned, of all suits at common law where the United States sue, and the matter in dispute amounts, exclusive of costs, to the sum or value of one hundred dollars. And shall also have jurisdiction exclusively of the courts of the several States, of all suits against consuls or vice-consuls, except for offences above the description aforesaid. And the trial of issues in fact, in the district courts, in all cases except civil causes of admiralty and maritime jurisdiction, shall be by jury. . . .

Sec. 11. That the circuit courts shall have original cognizance, concurrent with the courts of the several States, of all suits of a civil nature at common law or in equity, where the matter in dispute exceeds, exclusive of costs, the sum of value of five hundred dollars, and the United States are plaintiffs or petitioners; or an alien is a party, or the suit is between a citizen of the State where the suit is brought and a citizen of another State. And shall have exclusive cognizance of all crimes and offences cognizable under the authority of the United States, except where this act otherwise provides, or the laws of the United States shall otherwise direct, and concurrent jurisdiction with the district courts of the crimes and offences cognizable therein. . . . And the circuit courts shall also have appellate jurisdiction from the district courts under the regulations and restrictions hereinafter provided. . . .

Sec. 13. That the Supreme Court shall have exclusive jurisdiction of all controversies of a civil nature, where a state is a party, except between a state and its citizens; and except also between a state and citizens of other states, or aliens, in which latter case it shall have original but not exclusive jurisdiction. And shall have exclusively all such jurisdiction of suits or proceedings against ambassadors or other public ministers, or their domestics, or domestic servants, as a court of law can have or exercise consistently with the law of nations; and original, but not exclusive jurisdiction of all suits brought by ambassadors or other public ministers, or in which a consul or vice-consul shall be a party. And the trial of issues in fact in the Supreme Court in all actions at law against citizens of the United States shall be by jury. The Supreme Court shall also have appellate jurisdiction from the circuit courts and courts of the several states in the cases hereinafter specially provided for; and shall have power to issue writs of prohibition to the district courts, when proceeding as courts of admiralty and maritime jurisdiction, and writs of *mandamus,* in cases warranted by the principle and usages of law, to any courts appointed, or persons holding office under the authority of the United States. . . .

Sec. 25. That a final judgment or decree in any suit, in the highest court of law or equity of a State in which a decision in the suit could be had, where is drawn in question the validity of a treaty or statute of, or an authority exercised under, the United States, and the decision is against their validity; or where is drawn in question the validity of a statute of, or an authority exercised under, any State, on the ground of their being repugnant to the constitution, treaties, or laws of the United States, and the decision is in favour of such their validity, or where is drawn in question the construction of any clause of the constitution, or of a treaty, or statute of, or commission held under, the United States, and the decision is against the title, right, privilege, or exemption, specially set up or claimed by either party, under such clause of the said Constitution, treaty, statute, or commission, may be re-examined, and reversed or affirmed in the Supreme Court of the United States upon a writ of error, the citation being signed by the chief justice, or judge or chancellor of the court rendering or passing the judgment or decree complained of, or by a justice of the Supreme Court of the United States, in the same manner and under the same regulations, and the writ shall have the same effect as if the judgment or decree complained of had been rendered or passed in a circuit court, and the proceedings upon the reversal shall also be the same, except that the Supreme Court, instead of remanding the cause for a final decision as before provided, may, at their discretion, if the cause shall have been once remanded before, proceed to a final decision of the same, and award execution. But no other error shall be assigned or regarded as a ground of reversal in any such case as aforesaid, than such as appears on the face of the record, and immediately respect the before-mentioned questions of validity or construction of the said constitution, treaties, statutes, commissions, or authorities in dispute. . . .

Sec. 35. . . . And there shall also be appointed a meet person learned in the law to act as attorney-general for the United States, who shall be sworn or affirmed to a faithful execution of his office; whose duty it shall be to prosecute and conduct all suits in the Supreme Court in which the United States shall be concerned, and to give his advice and opinion upon questions of law when required by the President of the United States, or when requested by the head of any of the departments touching any matters that may concern their departments, and shall receive such compensation for his services as shall by law be provided.

THE MISSOURI COMPROMISE, 1819-21

In 1818 Missouri Territory, which had been part of the Louisiana Purchase, had gained sufficient population to warrant its consideration for admission into the Union as a state. By the terms of the original purchase the inhabitants of the Territory were guaranteed their property, liberty and freedom of religion. When Missouri petitioned for admission to the Union in 1818 the question arose as to whether this guarantee included the slaves in the Territory.

A Missouri statehood bill was introduced in the House of Representatives in 1818 which would forbid the importation of slaves and bring about the eventual emancipation of all slaves born in Missouri. Although the amendment passed the House in February of 1819, it was defeated by the Senate. The following summer and fall the Missouri question was the chief political issue before the country. The admission of Maine as a free state in 1820 and Alabama as a slave state in 1819 served to mollify the political and public sentiment and on March 6, 1820, Missouri was authorized to adopt a constitution having no restrictions on slavery.

The provisions contained, however, in the new Missouri constitution were objectionable to Northern politicians because it barred the immigration of free Negroes. And it was not until a conference committee pledged that nothing in the constitution would abridge the rights of citizens of the United States that Missouri was admitted to statehood on August 10, 1821.

MISSOURI ENABLING ACT
MARCH 6, 1820

An Act to authorize the people of the Missouri territory to form a constitution and state government, and for the admission of such state into the Union on an equal footing with the original states, and to prohibit slavery in certain territories.

Be it enacted That the inhabitants of that portion of the Missouri territory included within the boundaries hereinafter designated, be, and they are hereby, authorized to form for themselves a constitution and state government, and to assume such name as they shall deem proper; and the said state, when formed, shall be admitted into the Union, upon an equal footing with the original states, in all respects whatsoever.

Sec. 2. That the said state shall consist of all the territory included within the following boundaries, to wit: Beginning in the middle of the Mississippi river, on the parallel of thirty-six degrees of north latitude; thence west, along that parallel of latitude, to the St. Francois river; thence up, and following the course of that river, in the middle of the main channel thereof, to the parallel of latitude of thirty-six degrees and thirty minutes; thence west, along the same, to a point where the said parallel is intersected by a meridian line passing through the middle of the mouth of the Kansas river, where the same empties into the Missouri river, thence, from the point aforesaid north, along the said meridian line, to the intersection of the parallel of latitude which passes through the rapids of the river Des Moines, making the said line to correspond with the Indian boundary line; thence east, from the point of intersection last aforesaid, along the said parallel of latitude, to the middle of the channel of the main fork of the said river Des Moines; thence down and along the middle of the main channel of the said river Des Moines, to the mouth of the same, where it empties into the

Mississippi river; thence, due east, to the middle of the main channel of the Mississippi river; thence down, and following the course of the Mississippi river; in the middle of the main channel thereof, to the place of beginning: . . .

Sec. 3. That all free white male citizens of the United States, who shall have arrived at the age of twenty-one years, and have resided in said territory three months previous to the day of election, and all other persons qualified to vote for representatives to the general assembly of the said territory, shall be qualified to be elected, and they are hereby qualified and authorized to vote, and choose representatives to form a convention. . . .

Sec. 8. That in all that territory ceded by France to the United States, under the name of Louisiana, which lies north of thirty-six degrees and thirty minutes north latitude, not included within the limits of the state, contemplated by this act, slavery and involuntary servitude, otherwise than in the punishment of crimes, whereof the parties shall have been duly convicted, shall be, and is hereby, forever prohibited: *Provided always,* That any person escaping into the same, from whom labour or service is lawfully claimed, in any state or territory of the United States, such fugitive may be lawfully reclaimed and conveyed to the person claiming his or her labour or service as aforesaid.

1. The Tallmadge Amendment
February 13, 1819

(*Journal of the House of Representatives,* 15th Congress, 2nd. Sess. p. 272)

And provided also, That the further introduction of slavery or involuntary servitude be prohibited, except for the punishment of crimes, whereof the party shall be duly convicted; and that all children of slaves, born within the said state, after the admission thereof into the Union, shall be free but may be held to service until the age of twenty-five years.

2. The Taylor Amendment
January 26, 1820
(Annals of the Congress of the United States, 16th Cong. 1st. Sess. Vol. I, p. 947)

The reading of the bill proceeded as far as the fourth section; when

Mr. Taylor, of New York, proposed to amend the bill by incorporating in that section the following provision:

Section 4, line 25, insert the following after the word "States;" "And shall ordain and establish, that there shall be neither slavery nor involuntary servitude in the said State, otherwise than in the punishment of crimes, whereof the party shall have been duly convicted: *Provided, always,* That any person escaping into the same, from whom labor or service is lawfully claimed in any other State, such fugitive may be lawfully reclaimed, and conveyed to the person claiming his or her labor or service as aforesaid: *And provided, also,* That the said provision shall not be construed to alter the condition or civil rights of any person now held to service or labor in the said Territory."

THE MONROE DOCTRINE, 1823

Enunciated in President Monroe's message to Congress on December 2, 1823, the Monroe Doctrine grew out of two diplomatic problems. The first was a minor clash with Russia concerning the northwest coast of North America. In this debate Secretary of State John Quincy Adams expressed to President Monroe the principle that the American continents were not to be considered any longer as a place for colonization by European powers.

The other important issue of the Doctrine grew from the fear that a group of reactionary European governments commonly called the Holy Alliance would attempt to conquer and reduce to colonial status the Latin-American states that had recently revolted in Spain. The United States recognized the independence of those states and the presidential message therefore stated that the United States would not interfere in European affairs, but would view with displeasure any attempt by the European powers to subject the nations of the New World to their political systems.

Although the Monroe Doctrine did not obtain a place in international law, it became increasingly important in American policy, particularly when President Polk reasserted it in 1845 and 1848 with respect to disturbances over Texas and Oregon and the aspirations of European nations in Yucatan.

EXTRACTS FROM PRESIDENT MONROE'S SEVENTH ANNUAL MESSAGE TO CONGRESS DECEMBER 2, 1823.

. . . At the proposal of the Russian Imperial Government,

made through the minister of the Emperor residing here, a full power and instructions have been transmitted to the minister of the United States at St. Petersburg to arrange by amicable negotiation the respective rights and interests of the two nations on the northwest coast of this continent. A similar proposal had been made by His Imperial Majesty to the Government of Great Britain, which has likewise been acceded to. The Government of the United States has been desirous by this friendly proceeding of manifesting the great value which they have invariably attached to the friendship of the Emperor and their solicitude to cultivate the best understanding with his Government. In the discussions to which this interest has given rise and in the arrangements by which they may terminate the occasion has been judged proper for asserting, as a principle in which the rights and interests of the United States are involved, that the American continents, by the free and independent condition which they have assumed and maintain, are henceforth not to be considered as subjects for future colonization by any European powers. . . .

It was stated at the commencement of the last session that a great effort was then making in Spain and Portugal to improve the condition of the people of those countries, and that it appeared to be conducted with extraordinary moderation. It need scarcely be remarked that the result has been so far very different from what was then anticipated. Of events in that quarter of the globe, with which we have so much intercourse and from which we derive our origin, we have always been anxious and interested spectators. The citizens of the United States cherish sentiments the most friendly in favor of the liberty and happiness of their fellowmen on that side of the Atlantic. In the wars of the European powers in matters relating to themselves we have never taken any part, nor does it comport with our policy so to do. It is only when our rights are invaded or seriously menaced that we resent injuries or make preparation for our defense. With the movements in this hemisphere we are of necessity more immediately connected, and by causes which must be obvious to all enlightened and impartial observers. The political system of the allied powers is essentially different in this respect from that of America. This difference proceeds from that which exists in their respective Governments; and to the defense of our own, which has been achieved by the loss of so much blood and treasure, and matured by the wisdom of their most enlightened citizens, and under which we have enjoyed unexampled felicity, this whole nation is devoted. We owe it, therefore, to candor and to the amicable relations existing between the United States and those powers to declare that we should consider any attempt on their part to extend their system to any portion of this hemisphere as dangerous to our peace and safety. With the existing colonies or dependencies of any European power we have not interfered and shall not interfere. But with the Governments who have declared their independence and maintained it, and whose independence we have, on great consideration and on just principles, acknowledged, we could not view any interposition for the purpose of oppressing them, or controlling in any other manner their destiny, by any European power in any other light than as the manifestation of an unfriendly disposition toward the United States. In the war between those new Governments and Spain we declared our neutrality at the time of their recognition, and to this we have adhered, and shall continue to adhere, provided no change shall occur which, in the judgment of the competent authorities of this Government, shall make a corresponding change on the part of the United States indispensable to their security.

The late events in Spain and Portugal shew that Europe is still unsettled. Of this important fact no stronger proof can be adduced than that the allied powers should have thought it proper, on any principle satisfactory to themselves, to have interposed by force in the internal concerns of Spain. To what extent such interposition may be carried, on the same principle, is a question in which all independent powers whose governments differ from theirs are interested, even those most remote, and surely none more so than the United States. Our policy in regard to Europe, which was adopted at an early stage of the wars which have so long agitated that quarter of the globe, nevertheless remains the same, which is, not to interfere in the internal concerns of any of its powers; to consider the government *de facto* as the legitimate government for us; to cultivate friendly relations with it, and to preserve those relations by a frank, firm, and manly policy, meeting in all instances the just claims of every power, submitting to injuries from none. But in regard to those continents circumstances are eminently and conspicuously different. It is impossible that the allied powers should extend their political system to any portion of either continent without endangering our peace and happiness; nor can anyone believe that our southern brethren, if left to themselves, would adopt it of their own accord. It is equally impossible, therefore, that we should behold such interposition in any form with indifference. If we look to the comparative strength and resources of Spain and those new Governments, and their distance from each other, it must be obvious that she can never subdue them. It is still the true policy of the United States to leave the parties to themselves, in the hope that other powers will pursue the same course. . . .

THE EMANCIPATION PROCLAMATION, 1863

On July 13, 1862, President Abraham Lincoln mentioned his plan of issuing an edict freeing the slaves to Gideon Welles, a member of the Cabinet, and Secretary of State William H. Seward, but acquiesced to Seward's suggestion to wait until after a Union victory in the war going on between the states. The Antietam campaign presented just such an opportunity, and consequently on September 22, 1862, after reading a second draft of his edict, Lincoln issued a preliminary proclamation which stated that emancipation for the slaves would become effective on January 1, 1863. This was to be effective in those states "in rebellion" which had not laid down their arms by that date.

On January 1, 1863, the President, by virtue of his power as commander in chief, declared free all those slaves who were held in territory which was in rebellion against the Union. The Emancipation Proclamation was chiefly a document of policy which, it was hoped, would provide the beginning of the end to the South's manpower reserve. It was also aimed at impressing the Europeans, especially the British, which to some extent it did.

BY THE PRESIDENT OF THE UNITED STATES OF AMERICA: A PROCLAMATION

Whereas on the twenty-second day of September, in the year of our Lord one thousand eight hundred and sixty-two, a proclamation was issued by the President of the United States, containing, among other things, the following, to wit:

"That on the first day of January in the year of our Lord one thousand eight hundred and sixty-three, all persons held as slaves within any State or designated part of a State, the people whereof shall then be in rebellion against the

543

United States, shall be then, thence forward, and forever Free; and the Executive Government of the United States, including the military and naval authority thereof, will recognize and maintain the freedom of such persons, and will do no act or acts to repress such persons, or any of them, in any efforts they may make for their actual freedom.

That the Executive will, on the first day of January aforesaid, by proclamation, designate the States and parts of States, if any, in which the people thereof respectively, shall then be in rebellion against the United States; and the Fact that any State, or the people thereof, shall on that day be, in good faith, represented in the Congress of the United States by members chosen thereto at elections wherein a majority of the qualified voters of such State shall have participated, shall, in the absence of strong counter-vailing testimony, be deemed conclusive evidence that such State, and the people thereof, are not then in rebellion against the United States."

Now, therefore I, Abraham Lincoln, President of the United States by virtue of the power in me vested as Commander-in-Chief, of the Army and Navy of the United States in time of actual armed rebellion against the authority and government of the United States, and as a fit and necessary war measure for surpressing said rebellion, do, on this First day of January, in the year of our Lord one thousand eight hundred and sixty-three, and in accordance with my purpose so to do publicly proclaimed for the full period of one hundred days, from the day first above mentioned, order and designate as the States and parts of States wherein the people thereof respectively, are this day in rebellion against the United States, the following, to wit:

Arkansas, Texas, Louisiana, (except the Parishes of St. Bernard Plaquemines, Jefferson, St. John, St. Charles, St. James Ascension, Assumption, Terrebonne, Lafourche, St. Mary, St. Mantin, and Orleans, including the City of New Orleans) Mississippi, Alabama, Florida, Georgia,

South Carolina, North Carolina, and Virginia, (except the forty-eight counties designated as West Virginia, and also the counties of Berkley, Accomac, Northhampton, Elizabeth City, York, Princess Anne, and Norfolk including the cities of Norfolk and Portsmouth,) and which excepted parts are, for the present, left precisely as if this proclamation were not issued.

And by virtue of the power, and for the purpose aforesaid, I do order and declare that all persons held as slaves within said designated States, and parts of States, are and henceforward shall be free; and that the Executive government of the United States, including the military and naval authorities thereof, will recognize and maintain the Freedom of said persons.

And I hereby enjoin upon the people so declared to be free to abstain from all violence, unless in necessary self-defence; and I recommend to them that, in all cases when allowed, they labor faithfully for reasonable wages.

And I further declare and make Known, that such persons of suitable condition, will be received into the armed service of the United States to garrison forts, positions, stations, and other places, and to man vessels of all sorts in said service.

And upon this act, sincerely believed to be an act of justice, warranted by the Constitution, upon military necessity, I invoke the considerate judgment of mankind, and the gracious favor of Almighty God.

In witness whereof I have hereunto set my hand and caused the seal of the United States to be affixed.

Done at the city of Washington, this first day of January, in the year of our Lord one thousand eight hundred and sixty-three and of the Independence of the United States of America the eighty-seventh.

Abraham Lincoln

By the President:

William H. Seward,
Secretary of State.

CIVIL RIGHTS ACT, 1866

Passed in 1866 over President Johnson's veto, the Civil Rights Act was an attempt to give Negroes such common freedoms as the right to sue, to give evidence and to hold real and personal property. The Act was of special importance also because of the Dred Scott Decision, which had decided that Negroes were not citizens.

The first act, which was passed over Johnson's veto because he felt it was premature and perhaps unconstitutional, was re-enacted in 1870 only after the passage of the Fourteenth Amendment.

The third Civil Rights Act attempted to still further guarantee the social rights which had remained withheld from the Negro. It penalized proprietors of public establishments, railroads and other transportation owners for discriminating against the Negro in accommodations. Unfortunately this act was largely voided by the Supreme Court decision in 1883 in the Civil Rights Cases on the ground that these were not civil or property rights and so not the concern of Federal legislation. Consequently the civil rights issue was left open and most states subsequently passed legislation pertaining to civil rights law.

THIRTY-NINTH CONGRESS OF THE UNITED
STATES OF AMERICA;
AT THE FIRST SESSION,
BEGUN AND HELD AT THE CITY OF
WASHINGTON, ON MONDAY, THE FOURTH
DAY OF DECEMBER, ONE THOUSAND EIGHT
HUNDRED AND SIXTY-FIVE.

AN ACT
TO PROTECT ALL PERSONS IN THE UNITED STATES IN THEIR CIVIL RIGHTS, AND FURNISH THE MEANS OF THEIR VINDICATION.

Be it enacted by the Senate and House of Representatives of the United States of America in Congress assembled, that all persons born in the United States and not subject to any foreign power, excluding Indians not taxed, are hereby declared to be citizens of the United States; and such citizens, of every race and color, without regard to any previous condition of slavery or involuntary servitude, except as a punishment for crime whereof the party shall have been duly convicted, shall have the same right, in every State and Territory in the United States, to make and enforce contracts, to sue, be parties and give evidence, to inherit, purchase, lease, sell, hold, and convey real and personal property, and to full and equal benefit of all laws and proceedings for the security of person and property as is enjoyed by white citizens; and shall be subject to like punishment, pains, and penalties, and to none other, any law, statute, ordinance, regulation or custom, to the contrary notwithstanding.

Sec. 2. And be it further enacted, That any person who under color of any law, statute, ordinance, regulation, or custom, shall subject, or cause to be subjected, any inhabitant of any State or Territory to the deprivation of any right secured or protected by this act, or to different punishment, pains, or penalties on account of such person having at any time been held in a condition of slavery or involuntary servitude, except as a punishment for crime whereof the party shall have been duly convicted, or by reason of his color or race, than is prescribed for the punishment of white persons, shall be deemed guilty of a misdemeanor, and on conviction, shall be punished by fine not exceeding one thousand dollars, or imprisonment not exceeding one year, or both, in the discretion of the court.

Sec. 3. And be it further enacted, That the district courts

of the United States, within their respective districts, shall have, exclusively of the courts of the several States, cognizance of all crimes and offences committed against the provisions of this act, and also, concurrently with the circuit courts of the United States of all causes, civil and criminal, affecting persons who are denied or cannot enforce in the courts or judicial tribunals of the State or locality where they may be any of the rights secured to them by the first section of this act; and if any suit or prosecution, civil or criminal, has been or shall be commenced in any State court against any such person for any cause whatsoever, or against any office, civil or military, or other person, for any arrest or imprisonment, trespasses, or wrongs done or committed by virtue or under color of authority derived from this act or the act establishing a bureau for the relief of the freedmen and refugees, and all acts amendatory thereof, or for refusing to do any act upon the ground that it would be inconsistent with this act, such defendant shall have the right to remove such cause for trial to the proper district or circuit court in the manner prescribed by the "Act relating to habeas corpus and regulating judicial proceedings in certain cases," approved March three, eighteen hundred and sixty-three, and all acts amendatory thereof. The jurisdiction in civil and criminal matters hereby conferred on the district and circuit courts of the United States shall be exercised and enforced in conformity with the laws of the United States, so far as such laws are suitable to carry the same into effect, but in all cases where such laws are not adapted to the object, or are deficient in the provisions necessary to furnish suitable remedies and punish offences against law, the common law, as modified and changed by the constitution and statutes of the State wherein the court having jurisdiction of the cause, civil or criminal, is held, so far as the same is not inconsistent with the constitution and laws of the United States, shall be extended to and govern said courts in the trial and disposition of such cause, and, if of a criminal nature, in the infliction of punishment on the party found guilty.

Sec. 4. And be it further enacted, That the district attorneys, marshals and deputy marshals of the United States, commissioners appointed by the circuit and territorial courts of the United States, with powers of arresting, imprisoning, or bailing offenders against the laws of the United States, the officers and agents of the Freedmen's Bureau, and every other officer who may be specially empowered by the President of the United States, to institute proceedings against all and every person who shall violate the provisions of this act, and cause him or them to be arrested and imprisoned, or bailed, as the case may be, for trial before such court of the United States or territorial court as by this act has cognizance of the offence. And with a view to affording reasonable protection to all persons in their constitutional rights of equality before the law, without distinction of race or color, or previous condition of slavery or involuntary servitude, except as a punishment for crime, whereof the party shall have been duly convicted, and to the prompt discharge of the duties of this act, it shall be the duty of the circuit courts of the United States and the superior courts of the Territories of the United States, from time to time, to increase the number of commissioners, so as to afford a speedy and convenient means for the arrest and examination of persons charged with a violation of this act; and such commissioners are hereby authorized and required to exercise and discharge all the powers and duties conferred on them by this act, and the same duties with regard to offences created by this act, as they are authorized by law to exercise with regard to other offences against the laws of the United States.

Sec. 5. And be it further enacted, That it shall be the duty of all marshals and deputy marshals to obey and execute all warrants and precepts issued under the provisions of this act, when to them directed; and should any marshal or deputy marshal refuse to receive such warrant or other process when tendered, or to use all proper means diligently to execute the same, he shall, on conviction thereof, be fined in the sum of one thousand dollars, to the use of the person upon whom the accused is alleged to have committed the offense. And the better to enable the said commissioners to execute their duties faithfully and efficiently, in conformity with the Constitution of the United States and the requirements of this act, they are hereby authorized and empowered, within their counties respectively, to appoint, in writing, under their hands, any one or more suitable persons from time to time, to execute all such warrants and other process as may be issued by them in the lawful performance of their respective duties; and the persons so appointed to execute any warrant or process as aforesaid shall have authority to summon and call to their aid the bystanders or posse comitatus of the proper county, or such portion of the land or naval forces of the United States, or of the militia, as may be necessary to the performance of the duty with which they are charged, and to insure a faithful observance of the clause of the Constitution which prohibits slavery, in conformity with the provisions of this act; and said warrants shall run and be executed by said officers anywhere in the State or Territory within which they are issued.

Sec. 6. And be it further enacted, That any person who shall knowingly and willfully obstruct, hinder or prevent any officer, or other person charged with the execution of any warrant or process issued under the provisions of this act, or any person or persons lawfully assisting him or them, from arresting any person for whose apprehension such warrant or process may have been issued, or shall rescue or attempt to rescue such persons from the custody of the officer, other person or persons, or those lawfully assisting as aforesaid, when so arrested pursuant to the authority herein given and declared, or shall aid, abet, or assist any person so arrested as aforesaid, directly or indirectly, to escape from the custody of the officer or other person legally authorized as aforesaid, or shall harbor or conceal any person for whose arrest a warrant or process shall have been issued as aforesaid, so as to prevent his discovery and arrest after notice or knowledge of the fact that a warrant has been issued for the apprehension of such person, shall, for either of said offences, be subject to a fine not exceeding one thousand dollars, and imprisonment not exceeding six months, by indictment and conviction before the district court of the United States for the district in which said offence may have been committed, or before the proper court of criminal jurisdiction, if committed within any one of the organized Territories of the United States.

Sec. 7. And be it further enacted, That the district attorneys, the marshals, their deputies, and the clerks of the said district and territorial courts shall be paid for their services the like fees as may be allowed to them for similar services in other cases; and in all cases where the proceedings are before a commissioner, he shall be entitled to a fee of ten dollars in full for his services in each case, inclusive of all services incident to such arrest and examination. The person or persons authorized to execute the process to be issued by such commissioners for the arrest of offenders against the provisions of this act shall be entitled to a fee of five dollars for each person he or they may arrest and take before any such commissioner as aforesaid, with such other fees as may be deemed reasonable by such commissioner for such other additional services as may be necessarily performed by him or them, such as attending at the examination, keeping the prisoner in custody, and providing him with food and lodging during his detention, and until the final determination of such commissioner, and in general for performing such other duties as may be required in the premises; such fees to be made up in conformity with the fees usually charged by the officers of the courts of justice within the proper district or county, as near as may be practicable, and paid out of the treasury of the United States on the certificate of the judge of the district within which the arrest is made, and to be recoverable from the defendant as part of the judgment in case of conviction.

Sec. 8. And be it further enacted, That whenever the President of the United States shall have reason to believe that offences have been or are likely to be committed against the provisions of this act within any judicial district, it shall be lawful for him, in his discretion, to direct the judge, marshal, and district attorney of such district to attend at such place within the district, and for such time as he may designate for the purpose of the more speedy arrest and trial of persons charged with a violation of this act; and it shall be the duty of every judge or other officer, when any such requisition shall be received by him, to attend at the place and for the time therein designated.

Sec. 9. And be it further enacted, That it shall be lawful for the President of the United States, or such person as he may empower for that purpose, to employ such part of the land or naval forces of the United States, or of the militia, as shall be necessary to prevent the violation and enforce the due execution of this act.

Sec. 10. And be it further enacted, That upon all questions of law arising in any cause under the provisions of this act a final appeal may be taken to the Supreme Court of the United States.

———*Colfax*
Speaker of the House of Representatives

La Fayette T.———
President of the Senate, pro tempore.

IN THE SENATE OF THE UNITED STATES
APRIL 6, 1866

The President of the United States having returned to the Senate in which it originated, the bill entitled "An act to protect all persons in the United States in their civil rights, and furnish the means of their vindication." With his objections thereto, the Senate proceeded, in pursuance of the Constitution, to reconsider the same; and Resolved, That the

552

said bill do pass, two thirds of the Senate agreeing to pass the same.

Secretary of the Senate

In the House of Representatives, U.S. April 9th, 1866. The House of Representatives having proceeded, in pursuance of the Constitution, to reconsider the bill entitled "An act to protect all persons in the United States in their civil rights, and furnish the means of their vindication," returned to the Senate by the President of the United States, with his objections and sent by the Senate to the House of Representatives, with the message of the President returning the bill:—Resolved, That the bill do pass, two-thirds of the House of Representatives agreeing to pass the same.